T0353386

Quantum Cryptography and the Future of Cyber Security

Nirbhay Kumar Chaubey
Gujarat Technological University, India

Bhavesh B. Prajapati
Education Department, Government of Gujarat, India

A volume in the Advances in
Information Security, Privacy, and
Ethics (AISPE) Book Series

Published in the United States of America by
    IGI Global
    Information Science Reference (an imprint of IGI Global)
    701 E. Chocolate Avenue
    Hershey PA, USA 17033
    Tel: 717-533-8845
    Fax: 717-533-8661
    E-mail: cust@igi-global.com
    Web site: http://www.igi-global.com

Library of Congress Cataloging-in-Publication Data

Names: Chaubey, Nirbhay Kumar, 1971- editor. | Prajapati, Bhavesh B., 1975-
   editor.
Title: Quantum cryptography and the future of cyber security / Nirbhay
   Kumar Chaubey and Bhavesh B. Prajapati, editors.
Description: Hershey, PA : Information Science Reference, 2020. | Includes
   bibliographical references. | Summary: "This book explores the latest
   applications and advancements of quantum cryptography and cyber
   security"-- Provided by publisher.
Identifiers: LCCN 2019037762 (print) | LCCN 2019037763 (ebook) | ISBN
   9781799822530 (h/c) | ISBN 9781799822547 (s/c) | ISBN 9781799822554
   (eISBN)
Subjects: LCSH: Quantum communication--Security measures. | Cryptography. |
   Data encryption (Computer science)
Classification: LCC TK5103.592.Q83 Q38 2020 (print) | LCC TK5103.592.Q83
   (ebook) | DDC 005.8/24--dc23
LC record available at https://lccn.loc.gov/2019037762
LC ebook record available at https://lccn.loc.gov/2019037763

This book is published in the IGI Global book series Advances in Information Security, Privacy, and Ethics (AISPE) (ISSN: 1948-9730; eISSN: 1948-9749)

British Cataloguing in Publication Data
A Cataloguing in Publication record for this book is available from the British Library.

All work contributed to this book is new, previously-unpublished material.
The views expressed in this book are those of the authors, but not necessarily of the publisher.

For electronic access to this publication, please contact: eresources@igi-global.com.

Advances in Information Security, Privacy, and Ethics (AISPE) Book Series

ISSN:1948-9730
EISSN:1948-9749

Editor-in-Chief: Manish Gupta, State University of New York, USA

MISSION

As digital technologies become more pervasive in everyday life and the Internet is utilized in ever increasing ways by both private and public entities, concern over digital threats becomes more prevalent.

The **Advances in Information Security, Privacy, & Ethics (AISPE) Book Series** provides cutting-edge research on the protection and misuse of information and technology across various industries and settings. Comprised of scholarly research on topics such as identity management, cryptography, system security, authentication, and data protection, this book series is ideal for reference by IT professionals, academicians, and upper-level students.

COVERAGE

- IT Risk
- Security Classifications
- Privacy-Enhancing Technologies
- Global Privacy Concerns
- Tracking Cookies
- Internet Governance
- Computer ethics
- Cyberethics
- Cookies
- Information Security Standards

IGI Global is currently accepting manuscripts for publication within this series. To submit a proposal for a volume in this series, please contact our Acquisition Editors at Acquisitions@igi-global.com or visit: http://www.igi-global.com/publish/.

Titles in this Series

For a list of additional titles in this series, please visit:
https://www.igi-global.com/book-series/advances-information-security-privacy-ethics/37157

Internet Censorship and Regulation Systems in Democracies Emerging Research and Opportunities
Nikolaos Koumartzis (Aristotle University of Thessaloniki, Greece) and Andreas Veglis (Aristotle University of Thessaloniki Greece)
Information Science Reference • © 2020 • 200pp • H/C (ISBN: 9781522599739) • US $185.00

Impact of Digital Transformation on Security Policies and Standards
Sam Goundar (The University of the South Pacific, Fiji) Bharath Bhushan (Sree Vidyanikethan Engineering College, India) and Vaishali Ravindra Thakare (Atria Institute of Technology, India)
Information Science Reference • © 2020 • 300pp • H/C (ISBN: 9781799823674) • US $215.00

Handbook of Research on Intelligent Data Processing and Information Security Systems
Stepan Mykolayovych Bilan (State University of Infrastructure and Technology, Ukraine) and Saleem Issa Al-Zoubi (Irbid National University, Jordan)
Engineering Science Reference • © 2020 • 434pp • H/C (ISBN: 9781799812906) • US $345.00

Security and Privacy Issues in Sensor Networks and IoT
Priyanka Ahlawat (National Institute of Technology, Kurukshetra, India) and Mayank Dave (National Institute of Technology, Kurukshetra, India)
Information Science Reference • © 2020 • 323pp • H/C (ISBN: 9781799803737) • US $195.00

Modern Principles, Practices, and Algorithms for Cloud Security
Brij B. Gupta (National Institute of Technology, Kurukshetra, India)
Information Science Reference • © 2020 • 344pp • H/C (ISBN: 9781799810827) • US $195.00

For an entire list of titles in this series, please visit:
https://www.igi-global.com/book-series/advances-information-security-privacy-ethics/37157

701 East Chocolate Avenue, Hershey, PA 17033, USA
Tel: 717-533-8845 x100 • Fax: 717-533-8661
E-Mail: cust@igi-global.com • www.igi-global.com

This book is affectionately dedicated to my mother, the late Mrs. Subhraji Chaubey, who inspired me to live with purpose and meaning, always focus on giving back to the society, her love, courage, devotion have been the strength of my striving.
Nirbhay Kumar Chaubey

This book is dedicated to my parents, Lattaben and Babubhai, who taught me to practice truth, honesty and devotion. My brother, Amit, he is dear and special to me. My children, Riddhi and Aum, thanks for all they are augmentation of myself, they are my life. At last but not the least, my life partner, Asha, for her continuous love, care and inspiration....we are one.
Bhavesh Prajapati

Editorial Advisory Board

Table of Contents

Section 1
Quantum Cryptography

    *Amandeep Singh Bhatia, Center for Quantum Computing, Peng Cheng
Laboratory, China*
    *Shenggen Zheng, Center for Quantum Computing, Peng Cheng
Laboratory, China*

    *Bhavesh B. Prajapati, IT Department, Commissionerate of Technical
Education, Government of Gujarat, India & Gujarat Technological
University, India*
    Nirbhay Kumar Chaubey, Gujarat Technological University, India

    Sathish Babu B., RV College of Engineering, Bangalore, India
    K. Bhargavi, Siddaganga Institute of Technology, India
    K. N. Subramanya, RV College of Engineering, Bangalore, India

Section 2
Cyber Security

Detailed Table of Contents

Section 1
Quantum Cryptography

Chapter 1

Amandeep Singh Bhatia, Center for Quantum Computing, Peng Cheng Laboratory, China
Shenggen Zheng, Center for Quantum Computing, Peng Cheng Laboratory, China

In the last two decades, the field of post-quantum cryptography has had an overwhelming response among research communities. The ability of quantum computers to factorize large numbers could break many of well-known RSA cryptosystem and discrete log-based cryptosystem. Thus, post-quantum cryptography offers secure alternatives which are implemented on classical computers and is secure against attacks by quantum computers. The significant benefits of post-quantum cryptosystems are that they can be executed quickly and efficiently on desktops, smartphones, and the Internet of Things (IoTs) after some minor software updates. The main objective of this chapter is to give an outline of major developments in privacy protectors to reply to the forthcoming threats caused by quantum systems. In this chapter, we have presented crucial classes of cryptographic systems to resist attacks by classical and quantum computers. Furthermore, a review of different classes of quantum cloning is presented.

Chapter 2

*Bhavesh B. Prajapati, IT Department, Commissionerate of Technical
Education, Government of Gujarat, India & Gujarat Technological
University, India*
Nirbhay Kumar Chaubey, Gujarat Technological University, India

Quantum key distribution is an application of quantum cryptography which is based on quantum mechanics and optical physics. The word "quantum" means the smallest particle of matter and energy which inhibits unique special properties to make it different from normal matter. This chapter discusses underlying principles, and operations of quantum mechanics which are used to derive quantum key distribution protocols. This chapter also discusses elementary QKD protocols based on no cloning theorem and EPR correlations. Limitation of quantum key distribution is also discussed with reference to its implementation. Conceptual notes on quantum internet are also given.

Chapter 3

Sathish Babu B., RV College of Engineering, Bangalore, India
K. Bhargavi, Siddaganga Institute of Technology, India
K. N. Subramanya, RV College of Engineering, Bangalore, India

The advent of quantum computing is bringing threats to successful operations of classical cryptographic techniques. To conduct quantum key distribution (QKD) in a finite time interval, there is a need to estimate photon states and analyze the fluctuations statistically. The use of brute force and local search methods for parameter optimization are computationally intensive and becomes an infeasible solution even for smaller connections. Therefore, the use of quantum machine learning models with self-learning ability is useful in predicting the optimal parameters for quantum key distribution. This chapter discusses some of the quantum machine learning models with their architecture, advantages, and disadvantages. The performance of quantum convoluted neural network (QCNN) and Quantum Particle Swarm Optimization (QPSO) towards QKD is found to be good compared to all the other quantum machine learning models discussed.

Chapter 4

Padmapriya Praveenkumar, SASTRA University (Deemed), India
Santhiya Devi R., SASTRA University (Deemed), India
Amirtharajan Rengarajan, SASTRA University (Deemed), India
John Bosco Balaguru Rayappan, SASTRA University (Deemed), India

Nano industries have been successful trendsetters for the past 30 years, in escalating the speed and dropping the power necessities of nanoelectronic devices. According to Moore's law and the assessment created by the international technology roadmap for semiconductors, beyond 2020, there will be considerable restrictions in manufacturing IC's based on CMOS technologies. As a result, the next prototype to get over these effects is quantum-dot cellular automata (QCA). In this chapter, an efficient quantum cellular automata (QCA) based random number generator (RNG) is proposed. QCA is an innovative technology in the nano regime which guarantees large device density, less power dissipation, and minimal size as compared to the various CMOS technologies. With the aim to maximise the randomness in the proposed nano communication, a linear feedback shift register (LFSR) keyed multiplexer with ring oscillators is developed. The developed RNG is simulated using a quantum cellular automata (QCA) simulator tool.

Chapter 5
Bhanu Chander, Pondicherry University, India

Quantum cryptography is actions to protect transactions through executing the circumstance of quantum physics. Up-to-the-minute cryptography builds security over the primitive ability of fragmenting enormous numbers into relevant primes; however, it features inconvenience with ever-increasing machine computing power along with current mathematical evolution. Among all the disputes, key distribution is the most important trouble in classical cryptography. Quantum cryptography endows with clandestine communication by means of offering a definitive protection statement with the rule of the atmosphere. Exploit quantum mechanics to cryptography can be enlarging unrestricted, unfailing information transmission. This chapter describes the contemporary state of classical cryptography along with the fundamentals of quantum cryptography, quantum protocol key distribution, implementation criteria, quantum protocol suite, quantum resistant cryptography, and large-scale quantum key challenges.

Chapter 6
Manan Dhaneshbhai Thakkar, U. V. Patel College of Engineering,
Ganpat University, India
Rakesh D. Vanzara, U. V. Patel College of Engineering, Ganpat
University, India

We are leaving in the era where almost everyone in the world uses internet for the communication over social media site, shopping, E-commerce, online transaction and many more. The exponential growth in usage of internet resulted in security related challenges. Since last several years, traditional cryptography algorithms are found working well. Evolution of quantum computer and its high computing capability can break existing cryptography algorithms. To handle the security constraints, this chapter provides details on evolution of quantum cryptography, components involved to design network architecture for quantum internet, quantum key exchange mechanism and functionality wise stages for quantum internet. This chapter also includes challenges involved in evolution of quantum internet. Further, chapter also contains the details on e-governance, challenges in e-governance and solution using quantum cryptography.

Section 2
Cyber Security

Chapter 7

  Ayush Sinha, Indian Institute of Information Technology, Allahabad, India

  Ranjana Vyas, Indian Institute of Information Technology, Allahabad, India

  Venkatesan Subramanian, Indian Institute of Information Technology, Allahabad, India

  O. P. Vyas, Indian Institute of Information Technology, Allahabad, India

Cyber-physical security applied to the domain of critical infrastructure (CI) poses different challenges. To acknowledge the security concern of CI from a cyber-physical perspective becomes imperative since the failure of any one of the CI's components may not only lead to cascading effects, but also the overall services may shut-down state. The energy infrastructure is becoming the backbone in CI due to the complexity of environment, heterogeneous communication technologies, and different configurations of the energy infrastructure, so securing the communication among these devices and control centers becomes a central issue. Many significant works in the related domain has been done. The main focus of the chapter is identification of the attack vector formulation with prevention and detection mechanisms for different components, providing countermeasures cohesively against security threats.

Chapter 8

  Prisilla Jayanthi, K. G. Reddy College of Engineering and Technology, Hyderabad, India

  Muralikrishna Iyyanki, Defence Research and Development Organisation, India

Cryptography is an indispensable tool used to protect information in any organization; providing secure transmission over the Internet. The major challenge faced by health-sector is data security, and to overcome this several advancements in medicine and biomedical research have proven to increase computer processing in data security. The study focuses on cryptography, the most emerging field in computer industries. Both artificial intelligence and quantum technology are both transforming the health sector in regard to cybersecurity. In this study, the AES algorithm is a cryptographic cipher used. One such application is implemented and is responsible for handling a large amount of the information in the health sector. An application with a double Hashing algorithm is accomplished to can maintain the data in a secure fashion.

Chapter 9

Cybersecurity is essentials in today's era. An increase in cyberattacks has driven caution to safeguard data. An advanced persistent attack is an attack where the intellectual property of an organization is attempted to be misused. The attacker stays on the network for a long-time intruding into confidential files. The attacker switches into sleep mode, masking himself. Hence, the attacker is quite difficult to trace. The proposed work is suggested to tackle the problem. Public key cryptography is used to encrypt the data. The hash code is affixed to the transmitted message to provide reliability to the transmitted data. The work proves to be 4.9% stronger in authenticating the received packets, provides 4.42% greater data reliability, and decreases the load of the server by 43.5% compared to work.

Chapter 10

The Internet of Things (IoT) connects different IoT smart objects around people to make their life easier by connecting them with the internet, which leads IoT environments vulnerable to many attacks. This chapter has few main objectives: to understand basics of IoT; different types of attacks possible in IoT; and prevention steps to secure IoT environment at some extent. Therefore, this chapter is mainly divided into three parts. In first part discusses IoT devices and application of it; the second part is about cyber-attacks possible on IoT environments; and in the third part is discussed prevention and recommendation steps to avoid damage from different attacks.

Chapter 11

Kiritkumar J. Modi, Parul University, India

Prachi Devangbhai Shah, U. V. Patel College of Engineering, Ganpat
University, India

Zalak Prajapati, U. V. Patel College of Engineering, Ganpat University,
India

The rapid growth of digitization in the present era leads to an exponential increase of information which demands the need of a Big Data paradigm. Big Data denotes complex, unstructured, massive, heterogeneous type data. The Big Data is essential to the success in many applications; however, it has a major setback regarding security and privacy issues. These issues arise because the Big Data is scattered over a distributed system by various users. The security of Big Data relates to all the solutions and measures to prevent the data from threats and malicious activities. Privacy prevails when it comes to processing personal data, while security means protecting information assets from unauthorized access. The existence of cloud computing and cloud data storage have been predecessor and conciliator of emergence of Big Data computing. This article highlights open issues related to traditional techniques of Big Data privacy and security. Moreover, it also illustrates a comprehensive overview of possible security techniques and future directions addressing Big Data privacy and security issues.

Chapter 12

Binod Kumar, Jayawant Institute of Computer Applications, Pune, India

Sheetal B. Prasad, SRM Institute of Science and Technology, Chennai,
India

The purpose of the cyber security policy is to provide guidelines on how to secure public and private resources from cyberattacks. IoT devices are having challenges managing the personal information they collect and helps to people understand that information is managed by a system. Digital twins enhance development by allowing developers to directly manipulate the device's abstract version using programming instructions. It is required to think about possible attack vectors when tuning cyber security for the IoT environment concerns. So, a security administrator is required to think the about possible vulnerabilities of the environment. Supervision and protocols must also be developed for suppliers, manufacturers, vendors, etc. The deployment of consumer understanding to make best use of "smart" strategy, using their own "smart" minds is required. There is a need for a framework or other types of guidance for assessing IoT cyber security to provide an informed approach to securing devices and the ecosystems in which they are set up.

Chapter 13

Darshan Mansukhbhai Tank, Gujarat Technological University, Ahmedabad, India

Akshai Aggarwal, School of Computer Science, University of Windsor, Canada

Nirbhay Kumar Chaubey, Gujarat Technological University, India

Cybercrime continues to emerge, with new threats surfacing every year. Every business, regardless of its size, is a potential target of cyber-attack. Cybersecurity in today's connected world is a key component of any establishment. Amidst known security threats in a virtualization environment, side-channel attacks (SCA) target most impressionable data and computations. SCA is flattering major security interests that need to be inspected from a new point of view. As a part of cybersecurity aspects, secured implementation of virtualization infrastructure is very much essential to ensure the overall security of the cloud computing environment. We require the most effective tools for threat detection, response, and reporting to safeguard business and customers from cyber-attacks. The objective of this chapter is to explore virtualization aspects of cybersecurity threats and solutions in the cloud computing environment. The authors also discuss the design of their novel 'Flush+Flush' cache attack detection approach in a virtualized environment.

Foreword

It is a pleasure to write the Foreword for this important new book - "Quantum Cryptography and the Future of Cyber Security", edited by Professor (Dr.) Nirbhay Kumar Chaubey and Professor Bhavesh B. Prajapati. In this book, the editors have brought together an impressive and substantive array of important topics to explore recent advances in quantum computing and cybersecurity. This book contains thirteen chapters arranged in two sections: Section -1 Quantum cryptography comprises the first six chapters and the remaining seven chapters constitute Section -2 on Cyber security.

Quantum computing is a fast-emerging area of computer science and the research in Quantum Cryptography is intensifying since bottlenecks in the traditional methods of ensuring security of valuable digital data and communication are on the horizon. The clock frequency of the current computer processor systems may reach about 40GHz in the next 10 years. By then, one atom may represent one bit. Electrons under such conditions are no longer described by classical physics, and a new model of the computer may become necessary. A quantum computer represents information as a series of bits, called quantum bits or "qubits". Qubits can be either 0 or 1, but unlike a normal bit, qubits can exist in multiple states at the same time. This property allows the qubits to work on millions of computations in parallel. A quantum computer may be more powerful than the most advanced modern supercomputers available today and this could "lead to new breakthroughs in science, technology and life-sciences.

Quantum computing presents great opportunities and it will be adopted by several domains, including cyber security, cryptography, artificial intelligence, machine learning, biomedical simulations, financial services, weather forecasting and climate change etc.

Cyber security is becoming a larger issue every day as more computing power becomes easily available to every one, including those who want to attack the digital systems. We, the human beings, become more vulnerable as we increase our dependence upon digital systems. Ongoing cyberattacks, hacks, data breaches, and privacy concerns reveal vividly the inadequacy of existing techniques of cybersecurity and the need to continuously develop new and better ones. Quantum machine learning approaches can help develop new and powerful techniques to combat cyber security threats by recognizing the threats earlier and by helping mitigate the damage, that the cyber-attacks may do. Cybersecurity analysts and experts are worried that a new type of computer, based on quantum bits could break the most modern cryptographic techniques. In the future, even robust cryptographic algorithms (Finite Field Cryptography, RSA, Elliptic Curve Cryptography, SHA 256, AES 256,) may not remain secure in the face of attacks mounted by using quantum computers. Therefore, Quantum computing is at once both an opportunity and a threat. Researchers in Cyber security will have to use Quantum Computing to protect computer systems from attacks that could compromise the hardware, software or information even as the attacks, in the future, become sharper by use of new methodologies and more powerful Quantum Computers.

I would like to congratulate the editors and authors for this great effort, which will be highly useful to research scholars, cyber security analysts, industry experts, researchers in Social Studies and Public Policy, IT professionals and students of Computer Science & Engineering, Electronics & Communication Engineering, Computer Applications and Information & Communication Technology. The book is the product of the joint efforts by the authors, editors, reviewers, and advisory editorial board, who are all well-equipped to present the research & developments in the subject-matter, as they are educators with vast experiences in the field of computer science, quantum computing, cyber security, networking and communication engineering. I find that the book has turned out to be a comprehensive research handbook. I, therefore, recommend this book both for academic studies and research at universities and to all those in businesses and industries, who want to understand the new area of Quantum Cryptography.

Akshai Aggarwal
University of Windsor, Canada

Akshai Aggarwal, currently working as a Professor Emeritus in Computer Science, at Windsor, Canada, had served as Director, School of Computer Science, University of Windsor, Canada and as the Vice Chancellor, Gujarat Technological University, India for two successive terms (2010 - 2013, 2013-2016). Dr.Akshai Aggarwal holds Ph.D in Electrical Engineering from the prestigious Maharaja Sayajirao University of Baroda. In his distinguished career spanning over 45 years, he has served in premier institutions such as Maharaja Sayajirao University, Gujarat University, Gujarat Technological University and University of Windsor. He has also been invited to chair the International Advisory Committee, Industries Affairs Committee etc. of many Conferences. He has been honoured with the Governor's Award, IEEE Millennium Medal and Fellowships of IETE, M.S. University and Gujarat University.

Preface

Today's IT security depends on encryption and public key distribution to guarantee security of E-commerce, Government and corporate transactions and personal communications. These encryption techniques are based on complex mathematical algorithms, which are time safe and not possible to be broken by latest computation power for years. Brute force attack cannot be applied to algorithms like RSA-2048, AES-128 and ECDSA-256 having sufficient key length. Nevertheless, Quantum computers will pose a significant threat for existing cyber security mechanisms, when large fault - tolerant quantum computers are build the most commonly used cryptosystems will break. Therefore, dealing with this threat is crucial and need to study.

Quantum cryptography is a study of cryptographic techniques which applies quantum encryption and decryption based on principles of quantum physics. Theory of quantum physics which required to implement quantum cryptography is quite mature but practically still much remain to achieve. Quantum computing uses "qubit" as a basic unit of computing which is very sensitive to thermal and electromagnetic changes. Present implementations of quantum cryptography are still within the reach of universities, academia and research centers. Large scale commercial availability of quantum computer is still a far sight but can be a reality within a next decade. Current quantum computers are very expensive and limited to few qubit operations. Latest most powerful quantum computer can handle maximum 72 qubits at a time. Furthermore, quantum key distribution networks are limited by maximum distance of 100 kilometers as per latest implementation. Quantum cryptography is an application of quantum mechanics and quantum key distribution (QKD) is an example of that. QKD allows perfectly secure sharing of keys among parties. Any attempt to intercept transmitted key cannot become successful as one cannot deterministically find the states of qubit to get the information. Usually qubit is in super position state and when eavesdropper tries to measure, it takes one of the states from super position. Quantum key distribution schemes are usually classified in two categories based on: Prepare and measure scheme and entanglement based scheme. BB84 protocol, B92 protocol are examples of prepare and measure scheme which uses Heisenberg's uncertainty principle. Ekert's protocol and entangled BB84 protocol are using quantum entanglement. Device independent quantum cryptography, Bit commitment and oblivious transfer, coin flipping protocols, Delegated quantum computations, quantum storage models are latest research primitives in the field of quantum cryptography. Post quantum cryptography is new point for research which focuses on quantum safe algorithms. Quantum safe algorithms are capable to protect their data against most powerful quantum cryptographic algorithms and fastest quantum computers.

Cyber security deals with the protection of computer systems from attacks and minimizing risk of attack on hardware, software, transactions, data and information etc. Aim of cyber security is to provide authentication, confidentiality, integration, non-repudiation and availability. With the intent use of information and technology in the fields from social media to financial transactions, IT security concern is at its peak. The sphere of digital information is growing day by day. This sphere contains computer systems, networks and large amount of data. Security and privacy related problems are concerning users and distributers in their shift towards the ICT.

It is well-known that adapting to any new technology within our homes, work, or business environments opens doors to new security problems. It must be considered and dealt with cautions. IT security/ cyber security is utilized to provide the sustained functioning of such kind of systems. Industries and governments are implementing new rules or security rules/policies in collaboration with the international standards groups. Security operations can be complicated by regulations that lag behind the criminals' strategies. As criminals keep coming up with new ways to attack, regulation – while necessary and important – can sometimes make security harder. Organizations, many of which have limited IT and security resources, need to find a way to adapt to ensure compliance with these new regulations, while still managing day-to-day operations. IoT is combination of multiple devices connected together to serve a specific task e.g home appliances and services sensors. While these devices do not have any sensitive data but they can be also hacked to access information. With increased use of IoT, these devices are prime target of cyber-attacks. The reason for the same is many IoT implementations are not secured end-to-end. Attacks on these devices are also rising due to lack of standards concerning its security. Due to the lack of any industry-wide framework and standards, IoT security is left to respective vendors and device manufacturers, whose focus is often on the functionality of the device rather than the potential risks and consequences. In the backdrop of emerging threats, regulatory frameworks or guidelines addressing security concerns is the need of the hour. Digital transformation implies that effective security is no longer an option but it is mandatory. Attacks will be spread out and more number of small businesses and even individuals will come under the radar of cybercriminals. Large organizations have already done considerable work to protect themselves from attacks.

It is easier to target small and mid-size companies as they may not have adequate security measures and resources in place to protect themselves. Small companies must re-assess their security posture and ensure adequate measures and controls are implemented to safeguard against today's cyber-attacks.

AIM OF THE BOOK

The idea behind this book is to put researchers on the common theme of quantum cryptography and the future of cyber security with latest research topics of their work area.

Classical cryptography has very limited future with reference to availability of quantum computers in day-to-day life. Classical cryptography depends on complexity of mathematical algorithm and plenty of time required for breaking that complex algorithm with best computing resources. Quantum computers work exponentially fast with comparison to traditional ones. Quantum computers uses photon as a basic unit of transmission and security is derived from the fundamental laws of quantum mechanics.

Quantum cryptography is becoming the technology one cannot ignore for long. When we talk of quantum cryptography, cyber security will spontaneously come into the picture. Data is the most precious thing to be stolen in this new age. Even economies and technology platforms are becoming data driven and sensitive towards security of data. Rise in cyber crime and new methodologies adopted for cyber crime push us to study the new avenues of cyber security.

This book presents latest work of several researchers in field of quantum cryptography and cyber security to generate interest and discussion among post graduate, undergraduate, academic and research community.

INTENDED AUDIENCE AND USE

The intended audience for this book includes:

- Post graduate, graduate and undergraduate level students of Computer Science and Engineering, Electronics and Communication Engineering, Computer Applications and Information and Communication Technology.
- Ph.D and Research Scholar Students of Computer Science and Engineering, Electronics and Communication Engineering, Computer Applications and Information and Communication Technology.
- Systems Engineering, Social Studies, and Public Policy.

- Academician, Researchers and Industry experts engaged in quantum computing, quantum cryptography, cyber security related research from a wide range of perspectives including but not limited to the Computer Science and Engineering, Electronics and Communication Engineering, Computer Applications, Information and Communication Technology social studies and public administration.
- This book is intended for use as both a textbook and a comprehensive research handbook.
- The contributors to this edited volume book are renowned experts in their respective fields. Most of the chapters contained in this book provide an updated comprehensive survey of the related field and also specific findings from cutting-edging innovative research.

ORGANIZATION OF THE BOOK

This book is organized in thirteen chapters broadly divided among two sections:

Section 1: Quantum Cryptography
Chapters 1 to 6 discusses different areas of quantum cryptography.

Section 2: Cyber Security
Chapters 7 to 13 discusses different developments in the field of cyber security.

A brief description of each of the chapters are as follows:

Chapter 1: Post-Quantum Cryptography and Quantum Cloning

This chapter discusses basic notations of post quantum cryptography, different cryptosystems, lattice based cryptography, multivariate cryptography, hash based cryptography, quantum cloning and its classification.

Chapter 2: Quantum Key Distribution – The Evolution

This chapter presents fundamental concepts of quantum information, underlying principles and quantum processing. Qubit, its operations, basic postulates of quantum mechanics, quantum key distribution and its related protocols are also reviewed and discussed.

Chapter 3: Optimal Parameter Prediction for Secure Quantum Key Distribution Using Quantum Machine Learning Models

This chapter compare quantum key distribution, traditional public and private key distribution strategies. Authors of this chapter discuss the role of parameter prediction and optimization in achieving quantum key distribution (QKD) in a finite time interval. Several potential quantum machine learning algorithms like QFFNN, QRNN, QBNN, QCNN, QRL, QQL, QPSO, QA, and QDE are critically studied and found that the performances of the QCNN and QPSO is good amongst all the quantum machine learning models discussed towards quantum key distribution.

Chapter 4: LFSR Keyed MUX for Random Number Generation in Nano Communication Using QCA

Authors in this chapter proposed an efficient Quantum Cellular Automata (QCA) based Random Number Generator (RNG). To maximise the randomness in the proposed Nano communication, Linear Feedback Shift Register (LFSR) Keyed Multiplexer with Ring Oscillators is developed. The developed RNG is simulated using Quantum Cellular Automata (QCA) simulator tool.

Chapter 5: Quantum Cryptography Key Distribution – Quantum Computing

This Chapter discusses fundamentals of classical and quantum cryptography with different quantum key distribution protocols. Quantum key distribution characteristics, challenges and implementation concepts are also discussed. Idea of quantum resistant algorithm is also explored.

Chapter 6: Quantum Internet and E-Governance – A Futuristic Perspective

This chapter analyses evolution of quantum cryptography, components involved to design network architecture for quantum internet, quantum key exchange mechanism and functionality wise stages for quantum internet, E-governance, related challenges and solution using quantum cryptography.

Chapter 7: Critical Infrastructure Security – Cyber-Physical Attack Prevention, Detection, and Countermeasures

This chapter reviews NIST framework for cyber physical systems and discussed different views toward cyber physical security, attack categorization, attack against the smart grid, attacks against the customers, 3M architecture for cyber physical system, countermeasures. The authors of this chapter identify possible solution for defence against cyber physical system.

Chapter 8: Cryptography in Healthcare Sector With Modernized Cyber Security

This chapter identifies the necessity of cryptography in healthcare sector and related different techniques. It also discusses block chain health care data management system and the structure of block chain. Author investigate that face recognition and iris detection based on deep learning techniques.

Chapter 9: Improved Methodology to Detect Advanced Persistent Threat Attack

This chapter analyses security analysis, advanced persistent threat attacks and its characteristics. Authors of this chapter proposed a model based on Markov-chain property to tackle advanced persistent attack in the network. Experimental results with the help of simulator shows that the proposed model minimize load on the server and increases reliability.

Chapter 10: IoT and Cyber Security – Introduction, Attacks, and Preventive Steps

This chapter discusses about IoT and its hardware, experimental display for temperature and humidity sensing, IoT architecture, characteristics and applications. Author of this chapter also reviews possible attacks and preventive steps for IoT infrastructure.

Chapter 11: Security and Privacy in Big Data Computing – Concepts, Techniques, and Research Challenges

This chapter discusses fundamentals of big data and summarizes findings of many current research papers. It also discusses homographic encryption technique, certificate less proxy re encryption scheme, attribute based access control, block chain access control, de identification scheme. Open issues related to traditional techniques of big data privacy and security are also analysed by author. Moreover, it also illustrates comprehensive overview of possible security techniques and future directions addressing Big data privacy and security issues.

Chapter 12: Cyber Security Techniques for Internet of Things (IoT)

This chapter investigate IoT Security Maturity Model (SMM) set security targets and invest in security mechanisms. Authors conclude that the IoT device product lifecycle management (PLM) can be improved by accumulating IoT data with data from product specifications and digital twins. There is a need for a framework or other type of guidance for assessing IoT cybersecurity to provide an informed approach to securing devices and the ecosystems in which they are set up.

Chapter 13: Cyber Security Aspects of Virtualization in Cloud Computing Environment – Analyzing Virtualization Specific Cyber Security Risks

This chapter discusses quantum key distribution fundamentals with reference to secure cloud computing. It also focuses on virtualization security, taxonomy, threats, vulnerability and different attacks. Author analyzed that the side-channel attacks are flattering big security concerns which needs to be reviewed from a new point of view. A CPU cache which is shared between Virtual Machines (VMs) leaks information on cache access patterns of running instances. The authors also discuss the design of their novel 'Flush+Flush' cache attack detection approach in a virtualized environment.

CONCLUSION

Quantum cryptography still have many miles to go but today's cyber security solutions have already started to think about inclusion of quantum cryptographic techniques as part of their implementation. Research community has even started representing different solutions for post quantum cryptography and quantum resistant solution thinking of quantum reality. Quantum Cryptography and Cyber Security are at the center of research and practitioner interests in an increasingly inter-connected world. Quantum technologies have a positive impact on cyber security. Quantum device with the current state-of-the art technology can be used to enhance the security by achieving tasks impossible classically, such as, secret key expansion with perfect security. Since, quantum computers will become an integral part of our future network of communications and computations, we need to develop practical way to use the quantum computers with same security guarantees with those of secure (classical) computing. Security scenario is changing drastically fast, from the perception of attacker and preventer both side. We need to remain open to new invention and its adaptation to the existing solutions and this book share latest development of quantum cryptographic and cyber security. In the future, the part of everyday life and economy requiring computer systems is bound to increase further and become fully dominant. Cyber warfare and cybercrime will be common and the role of cyber security crucial. We hope that this book continues to engage researchers, practitioners and students on this important topic.

Nirbhay Chaubey
Gujarat Technological University, India

Bhavesh Prajapati
Education Department, Government of Gujarat, India

Acknowledgment

The editors would like to acknowledge the help of all the people involved in this project and, more specifically, the authors, as without their contribution and support this book would not have become a reality. The editors would like to thank each one of the authors for their contributions. Our sincere gratitude goes to the chapters' authors who contributed their time and expertise to this book.

We wish to acknowledge the valuable contributions of the reviewers, editorial board members regarding the improvement of quality, coherence, and content presentation of chapters. Few authors also served as referees; we highly appreciate their double task.

We are highly grateful and express deep appreciation to our source of inspiration, Dr. Akshai Aggarwal, Professor Emeritus, School of Computer Science, University of Windsor, Canada and Ex. Vice Chancellor, Gujarat Technological University (GTU), India for the insights and guidance he provided throughout the execution of this book project.

We acknowledge and thank Dr. Savita Gandhi, Professor and Head, Department of Computer Science, Gujarat University, Ahmedabad, India for her encouragement and support to write this book. Her continuous support and excellent guidance have been our strongest motivation to bring our book in its present form. We would like to acknowledge the help rendered by our family members for their patience and support throughout the process of our book project.

We acknowledge and thank Dr. Chetan B. Bhatt, Professor and Principal, Government MCA College, Maninagar, Ahmedabad for his continuous support, guidance and inspiration throughout this work.

We acknowledge and thank Dr. Vinay S. Purani, Professor and Principal, Government Engineering College, Valsad and Ex. Joint Director, Technical Education department, Government of Gujarat for his support, motivation and constructive feedback for excellence.

Acknowledgment

The editors would like to give a special thanks to IGI Global, the publishers, who believed in us and published our book for their constant support and guidance throughout the entire process.

Nirbhay Kumar Chaubey
Ganpat Technological University, India

Bhavesh B. Prajapati
Education Department, Government of Gujarat, India

Section 1
Quantum Cryptography

Chapter 1
Post–Quantum Cryptography and Quantum Cloning

Amandeep Singh Bhatia
Center for Quantum Computing, Peng Cheng Laboratory, China

Shenggen Zheng
Center for Quantum Computing, Peng Cheng Laboratory, China

ABSTRACT

In the last two decades, the field of post-quantum cryptography has had an overwhelming response among research communities. The ability of quantum computers to factorize large numbers could break many of well-known RSA cryptosystem and discrete log-based cryptosystem. Thus, post-quantum cryptography offers secure alternatives which are implemented on classical computers and is secure against attacks by quantum computers. The significant benefits of post-quantum cryptosystems are that they can be executed quickly and efficiently on desktops, smartphones, and the Internet of Things (IoTs) after some minor software updates. The main objective of this chapter is to give an outline of major developments in privacy protectors to reply to the forthcoming threats caused by quantum systems. In this chapter, we have presented crucial classes of cryptographic systems to resist attacks by classical and quantum computers. Furthermore, a review of different classes of quantum cloning is presented.

DOI: 10.4018/978-1-7998-2253-0.ch001

INTRODUCTION

In cryptography, several public-key cryptosystems are based on hard problems (not easily tractable on classical computers) such as discrete logarithms and integer factorization. Over the years, number of cryptography algorithms have been introduced and played a crucial role in cybersecurity such as Rivest-Shamir-Adleman (RSA) cryptosystem, Diffie-Hellman key exchange, elliptic curve cryptosystems (ECC) and digital signature algorithm (DSA). Nowadays, quantum computing is an exceptionally hot area of research. The era of quantum computing is nearly upon us, and quantum computers will be able to perform certain operations more quickly and efficiently than classical ones. It is based on quantum mechanical principles of superposition and entanglement. Feynman (1982) stated that the simulation of quantum mechanics was performed on a classical computer. Initially, it was thought to be only a theoretical interest, but now the race to develop a truly useful quantum computer is on among major IT companies and research communities.

Shor (1994) developed a polynomial quantum algorithm which can solve the above intractable problems easily on a quantum computer. As the rapid advancement in quantum computers is catching up, Shor's factorization algorithm will completely end the RSA encryption. It take $O(\log n)$ space complexity and $O((\log n)^2 * \log \log n)$ time on a quantum computer and $O(\log n)$ time on a classical computer to find factors of a large number n. Therefore, current popular public-key cryptosystems can be attacked in polynomial time. Bernstein (2009) shown the status of several present public-key cryptosystems, given in Table 1.

Till now, various public-key cryptosystems have been introduced to reply to security concerns with quantum systems in the post-quantum era. Post-quantum

Table 1. The present status of public-key cryptosystems

Cryptosystems	Cracked by Quantum algorithms?
Diffie-Hellman key-exchange by Diffie and Hellman (1976)	Yes
McEliece public-key encryption by McEliece (1978)	No
Algebraically Homomorphic by Rivest et al. (1978)	Yes
RSA public-key encryption by Rivest et al. (1978)	Yes
Algebraically Homomorphic by Rivest et al. (1978)	Yes
Elliptic curve cryptography by Koblitz (1987)	Yes
Buchmann-Williams key-exchange by Buchmann and Williams (1988)	Yes
Lattice-based public-key encryption by Cai and Cusick (1998)	No
NTRU public-key encryption by Hoffstein et al. (1998)	No

cryptography provides secure substitutes. The objective is to unfold different public-key cryptosystems, which can be adaptable to present communication networks and resist the attacks by both classical and quantum computers. Besides, RSA, DSA, and Elliptic curve digital signature algorithm (ECDSA), there exist several crucial classes of cryptographic systems which consist of code-based, hash-based, lattice-based, and multivariate-quadratic-equations. Indeed, Shor's algorithm has not been employed in these classes yet.

Although there exist several challenges for the implementation of the post-quantum algorithms. The requirement is to expand the effectiveness and make practicable these algorithms. Secondly, the time is required to get assuredness in post-quantum algorithms. Recently, Bhatia and Kumar (2019) mentioned that these challenges need to be focused before shifting completely to the post-quantum era. In this chapter, the details of different post-quantum cryptosystems to resist completely every attack are given. Moreover, the various classes of quantum cloning are described.

Basic Notations

In this section, some basic notations and terminologies are given, which will be used in the rest of this chapter.

- **Hamming Distance:** A Hamming distance $d_H(x, y)$ is the number of positions in which two codewords *(x, y)* differ. Let C be a [n, k] linear code over F_q^n and $x = \left(x_1, x_2, ..., x_n \right), y = (y_1, y_2, ..., y_n)$ are codewords by Löndahl et al. (2016).

$$d_H(x, y) = \left| i : x_i \neq y_i, 1 \leq i \leq n \right| \tag{1}$$

- **Hamming Weight:** A Hamming weight $wt_H(x)$ is defined as the number of non-zero positions in the codeword x. Let C be a [n,k] linear code over F_q^n and $x = \left(x_1, x_2, ..., x_n \right)$ is a codeword by Löndahl et al. (2016), such that

$$wt_H(x) = \left| i : x_i \neq 0, 1 \leq i \leq n \right| \tag{2}$$

- **Generator Matrix:** A generator matrix for C is a $k \times n$ matrix G having the vectors of $V = (v_1, v_2, ..., v_k)$ as rows, which forms a basis of C such that

3

$$C = \{mG : m \in F_q^n\}, G = \begin{bmatrix} v_1 \\ v_2 \\ \dots \\ v_k \end{bmatrix} \tag{3}$$

The matrix G generates the code as a linear map: for each message $m \in F_q^n$, the corresponding codeword mG is obtained by Bhatia and Kumar (2019).

- **Parity Matrix:** A $(n-k) \times n$ generator matrix H is called a parity-check matrix for codeword C defined by Löndahl et al. (2016), which is described by

$$C = \{m \in F_q^n : mH^T = 0\} \tag{4}$$

- **Lattice (L):** It is defined as a set of all integer combinations of linearly independent vectors $(a_1, a_2, \dots, a_n)$ of length n in R^n, which are called basis in a lattice by Peikert (2016).

$$L(a_1, a_2, \dots, a_n) = \sum_{i=1}^{n} x_i a_i \mid x_i \in Z, \tag{5}$$

It can be represented in matrix form such that $A = (a_1, a_2, \dots, a_n) \in R^{n \times n}$, columns act as basis vectors.

- **Polynomial Ring:** Let R be a commutative ring, then
$R[x] = \{a_n x^n + a_{n-1} x^{n-1} + .. + a_1 x. + a_0\}$, is called the ring of polynomials over R in the intermediate x, where x is the set of polynomials with $a_0, a_1, \dots, a_n$ coefficients and $n \in Z$ and defined by Buchmann (2013).

CODE-BASED CRYPTOGRAPHY

Code-based cryptography refers to the study of public-key cryptosystems based on error-correcting codes to resist the attacks by quantum computers. It is among the most popular post-quantum algorithms. The error code is added intentionally to a message and syndrome is computed corresponding to the parity matrix of a code.

The main public-key code-based cryptosystems are McEliece and Niederreiter. These algorithms provide a significant trade-off between security and efficiency.

McEliece Cryptosystem

In the 1950s, the concept of Golay code was proposed and has got an overwhelming response in the last two decades. Based on extended binary Golay code [24, 12, 8], McEliece cryptosystem provides a unique way to encode 12 bits of data into 24-bit long word and can correct up to 3 bits of error. A public-key cryptosystem based on binary Goppa codes is developed by McEliece (1978). It is one of the oldest asymmetric encryption algorithms and considered to be post-quantum secure. The security of McEliece cryptosystem depends upon the decoding algorithm to decode the linear block of code unknowing the internal structure.

Till now, several modified variants of the original McEliece cryptosystem were introduced on the basis of a family of error-correcting codes such as Reed-Muller codes, Reed-Solomon codes, sub-codes of Reed-Solomon codes, Gabidulin codes, concatenated codes, and convolutional codes. The McEliece cryptosystem based on the concept of extended Golay code is proposed, and its security is analyzed by Bhatia and Kumar (2018). The description of the original McEliece cryptosystem algorithm is given in Table 2. The working of McEliece public-key cryptosystem is shown in Figure 1.

Figure 1. Encryption and decryption process of a McEliece public-key cryptosystem

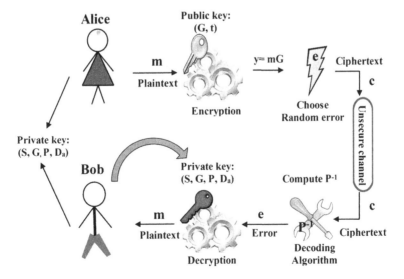

Table 2. McEliece public-key cryptosystem

The McEliece cryptosystem is defined as a triple (KeyCr, Encr, Decr):
Key Creation (KeyCr)
• Choose a random [n, k, 2t+1] decodable linear code C. • Compute the matrix $(k \times n)$ $G' = SGP$, where G is $(k \times n)$ generator matrix, S $(k \times k)$ and P $(n \times n)$ are randomly chosen non-singular and permutation matrix respectively.
• The private key: *(S, G, P, D_a)* and public key: (G', t).
Encryption (Encr)
• Select a random vector $e \in \{0,1\}^n$ consists of exactly t ones.
• Encrypt the *k*-length message $m \in \{0,1\}^k$. Finally, compute the ciphertext $c = mG' + e$.
Decryption (Decr)
• The inverse of the permutation matrix P^{-1} is computed.
• Compute $cP^{-1} = mSG + eP^{-1}$.
• An efficient decoding algorithm (D_a) is used to decrypt $c_1 = cP^{-1}$ to *m*.
• Retrieve the original message $m = m'S^{-1}$.

Sendrier (1998) mentioned that the original McEliece algorithm is unbroken today no doubt. But, there are some of its disadvantages. It is not symmetric in nature. The size of the key is large, which can influence its execution process. The transmission rate is also very low. Due to the enlarging bandwidth size, the implementation can be exposed to errors.

Security

The McEliece algorithm is observed to be fully secure based on decoding algorithm and rigorous search on key. There exist two types of attacks, namely decoding and structural attacks on original Mcliece public-key cryptosystem:

1. Decoding attacks

As the name suggests, the attack consists of decrypting the ciphertext. In case, it becomes successful; then the plaintext can be retrieved easily. Loidreau (2000) has determined that on considering 1024-length of code, the requirement is to compute total 2^{64} binary operations for decoding ciphertext in addition to 524 key-size and 50 error-correcting capability. Hence, as the computational power grows, the original McEliece cryptosystem will not remain secure.

2. Structural attacks

The main attempt in structural attacks is to recreate the definite form of code from the public key. It is easy to retrieve the private key after the successful structural attack, which results in broken of the complete cryptosystem. On considering 1024-length of code, the need is to scan 2^{466} codes with 524-key size and 50 error-correcting capability. The internal structure of generator matrix G after the attack on the original McEliece cryptosystem was revealed by Loidreau and Sendrier (2001). So far, several structural attacks have been tried on different versions of McEliece cryptosystem.

Niederreiter Cryptosystem

In 1986, Niederreiter introduced the public-key cryptosystem based on Reed-Solomon codes. From a security perspective, it is similar to McEliece cryptosystem. The only difference lies in the illustration of codes, where McEliece uses a generator matrix, and Niederreiter utilizes a parity check matrix. Sidelnikov et al. (1992) proved that Niederreiter cryptosystem is insecure with Goppa and Reed-Solomon codes. Till now, several researchers tried to reduce the size of the public key of original McEliece cryptosystem. But, all existing variants remain ineffective and insecure on comparison with McEliece public-key cryptosystem. The description of Niederreiter cryptosystem is given in Table 3.

In Niederreiter cryptosystem, the plaintext m is demonstrated as an error of C rather than the original word. Besides, the decoding of code can be implemented more efficiently as compared to original McEliece cryptosystem. It can be noted that the generator matrix can be easily calculated from the party matrix and vice versa. Therefore, McEliece and Niederreiter cryptosystems are dual to each other. Niederreiter cryptosystem is useful to represent a digital signature scheme.

Table 3. Niederreiter cryptosystem

The Niederreiter cryptosystem is defined as a triple (KeyCr, Encr, Decr):
Key Creation (KeyCr)
• Choose a random [n, k, 2t+1] decodable linear code C . • Compute the matrix $(n-k) \times n$ $H' = SHP$, where H is $(n-k) \times n$ parity-check matrix, S $(n-k) \times (n-k)$ and P $(n \times n)$ are randomly chosen a binary non-singular matrix and permutation matrix respectively.
• The Private key: *(S, H, P, D)* and public key: (H', t)
Encryption (Encr)
• Encrypt the k-length message $m \in \{0,1\}^k$ of weight t, compute the ciphertext $c = mH'^T$.
Decryption (Decr)
• The inverse of non-singular matrix S^{-1} is computed.
• Compute $S^{-1}c^T = HPm^T$
• Find a vector (v) such that $Hv^T = HPm^T$
• Employ an efficient decoding algorithm D_a on v to retrieve the original message m.

LATTICE-BASED CRYPTOGRAPHY

The construction of lattice-based cryptosystems holds strong security proofs on the basis of worst-case resistance of lattice problems, which offers efficient execution and simplicity. Moreover, such cryptosystems are reliable and secure against the attacks of quantum computers. Basically, a lattice representing arbitrary basis is given as input and expected the output to be the shortest non-zero vector. The concept of lattice-based cryptosystem for the shortest vector problems is proposed by Lenstra et al. (1993). It runs in polynomial time. It is the most extensively studied algorithm for lattice problems, but later on, its various extensions have been introduced. The main lattice-based cryptosystems are described that have been introduced so far. Begin with the NTRU cryptosystem, which is the most well-known practically implemented lattice-based encryption scheme till now.

NTRU Algorithm

Hoffstein, Pipher, and Silverman (1998) proposed ring-based public-key cryptosystem. Since the NTRU algorithm is introduced, numerous researchers tried to enhance its security and to speed up the procedure. It contains q-ary sub lattices which are closed under linear modification. Futhermore the different attacks attempted to find the private key instead of retrieving the original message. So far, several variants have been introduced and evaluated on the basis of selected variables. The description of NTRU algorithm is given in Table 4.

The decryption of NTRU algorithm can be executed successfully, if the selected parameters (n, p, q, d) satisfy that $q > (6d + 1)p$. It has been demonstrated that NTRU algorithm can be implemented efficiently in hardware and software by Bu and Zhou (2009) and Hoffstein, Pipher and Silverman (1998). In NTRU, the less memory is needed, and keys can be produced quickly. Therefore, it can be practically implemented for devices with less memory, for example, mobile phones and smart cards (integrated circuits).

On comparing with the most popular public-key cryptosystems ECC and RSA, the NTRU algorithm is effective and secure. Several attacks are attempted on NTRU algorithms such as alternate secret keys, simultaneously transmission attack and brute force attack to decode the original message m. Thus, NTRU takes less time as compared to RSA and ECC and more time as compared to McEliece public-key cryptosystem for key creation, encryption, and decryption process.

Goldreich-Goldwasser-Halevi (GGH)

It is the most instinctive encryption scheme based on lattices. There exist many components of GGH encryption scheme in other lattice-based cryptosystems, but original GGH is practical, which offers simplicity. Goldreich, Goldwasser, and Halevi (1997) introduced lattice equivalent of McEliece cryptosystem in which short orthogonal vectors used as a private key. It acts as a good lattice basis. Till now, asymptotically good attack to GGH public encryption scheme is not identified because the security and correctness depend upon the selection of private basis and error vector. It is based on solving the problem "Close vector problem (CVP)" in a lattice, i.e., finds the lattice point closest to a given vector. As compared to RSA, Diffie-Hellman, and ElGamal, it offers high performance due to simple matrix operations.

The security of GGH cryptosystem depends upon selecting a suitable perturbation vector r. If it is selected very small, then the closest vector v can be easily retrieved without any difficulty. If it is selected very large, then it may be not possible to decrypt using the private key. Hence, the perturbation vector r must be chosen

Table 4. NTRU cryptosystem

Public Parameters
• Operations are formed on objects in a polynomial ring (R) that is truncated having coefficients to a certain degree such that $R = Z[X]/(X^N - 1)$. Choose two moduli p and q relatively prime in R. The moduli q is smaller than N and p is smaller than q such that $\gcd(p,q) = 1$.
• Additional parameters, d_f is set of polynomial in R having exactly d -1's and $(d+1)$ 1's; d_g and d_r is set of polynomials in R having exactly similar d -1's and d 1's and d_m is set of polynomials in R_p such that coefficients are in between -1/2(p+1) and 1/2(p+1).
Key Creation
• Choose a random $f \in d_f$ and invertible in $R = Z[X]/(X^N - 1) \bmod p$ and q. In case, if does not satisfy, then new random f is selected.
• Compute the inverse of $f \bmod p$ and $f \bmod q$ such that $f_q^{-1}.f \equiv 1 \bmod q$ and $f_p^{-1} \star f \equiv 1 \bmod p$.
• Hence, the pair $\left(f, f_q^{-1}\right)$ is a private key.
• For the public key h, compute the polynomial $h = f_q^{-1} \star g(\bmod q)$.
Encryption
• Select a polynomial randomly $r \in d_r$.
• Select a message $m \in d_m$.
• Calculate the ciphertext (c): $c = pr \star h + m \ (\bmod q)$.
Decryption
• Evaluate a polynomial a using private key polynomial such that $a = f \star c \ (\bmod q)$.
• Calculate $b = a \ (\bmod q)$ and reduces each of the coefficients of $b \bmod p$.
• Determine $z = f_p^{-1} \star b \ (\bmod p)$ by using private key polynomial f_p^{-1} to get the original message m.

Table 5. GGH cryptosystem

Construction of Keys
• For private key: Choose a full-column rank integer matrix *V* such that columns are orthogonal to each other.
$V = [v_1 v_2, v_3, ..., v_n], v_j \in Z^n, 1 \le j \le n$
• Select a random $n \times n$ unimodular matrix (*U*), such that $det(U) = \pm 1$.
• For public key: compute a matrix *W=VU*.
Encryption
• Choose a perturbation vector *r*, i.e., acts as an ephemeral key
• Select a plaintext message *m* of the same dimension, belongs to a lattice.
• Encrypt the message *m* using public key *W* and ephemeral key *r*, compute the ciphertext
$c = Wm + r$
Decryption
• Decrypt the closest vector *v* belongs to a lattice of ciphertext (*c*) using private key *V* and any decoding algorithm.
• Compute the inverse of *V* to decrypt the ciphertext such that $x = c.V^{-1}$.
• Then, retrieve the original message *m* by multiplying with the inverse of a unimodular matrix such as $m = x.U^{-1}$. At the end, its correctness can be checked by differentiating *m* with hashed value.

balanced, i.e., relatively small as compared to the vectors in public key *W*. Following are the advantages of lattice-based cryptography: Till now, any quantum attacks do not exist to break lattice-based cryptosystems. It is one of chief substitute for post-quantum cryptosystems. Nguyen and Regev (2009) analyzed that lattice-based cryptosystems are not employed much yet due to security reasons. NTRU is efficient in implementation but lack of security.

Nguyen and Regev (2009) shown the imperfection in design of GGH cryptosystem. The challenges in the execution of GGH are solved and came with partial information about the lattice. No doubt, GGH cryptosystem offers security with a suitable selection of parameters. But, on selecting the high dimension of lattice, it provides great improvement. Although the key size increases quadratically. Micciancio (2001) demonstrated that GGH cryptosystem promises security if the lattice dimension is larger than 350.

MULTIVARIATE CRYPTOGRAPHY

Over finite fields, Multivariate cryptosystems are based on non-linear equations that are difficult to solve. Thus, it is said to be very light-weight cryptography which is effective and efficient to be employed in embedded devices (microcontrollers). The security of multivariate cryptosystems is based on the NP-hardness of the problem. In the last two decades, an enormous development occurs in multivariate cryptography. It is defined as the study of public-key cryptosystem (Diffie and Hellman) in which one-way trapdoor function is based on the mapping of multivariate quadratic equations. There exist several multivariate public-key cryptography schemes such as Oil and vinegar signature scheme by Patarin (1997), Quartz signature scheme $(2,129,103,3,4)$ by Patarin et al. (2001), and Rainbow signature scheme $(2^8,18,12,12)$ by Ding and Schmidt (2005). These multivariate public key encryption algorithms are developed in several ways and all have their own benefits and drawbacks. It can also be called as trapdoor multivariate quadratic because most of the schemes are constructed using higher-order quadratic polynomial equations. Generally, the public key is a set of quadratic polynomials over a finite field

$$
\begin{aligned}
p_1(x_1,...,x_n) &= \sum_{1 \leq i \leq j \leq n} a_{ij}^1 x_i x_j + \sum_{1 \leq i \leq n} b_i^1 x_i + c^1 \\
p_2(x_1,...,x_n) &= \sum_{1 \leq i \leq j \leq n} a_{ij}^2 x_i x_j + \sum_{1 \leq i \leq n} b_i^2 x_i + c^2 \\
&\vdots \\
p_m(x_1,...,x_n) &= \sum_{1 \leq i \leq j \leq n} a_{ij}^m x_i x_j + \sum_{1 \leq i \leq n} b_i^m x_i + c^m
\end{aligned}
\tag{6}
$$

where $p_1, p_2,..., p_m$ are m quadratic polynomials with n variables such as $x_1, x_2,...x_n$. Chen et al. (2016) investigated that the multivariate public key cryptosystem encrypts the message faster as compared to RSA and ECC. The security depends upon the multivariate quadratic polynomial problem (MQP) where the need is to find a vector $x' = (x_1', x_2',...x_n')$ such that $p_1(x') = ... = p_m(x') = 0$. It has been demonstrated that such MQP problem is NP-hard over any field (Fraenkel and Yesha, 1979). The following are the multivariate public key cryptosystems:

Oil and Vinegar Signature Scheme (OV)

The first method of multivariate quadratic systems, namely oil and vinegar (OV) signature scheme is introduced by Patarin (1997). The logic behind the name oil and vinegar is that they cannot be blended in terms of quadratic variables.

Let oil (o) and vinegar (v) are two integers, and k be a finite field, such that $n = o + v$. Then, set $O=\{v+1,..., \text{n}\}$ and $V=\{1,..., v\}$, where $x_v + 1,..., x_n$ and $x_1,...x_v$ are oil and vinegar variables, respectively. It was indicated to choose $o=v$, then it is known as balanced OV scheme, if $v > 0$, then it is named as unbalanced OV scheme. The key generation consists a mapping F: $k^{0+v} \rightarrow k^0$ such that o quadratic polynomials is in form

$$f^k(x) = \sum_{i \in V}\sum_{j \in V} a_{ij}^k x_i x_j + \sum_{i \in V}\sum_{j \in O} b_{ij}^k x_i x_j + \sum_{i \in O \cup V} c_i^k x_i + d^k \qquad (7)$$

where $x_j, j = 1,...,o$ and $x_i, i = 1,...,v$ are oil and vinegar variables and $a_{ij}^k, b_{ij}^k, c_i^k x_i$ and d^k are randomly selected coefficients. It can be noted that mapping $F = (f_{v+1}(x),...,f_n(x))$ is simply invertible. Firstly, select vinegar variables randomly. Further, solve the linear equations with o variables by using Gaussian elimination method. If in case, we do not get any solution, then the need is to select vinegar variables again.

Quartz Signature Scheme (F, d, n, a, v) = (2,129,103,3,4)

Patarin et al. (2001) introduced the Quartz signature scheme based on the HFEv-trapdoor function. It was designed to produce very short signatures i.e. of only 128 bits. It has been designed for specific applications. Although, there are already exists several classical algorithms (RSA, ECC, DSA etc) which can generate signatures of length greater than equal to 320 bits. The public and private keys are HFEv that maps with the following parameters: $(F, d, n, a, v) = (GF(2), 129, 103, 3, 4)$, where F represents finite field, d denotes the polynomial degree, n signifies the size of an extended field, a is used to denote the number of removed equations and v signifies the vinegar variables.

In quartz algorithm, the public key (Pu_k) is used which maps quadratic equations from F^{107} to F^{100} and give input $n - a = 100$ bits. Firstly, compute four signatures for the messages

$$m_0 = SHA - 1(m), SHA - 1(m_0 \| 0x00), SHA - 1(m_0 \| 0x01)$$

and $SHA - 1(m_0 \| 0x02)$, where SHA stands for secure hash algorithm. Then, combine all of them in to one 128-bit long signature. During its verification, apply public key (Pu_k) four times. Generally, there are two known attacks MinRank proposed by Kipnis and Shamir (1999) and direct algebraic attacks. It has not been used much practically because of slow process of signature generation and production of short signatures.

Rainbow Signature Scheme

$$f^k(x) = \sum_{i \in V_l}\sum_{j \in V_l} a_{ij}^k x_i x_j + \sum_{i \in V_l}\sum_{j \in O_l} b_{ij}^k x_i x_j + \sum_{i \in O_l \cup V_l} c_i^k x_i + d^k \tag{8}$$

where $l \in \{1, 2, ..., u\}$ such that $k \in O_l$. The steps of rainbow signature scheme's construction are explained as follows:

- **Key Creation:** Public-key contains k and map of the form $P(x) = S_1 \circ F \circ S_2(x)k^n$, $\rightarrow k^m$ where S_1, S_2 are two invertible or linear maps $S_1 : k^m \rightarrow k^m$ and $S_2 : k^n \rightarrow k^n$. A private-key contains (F, S_1, S_2), where $F = (f^{v_1+1}, ..., f^n)$ is central rainbow map.

- **Signature a Document:** To sign a document d, the need is to observe a solution of an equation

$$S_1 \circ F \circ S_2 \left(x_1, x_2, ..., x_n \right) = F'\left(x_1, x_2, ..., x_n \right) = T'$$

On applying inverse of S_1,

$$F \circ S_2 \left(x_1, x_2, ..., x_n \right) = S_1^{-1} T' = T''$$

The equation is computed recursively to the inverse of F such that

$$F\left(x_1, x_2, ..., x_n \right) = T'' = \left(y_1'', ..., y_{n-v_1}'' \right)$$

In the end, apply the inverse of S_2 such that $z = S_2^{-1}(y)$, which gives us the signature T' of document d i.e. $T' \in k^n$.

- **Verification:** To demonstrate the authenticity of signature d, check $F'\left(x_1', x_2', ..., x_n' \right) = T'$.

14

If there is a need to sign a large size document, then apply the hash function and compute the hash value to verify its authenticity. The rainbow signature scheme offers simplicity due to simple matrix operations (multiplication and inversion) over a finite field. It is more efficient than oil and vinegar scheme due to small key and concise signatures in size. Although, there exists several attacks MinRank attack by Kipnis and Shamir (1999) and Rainbow-Band-Separation attack by Fraenkel and Yesha (1979), which find the linear mapping to change the polynomials into quadratic mapping.

HASH-BASED CRYPTOGRAPHY

The security of currently used digital signature algorithms is based on the hardness of factorization of sizeable composite numbers. Such algorithms are not quantum resistant. Therefore, hash-based cryptography is based on the cryptographic hash function. as an alternative solution and its security depends upon the collision resistance of hash function. Hash-based cryptosystems are the prominent candidate of post-quantum cryptography due to their minimal security requirements. There exist various hash-based cryptography schemes which are beneficial for an era of quantum such as Lamport-Diffie one-time signature scheme (LD-OTS) introduced by Lamport (1979), Winternitz one-time signature scheme (W-OTS) by MErkle (1989). These one-time digital signature schemes are not suitable for practical states because every pair of a key can be utilized per signature only. Hence, Merkle defined MErkle's tree authentication scheme based on a complete binary hash tree to lessen the validity of one-time verification keys

Lamport-Diffie One-Time Signature Scheme (LD-OTS)

A one-time signature scheme (LD-OTS) is proposed by Lamport (1979). For security reasons, most of the signature schemes are based on hash functions, whereas the security of Lamport signature scheme is based on one-way functions $f : \{0,1\}^n \rightarrow \{0,1\}^n$ and cryptographic hash function $h : \{0,1\}^n \rightarrow \{0,1\}^n$. The construction of Lamport–Diffie one-time signature scheme is explained as follows:

- **Key Creation:** The signature key (S_k) and verification key (V_k) are selected randomly which consists of $2n$ bit strings of length n such that

$$S_k(x) = \left\{ x_{n-1}[0]x_{n-1}[1],..., x_1[0]x_1[1], x_0[0]x_0[1] \right\} \in \{0,1\}^{(n,2n)} \tag{9}$$

$$V_k(y) = \left\{y_{n-1}[0]y_{n-1}[1], \ldots, y_1[0]y_1[1], y_0[0]y_0[1]\right\} \in \{0,1\}^{(n,2n)} \tag{10}$$

where $y_j[k] = f(x_j[k])$, for $0 \le j \le n-1$, $k = 0,1,\ldots$ Thus, key generation needs $2n$ assessments of f.

- **Signature Generation:** Consider a document $d \in \{0,1\}^*$ which is signed by exploiting signature key (S_k). Suppose a message digest be a $g(D) = M\{m_{n-1}, \ldots, m_0\}$. Then, its signature becomes

$$\sigma = \left\{x_{n-1}[d_{n-1}], \ldots, x_1[d_1], x_0[d_0]\right\} \in \{0,1\}^{(n,n)} \tag{11}$$

where σ is group of n bit strings of length n, which are selected as a f(D). So, the length of signature becomes n^2.

- **Verification:** To verify the signature (σ), the verifier determines the message digest $M = \{m_{n-1}, \ldots, m_0\}$. It needs n evaluations of f to check equality such that

$$(f(\sigma_{n-1}), \ldots, f(\sigma_0)) = (y_{n-1}[d_{n-1}], \ldots, y_0[d_0]) \tag{12}$$

Winternitz One-Time Signature Scheme (W-OTS)

After the introduction of LD-OTS, MErkle has written that Winternitz suggested him the method and named it as Winternitz one-time signature scheme. The main notion is to use a string in (S_k) to sign various bits in message digest at same time. It uses same one-way functions and cryptographic functions like LD-OTS and produces shorter signatures efficiently. The construction of original W-OTS is explained as follows:

- **Key Creation:** Firstly, set the number of bits to be signed at same time i.e. $w \ge 2$. Then, compute

$$t_1 = \left\lceil \frac{n}{w} \right\rceil, t_2 = \left\lceil \frac{\lfloor \log_2 t_1 \rfloor + 1 + w}{w} \right\rceil, t = t_1 + t_2 \tag{13}$$

The signature key (S_k) is selected at random such that

$$S_k(x) = (x_{t-1}, ..., x_1, x_0) \in \{0,1\}^{(n,t)} \tag{14}$$

and the verification key (V_k) is computed by applying one-way function $f : \{0,1\}^n \rightarrow \{0,1\}^n$, $2^w - 1$ times to each bit string in S_k.

$$V_k(y) = (y_{t-1}, ..., y_1, y_0) \in \{0,1\}^{(n,t)} \tag{15}$$

where $y_i = f^{2^w - 1}(x_i)$ for $0 \le i \le t-1$.

- **Signature Generation:** Consider a message digest $g(D) = M = (m_{n-1}, ..., m_0)$ to be signed. In order to divide the message digest d with w, prepend the minimum number of 0's to it. Now, the string d is split into t-1 bit strings such that $d = a_{t-1} \| ... \| a_{t-t_1}$, where $\|$ signifies concatenation of strings and a_i are integers belong to $(0,1, ..., 2^w - 1)$. Next, the checksum is computed

$$c = \sum_{i=t-t_1}^{t-1} (2^w - a_i) \tag{16}$$

Then, in order to divide a binary representation by w, prepend a minimum number of 0's, and the string is split into t_2 groups such that

$$c = a_{t_2-1} \| ... \| a_0 \tag{17}$$

In the end, the signature is calculated as

$$\sigma = \{f^{a_{t-1}}(x_{t-1}), ..., f^{a_1}(x_1), f^{a_0}(x_0)\} \tag{18}$$

- **Verification:** In order to verify the signature above, the bit strings $a_{t-1}, ..., a_1, a_0$ are computed and check the equality such that

$$(f^{2^w - 1 - a_{t-1}}(\sigma_{n-1}), ..., f^{2^w - 1 - a_0}(\sigma_0)) = (y_{n-1}, ..., y_0) \tag{19}$$

If the computed signature is logically correct, then, the following equation holds such that

$$f^{2^w-1-a_i}(\sigma_i) = f^{2^w-1}(x_i) = y_i \qquad (20)$$

where $i = t - 1, ...0$. It needs $t(2^w - 1)$ assessment of f in the worst case.

Till now, various generalizations of W-OTS has been occurred, such as W-OTS (used in MAC) and W-OTS$^+$ introduced by Hülsing (2013). The main purpose is to upgrade the W-OTS to increase the security and shorten the size of signatures.

QUANTUM CLONING

Until the mid-1990s, the people did not acknowledge the concept of quantum cloning due to no-cloning theorem. The concept of "Universal Quantum Cloning Machine" is introduced by Buzek and Hillery (1996). It generates imperfect copies of a qubit, where the quality of the cloned state is not dependent on the input state. The no-cloning theorem states that there is no such quantum operation exists that can exactly produce a priori unknown pure state $|\varphi\rangle$, such that $U|\varphi\rangle|0\rangle = |\varphi\rangle|\varphi\rangle$, i.e., there is no unitary operator exists for pure state $|\varphi\rangle$. The "quantum cloning machines" are crucial to study eavesdropping on quantum cryptosystems and state estimation. There exist several versions of universal quantum cloning, but the main objective is to produce a cloned state of the arbitrary pure state in a finite-dimensional Hilbert space.

Figure 2. N → M deterministic quantum cloning with the ancilla qubit

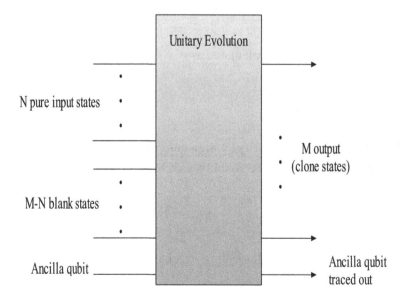

In 2005, the deterministic cloning of arbitrary pure states was mapped as a linear trace-preserving completely positive (TPCP). Scarani et al. (2005) indicated that the exchange of quantum information between the systems is intermediate with the ancilla qubit, which can redistribute the information among numerous quantum systems. Thus, the process of deterministic quantum cloning of an input state is investigated as follows:

$$\left(\left|\varphi\right\rangle^{\otimes N}\right) \otimes \left(\left|0\right\rangle^{\otimes M-N}\right) \otimes \left|C\right\rangle \xrightarrow{\quad U \quad} \left|\Psi\right\rangle \tag{21}$$

where N denotes the input states and M-N represent the blank copies associated with an ancilla qubit and performs a unitary operator U into the final state. Initially, the universal quantum cloning machine is introduced for optimal $1 \rightarrow 2$ qubits, which generates two clones from an input state of the same fidelity. Later on, the extended variant for $N \rightarrow M$ qubits is proposed. If the quality of all output (cloned states) M is equivalent, the t quantum machine is referred as symmetric, else asymmetric. The different classes of quantum cloning are shown in Figure 3.

State-Dependent Quantum Cloning

When the quality of output (cloned states) is generated by the cloning evolution depends on the input state, the evolution of the cloning process is said to be state-dependent quantum cloning. In fact, the quality of output is produced by state-dependent cloning is better than the universal quantum cloning machine, but at the cost of poor cloning of other states. In state-dependent cloning, it is possible to improve the quality of output cloned states by getting some information about the initial state.

Figure 3. Classification of quantum cloning

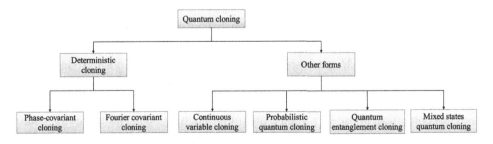

It should be noted that the information about the initial state does not always result in superior cloning. Bruss et al. (1998) stated that the universal quantum cloning machine can be used for the six-state quantum key distribution protocol. It is stated that it is not possible to produce exact output (clone states) of the six-state protocol using state-dependent cloners. Consider two input states $|\alpha\rangle$ and $|\beta\rangle$, related by $\langle\alpha|\beta\rangle = z$, where z can be 0 or 1. It is investigated that the perfect cloning can be attained for z, and results shown that minimum fidelity (F=0.987) is achieved for z=1/2. The find the minimum input sets for defining the universal cloning machine is a problem. Jing et al. (2012) explored that the minimum four states on the vertices of the polyhedron are required for cloning $1 \rightarrow 2$ states optimally.

Phase-Covariant Cloning

In phase-covariant cloning, the quality of cloned states is not controlled by phase. Consider a pure state of form

$$|\varphi\rangle = \left(|\varphi\rangle + e^{i\phi}|1\rangle\right) / \sqrt{2} \tag{22}$$

The qubits of such form are equatorial qubits of the Bloch sphere, i.e., the Bloch vector is confined to xy-plane only, and z-component is zero. The parameter $\phi \in [0, 2\pi)$ defines the angle between x-axis and Bloch vector. The output of phase-covariant cloners does not depend upon the value of phase ϕ. It can be symmetric or asymmetric. Fuchs et al. (1997) and Fan et al. (2001) described the major difference with the universal quantum cloning. It has been demonstrated that phase-covariant cloning depends upon global fidelity or single-copy.

Initially, the concept of phase-covariant cloner as an eavesdropping attack on the most popular quantum key distribution protocol BB84 is studied by Fuchs et al. (1997) with respect to single-copy fidelity. The phase-covariant $1 \rightarrow M$ was studied for qubits. Till now, the optimal $1 \rightarrow 2$ phase-covariant cloner for qudits (It can have 10 or more quantum states simultaneously compared to just two for qubits). It has been demonstrated by different researchers Buscemi et al. (2005) and Fan et al. (2003), but the $N \rightarrow M$ phase-covariant cloner for qudits is not introduced yet. The phase-covariant cloners can be constructed economically without using ancilla qubit.

The economical phase-covariant cloners (symmetric and asymmetric) for a pure state (given in Eq. 22) are introduced by Niu and Griffiths (1999) and compared with the counterparts based on the same fidelity. Fan et al. (2014) stated that the clone states of phase-covariant cloners and economical cloners can be different, even they have the same fidelity. It has been determined on several occasions that state-dependent cloners are superior to the universal quantum cloners. The phase-covariant $1 \rightarrow 3$ quantum clone machines attain 5/6 fidelity, as similar to $1 \rightarrow 2$ universal quantum clone machines. Although, the third clone with the same fidelity is obtained for equatorial input states.

Fourier-Covariant Cloning

As the name indicates, the covariant evolutions are covariant with regards to a Fourier-transform and clones are mutually unbiased bases to each other. The eigenstates of Pauli matrices are used to produce clones of three qubits mutually unbiased bases. Thus, the phase covariant cloner can be generated with the states of two mutually unbiased bases. In two-dimensional Hilbert space, all pairs of mutually unbiased based are unitarily identical. Hence, Cerf et al. (2006) stated that Fourier-covariant cloner is corresponding to phase-covariant cloner. It has been investigated that the fidelity of Fourier-covariant cloner is more than phase-covariant cloner in case of three-level $1 \rightarrow 2$ qutrit asymmetric cloner. Later on, the $1 \rightarrow 2$ qutrit cloner is expanded in arbitrary finite dimension by Cerf et al. (2002).

Other Forms

The aforementioned classes of cloning are focusing on cloning of states deterministically. The following are the other forms of quantum cloning.

Continuous-Variable Quantum Cloning

In infinite-dimensional Hilbert space, the continuous-variable quantum cloning is the most studied quantum cloning. Universal quantum cloning machine for coherent states is not widely studied. Initially, Gaussian cloner and produced similar copies of two conjugate variables for $1 \rightarrow 2$ cloning evolution is presented by Cerf et al. (2000). Till now, the concept of Gaussian continuous-variable cloning has been considered enormously. Further, the fidelity of $N \rightarrow M$ Gaussian cloner based on coherent states is determined by Cerf et al. (2000). It has been demonstrated that Gaussian cloner can be used to produce clones of squeezed states optimally with minor changes.

The $N \rightarrow M$ Gaussian cloner using beam splitter network and linear phase-sensitive amplifier is implemented by Braunstein et al. (2001). The cloning evolution relies on global or single-copy fidelity. Cerf et al. (2005) shown that continuous-variable quantum cloning is Gaussian with respect to global fidelity, but if the number of cloned states (M) is finite, then the quantum cloners are non-Gaussian with respect to single-copy fidelity.

Probabilistic Quantum Cloning

The cloning transformation of probabilistic quantum cloning consists of unitary operator and measurement. There is less than 1% probability of producing exact clone; otherwise, it is unsuccessful. In the end, the measurement is carried out on ancilla qubit, which shows whether the process of cloning evolution is successful or not. Regardless of higher fidelity than deterministic cloning schemes, it can produce cloned copies approximately.

The concept of probabilistic cloning was proposed independently by Duan and Guo (1998) and Chefles and Barnett (1998). It has been determined that a perfect copy of linearly independent states can be produced with some probability. Later on, the concept of Probabilistic cloning is expanded to infinite-dimensional space and stated that the quality of cloned states by universal quantum cloning machine could not be enhanced by probabilistic cloning machine. Although, Hardy and Song (1999) investigated that it can be helpful if the number of states is limited. Probabilistic cloning plays a crucial role in quantum information processing. Duan and Guo (1998) described the relationship in state discrimination and probabilistic cloning, and can be applied in the security analysis of quantum key distribution protocols.

Quantum Entanglement Cloning

Quantum entanglement and superposition are fundamental principles of quantum mechanics and play an important role in quantum information processing. Koashi and Imoto (1998) determined that the exact clone copies of quantum entanglement cannot be produced due to the principles of quantum mechanics. So far, several methods were presented on quantum entanglement cloning. It has been shown that the copies of two-qudit state cannot be generated exactly. Furthermore, the fidelity of $1 \rightarrow 2$ quantum entanglement cloners over the $n \times n$-dimensional entangled states is studied by Karpov et al. (2005).

Mostly, the concept of quantum entanglement is demonstrated under local operations and classical communication (LOCC). Under the effect of LOCC, the entanglement cannot be expanded. It has been stated that the perfect cloning of a pair of Bell states can be performed. Therefore, the cloning of $1 \rightarrow 2$ is shown with LOCC by Bennett et al. (1996). Later on, the possibility to produce clone copies of unknown Bell state without the supervision of LOCC is presented. It can be performed using CNOT gates and entangled ancilla qubits.

Mixed States Quantum Cloning

It is known that the broadcast of non-commuting mixed states is not possible. As a result, most researchers studied the concept of cloning for pure quantum states until now. Initially, Barnum et al. (1996) proved that the no-cloning theorem can also be used for mixed states. Rastegin (2003) determined that the global fidelity for state-dependent mixed state and stated that the cloning evolutions are cannot be generated for mixed states. The mixed-state quantum cloning for qubits is presented and proved that $N \to M$ universal quantum clone machine is optimal by Aiano et al. (2005). Further, it has been determined that $1 \to M$ universal quantum cloning machine is not available based on fidelity as the parameter. It has been proved that the probabilistic cloning of mixed states can be performed by Li et al. (2009).

CONCLUSION

After the introduction of Shor's algorithm, quantum computing can decrypt any data secured by present algorithms. Post-quantum cryptosystems are focused on defending the encrypted data against the attacks of classical and quantum computers in the future. Due to lack of hardware and resources for their implementation, more efforts are needed to build confidence for using post-quantum cryptosystems extensively. Hence, there exist several essential questions that need to be addressed. Although, there are several tech giants already conducting experiments with promising post-quantum cryptography algorithms. The requirement is to reduce the public-key size and the actual implementation of post-quantum algorithms in quantum-safe systems. In this chapter, numerous post-quantum public-key cryptosystems are illustrated. Moreover, the classes of quantum cloning machines are described for several quantum information processing tasks.

REFERENCES

Barnum, H., Caves, C. M., Fuchs, C. A., Jozsa, R., & Schumacher, B. (1996). Noncommuting mixed states cannot be broadcast. *Physical Review Letters*, *76*(15), 2818–2821. doi:10.1103/PhysRevLett.76.2818 PMID:10060796

Bennett, C. H., Bernstein, H. J., Popescu, S., & Schumacher, B. (1996). Concentrating partial entanglement by local operations. *Physical Review A*, *53*(4), 2046–2052. doi:10.1103/PhysRevA.53.2046 PMID:9913106

Bernstein, D. J. (2009). *Introduction to post-quantum cryptography. Post-quantum cryptography* (pp. 1–14). Berlin: Springer. doi:10.1007/978-3-540-88702-7

Bhatia, A. S., & Kumar, A. (2018). McEliece Cryptosystem Based On Extended Golay Code.

Bhatia, A. S., & Kumar, A. (2019). Post-Quantum Cryptography. In *Emerging Security Algorithms & Techniques* (1st ed.). New York: Chapman and Hall/CRC Press. doi:10.1201/9781351021708-9

Braunstein, S. L., Cerf, N. J., Iblisdir, S., van Loock, P., & Massar, S. (2001). Optimal cloning of coherent states with a linear amplifier and beam splitters. *Physical Review Letters, 86*(21), 4938–4941. doi:10.1103/PhysRevLett.86.4938 PMID:11384386

Bruß, D., DiVincenzo, D. P., Ekert, A., Fuchs, C. A., Macchiavello, C., & Smolin, J. A. (1998). Optimal universal and state-dependent quantum cloning. *Physical Review A., 57*(4), 2368–2378. doi:10.1103/PhysRevA.57.2368

Bu, S., & Zhou, H. (2009). A secret sharing scheme based on NTRU algorithm. In *Proceedings of the 5th International Conference on Wireless Communications, Networking and Mobile Computing, WiCom'09*. IEEE. 10.1109/WICOM.2009.5302743

Buchmann, J. (2013). *Introduction to cryptography*. Springer Science & Business Media.

Buchmann, J., & Williams, H. C. (1988). A key-exchange system based on imaginary quadratic fields. *Journal of Cryptology, 1*(2), 107–118. doi:10.1007/BF02351719

Buscemi, F., D'Ariano, G. M., & Macchiavello, C. (2005). Economical phase-covariant cloning of qudits. *Physical Review A., 71*(4), 042327. doi:10.1103/PhysRevA.71.042327

Bužek, V., & Hillery, M. (1998). Universal optimal cloning of arbitrary quantum states: From qubits to quantum registers. *Physical Review Letters, 81*(22), 5003–5006. doi:10.1103/PhysRevLett.81.5003

Cai, J. Y., & Cusick, T. W. (1998). A lattice-based public-key cryptosystem. In *Proceedings of the International Workshop on Selected Areas in Cryptography* (pp. 219-233). Springer.

Cerf, N., Durt, T., & Gisin, N. (2002). Cloning a qutrit. *Journal of modern optics, 49*(8), 1355-1373.

Cerf, N. J., Bourennane, M., Karlsson, A., & Gisin, N. (2002). Security of quantum key distribution using d-level systems. *Physical Review Letters, 88*(12), 127902. doi:10.1103/PhysRevLett.88.127902 PMID:11909502

Cerf, N. J., & Fiurasek, J. (2006). Optical quantum cloning. *Progress in Optics, 49*, 455–545. doi:10.1016/S0079-6638(06)49006-5

Cerf, N. J., & Iblisdir, S. (2000). Optimal N-to-M cloning of conjugate quantum variables. *Physical Review A., 62*(4). doi:10.1103/PhysRevA.62.040301

Cerf, N. J., Ipe, A., & Rottenberg, X. (2000). Cloning of continuous quantum variables. *Physical Review Letters, 85*(8), 1754–1757. doi:10.1103/PhysRevLett.85.1754 PMID:10970606

Cerf, N. J., Krüger, O., Navez, P., Werner, R. F., & Wolf, M. M. (2005). Non-Gaussian cloning of quantum coherent states is optimal. *Physical Review Letters, 95*(7), 070501. doi:10.1103/PhysRevLett.95.070501 PMID:16196769

Chefles, A., & Barnett, S. M. (1998). Quantum state separation, unambiguous discrimination and exact cloning. *Journal of Physics. A, Mathematical and General, 31*(50), 10097–10103. doi:10.1088/0305-4470/31/50/007

Chen, A. I. T., Chen, M. S., Chen, T. R., Cheng, C. M., Ding, J., Kuo, E. L. H., & Yang, B. Y. (2009). SSE implementation of multivariate PKCs on modern x86 CPUs. In *Cryptographic Hardware and Embedded Systems-CHES* (pp. 33–48). Berlin: Springer. doi:10.1007/978-3-642-04138-9_3

D'Ariano, G. M., Macchiavello, C., & Perinotti, P. (2005). Superbroadcasting of mixed states. *Physical Review Letters, 95*(6), 060503. doi:10.1103/PhysRevLett.95.060503 PMID:16090933

Diffie, W., & Hellman, M. (1976). New directions in cryptography. *IEEE Transactions on Information Theory, 22*(6), 644–654. doi:10.1109/TIT.1976.1055638

Ding, J., & Schmidt, D. (2005), Rainbow, a new multivariable polynomial signature scheme. In *Proceedings of the Conference on Applied Cryptography and Network Security ACNS 2005* (pp. 164-175). Springer. 10.1007/11496137_12

Duan, L. M., & Guo, G. C. (1998). Probabilistic cloning and identification of linearly independent quantum states. *Physical Review Letters, 80*(22), 4999–5002. doi:10.1103/PhysRevLett.80.4999

Fan, H., Imai, H., Matsumoto, K., & Wang, X. B. (2003). Phase-covariant quantum cloning of qudits. *Physical Review A., 67*(2). doi:10.1103/PhysRevA.67.022317

Fan, H., Matsumoto, K., Wang, X. B., & Wadati, M. (2001). Quantum cloning machines for equatorial qubits. *Physical Review A, 65*(1), 012304. doi:10.1103/PhysRevA.65.012304

Fan, H., Wang, Y. N., Jing, L., Yue, J. D., Shi, H. D., Zhang, Y. L., & Mu, L. Z. (2014). Quantum cloning machines and the applications. *Physics Reports, 544*(3), 241–322. doi:10.1016/j.physrep.2014.06.004

Feynman, R. P. (1982). Simulating physics with computers. *International Journal of Theoretical Physics, 21*(6), 467–488. doi:10.1007/BF02650179

Fraenkel, A. S., & Yesha, Y. (1979). Complexity of problems in games, graphs and algebraic equations. *Discrete Applied Mathematics, 1*(1-2), 15–30. doi:10.1016/0166-218X(79)90012-X

Fuchs, C. A., Gisin, N., Griffiths, R. B., Niu, C. S., & Peres, A. (1997). Optimal eavesdropping in quantum cryptography. I. Information bound and optimal strategy. *Physical Review A., 56*(2), 1163–1172. doi:10.1103/PhysRevA.56.1163

Goldreich, O., Goldwasser, S., & Halevi, S. (1997). Public-key cryptosystems from lattice reduction problems. In *Proceedings of the Annual International Cryptology Conference* (pp. 112-131). Springer.

Hardy, L., & Song, D. D. (1999). No signalling and probabilistic quantum cloning. *Physics Letters. [Part A], 259*(5), 331–333. doi:10.1016/S0375-9601(99)00448-X

Hoffstein, J., Pipher, J., & Silverman, J. H. (1998). NTRU: a ring based public key cryptosystem. In *Proceedings of ANTS-III* (pp. 267-288). Springer. 10.1007/BFb0054868

Hülsing, A. (2013). W-OTS+–shorter signatures for hash-based signature schemes. *In Proceedings of the International Conference on Cryptology* (pp. 173-188). Springer. 10.1007/978-3-642-38553-7_10

Jing, L., Wang, Y. N., Shi, H. D., Mu, L. Z., & Fan, H. (2012). Minimal input sets determining phase-covariant and universal quantum cloning. *Physical Review A., 86*(6), 062315. doi:10.1103/PhysRevA.86.062315

Karpov, E., Navez, P., & Cerf, N. J. (2005). Cloning quantum entanglement in arbitrary dimensions. *Physical Review A., 72*(4), 042314. doi:10.1103/PhysRevA.72.042314

Kipnis, A., & Shamir, A. (1999). Cryptanalysis of the HFE public key cryptosystem by relinearization. In *Proceedings of the Annual International Cryptology Conference* (pp. 19-30). Springer. 10.1007/3-540-48405-1_2

Koashi, M., & Imoto, N. (1998). No-cloning theorem of entangled states. *Physical Review Letters*, *81*(19), 4264–4267. doi:10.1103/PhysRevLett.81.4264

Koblitz, N. (1987). Elliptic curve cryptosystems. *Mathematics of Computation*, *48*(177), 203–209. doi:10.1090/S0025-5718-1987-0866109-5

Lamport, L. (1979), Constructing digital signatures from a one-way function. SRI International Computer Science Laboratory.

Lenstra, A. K., & Hendrik Jr, W. (1993). The development of the number field sieve. Springer Science & Business Media. doi:10.1007/BFb0091534

Li, L., Qiu, D., Li, L., Wu, L., & Zou, X. (2009). Probabilistic broadcasting of mixed states. *Journal of Physics. A, Mathematical and Theoretical*, *42*(17), 175302. doi:10.1088/1751-8113/42/17/175302

Loidreau, P. (2000). Strengthening McEliece cryptosystem. In *Proceedings of the International Conference on the Theory and Application of Cryptology and Information Security* (pp. 585-598). Springer.

Loidreau, P., & Sendrier, N. (2001). Weak keys in the McEliece public-key cryptosystem. *IEEE Transactions on Information Theory*, *47*(3), 1207–1211. doi:10.1109/18.915687

Löndahl, C., Johansson, T., Shooshtari, M. K., Ahmadian-Attari, M., & Aref, M. R. (2016). Squaring attacks on McEliece public-key cryptosystems using quasi-cyclic codes of even dimension. *Designs, Codes and Cryptography*, *80*(2), 359–377. doi:10.100710623-015-0099-x

McEliece, R. J. (1978). A public-key cryptosystem based on algebraic coding theory. *Deep Space Network Progress Report*, *44*, 114–116.

MErkle., R. C. (1989). A certified digital signature. In *Proceedings of the Conference on the Theory and Application of Cryptology* (pp. 218-238). Springer.

Mersin, A. (2007). The comparative performance analysis of lattice based NTRU cryptosystem with other asymmetrical cryptosystems [Master's thesis]. İzmir Institute of Technology.

Micciancio, D. (2001). Improving lattice-based cryptosystems using the Hermite normal form. In *Cryptography and lattices* (pp. 126–145). Berlin: Springer. doi:10.1007/3-540-44670-2_11

Nguyen, P. Q., & Regev, O. (2009). Learning a parallelepiped: Cryptanalysis of GGH and NTRU signatures. *Journal of Cryptology*, *22*(2), 139–160. doi:10.100700145-008-9031-0

Niederreiter, H. (1986). Knapsack-type cryptosystems and algebraic coding theory. *Problems of Control and Information Theory*, *15*, 19–34.

Niu, C. S., & Griffiths, R. B. (1999). Two-qubit copying machine for economical quantum eavesdropping. *Physical Review A.*, *60*(4), 2764–2776. doi:10.1103/PhysRevA.60.2764

Patarin, J. (1997). The oil and vinegar signature scheme. *Presented at the Dagstuhl Workshop on Cryptography*. Academic Press.

Patarin, J., Courtois, N., & Goubin, L. (2001). Quartz, 128-bit long digital signatures. In *Cryptographers' Track at the RSA Conference* (pp. 282-297). Springer.

Peikert, C. (2016). A decade of lattice cryptography. *Foundations and Trends in Theoretical Computer Science*, *10*(4), 283–424. doi:10.1561/0400000074

Rastegin, A. E. (2003). Upper bound on the global fidelity for mixed-state cloning. *Physical Review A.*, *67*(1), 012305. doi:10.1103/PhysRevA.67.012305

Rivest, R. L., Adleman, L. Dertouzos, M. L. (1978). On data banks and privacy homomorphisms. *Foundations of secure computation*, *4*(11), 169-180.

Rivest, R. L., Shamir, A., & Adleman, L. (1978). A method for obtaining digital signatures and public-key cryptosystems. *Communications of the ACM*, *21*(2), 120–126. doi:10.1145/359340.359342

Scarani, V., Iblisdir, S., Gisin, N., & Acin, A. (2005). Quantum cloning. *Reviews of Modern Physics*, *77*(4), 1225–1256. doi:10.1103/RevModPhys.77.1225

Shor, P. W. (1994). Algorithms for quantum computation: discrete logarithms and factoring. In *Proceedings of 35th Annual Symposium on Foundations of Computer Science* (pp. 124–134). IEEE. 10.1109/SFCS.1994.365700

Sidelnikov, V. M., Vladimir, M., & Shestakov, S. O. (1992). On insecurity of cryptosystems based on generalized Reed-Solomon codes. *Discrete Mathematics and Applications*, *2*(4), 439–444. doi:10.1515/dma.1992.2.4.439

Chapter 2
Quantum Key Distribution:
The Evolution

Bhavesh B. Prajapati
*IT Department, Commissionerate of Technical Education, Government of
Gujarat, India & Gujarat Technological University, India*

Nirbhay Kumar Chaubey
https://orcid.org/0000-0001-6575-7723
Gujarat Technological University, India

ABSTRACT

Quantum key distribution is an application of quantum cryptography which is based on quantum mechanics and optical physics. The word "quantum" means the smallest particle of matter and energy which inhibits unique special properties to make it different from normal matter. This chapter discusses underlying principles, and operations of quantum mechanics which are used to derive quantum key distribution protocols. This chapter also discusses elementary QKD protocols based on no cloning theorem and EPR correlations. Limitation of quantum key distribution is also discussed with reference to its implementation. Conceptual notes on quantum internet are also given.

INTRODUCTION

Today's world is flooded by exponentially increasing small mobile devices having enormous computing power and giant central servers. The need of communicating secret messages among parties is basic demand and hence need to be attained by cryptographic solutions. Cryptographic solutions should not only be used for solving

DOI: 10.4018/978-1-7998-2253-0.ch002

current needs but it should also address the assumptions of increasing computational power in future with reference to technological advancement.

Current classical cryptographic techniques solely depend on complexity of mathematical algorithms and limitation of current computational power to break it with reference to time constraints. Application of basic principles of quantum physics for cryptographic solutions proves almost all classical cryptographic solutions are inadequate for use and promises to provide unconditional security in quantum key distribution which is unattainable task using classical techniques.

Quantum technology is an emerging field now a days and current quantum devices are capable enough to break the latest classical cryptographic solutions in fraction of time. Quantum factoring algorithm developed by Shor can break RSA scheme easily. New emerging field Post Quantum Cryptography aims to develop cryptographic algorithms which are future safe against quantum computers. Such technological developments point out towards the need of more challenging and complex protocols for security.

How It Started

At MIT in 1981, Richard Faynman coined the idea of Quantum Computer and proposed a conceptual model of quantum Computer. He assumed that quantum computer will replace classical computers in near future but the first break through was achieved almost after 10 years when in 1994, Peter Shor proposed Shor's algorithm. Shor's algorithm can efficiently factorize large integer exponentially faster compared to classical computers. To factor large numbers like a 300 digit number, classical computer may take millions of years but the same can be done by the quantum computer in few minutes. Quantum computers and related research are gaining attention of many due to the ability of breaking cryptosystems in negligible time.

In 1996, Lov Grover presented a database search algorithm based on quantum techniques which solves the problem of random search or brute force search four times faster than search techniques using classical computers. First functioning 2-qubit quantum computer was built in 1998 which was capable to solve Grover's algorithm. This development started a new era of technical advancement in quantum computing and its applications. Recently in 2017, IBM built a commercial quantum computer and raised the bar to new level.

Quantum Information and Quantum Processing

A quantum computer is a device which is based on the underlying principles of quantum mechanics. The basic unit of operation which is used for quantum computer is quite different in structure and characteristics than in classical computer. This unit of operation is called a "Qubit." When quantum computer is being operated with classical data gives normal efficiency but key to outperform classical computer is the use of qubit because of its properties which are discussed in later sections.

Quantum computers differ with classical computers in following points:

- Quantum operations are exponentially faster than classical operations and hence result in great efficiency.
- Inhibit properties of a qubit allows its use in multiple ways which is not the case with classical bits.
- One cannot measure the position of qubit due to its super position state. If one tries to measure its position, it collapses to either of the states and this feature is essential in achieving privacy.
- No-Cloning property of qubit ensures that quantum information is impossible to be copied.

Qubit

Classical computers are driven by bits 0 and 1 used to represent digital signals. For a vector having length n, possible number of bit vectors can grow up to 2^n. Quantum information is represented as a Qubit. Qubit may have two possible states 0 and 1, but in contradiction with classical bits, it may remain in super position of 0 and 1. This combined state ψ can be represented as follows.

$$|\psi\rangle = |\alpha\rangle + |\beta\rangle,$$

where α and β are representing complex numbers and

$$|\alpha|^2 + |\beta|^2 = 1$$

As being in super position of two states, qubit can be represented as two-dimensional complex vector space forming ortho-normal basis. Qubits 0 and 1 can be associated with vectors in standard basis $\{|0\rangle, 1\rangle\}$ as

$$0 \rightarrow |0\rangle = \begin{pmatrix} 1 \\ 0 \end{pmatrix} and\, 1 \rightarrow |1\rangle = \begin{pmatrix} 0 \\ 1 \end{pmatrix}$$

The states 0 and 1 of qubit can also be perceived as ground and excited state of atoms. An example qubit state in Hadamard basis $\left\{\left|+\right\rangle, \left|-\right\rangle\right\}$ can be given as

$$\left|+\right\rangle = \frac{1}{\sqrt{2}}\left(\left|0\right\rangle + 1\right) = \frac{1}{\sqrt{2}}\begin{pmatrix}1\\1\end{pmatrix}$$

$$\left|-\right\rangle = \frac{1}{\sqrt{2}}\left(\left|0\right\rangle - \left|1\right\rangle\right) = \frac{1}{\sqrt{2}}\begin{pmatrix}1\\-1\end{pmatrix}$$

Multiple Qubits

Classical information system represents two bits as '00', '01' and so forth. But this is not the case for multiple qubit representation. By naming qubits as A and B for understanding and associating them with two classical bits X_1, $X_2 \in \{0,1\}^2$, strings can be mapped to orthonormal vectors as

$$0_A 0_B \rightarrow \left|00\right\rangle_{AB} = \begin{pmatrix}1\\0\\0\\0\end{pmatrix} 0_A 1_B \rightarrow \left|01\right\rangle_{AB} = \begin{pmatrix}0\\1\\0\\0\end{pmatrix}$$

$$1_A 0_B \rightarrow \left|10\right\rangle_{AB} = \begin{pmatrix}0\\0\\1\\0\end{pmatrix} 1_A 1_B \rightarrow \left|11\right\rangle_{AB} = \begin{pmatrix}0\\0\\0\\1\end{pmatrix}$$

These resulting vectors are in C^d, where d is dimension (d = 2^2 = 4). Numbers of possible strings are considered as dimension. Two qubit state $\left|\psi\right\rangle_{AB} \varepsilon C^4$ can be represented as equal superposition of standard basis vectors.

$$\left|\psi\right\rangle_{AB} = \frac{1}{2}\left|00\right\rangle_{AB} + \frac{1}{2}\left|01\right\rangle_{AB} + \frac{1}{2}\left|10\right\rangle_{AB} + \frac{1}{2}\left|11\right\rangle_{AB}$$

$$= \frac{1}{2} \begin{pmatrix} 1 \\ 1 \\ 1 \\ 1 \end{pmatrix}$$

Tensor Product

Tensor product can be used to find the combined state of qubits. If the state of the qubit A is $|\psi\rangle_A$ and qubit B is $|\theta\rangle_B$, joint state of these two qubits can be calculated as follows.

$$|\psi\rangle_A = \alpha_A |0\rangle_A +^2_A |1\rangle_A = \begin{pmatrix} \alpha_A \\ 2 \end{pmatrix}_A$$

$$|\theta\rangle_B = \alpha_B |0\rangle_B + \beta_B |1\rangle_B = \begin{pmatrix} \alpha_B \\ \beta_B \end{pmatrix}$$

The joint state $|\psi\rangle_{AB}$ can be expressed by applying tensor product on individual vectors $|\psi\rangle_A$ and $|\theta\rangle_B$.

$$|\psi\rangle_{AB} = |\psi\rangle_A \otimes |\theta\rangle_B = \begin{pmatrix} \alpha_A \\ \beta_A \end{pmatrix} \otimes |\theta\rangle_B$$

$$= \begin{pmatrix} \alpha_A |\theta\rangle_B \\ \beta_A |\theta\rangle_B \end{pmatrix} = \begin{pmatrix} \alpha_A \alpha_B \\ \alpha_A \beta_B \\ \beta_A \alpha_B \\ \beta_A \beta_B \end{pmatrix}$$

Foundation of Quantum Cryptography

Quantum cryptography is an application of quantum computing based on quantum information processing which can be achieved by applying fundamental principles of quantum mechanical systems. Quantum mechanics and related mathematical problems are set of rules to construct quantum physical system. Quantum mechanics possesses some simple rules, but researchers find them counterintuitive to understand. This leads to the need of better understanding towards the application of the same.

Entanglement

Entanglement is a unique quantum property which makes quantum computing different from classical computing. Entanglement plays a key role in many of the quantum cryptographic applications. Researchers try to explore more properties of entanglement to understand nature for the solutions of energy, entropy and fundamental operations.

Entanglement of correlated systems and counterintuitive predictions were first challenged in joint paper by Albert Einstein, Boris Podolsky and Nathan Rosenin in 1935. A thought experiment was represented to prove the impossibility of quantum mechanics. In a communication to Einstein, Erwin Schrodinger first coined the word "Entanglement" to describe that two particles can interact even in a space like separated situations (1935a, 1935b). Horodecki, Horodecki, and Horodecki (2009) have shown that entanglement is generated by direct interactions at subatomic level among particles.

Two systems A and B are in their respective Hilbert space H_A and H_B and are not interacting. Tensor product $H_A \otimes H_B$ will be the Hilbert space of composite system. State of the system A is $\left| \psi \right\rangle_A$ and the state of the system B is $\left| \psi \right\rangle_B$, the state of the composite system can be given as $\left| \psi \right\rangle_A \otimes \left| \psi \right\rangle_B$. This composite state is a product state and is separable, but all states are not separable. If states are not separable, they are considered as entangled states. For example, basis vectors $\left\{ \left| 0 \right\rangle_A, \left| 1 \right\rangle_A \right\}$ in H_A and $\left\{ \left| 0 \right\rangle_B, \left| 1 \right\rangle_B \right\}$ in H_B, the entangled state can be given as

$$\frac{1}{\sqrt{2}} \left(\left| 0 \right\rangle_A \left| 0 \right\rangle_B + \left| 1 \right\rangle_A \left| 1 \right\rangle_B \right)$$

For a given composite system, it is impossible to define pure states from either system separately. One cannot address the attributes of individual states separately.

No Cloning Theorem

In 1982, Wootters, Zurek, and Dieks discussed "no cloning theorem" which is key contributor in many of the protocols and applications of quantum cryptography. As per the theorem, an arbitrary quantum state cannot be copied perfectly without affecting its properties.

Linearity of quantum physics is the key trait behind no cloning theorem. When one tries to measure the state or to gain the information about the state of the system, the state gets disturbed and changes its attributes. This constraint or weird property surprisingly turns advantageous for quantum cryptography. If eavesdropper attempts to gain any information which is encoded using quantum operations, the state of the information will change and in turn it will reveal the presence of eavesdropper. This can lead to achieve unconditionally secure key distribution.

As per the properties of no cloning theorem, one cannot apply classical error correction techniques to quantum states. One needs to create backup copies of quantum states for error correction and to prevent sub sequent errors, but this is not possible as per no cloning theorem. As error correction being the significant substage of quantum cryptography, this limitation has created bottleneck problem for some time. In 1996, Shor and Steane removed this bottleneck problem by providing first quantum error correction code.

Heisenberg Uncertainty Principle

Heisenberg's uncertainty principle (HUP) represents fundamental concept of quantum physics which states about realization of fundamental uncertainty in measuring more than one attribute of quantum variable simultaneously. For example, if position and momentum are two attributes of quantum variable, when one tries to measure position of elementary particle with highest accuracy, the uncertainty in measurement of momentum of that elementary particle with highest accuracy increases. In quantum communication, messages are represented by photons, the small light particles. Due to uncertainty, when one performs same measurement several times, gets different result every time. So, when eavesdropper tries to measure one attribute of quantum variable, inevitably other attribute gets disturbed. HUP is key component in design of many quantum cryptographic protocols.

Quantum Key Distribution

In his rejected paper, Stephen Wiesner in early 70's proposed quantum multiplexing and counterfeit free bank note. In 1980, based on Wiesner's work, Charles H. Bennett and Gilles Brassard proposed solution to key distribution protocol using quantum computing. In 1984, they published very well-known BB84 protocol for quantum key distribution which provided key distribution over untrusted channel where output key was not correlated and dependent with input given. Lo and Chau (1999) had been given the simpler proof for security based on privacy amplification. Mayers (2001) provided the proof of unconditional security for BB84 protocol.

Figure 1. Quantum key distribution phases

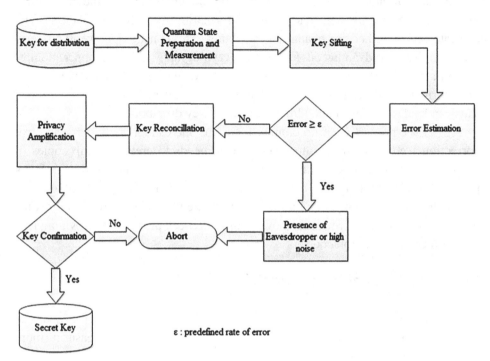

Figure 1 displays the flow of different phases of Quantum Key Distribution. Alice and Bob have quantum bits which they measure using different polarization angles. To generate the secret key, their measurement results should be same and in the process some bits are discarded during the process of sifting. Error rate is calculated after sifting and if error rate is greater than predefined threshold, then key distribution process will be aborted. This may be caused due to the presence of eavesdropper or higher amount of noise. If error rate is below threshold, privacy amplification is performed to reduce the information gain by eavesdropper further.

The BB84 Protocol

First phase of BB84 protocol is quantum communication phase having following steps.

- Alice sends photon sequence to Bob using insecure quantum channel. Alice and Bob use four polarizations: vertical, horizontal, 45-degrees, 135-degrees.
- For each received photon, Bob chooses randomly any one base from two bases, rectilinear or diagonal.

- Bob stores the bases used and measurement results are achieved. Bob publically announces the receipt of the signals.

Second phase of BB84 protocol is public discussion phase having following steps.

- Alice and Bob both broadcast their bases of measurements.
- Alice and Bob keep only those events where they have used same bases for measurement; they discard all others where measurement bases used by them are different.
- To check for presence of eavesdropper, small fraction of remaining events is chosen as test events by Alice. For these events, Alice publicly broadcasts positions and polarizations.
- Bob also broadcasts the polarizations.
- Alice and Bob compute the error rate for test events and if it is higher than some predefined threshold, they abort the procedure. Else they proceed with next step.
- Alice and Bob convert the polarization data to classical bits 0 and 1 known as raw key. They can now apply classical processes for error correction and privacy amplification to achieve final key.

Security of BB84 protocol can be understood with the understanding of no cloning theorem. Eavesdropper's presence can be detected by observing Quantum Bit Error Rate (QBER) and deciding value of QBER by quantifying eavesdropper's probability to gain information.

Table 1. BB84 protocol procedure with sample values

Alice's Bits	0	1	0	1	0	1	1	1
Alice's basis	+	X	+	X	+	X	X	+
Alice's polarization	↑	↗	→	↘	↑	↘	↗	→
Bob's basis	+	+	X	X	X	+	X	+
Bob's polarization	↑	→	↘	↘	↗	→	↗	→
Public discussion of measurements								
Shared secret key	0			1			1	1

QKD Using EPR Correlations

Entanglement property of qubit and Einstein-Podolsky-Rosen (EPR) correlations are used by ArturEkert (1991) and Bennett, Brassard, and Mermin (1992) to develop a secret key. Entangled photons are not independent from each other even though being space like separated. If one has entangled pair of photons and measurement outcome is horizontal polarization when measured using rectilinear bases for one particle then other particle must have horizontal polarization if measured using on the same rectilinear basis.

Ekert in his 1991 paper discussed that Bell inequality which proves that local classical theory is not able to achieve the same correlations as produced by quantum mechanics. Third bases are used by both to reduce the probability of the same base selection drastically to check for Bell inequality.

Steps are as follows to develop a secret key using entanglement and EPR correlations.

- Alice forms EPR pair of photons, keeps one particle to her and sends the other particle to Bob from each pair.
- Alice randomly performs measurement of polarization for each photon either using rectilinear or circular basis and inscribes measurement type and polarization.
- Bob also randomly performs measurement of polarization for each photon either using rectilinear or circular basis and inscribes measurement type and polarization.
- Alice and Bob publicly discuss the measurement types they have used and keep events for which they have used the same measurement types.
- They convert the data to classical string bits using a predefined convention.

In case of BB84 protocol, the key is generated classically and stored for distribution using quantum key distribution protocol. So the security of key is as strong as the security of storage. This is not the case with protocol with EPR method. With EPR approach, Alice and Bob can store their entangled photon pairs and can use them to generate key on the go when needed. This approach removes the constraint of insecurity related to storage.

Limitations of QKD

Quantum cryptography theory is mature enough to provide proofs for different algorithms, but real life commercial practical implementation is far away from future. Following key issues need to be taken care while implementing QKD systems.

High Bit Error Rate

As compared to classical communication system, bit error rate in quantum communication system is significantly high. This may affect accuracy of operations in practical situations.

Denial of Service and Point to Point Links

Quantum channel is a special channel which connects two parties point to point. Both parties must be there at the end of the channel with their photon source and detector. Point to point kind of link increases the chances of denial of services. If any third party is not able to intercept the messages and break the link then legitimate parties cannot communicate even.

Authentication

QKD does not provide authentication in itself. Current techniques are used to provide authentication for preposition of secret keys which is applied in hash-based authentication scheme or even hybrid approach can also be considered. Prepositioning of keys require to share the keys before the key distribution starts and once again need to depend on traditional and classical approaches of key distribution. Hybrid quantum classical public system also comes with constraints of classical system and related security issues.

Ample Rapid Key Delivery

Key distribution systems need to deliver keys at required speed as per the requirement of encryption devices employed, otherwise they might get exhausted for their input requirement. Latest QKD systems can achieve up to 1000 bits/second throughput in ideal case. Actual rate may be even very low.

Distance and Location Independence

In case of classical key distribution, any party can agree upon or transfer keys from any distance or from any location using internet protocols. This is not feasible with quantum key distribution. Underlying internet framework which can communicate photons across distance and different location is still at very primary level and limited to few kilometers using fiber.

Quantum Internet: The Future

By connecting multiple quantum devices and make such interconnection able to share quantum information on remote nodes, one need to design a quantum internet. Compare to classical internet, this will speed up the information sharing exponentially. Quantum internet design has many constraints asit will be operated only by rules of quantum mechanics. Quantum key transmission is key task for quantum internet which can be accomplished by using either entanglement or quantum teleportation.

Quantum teleportation does not require a particle to be transferred physically. EPR pair is shared between source and destination, Bell state measurement is done by C. H. Bennett, G. Brassard, C. Crépeau (1993). But deployment of quantum internet has many constraints. Optical hardware is required for implementation of quantum computers while network is very costly and difficult to implement. Quantum communication is also limited by distance. At present quantum network can be established for maximum 150 Km distance. Hybrid architecture needs to be applied and at one level interface with classical world must be provided. Small clusters of quantum processors and data center architecture need to be designed and optimized for performance.

Quantum internet has passed the inception stage and now moving towards realization stage. It requires heterogeneous skill set like classical computing, telecommunication engineering, quantum physics and optics, quantum cryptography and many interdisciplinary fields.

CONCLUSION

With the current progress in practical implementation of quantum technology, one can predict multi qubit system in near future. Still commercially available quantum cryptographic system and large-scale quantum network implementation seem far away. As classical cryptographic algorithms have mature mathematical foundations and well installed infrastructure, quantum cryptography technology should be combined with classical implementations. In the combined approach, quantum technology can be used for enhancing efficiency and security of current classical cryptographic approaches towards the security. Vice versa many proven concepts of classical cryptography like a one-time pad, two party / multi-party cryptography, delegated computing and homographic encryption can be used to implement quantum fundamentals.

REFERENCES

Alleaume, R. (2007). SECOQC white paper on quantum key distribution and cryptography.

Barrett, J, Hardy, L, & Kent, A. (2005). No signaling and quantum key distribution. *Physical Review Letters, 95*(1).

Bennett, B., Brassard, G., Crépeau, C., Jozsa, R., Peres, A., & Wootters, W. K. (1993, March). Teleporting an unknown quantum state via dual classical and Einstein-Podolsky-Rosen channels. *Physical Review Letters, 70*(13), 1895–1899. doi:10.1103/PhysRevLett.70.1895 PMID:10053414

Bennett, C. H., & Brassard, G. (1984). Quantum cryptography: Public key distribution and coin tossing. In *Proceedings of IEEE International Conference on Computers, Systems, and Signal Processing*. IEEE Press.

Bennett, C. H., Brassard, G., & Mermin, N. D. (1992). Quantum cryptography without Bell's theorem. *Physical Review Letters, 68*(5), 557–559. doi:10.1103/PhysRevLett.68.557 PMID:10045931

Brassard, G. (2005). Brief history of quantum cryptography: A personal perspective. In *Proceedings of IEEE Information Theory, Workshop on Theory and Practice in Information Theoretic Security* (pp. 19-23). 10.1109/ITWTPI.2005.1543949

Brassard, G. (2006). Brief history of quantum cryptography: a personal perspective.

Dowling, J. P., & Milburn, G. J. (2003). Quantum technology: The second quantum revolution. *Philosophical Transactions of the Royal Society of London. Series A, Mathematical and Physical Sciences, 361*(1809), 1655–1674. doi:10.1098/rsta.2003.1227 PMID:12952679

Einstein, A., Podolsky, B., & Rosen, N. (1935). Can Quantum-Mechanical Description of Physical Reality Be Considered Complete? *Physical Review, 47*(10), 777–780. doi:10.1103/PhysRev.47.777

Ekert, A. K. (1991). Quantum cryptography based on Bell's theorem. *Physical Review Letters, 67*(6), 661–663. doi:10.1103/PhysRevLett.67.661 PMID:10044956

Feynman, R. P. (1982). Simulating physics with computers. *International Journal of Theoretical Physics, 21*(6-7), 467–488. doi:10.1007/BF02650179

Gisin, N., Ribordy, G., Tittel, W., & Zbinden, H. (2002). Quantum cryptography. *Reviews of Modern Physics, 74*(1), 145–195. doi:10.1103/RevModPhys.74.145

Horodecki, R., Horodecki, P., Horodecki, M., & Horodecki, K. (2009). Quantum entanglement. *Reviews of Modern Physics*, *81*(2), 865–942. doi:10.1103/RevModPhys.81.865

Kimble, H. J. (2008). The quantum internet. *Nature*, *453*(7198), 1023–1030. doi:10.1038/nature07127 PMID:18563153

Lo, H.-K., & Chau, H. F. (1999). Unconditional Security of Quantum Key Distribution over Arbitrarily Long Distances. *Science*, *283*(5410), 2050–2056.

Lo, H.-K., & Chau, H. F. (1999). Unconditional security of quantum key distribution over arbitrary long distances. *Science*, *283*(5410), 2050–2056. doi:10.1126cience.283.5410.2050 PMID:10092221

Lo, H.-K., & Zhao, Y. (2007). Quantum cryptography.

Mayers, D. (1996). Advances in Cryptology. In N. Koblitz (Ed.), *Proceedings of Crypto '96* (pp. 343–357). New York: Springer.

Mayers, D. (1997). Unconditionally Secure Quantum Bit Commitment is Impossible. *Physical Review Letters*, *78*(17), 3414–3417. doi:10.1103/PhysRevLett.78.3414

Mayers, D. (2001). Unconditional security in quantum cryptography. *Journal of the Association for Computing Machinery*, *48*(3), 351–406. doi:10.1145/382780.382781

Scarani, V., Bechmann-Pasquinucci, H., Cerf, N. J., Dušek, M., Lütkenhaus, N., & Peev, M. (2009). The security of practical quantum key distribution. *Reviews of Modern Physics*, *81*(3), 1301–1350. doi:10.1103/RevModPhys.81.1301

Schrodinger, E. (1935a). Diegegenwärtige Situation in der Quantenmechanik. *Naturwissenschaften*, *23*, 807–812, 823–828, 844–849.

Schrodinger, E. (1935b). Discussion of probability relations between separated systems. *Proceedings of the Cambridge Philosophical Society*, *31*(4), 555–563. doi:10.1017/S0305004100013554

Shor, P. W., & Smolin, J. A. (1996). Quantum error correcting codes need not completely reveal the error syndrome.

Singh, S. (1999). *The code book: the science of secrecy from ancient Egypt to quantum cryptography*. London: Fourth Estate.

Steane, A. M. (1996b). Error correcting codes in quantum theory. *Physical Review Letters*, *77*(5), 793–797. doi:10.1103/PhysRevLett.77.793 PMID:10062908

Steane, A. M. (1996c). Simple quantum error-correcting codes. *Physical Review A.*, *54*(6), 4741–4751. doi:10.1103/PhysRevA.54.4741 PMID:9914038

Tan, X. (2013). *Introduction to Quantum Cryptography, Theory and Practice of Cryptography and Network Security Protocols and Technologies*. Intechopen.

Umesh, V., & Thomas, V. (2014). Fully Device-Independent Quantum Key Distribution *Physical Review Letters*, *113*(14), 140501. doi:10.1103/PhysRevLett.113.140501 PMID:25325625

Wang, X.-B. (2005). Beating the Photon-Number-Splitting Attack in Practical Quantum Cryptography. *Physical Review Letters*, *94*(23), 230503. doi:10.1103/PhysRevLett.94.230503 PMID:16090451

Wehner, S. (2010). How to implement two-party protocols in the noisy-storage model.

Wiesner, S. (1983). Conjugate coding. *SIGACT News*, *15*(1), 78–88. doi:10.1145/1008908.1008920

Wootters, W. K., & Zurek, W. H. (1982). A single quantum cannot be cloned. *Nature*, *299*(5886), 802–803. doi:10.1038/299802a0

Chapter 3
Optimal Parameter Prediction for Secure Quantum Key Distribution Using Quantum Machine Learning Models

Sathish Babu B.
RV College of Engineering, Bangalore, India

K. Bhargavi
Siddaganga Institute of Technology, India

K. N. Subramanya
RV College of Engineering, Bangalore, India

ABSTRACT

The advent of quantum computing is bringing threats to successful operations of classical cryptographic techniques. To conduct quantum key distribution (QKD) in a finite time interval, there is a need to estimate photon states and analyze the fluctuations statistically. The use of brute force and local search methods for parameter optimization are computationally intensive and becomes an infeasible solution even for smaller connections. Therefore, the use of quantum machine learning models with self-learning ability is useful in predicting the optimal parameters for quantum key distribution. This chapter discusses some of the quantum machine learning models with their architecture, advantages, and disadvantages. The performance of quantum convoluted neural network (QCNN) and Quantum Particle Swarm Optimization (QPSO) towards QKD is found to be good compared to all the other quantum machine learning models discussed.

DOI: 10.4018/978-1-7998-2253-0.ch003

INTRODUCTION

Today's e-manufacturing, digital world provides a variety of services for the benefit of mankind, which includes e-Health, e-Bank, e-Hotel, e-Government and e-Commerce. For successful operation of these services several factors, like privacy, security, confidentiality, cost, trust, compatibility, and standardization. need to be taken into account. Among all the factors security is given paramount importance as the data being exchanged need to be protected from third party attacks. Traditional cryptography is one of the methods that allow us to store and send the data via encryption and reverse decryption process and established secure communication between two parties by protecting the data from attackers using public and private key distribution strategies (Van & Thijssen, 2015).

Some of the consequences of traditional cryptography are listed below.

- The message which is strongly authenticated using cryptographic mechanism sometimes makes it difficult to take legitimate decisions at crucial time.
- The speed of execution slows down due to complex mathematical operations.
- Providing selective access to the data is difficult suing crypto system.
- The design of the crypto system is poor in terms of architecture, protocol, and procedures used for encoding and decoding.
- Cost of setup and operation of public key cryptosystem is high as it demands separate public key infrastructure.

QUANTUM COMPUTING: AN OVERVIEW

Quantum computing is a revolutionary technology which leverages the characteristics of quantum mechanics such as superposition and entanglement to perform computation extremely faster than classical computing technologies (Feynman, 1982).

Many forms of quantum technologies are already in use, out of which quantum key distribution has been pioneered by using commercially available quantum computers. Quantum sensors and actuators are allowing scientists to work at nano-scale levels with remarkably higher precision and sensitivity. Development of quantum processors is another main stream activity which is seriously taken up by some of the top-notch technology companies. A generic representation of quantum computing process is given in figure 1, consists of quantum states whose output is processed by quantum gates to yield quantum outputs.

The advent of quantum computers is bringing in the following threats to successful operations of classical cryptographic techniques.

Figure 1. Quantum computing process

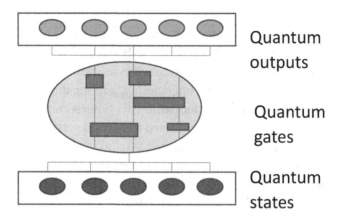

Quantum outputs

Quantum gates

Quantum states

- Classical cryptographic algorithms rely on the complexity of the mathematical function used for encryption and decryption, which can be easily tackled by quantum computers using photon properties.
- Shors quantum computer algorithm is an attack on asymmetric cryptographic algorithms as it can easily find prime factors for the given integer (Yimsiriwattana & Lomonaco, 2004).
- Grover's quantum computing algorithm weakens symmetric cryptographic algorithms as it can determine the unique input to a black box output generating function using $O\sqrt{N}$ function evaluation, where N represent the size of the evaluation function (Zalka, 1999).
- Quantum hacking affects the security and privacy of key agreement-based protocols like Diffie–Hellman (DH), and Menezes–Qu–Vanstone (MQV) through photon polarization.
- Encryption algorithms like Rivest-Shamir-Adleman (RSA), Digital Signature Algorithm (DSA), and elliptic curve cryptography (ECC) are breakable as a quantum computer can easily factor the large keys.

QUANTUM CRYPTOGRAPHY: AN OVERVIEW

The consequence of classical cryptography led to the innovation of quantum cryptography which was developed by Stephen Weisner in the year 1970 (Brassard & Crepeau 1996). In quantum cryptography the cryptographic operations are performed and the data is stored in qubits i.e., each bit can be on, off, or both which is obtained by superposition of the multiple quantum states whereas in traditional

Figure 2. High level view of quantum cryptography

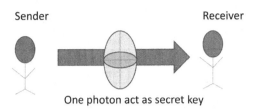

Sender   Receiver

One photon act as secret key

cryptography the cryptographic operations are carried out by storing the data in binary format i.e., either on or off. As a result the quantum cryptography allows quantum computation to be performed in order of magnitude which is super faster than the conventional processors in the system (Goyal, Aggarwal, & Jain,, 2011),(Lakshmi & Murali, 2017). A high level view of quantum cryptography is shown in figure 2. The major differences between classical cryptography and quantum cryptography are given in Table 1.

APPLICATIONS OF QUANTUM CRYPTOGRAPHY

The quantum cryptography is being used in variety of applications where the traditional cryptography fails to provide required amount of security (Ellie, 2018), (Lee, Barnum, Bernstein, & Swamy, 1999). Few of the important applications of quantum cryptography are given below.

- Developing an ultra-secure voting system which supports safe transfer of votes from one counting station to another counting station and prevents fraudulent elections from being conducted.
- Transition from traditional internet to quantum internet which prevents hacking of confidential data.
- Establishing secure communication between national and international bank for safe exchange of financial data and the transmission channels used are not susceptible to security threats.
- Maintaining and transferring the defense documents over the internet by preventing the threats of copying the data from eavesdropper.
- Establishing secure communication over open space environment between the satellites and astronomers by preventing the attacks from adversaries.
- Facilitating fast search mechanisms over the database in which every record is visited individually using quantum computer enabled with qubit superposition principle.

Table 1. Classical cryptography versus quantum cryptography

Classical Cryptography	Quantum Cryptography
Relies on mathematical formulas.	Relies on the law of quantum physics.
It is vulnerable to the improvement in technologies.	It is not vulnerable to the improvement in the technologies.
Extent of security achieved is dependent on the complexity of factoring the large integer number.	Extent of security is dependent on the quantum superposition and photon polarization rate.
Classical cryptography protocols are usually device dependent and rarely device independent.	Quantum cryptography protocols are device independent.
The bit rate is limited by the limitation of the computational resources.	The bit rate supported extends up to 1Mbits/second.
The communication range supported is millions of miles.	The communication range supported is limited to few 10's of miles.
Register storage is up to 2^n bit strings.	Register storage is up to one n bit strings.
The life expectancy of the classical cryptographic algorithms keeps changing due to the changes in mathematical computation.	The life expectancy of the quantum cryptographic algorithms does not change as the laws of physics remain constant.
Stand alone systems with portable software are enough to perform classical cryptographic computations.	Dedicated quantum computers are required to perform quantum operations.
It is independent of the transmission medium used for data exchange.	It is dependent of the transmission medium used for data exchange.
It is appropriate for long distance communication.	It is inappropriate for long distance communication.
It is not costly as the mathematical computations can be performed on resource constrained devices.	It is costly as for transmission of every photon a separate quantum channel is required.
Supports sequential execution of computational tasks.	Supports parallel execution of computational tasks.

- Optimal solutions to NP-hard and unpredictable problems like travelling salesman, rice's theorem, halting problem, and so on are given quickly using quantum algorithms.
- Performing predictive analytics over the business database to forecast the future trends by mining the hidden patterns in the data collected.
- Analysis of complex structure of human brain in which billions of neurons are interconnected in microscopic manner.
- Understanding chemical and physical properties of DNA structure and even to predict the future dynamics of the molecular structures of DNA.
- Exploring the power of genetic programming using quantum computing to simulate the mechanism of selection, crossover, and mutation.
- Real time processing and exact analysis of drug discovery process using quantum computers.

- Controlling of air traffic by streamlining the traffic and maintaining the confidentiality of the operational data.
- Securing the IoT-based smart grids using quantum cryptography and secure transmission of power data.

QUANTUM-BASED KEY DISTRIBUTION (QKD)

There is a tremendous pressure in the industry to make the classical cryptographic techniques quantum safe, which has given rise to intense research in the domain of quantum-based key distribution (QKD) which makes use of properties of photons to securely exchange the keys or key related information between the communication entities. Quantum key distribution is considered as replacement for traditional key distribution strategies due to the several reasons like ease detection of eavesdropper, suitable for long-term security, capacity to deliver unrestricted security, uses minimum resources for key exchange, exhibits continuously improving features, cannot be virtually hacked, relies on physics laws instead of mathematical functions, and so on (Gottesman, Lo, Lutkenhaus, & Preskill, 2004). A sample depiction of the QKD process is given in figure 3.

To conduct QKD in a finite time interval there is a need to estimate photon states and analyze the fluctuations statistically. The choice of the intensity and the probability of sending the message, are difficult to estimate in quantum cryptography and is directly related to the optimal performance of the system. Many of the existing QKD protocols over symmetric and asymmetric security channels, uses coordinate descent algorithm to determine the intensity and probability of sending the message were suffered from delay and the increased requirements of quantum computing resources (Bennett & Brassard, 2014). As there are many efforts to carry out QKD

Figure 3. QKD process

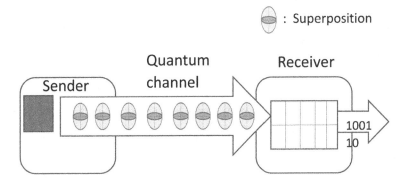

49

on mobile devices like the drone, mobile phones, satellites which demands the performance over large scale networks. Some of the practical challenges for QKD are listed below.

- Parameter optimization during key distribution is computationally intensive for both smaller and larger connections.
- Compared to classical key distribution quantum key distribution is complex as it just extends the existing secret key model.
- The use of quantum key does not prevent hypothetical hacking i.e. the hacker tries to insert large amount of data during decryption.
- QKD strategy works at lower rate as some of the existing optical fibers are incompatible with the developed QKD.
- The success rate of QKD is limited to individual system but they don't span towards global large-scale networks.
- The certification of security of QKD pertaining to market and laws are not completely defined.
- The QKD strategy is vulnerable to some of the attacks like man-in-the-middle, side channel, device imperfections, and errors in calibration.
- The scalability factor of QKD chip is still less as it incorporates single photon detectors with amplitude modulator and homodyne detectors.
- The cost of integration of light weight QKD models in the mobile devices is high due to high level of miniaturization.

Among all the challenges listed, parameter optimization for secure QKD is addressed in the chapter using quantum machine learning models with a self-learning ability. These models are useful in predicting the optimal parameters for quantum key distribution as they offer several prospects in terms of speed, storage capacity, accuracy, and efficiency.

QUANTUM MACHINE LEARNING (QML)

QML is an interdisciplinary research which combines quantum physics with machine learning. It is a study to build the suit of machine learning techniques as quantum algorithms to run on quantum computers. Learning basically deals with how energy evolution takes place in the quantum circuits (Biamonte, Wittek, Pancotti, Rebentrost, Wiebe, & Lloyd, 2017), a diagrammatic representation of the QML process is given in Figure 4. The driving force for QML process is the dataset, which gets encoded and are passed to the quantum circuit via gate parameters then the results obtained are verified against the objectives set. The process of reading the input from the gate parameters and passing through quantum circuit for verification of the output is repeated until desired level of accuracy is obtained.

QML can also be employed over the data generated by quantum experiments and there are also efforts to propose quantum learning theory. Some of the applications of QML are listed below.

- Simulation of movements of the molecules and establishing interaction between the molecules.
- Discovery of advancement in the field of medical science and discovery of drug materials.
- Topological analysis of the big data with accelerated speed.
- Used to train classical Boltzmann machines to perform scientific computations.
- Preserving the cryptographic data from hackers.
- Establishing the quantum awareness in brain cognition.
- Used to generate music which leads to creative productions.
- Generation of TV scripts by mimicking the realistic set of dialogues.
- Generation of text using high level quantum enabled machine learning APIs.
- Detection and classification of objects from complex image scenario.
- Scenario based classification of lanes for automated driving.
- Safety critical classification of car and cyclist scenarios using trajectory data.
- Automatic generation of dramatic and piano music using popular projects like Magenta, DeepJazz, BatchBot, FlowMachines, WaveNet, and GRUV.
- Voice recognition and classification with quadratic speedup.
- Anomaly and fraud detection using elastic quantum search APIs.
- Segmentation and analysis of market using quantum machine learning classification models.
- Automatic translation of scripts written in one language into another language.
- Identification of abnormalities in the financial contracts and development of precise credit lending applications for banking sectors.
- Quick information retrieval based on the images and texts in popular search engines and shopping sites.

Some of the potential quantum machines learning models used for parameter optimization are: Quantum Feed Forward Neural Network (QFFNN), Quantum Recurrent neural network (QRNN), Quantum Backpropagation Neural Network (QBNN), Quantum Convoluted Neural Network (QCNN), Quantum Reinforcement Learning (QRL), Quantum Q learning (QQL), Quantum Particle Swarm Optimization (QPSO), Quantum Annealing (QA), and Quantum Differential Evolution (QDE). We provide the detailed discussion on these models in the following subsections.

Figure 4. QML process

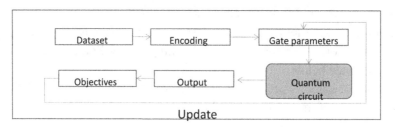

QUANTUM FEED FORWARD NEURAL NETWORK (QFFNN)

The QFFNN includes the generalization of the classical neural network model with coherent quantum inputs. The individual neurons are made revisable, and they are generalized to become quantum reversible. The networks of neurons are trained using the global gradient descent algorithm, which generalizes the cost function. The performance of QFFNN is found to be excellent over the conventional feed forward neural network models for training dense, large-scale, fully connected networks (Wan, Dahlsten, Kristjansson, Gardner, & Kim, 2017).

The simple architecture of QFFNN is given in figure 5. It mainly consists of three layers i.e., quantum enabled input layer, several hidden layers, and an output layer. The QFFNN is used for classification jobs and the quantum enabled neurons are referred as qurons, and qurons are predefined in input layer, hidden layers, and the output layer. The qurons offer several prospects over the classical neurons in terms of integration, dissipative dynamics and unitary quantum theory. The input is processed sequentially from the input layer through several hidden layers and aggregated at the output layer. The summary of the QFFNN machine learning model are given in Table 2.

Figure 5. |X>|Z>*|Y> QFFNN architecture*

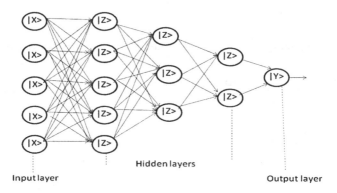

The optimality in parameter prediction for secure key distribution using QFFNN is dependent on the type of the algorithm used for training of the QFFNN model. The model is able learn the complex, nonlinear relationship among the input data samples easily in which the connection between the data samples do not form a cycle. The convergence rate is also high due to the deployment of multi level neurons in the output layer and its training is easy compared to the training of the single level neurons in the output layer. In parameter prediction continuous input is fed into the neural network to generate continuous parameter prediction as output. The flow of data from the input layer of the network to the output layer is strictly pre-calculated which makes the model to work in a more efficient manner compared to traditional systems.

QUANTUM RECURRENT NEURAL NETWORK (QRNN)

The QRNN includes quantum algorithms among the connections between the nodes to form a directed graph using the temporal sequence. The performance of QRNN is excellent over large scale data as it operates at exponentially high speed compared to classical recurrent neural network models. Hence QRNN is extensively applied to a variety of applications including pattern recognition, pattern mining, pattern reconstruction, and optimization (Luitel, & Venayagamoorthy, 2010), (Kutvonen, Sagawa, & Fujii, 2018).

Most popular QRNN is Hopfield network which is used in applications like pattern recognition and optimization. The architecture of QRNN is given in figure 6. Which mainly consists of quantum enabled input layer, hidden layer, output layer, and contextual units. The connection from output layer is given to contextual units, at every time interval the input sample is forwarded from one layer to another and the learning rule gets updated. The qurons in QRNN stores the previous values in the hidden states which are used in generating highly precise output even in the presence of the uncertainty. The summary of the QRNN machine learning model is given in Table 3.

The optimality in parameter prediction for secure key distribution using QRNN model dependent on the type of the data labels used for labeling the data samples. The data samples can be labeled either sequentially or non-sequentially, after feeding the data samples the training of QRNN model is easy as it is composed of very few training parameters. The QRNN model is able to model the sequence of inputs in which every current input is dependent on the previous input. The capability of the QRNN model to remember each and every interaction throughout the process of learning makes it suitable for parameter prediction applications. It allows for the formation of the loops within the QRNN model as a result the information will stay

Table 2. Summary of QFFNN

Prospects: 1. Exponential storage capacity to process huge amount of information.   2. Accelerated speed of processing.   3. Ability to learn easily from large neural networks through empirical observations.   4. Easily captures non-linear relationship between input and output variables.   5. Prediction accuracy is high and is also towards the actual value.   6. Errors are assessed very easily and are prevented from propagating to other stages of the network.   7. Ability to process unseen relationships in the input data is high which helps in generalization of the input model and even predict from unseen data.   8. Self-associative nature of qurons in QFFNN leads to efficient implementation of multi modular recognition schemes.   9. Quantum associative memory leads to store complicated patterns and even recall it within the specified time interval.
Consequences: 1. There might be chances of deviation in the QFFNN output achieved due to sub-quantum level fluctuation.   2. The randomness in sub quantum level causes problems during quantum experiments.   3. Treating individual qubits as neuron in the QFFNN becomes complex during initial iterations.   4. The architecture of QFFNN is difficult to understand due to non-evolutionary behavior of qurons in feedforward network.
Training methods: Trainlm, gradient descent, content based filtering, delta rule, and genetic algorithms,
Precision: 1. For uniform datasets after sufficient training iterations the QFFNN model achieved an accuracy of 60%.   2. For non-uniform datasets the accuracy of prediction is below 50% as even with several iterations of training the exact number of hidden layers and number of hidden nodes in every layer could not be determined easily.
Activation functions: Sigmoid, TanH, and ReLU.

inside the network for long duration of time. Compared to other traditional neural

Figure 6. |X>*|Z>*|Y> architecture of QRNN with contextual units

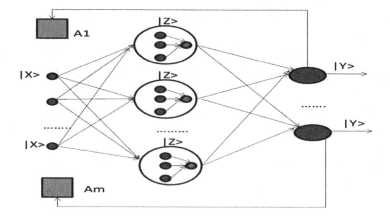

networks the recurrent neural network can learn long sequences of the input with long time gaps between the input samples easily and efficiently in parallel.

QUANTUM BACKPROPAGATION NEURAL NETWORK (QBNN)

The QBPNN is used exhaustively in pattern recognition by back-propagating the errors using various kinds of activation functions. The backpropagation of the errors through a neural network makes the network self-programmable, self-organizable, interactive, and are capable enough for solving computation intensive problems (Gonçalves, 2016). The performance of QBPNN is faster and more accurate compared to conventional BPNN models in prediction problems.

Table 3. Summary of QRNN

Prospects:
1. Exponentially sized polynomial numbers can be easily stored in QRNN qubits.
2. The computational complexity of QRNN is very low i.e., logarithmic value.
3. Achieves exponential speedup compared to classical RNN.
4. QRNN uses quantum algorithm to perform large matrix multiplication.
5. Easy to extract the hidden pattern in the input sample which reduces the runtime of the QRNN model.
6. The training of the QRNN is done using Hebbian model approach which helps in solving complex linear equations in quadratic time interval.
7. The transfer of data in quantum states to quantum devices is easy due to the availability of the pure state data in the hidden layers of the QRNN model.
8. The QRNN model is data-driven and generalized approach can be easily applied to any of the new fields without prior knowledge about the field.

Consequences:
1. The QRNN model still suffers from inherent stability problem as several architectures of RNN into a single QRNN.
2. If gradient descent optimization method is used while training the QRNN the chances of network getting exploded is more.
3. The QRNN model demands frequent updating of the architecture elements along with the coefficient parameters which causes problems during practical implementation of the model.
4. Embedding the QRNN model inside the deep learning model is difficult using tanh and ReLu activation function.

Training methods:
Stochastic gradient descent, recursive filter, correlation rule, Bayes filter, and convolution filter

Precision:
1. For uniform data samples with sequential labeling the performance of the QRNN model falls in the range of 70% as it efficiently handles the problems like gradient vanishing, and exploding tendency in the network.
2. For non-uniform data samples with non-sequential labeling the performance of the QRNN model is in average range i.e., 50% as it fails to process the long sequence of non-sequential data samples and it gets stuck in recurring gradient vanishing problem.

Activation functions:
Softmax, kernel activation function, and linear.

The simple architecture of QBNN model is given in figure 7. It mainly consists of two stages: the first stage is the learning stage and the second stage is the Backpropogation stage. During the learning stage the network learns from the input samples through several layers of feed forward neural network and in the backpropogation stage the neurons in output layer back propagates the error and make the network to get self-stabilized. The summary of QBNN machine learning model is given in Table 4. The optimality in parameter prediction for secure key distribution using QBNN model is dependent on number of qurons considered in every layer of the network. The poor performance is due to several factors like extremely sensitive to noise and outliers, the use of matrix based approach for Backpropogation leads to lot of errors, requires smaller learning rate to stabilize the learning process, too few qurons in the layers causes underfitting problem, finding accurate weights for Backpropogation of the errors takes too long time, and so on.

QUANTUM CONVOLUTED NEURAL NETWORK (QCNN)

The quantum inspired CNN deep learning models uses a variable sized small set of parameters for training and implementation of the quantum neural networks for image analysis. The QCNN is capable of performing both encoding and decoding tasks in parallel which outperforms the conventional CNN by removing the problem of exploding gradients in image recognition and classification tasks (Cong, Choi, & Lukin, 2019).

Figure 7. |X>|Z>*|Y> QBNN architecture*

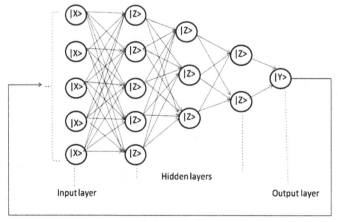

Table 4. Summary of QBNN

Prospects: 1. It is more efficient in terms of energy as the quantum states are embodied easily inside the multi-layer backpropagation network. 2. Exhibits exponential speed due to parallel computation of quantum states. 3. The QBNN model is easily adaptable in nature due to the back propagation of errors. 4. The use of NOT gates with lowered decoherence level along with the qurons makes the topology of the QBNN model more generic. 5. The ability to solve complex non-linear problem is high as qurons in QBNN model are self-adaptable and can easily understand the dynamic stochasticity and periodic variation in the learning environment. 6. The learning rate of the qurons decreases from larger value to smaller value and adjusts the weights between the qurons automatically which leads to rapid learning.
Consequences: 1. Convergence speed of the QBNN model is very slow as the gradient descent method is used for error back propagation. 2. Validating the learning ability of the QBNN model is difficult to the reoccurrence of the XOR problems in the hidden and output layers of the QBNN model. 3. The error propagation rate during training phase of the QBNN model is high due to inappropriate updating of the weights associated with the learning phase of the QBNN model. 4. The random superposition of qurons during training and testing period of the QBNN model leads to weak connection between the qurons among various layers of the QBNN model.
Training methods: Genetic algorithms, evolutionary theory, and chain rule
Precision: With respect to both uniform and non-uniform data samples the QBNN model suffers from poor performance in terms of parameter prediction for key distribution.
Activation functions: Logistic, gradient backpropogation, and threshold.

The architecture QCNN is given in figure 8, which mainly consists of three layers i.e., convolution layer, pooling layer, and fully connected layer. The parameters unitaries in the three layers of the QCNN will be initialized and training happens through gradient descent learning. The convolution layer is composed of several unitaries and processes images of varying dimensions. The pooling layer is mainly used to reduce the size of the QCNN model by computing final mean unitary over several the initial unitaries. The fully connected layer consists of non-local measurements used to do classification jobs. The summary of the QBNN machine learning model are given in Table 5.

The use of QCNN in predicting the optimal parameters for quantum key distribution is beneficial in terms of learning rate, convergence speed, and accuracy. The QCNN model can quickly capture the patterns in the both uniform and non-uniform data samples and they involve less complexity and even save lot of memory compared to conventional CNN model. The QCNN model consists of only $O(\log(N))$ variational input parameters for any input of size N qubits. As a result it is very easy to train and test the realistic quantum key distribution applications and achieves near

Figure 8. Architecture of QCNN

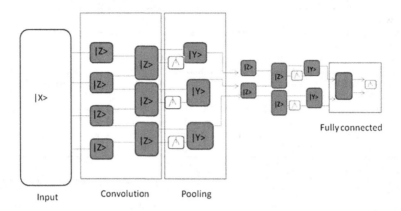

optimal accuracy. It can also recognize any infinitesimal quantum states during key distribution using a single dimensional topological analysis mechanism. It also has inbuilt error correction model which prevents the propagation of errors from one phase to another phase during key distribution. The performance of the QCNN model is found to be good due to the reasons like use of local spatial coherence in the input data samples, parameter sharing using convolutional and pooling layers, ability to easily locate the features in the input data samples, easily adaptable model due to the use of data augmentation and regularization, and so on.

QUANTUM REINFORCEMENT LEARNING (QRL)

The QRL model combines the quantum theory with a reinforcement learning agent, which works based on state superposition principle and also exploits the quantum parallelism for updating over time. The QRL model decides the probability of Eigen value based on the amplitude which gets updated by collecting the rewards which increase the convergence rate of the learning model and increases the learning ability of the agent by achieving the proper balance between exploration and exploitation (Dong, Chen, Li, & Tarn, 2008).

The architecture of QRL is given in figure 9 which mainly consists of four main components i.e., agent, environment, register-1, and register-2. The interaction happens in several forms like agent to environment, agent to register-1, agent to register-2, register-1 to register-2, environment to register-1, and environment to register-2. To facilitate accelerated learning logical quantum gates and XOR gates are embedded inside the reinforcement learning protocol. The representation of QRL can be extended easily for multiple qubits systems which are useful for demonstration

Table 5. Summary of QCNN

Prospects:
1. The speed of operation increases exponentially using qHob and qHeb training algorithms.
2. The accuracy achieved in classification jobs is high due to quantum enabled error correction mechanism.
3. The addition of quantum convolution layer into the conventional CNN architecture increases the power of computation.
4. The hypothesis generated by the QCNN is correct due to the use of quantum-convolutional circuits.
5. The QCNN model is highly scalable as quantum-convolutional layers are free from error and can operate with a smaller number of quantum circuits.
6. Able to model complex non-linear relationship in cellular automata as flexibility is provided to keep layer specific configuration attributes.
7. Polynomial sized image classification problems can be solved easily as the QCNN model allows several quantum-convolutional layers to be stacked one after the other.
Consequences:
1. In order to achieve higher accuracy, the QCNN model demands large data samples.
2. The chance of converging to local optimal solutions is high as the QCNN model exhibits higher dependency on the initial parameter tuning.
3. The QCNN model fails to handle the invariance caused during translation i.e., when the images with slight variation is fed during training the qurons in the quantum-convolutional layers won't get triggered as they cannot encode the position and orientation of the images.
4. The use of qurons in pooling layer leads to loss of information.
Training methods:
Backprop, RMSProp, and Adadelta
Precision:
The performance of the QCNN model goes above 85% for all forms of data i.e., uniform and no uniform samples considered for training and testing.
Activation functions:
tanh, ReLu, and LeakyReLu

Figure 9. Architecture of QRL

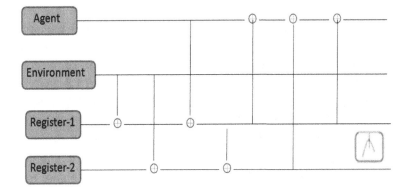

of applications like harmonic oscillators, superconductors, movement of atoms, and so on. The agent in QRL model easily learns about the environment and meanwhile environment also gains knowledge about the agent and more number of registers can be updated simultaneously which increases the learning speed by receiving maximum possible rewards. The summary of the QRL machine learning model are given in Table 6.

QUANTUM Q LEARNING (QQL)

The QQL model appears in several forms like single valued Q learning, double valued Q learning, multiple agents-based Q learning, these algorithms are combined with the quantum states and action space for parameter optimization in the high-performance computing environment. The application of quantum mechanics in Q learning resolves the contextual bandit problem by preventing the long-delayed reward signals generation (Dunjko, Taylor, & Briegel, 2017).

The architecture of quantum Q learning is given in figure 10 which stores the quantum reinforcement learning policies by super-positioning it in the qubits. The value function of the conventional Q learning algorithm is replaced by the quantum enabled action-value function. The quantum agent performs action to get highest possible reward and the learning process is controlled by the discount factor. In QQL the quantum states are based on Markov property that output of each state depends on previous state. By storing the previous experience in every quantum states memory, the actions are taken to maximize the throughput of QQL network and the loss function is also minimized. The summary of the QQL machine learning model are given in Table 7.

QUANTUM PARTICLE SWARM OPTIMIZATION (QPSO)

The QPSO model applies quantum laws of mechanics to improve the behavior of conventional PSO to achieve guaranteed global convergence. With the introduction of interpolation operator in QPSO, it is possible to find new globally best solutions in the search space. The QPSO is applied to solve multimodal complex and constrained problems containing too many varying parameters (Liu, Chen, Chen, & Xie, 2019).

The architecture of quantum Q learning is given in figure 11 which mainly consists of particles with global and local positions. The small particles tend to move towards the larger particles by following the bigger arrow which exhibits highest probability path i.e., the path which moves the small particles towards larger particles. In conventional PSO there might be some smaller particles which are misleading

Table 6. Summary of QRL

Prospects:
1. The quantum reinforcement learning is useful for epoch type environment in which the state of the environment keeps changing rapidly.
2. Achieves accelerated speed in object classification by receiving maximum possible rewards over iterations using multi qubits enabled quantum states.
3. The chances of quantum agent failing to perform any desired action is exponentially small due to quadratic improvement in forming high quality learning policies.
4. The quantum agents are adaptable to complex environment as it always takes valuable steps towards the reward in incremental manner.
5. The quantum agent is equipped with hyper parameters or meta parameters which help in fixing any undeterministic problems.
6. The convergent speed rate of the quantum agent is optimal as it perfectly balances between exploration and exploitation.

Consequences:
1. It is difficult to realize the fully quantum-controlled environment exactly using quantum agents.
2. The use of progressive wavelet decoders in QRL is infeasible due to the uncertainty involved during decoding.
3. The accuracy achieved in classification jobs is low due to piecewise representation of trajectories in the environment.
4. While dealing with high dimensional environment the use of XOR, NOT, and CNOT causes problems during generalization.
5. Too much reinforcement of the quantum agents can lead to overloading of the quantum states and may produce wrong results.

Training methods:
Trial and error approach, cut and try, reward based, and session backpropogation.

Precision:
1. The performance of QRL towards parameter prediction for quantum key distribution is satisfactory and lies in the range of 50% for the data samples which are having continuous states.
2. The QRL is a probability-based model with dynamic programming ability which exhibits high accuracy in terms of recall precision, true positive and true negative classification. But when the QRL model is exposed to data samples with discontinuous high dimensional states the model becomes infeasible and significantly slower.

Activation functions:
Rectified linear function, softmax, sigmoid, and tanh.

Figure 10. Architecture of QQL

Table 7. Summary of QQL

Prospects:
1. The accuracy of the result obtained is high as it consistently updates the policy of learning at regular period of intervals. 2. The convergence rate of the QQL is high as it replaces the value function with the quantum action-value function. 3. Achieves perfect balance between the exploration and exploitation due to the use of quantum states while deriving the action policies. 4. The speed of learning is good as the quantum state-action pair holds most accurate information compared to the ordinary state-action pair of Q learning. 5. The amount of time required to traverse every state of the quantum table decreases due to the use of quantum reinforcement policies. 6. Even when the target function is unstable the training phase of the QQL model remains in steady state.
Consequences:
1. The quantum agents give equal weightage to optimal and sub-optimal paths which reduces the quality of Q learning policies formed over high dimensional environment. 2. The chance of trapping in local minimal solution is high when the policies formed are similar to each other. 3. Even the quantum reinforcement learning agents express the inability to deal with the long horizons. 4. The samples required to train the quantum agent's increases with the increase in the number of the quantum states and action pairs.
Training methods:
Backpropogation, random batch transition, experience replay, and neural fitted Q iteration.
Precision:
1. The performance of QQL model in parameter prediction for quantum key distribution is satisfactory and lies in the range of 50%. 2. For uniform data samples the QQL model quickly learns the pattern by calculating fixed rewards, the use of policy gradient method always leads to perform an action which has highest expected target value. 3. But for non-uniform data samples the performance of the QQL model gets affected as too much of reinforcement leads to overloading of the quron states and which in turn diminishes the quality of results.
Activation functions:
Policy gradient, Piece-wise, and min-max.

in nature if more number of particles gets attracted towards the misleading smaller particles the chances of getting trapped in local optimal solution is more. This problem is prevented by using Gaussian distribution strategy which determines the misleading local particles easily in the wider search space and prevents the situation of falling into local optima solutions. The summary of the QPSO machine learning model are given in Table 8.

QPSO guarantees to produce global optimal key distribution policies using probabilistic approach for searching better solution within the limited time interval. In QPSO the state of the particles are represented in wave form instead of choosing position and velocity of the particle which makes the technique to be suitable for cryptographic applications. Here the probability of a particle to be present a quantum state is determined using quantum density function which prevents the explosion rate during key distribution. The walking mechanism of QPSO is in isotropic direction

Figure 11. Architecture of QPSO

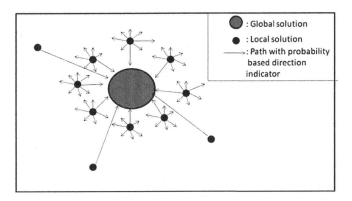

which helps in searching global optimal parameters among the wide range of highly dense parameter set for training the quantum neural network. The QPSO model exhibits high optimality in parameter prediction due to several features like ability to search global optimal solution using levy flight mechanism, successful quantum logic gate operations over the noisy data samples, computation overhead is less due to the involvement of fewer tuning and control parameters, adaptive quantum states update mechanism which avoids the particles from falling into local optimum solutions, and so on.

QUANTUM ANNEALING (QA)

The QA is one of the metaheuristic models used to find the global solution among the available set of candidate solutions based on quantum fluctuations. The model finds the global best solution in the existence of several local minima solutions as it applies the quantum mechanical superposition on all possible states with equal weights. Its speed is 100 times faster than conventional simulated annealing and is not sensitive to the missing information during prediction. The quantum annealing is used in variety of complex applications like artificial intelligence, aerospace, rocket launching, and so on (Chancellor, 2017).

Sample architecture of quantum annealing is given in figure 12 the energy applied to the quantum annealing changes with respect to time and it take the shape of D-shaped curve. The amplitude of all the states of quantum annealing is found to vary in parallel whereas in simulated annealing it is totally dependent on energy of the states. The states of the system keep changing continuously by using more number of quantum cost factors which helps in doing the quantum operations in parallel. The use of quantum fluctuation in annealing make sure that that it will never

Table 8. Summary of QPSO

Prospects: 1. The chances of falling into local optimal solution are prevented by detecting misleading particles early. 2. The speed of computation is high as a smaller number of control parameters are involved in the QPSO and overhead caused by them is also less. 3. The QPSO can easily explore larger search space and consists of very little assumption during computation. 4. By using the uncertainty principle of quantum mechanics, the particles are made capable enough to appear in the search space. 5. The QPSO convergence to globally optimal solution easily compared to classical PSO as it reaches the stopping criteria in very little iteration. 6. The error propagation is also less in the QPSO architecture as it consists of only a smaller number of local optimal solutions. 7. The use of quantum mechanics in PSO algorithms is able to solve any real-world problems in logarithmic time interval. 8. The QPSO follows probabilistic approach in finding the solution in discrete manner which makes it suitable to solve large scale multiple valued real time problems.
Consequences: 1. It is difficult to estimate the quantum particles values during beginning interval of learning in QPSO. 2. If the local and global solutions are highly scattered in the wide search space the accuracy of the solution drops. 3. The approach is not suitable for system which is non-coordinated in nature due to its randomness in computation. 4. It demands frequent updating of quantum velocity in the memory which might slow down the convergence rate.
Training methods: Gradient descent, error backpropogation, and wrapper method.
Precision: The optimality in parameter prediction for quantum key distribution using QPSO model is very good and is in the range of above 80% for both uniform and non-uniform data samples.
Activation functions: Hyperbolic tangent, radial basis, and log sigmoid.

produce a solution which gets trapped in local minima. To perform the tunneling operation quantum computers are preferred than the traditional computers and even the propagation of errors is prevented by using the methodology of quantum entanglement. The summary of the QA machine learning model are given in Table 9.

Some of the characteristics of the quantum annealing which contributes to good performance are reduction in error propagation rate due to qubits computation, ability to solve the problems quickly due to the availability of D-wave processors, arriving at global optimal solution is easy as it the candidate solution can be searched easily by mimicking tunneling with semi-classical energy landscape.

Figure 12. Architecture of quantum annealing

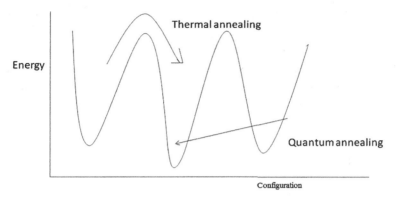

Table 9. Summary of QA

Prospects:
1. The quantum fluctuations methodology of quantum annealing is helping in performing prime number factorization with high speed.
2. The speed of operation is 10^8 times faster than the traditional annealing.
3. Quantum annealing is preferred over the simulated annealing to solve optimization problems as it provides runtime polymorphism.
4. With the increase in the size of the problem the annealing time takes the shape of D formed curve and it is exponentially very lower.
5. The energy required to solve high dimensional problems is very less due to annealing of quantum states.
Consequences:
1. If the quantum states are annealed repeatedly over the iteration then it might slow down the quantum annealing process.
2. Often the behavior of quantum annealing is application specific which limits its generality in terms of operation.
3. While solving complex problem with uncertainty the time taken to find global optimal solution is high.
Training methods:
Ensemble learning, stochastic gradient descent, and Monte Carlo
Precision:
The performance of the QA model with respect to parameter prediction for quantum key distribution is satisfactory in the range of 60% for both uniform and non-uniform data samples.
Activation functions:
Periodic function, Boltzmann distribution function, and radial activation function.

Quantum Differential Evolution (QDE)

The QDE model applies the operators like mutation, crossover, and vector selection over the input sample to select optimal global parameter among the existing several local optimal parameters. The use of quantum-based differential evolution is excellent in terms of speed of operation and rate of convergence (Fu, Ding, Zhou, & Hu, 2013). Sample architecture of quantum differential evolution is given in figure 13. After setting the initial parameters in quantum states the individual trails of candidate solutions are generated by using crossover operation and the highly fit solutions is selected using selection operator. The quantum states are embedded inside the class states of the candidate solution by using the Monte Carlo method. The position of the individual candidate solutions are updated using the position iteration policy until the stopping criteria is reached. The summary of the QDE machine learning model are given in Table 10.

The performance comparison of all quantum machine learning models is summarized in the Table 11. This shows the performance of various quantum machine learning algorithms with respect to parameters like convergence rate, accuracy, speed of execution, and scalability on a scale of low, medium, or high.

CONCLUSION

This chapter provides a brief introduction to quantum cryptography, comparison between quantum key distribution and traditional public and private key distribution strategies. Also discuss the role of parameter prediction and optimization in achieving quantum key distribution in a finite time interval. Several potential quantum machine learning algorithms like QFFNN, QRNN, QBNN, QCNN, QRL, QQL, QPSO, QA, and QDE are discussed. Among all the quantum machine learning models discussed the performances of the QCNN and QPSO are found to be good towards quantum key distribution.

Figure 13. Architecture of quantum differential evolution

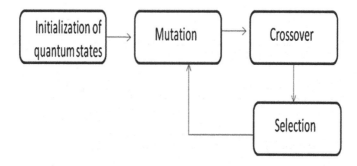

Table 10. Summary of QDE

Prospects: 1. Due to the use of quantum search mechanism in differential evolution the tendency of premature convergence gets prevented. 2. It also achieves perfect balance between exploration and exploitation phases which results high optimal solutions. 3. The accuracy in determining the potential candidate solution is high due to the use of quantum states. 4. Ability to process the input data without explicit segmentation and separation is high. 5. The representation of the input data in quantum states is in terms of Q-bit strings which makes the processing stage easier. 6. It guarantees global optimal solution with least concern about the initial parameters setting. 7. The time taken to convergence to global optimal solution is very less due to the involvement of fewer control parameters and use of differential evolution operators. 8. The potential to balance between exploration and exploitation is high as the tendency to converge to sub-optimal solutions is very less.
Consequences: 1. The efficiency of the quantum differential evolution algorithms are depended on the initial parameter setting for control parameters and is difficult to select appropriate values for the control parameters which in turn affects efficiency. 2. The efficiency of the quantum differential evolution fails when it is applied over the epistatic problems as it cannot capture the valid expressions in phenotypes with uncertainty. 3. The time taken to find global optimal values for control parameters of quantum differential evolution is high as it requires more number of quantum iterations.
Training methods: Ensemble averaging, error backpropagation, and affinity propogation.
Precision: 1. The performance of the QDE model towards parameter prediction for quantum key distribution is not satisfactory as it falls in the range 30% to 50% for uniform and non-uniform data samples. 2. The poor performance of QDE model is due to the reasons like inability to capture exact pattern in the input data sample due to influence of noise, high tendency to fall into local optimal solution due to improper choice of genetic operators, and so on.
Activation functions: Radial basis function, penalty function, and nondifferential neuron function.

Table 11. Comparison of quantum machine learning models

Technique	Convergence Rate	Accuracy	Speed	Scalability
QFFNN	Low	Medium	Low	Low
QRNN	Low	Medium	Medium	Medium
QBNN	Low	Low	High	Low
QCNN	High	High	Medium	High
QRL	Low	Medium	Medium	Low
QQL	High	Medium	Low	Low
QPSO	High	High	High	Medium
QA	Low	Medium	Low	Low
QDE	Low	Medium	Low	Low

REFERENCES

Bennett, C. H., & Brassard, G. (2014). Quantum cryptography: Public key distribution and coin tossing. *Theoretical Computer Science*, *560*(12), 7–11. doi:10.1016/j.tcs.2014.05.025

Biamonte, J., Wittek, P., Pancotti, N., Rebentrost, P., Wiebe, N., & Lloyd, S. (2017). Quantum machine learning. *Nature*, *549*(7671), 195–202. doi:10.1038/nature23474 PMID:28905917

Brassard, G., & Crepeau, C. (1996). 25 years of quantum cryptography. *ACM Sigact News*, *27*(3), 13–24. doi:10.1145/235666.235669

Chancellor, N. (2017). Modernizing quantum annealing using local searches. *New Journal of Physics*, *19*(2), 23–24. doi:10.1088/1367-2630/aa59c4

Cong, I., Choi, S., & Lukin, M. D. (2019). Quantum convolutional neural networks.

Dong, D., Chen, C., Li, H., & Tarn, T. J. (2008). Quantum reinforcement learning. *IEEE Transactions on Systems, Man, and Cybernetics. Part B, Cybernetics*, *38*(5), 1207–1220. doi:10.1109/TSMCB.2008.925743 PMID:18784007

Dunjko, V., Taylor, J. M., & Briegel, H. J. (2017). Advances in quantum reinforcement learning. In *Proceedings of the IEEE International Conference on Systems, Man, and Cybernetics (SMC)* (pp. 282-287). IEEE Press. 10.1109/SMC.2017.8122616

Ellie, M. (2018). *4 Amazing Quantum Computing Applications*. DevOps. Retrieved from https://devops.com/4-amazing-quantum-computing-applications/

Feynman, R. P. (1982). Simulating physics with computers. *International Journal of Theoretical Physics*, *21*(6), 467–488. doi:10.1007/BF02650179

Fu, Y., Ding, M., Zhou, C., & Hu, H. (2013). Route planning for unmanned aerial vehicle (UAV) on the sea using hybrid differential evolution and quantum-behaved particle swarm optimization. *IEEE Transactions on Systems, Man, and Cybernetics. Systems*, *43*(6), 1451–1465. doi:10.1109/TSMC.2013.2248146

Gonçalves, C. P. (2016). Quantum neural machine learning-backpropagation and dynamics.

Gottesman, D., Lo, H. K., Lutkenhaus, N., & Preskill, J. (2004). Security of quantum key distribution with imperfect devices. In *Proceedings of the International Symposium on Information Theory*. Academic Press. 10.1109/ISIT.2004.1365172

Goyal, A., Aggarwal, S., & Jain, A. (2011). Quantum Cryptography & its Comparison with Classical Cryptography: A Review Paper. In *Proceedings of the 5th IEEE International Conference on Advanced Computing & Communication Technologies ICACCT-2011*. IEEE Press.

Kutvonen, A., Sagawa, T., & Fujii, K. (2018). Recurrent neural networks running on quantum spins: memory accuracy and capacity.

Lakshmi, P. S., & Murali, G. (2017). Comparison of classical and quantum cryptography using QKD simulator. In *Proceedings of the International Conference on Energy, Communication, Data Analytics and Soft Computing (ICECDS)* (pp. 3543-3547). Academic Press. 10.1109/ICECDS.2017.8390120

Liu, G., Chen, W., Chen, H., & Xie, J. (2019). A Quantum Particle Swarm Optimization Algorithm with Teamwork Evolutionary Strategy. *Mathematical Problems in Engineering*.

Luitel, B., & Venayagamoorthy, G. K. (2010). Quantum inspired PSO for the optimization of simultaneous recurrent neural networks as MIMO learning systems. *Neural Networks*, *23*(5), 583–586. doi:10.1016/j.neunet.2009.12.009 PMID:20071140

Spector, L., Barnum, H., Bernstein, H. J., & Swamy, N. (1999). Quantum computing applications of genetic programming. In *Advances in genetic programming* (pp. 135-160). Academic Press.

Van Waart, O., & Thijssen, J. (2015). Traditional Cryptography.

Wan, K. H., Dahlsten, O., Kristjansson, H., Gardner, R., & Kim, M. S. (2017). Quantum generalisation of feedforward neural networks. *NPJ Quantum Information*, *3*(1), 36.

Yimsiriwattana, A., & Lomonaco, S. J. Jr. (2004). Distributed quantum computing: A distributed Shor algorithm. *Quantum Information & Computation*, *2*(5436), 60–372.

Zalka, C. (1999). Grover's quantum searching algorithm is optimal. *Physical Review A.*, *60*(4), 2746–2751. doi:10.1103/PhysRevA.60.2746

Chapter 4
LFSR–Keyed MUX for Random Number Generation in Nano Communication Using QCA

Padmapriya Praveenkumar
SASTRA University (Deemed), India

Santhiya Devi R.
SASTRA University (Deemed), India

Amirtharajan Rengarajan
iD https://orcid.org/0000-0003-1574-3045
SASTRA University (Deemed), India

John Bosco Balaguru Rayappan
iD https://orcid.org/0000-0003-4641-9870
SASTRA University (Deemed), India

ABSTRACT

Nano industries have been successful trendsetters for the past 30 years, in escalating the speed and dropping the power necessities of nanoelectronic devices. According to Moore's law and the assessment created by the international technology roadmap for semiconductors, beyond 2020, there will be considerable restrictions in manufacturing IC's based on CMOS technologies. As a result, the next prototype to get over these effects is quantum-dot cellular automata (QCA). In this chapter, an efficient quantum cellular automata (QCA) based random number generator (RNG) is proposed. QCA is an innovative technology in the nano regime which guarantees

DOI: 10.4018/978-1-7998-2253-0.ch004

large device density, less power dissipation, and minimal size as compared to the various CMOS technologies. With the aim to maximise the randomness in the proposed nano communication, a linear feedback shift register (LFSR) keyed multiplexer with ring oscillators is developed. The developed RNG is simulated using a quantum cellular automata (QCA) simulator tool.

INTRODUCTION

The present Semiconductor technology is approaching its scaling limitation due to disadvantages like the transistor number will be doubled about every two years, as stated by Gordon Moore in Moore's law during the mid-1960(Cavin, Lugli, & Zhirnov, 2012; Das & De, 2017; Walus, Dysart, Jullien, & Budiman, 2004). Therefore, it is necessary to devise modern technology with a reduction in the size, high-speed, low power consumption, and high-density transistor. These issues have led researchers to find an alternative technology named Quantum dot Cellular Automata (QCA), which was proposed by Lent et al. (Lent, Tougaw, Porod, & Bernstein, 1993). QCA will have four quantum dots at the corners of the structure (Kim, Wu, & Karri, 2006; Lent & Tougaw, 1997; Vacca, Wang, Graziano, Roch, & Zamboni, 2015)and instead of using the current charge, it uses a polarized method for transferring the digital information thereby reducing the need of energy for operations(Kianpour & Sabbaghi-Nadooshan, 2014; Vacca et al., 2015)and can be used as an alternate for CMOS technology.

BACKGROUND

In the past, a significant hazard to the CMOS based cryptographic circuits is the side channel attack (Kelsey, Schneier, Wagner, & Hall, n.d.; Kocher, 1996; Liu, Srivastava, Lu, O'Neill, & Swartzlander, 2012) that is based on power analysis. There is a possibility that with the power analysis, the secret key can be exposed just by measuring the encryption and decryption power consumption. As there is no current flow in QCA, this can be avoided (Kianpour & Sabbaghi-Nadooshan, 2014; Liu et al., 2012). In this aspect, many researchers have developed new cryptographic algorithms. Pain et al. (Pain, Das, Sadhu, Kanjilal, & De, 2019) have developed a True Random Number Generator (TRNG) intending for secure communication by encompassing a smaller amount of QCA cells. An architecture that is based on

QCA for hiding the information in images has been proposed by Debnath et al. (Debnath, Das, & De, 2017). Amiri et al. (Amiri, Mahdavi, & Mirzakuchaki, 2009) incorporated QCA technology for implementing 4×4 S-Box that can be used for confusing the information in a cryptosystem.

Jadav et al. (Das et al., 2019) designed a QCA based even parity generator and checker circuits for utilizing in Nano communication networks using XOR gates. The proposed QCA nano architecture is exceptional in high device density and faster speed as compared to the existing ones. The general characteristics of QCA are enumerated by Criag et al. (Lent et al., 1993) in his invited paper, where the switching sequences of the QCA device for various clocking is elaborated. Also, the various pipelining stages like switch, hold, release and relax phases of the QCA cell is depicted with respect to time. Bikash et al. (Debnath et al., 2017) establishes a secure communication by using reversible image steganography using quantum dots. QCA parameters like latency, area, cell count for the secured QCA circuit was analyzed (Sabbaghi-Nadooshan & Kianpour, 2014). Moreover, LSB based embedding was carried using QCA array and the metrics like PSNR, SNR and MSE were estimated as like normal secure communication. Later, Himanshu et al. (Thapliyal, Ranganathan, & Kotiyal, 2013) realizes two test vector based completely reversible sequential circuits using quantum dots. Fredkin and Mux (Ahmad et al., 2016; Angizi, Alkaldy, Bagherzadeh, & Navi, 2014) based QCA layouts were constructed and tested for completely stuck at fault conditions. From the analysis, MUX based gates outshine than Fredkin in terms of majority gates, speed and device density.

- By analyzing the various QCA techniques in literature this chapter proposes a QCA based RNG using LFSR and ROs. The main contribution of this chapter is as follows:
- Two EXOR structures using QCA were designed
- MUX, ROs and LFSR were depicted using QCA cell structure
- Parameters like area, latency, cell count, energy dissipation and cost were estimated and
  compared with the available literature
- Initial key sequences were generated by LFSR and given as select signals to MUX
- Select lines in MUX decides the ROs for random number generation
- Clock circuitry in QCA simulation tool acts as an initial seed to the LFSR circuitry

PRELIMINARIES

QCA Cell Structure

It consists of 4 Q dots in a square array format with 2 electrons to facilitate encoding and transmission of information. The Q dots are joined through the potential barriers allowing the electrons to tunnel through the barriers as in Figure 1(a). The potential barrier heights decide the electron tunnelling. The position of the electrons in a cell is used to encode the binary states and is denoted by polarizations. The states 1, 0, and null are represented by the cells with polarization $P = +1$, $P = -1$ and $P = 0$, respectively.

QCA Polarization

Quantum dots are small diametric semi-conductors whose charging energy is always greater than KBT. KB represent Boltzmann's constant and T is the operating temperature. Due to electron tunnelling, the loaded electrons in the cell and can make their transition to any of the Quantum dot in the QCA cell structure. The path connecting the quantum dots are called as tunnels. Due to columbic repulsion force, the electrons always occupy any of the corners based on the polarization. When the cell is polarized by 1, it is represented by binary '1' else binary '0' state as in Figure 1(b).

Majority Gate

It contains a minimum of five QCA cells, where three acts as inputs while the fourth one as output as in Figure 1 (a). The fifth one in the middle is termed as device cell. The logical implementation of a three-input majority gate is represented by Majority $(I_1, I_2, I_3) = I_1I_2 + I_2I_3 + I_3I_1$. The majority gates can be utilized as AND/ OR gate by fixing the polarity of the inputs.

Figure 1. (a) QCA Cell structure and (b) QCA polarization

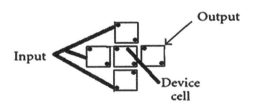

PROPOSED METHODOLOGY

QCA Random Number Generator

The proposed QCA RNG was simulated using QCA simulation tool. The proposed scheme involves various QCA structures:

1.   EXOR gates
2.   Ring oscillators acting as random key generator
3.   2:1 MUX
4.   Linear Feedback Shift register

EXOR Gate Realization Using QCA

The EXOR expression is given by $A \oplus B = \overline{A}.B + \overline{B}.A$. Two different realizations were made using QCA layouts as in Figure 2 and 3. Figure 2 was implemented using NOT-AND-OR structure and Figure 3 was implemented using NAND-AND –OR structure.

Ring Oscillators Acting as Random Key Generator

In Ring oscillator, the NOT gates are connected in a ring fashion with the output of the last NOT gate is connected to the first one. Ring oscillators act as the input to the 2:1 MUX. Ring Oscillator is a Random Key Generator (RKG) (Figure 4) which comprises of the odd number of NOT gates aligned in a feedback ring structure.

The projected scheme uses two ROs with different initial seeds provided by the clock circuitry in the QCA simulator tool. Also, the LSB and MSB positions are reversed with different output EXOR structures for each of the ROs as Figure 2 and 3 respectively. The feedback polynomials used by ROs are $1+x_2+x_3$ and $1+x_1+x_2$, respectively.

2:1 MUX

A 2:1 MUX is designed using QCA structure, which accepts two inputs based on the selection line. The select input decodes one of the inputs to the output of the MUX unit. The designed QCA MUX is depicted in Figure 5. Based on the LFSR input, the 2:1 MUX selects either RO1 or RO2 to produce the random key sequences.

Figure 2. EXOR 1 using QCA

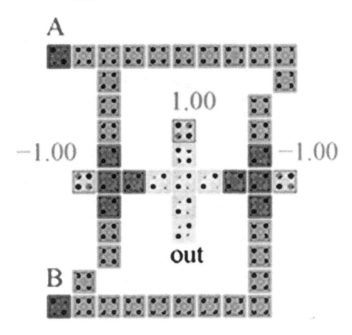

Linear Feedback Shift Register

LFSR is a type of shift register whose input is a linear function of its previous state values. In the proposed scheme, the LFSR is designed using D flip-flops with the clock input set to 1. The input of the flip flop is decided by the EXOR gate output which is being tapped by third and fifth flip flop. LFSR QCA structure constructed using D flip flops is shown in Figure 6.

The proposed scheme involves structures like ROs (Figure 4), 2:1 MUX (Figure 5), LFSR (Figure 6), and two different EXOR structures (Figure 2& 3). In the projected methodology, random number generating was carried out using QCA cell structure. The following steps were carried out for Random number generation as shown in Figure 7.

- The clock circuitry in the QCA simulation tool decides the initial seed to LFSR
- Key sequence in LFSR act as a selection line to the 2:1 MUX circuitry
- ROs are attached as the inputs to the MUX circuit
- Further the selection line from LFSR triggers one of the ROs to the MUX architecture
- RNG outputs the random sequence at the MUX output

Figure 3. EXOR 2 using QCA

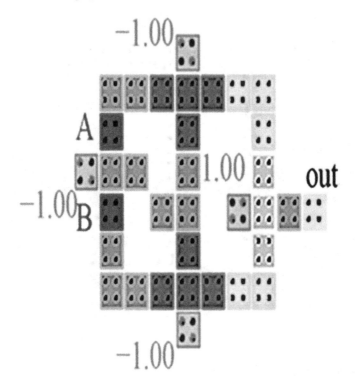

RESULTS AND DISCUSSION

In the projected QCA structure, Area in (μm^2), cell count, latency in clock cycles, total energy dissipation in (eV) and the cost function were estimated, and it is provided in Table 1. The cost function can be estimated by the product of the area of the QCA cell by the latency in clock cycles. Cost function = Area of the QCA cell × latency period.

From the estimated parameters, it is evident that the proposed QCA RKG provides 50% improvement over (Angizi et al., 2014) and (Ahmad et al., 2016) in terms of cell count, area, latency, total energy dissipation and in the cost function.

The QCA simulation layout output of the designed random number generator using MUX, ROs and LFSR is shown in Figure 8. The timing waveform shows the simulation results of the RNG realized using QCA layout. The generated random output sequence has a latency of one clock cycle.

Figure 4. Ring oscillator design using QCA

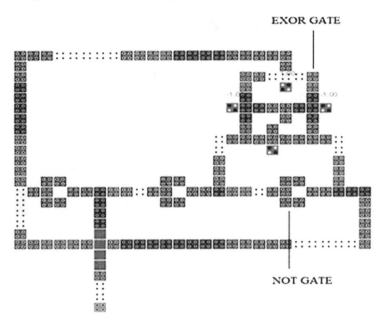

Figure 5. MUX design using QCA

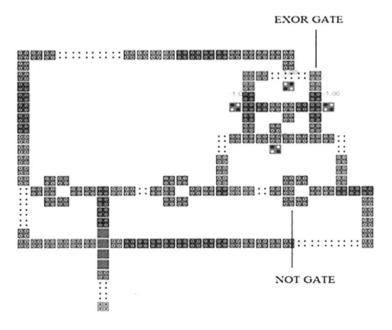

Figure 6. LFSR using QCA

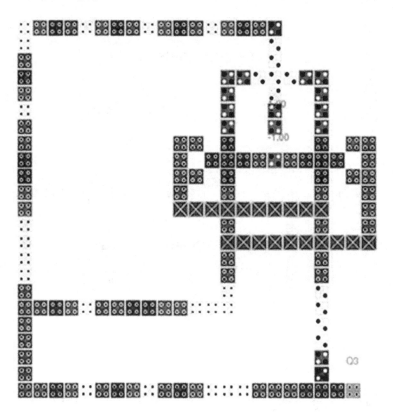

FUTURE RESEARCH DIRECTIONS

QCA design can be extended to a devise a complete model to perform encryption and decryption algorithms using generated RNG sequences. Further, memory can be constructed to store the QCA encrypted data.

CONCLUSION

In this chapter, a new random key generation scheme has been proposed by using MUX and LFSR in QCA platform. The developed random key generation scheme has used two Ring Oscillators as input to the MUX with LFSR as a select input in the developed secret Nano communication circuit. The initial seeds to the LFSR and the Ring oscillators are decided by the clock circuitry available in the QCA simulation tool. Hence the initial seeds are highly sensitive and absolutely unpredictable. To

Figure 7. Proposed LFSR keyed QCA random number generator circuit

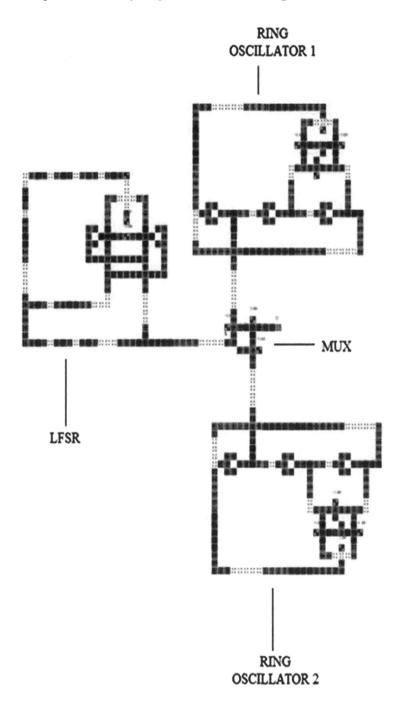

Table 1. Parameter analysis of the proposed QCA RKG circuit

Structure	Cell Count	Area (µm²)	Latency (Clock Cycle)	Total Energy Dissipation (eV)	Cost
LFSR	153	0.22	1	2.70 e-2	0.22
Ring Oscillator	159	0.27	1	4.54 e-2	0.27
2:1 MUX	21	0.02	1	1.34 e-2	0.02
RNG (1-bit)	512	1.41	1	1.29 e-1	1.41
EXOR 1	48	0.05	1	1.78 e-2	0.05
EXOR 2	34	0.04	1	2.33 e-2	0.04
EXOR (Angizi et al., 2014)	75	0.08	2	NA	0.16
EXOR (Ahmad et al., 2016)	93	0.07	1.25	NA	0.0875

prove the effectiveness of the proposed QCA random number generator, extensive analysis was carried out concerning device density and power dissipation for all the individual structures involved in the QCA layout.

ACKNOWLEDGMENT

The authors wish to acknowledge SASTRA Deemed University, Thanjavur, India for extending infrastructural support to carry out this work.

Figure 8. Simulation results of designed random number generator

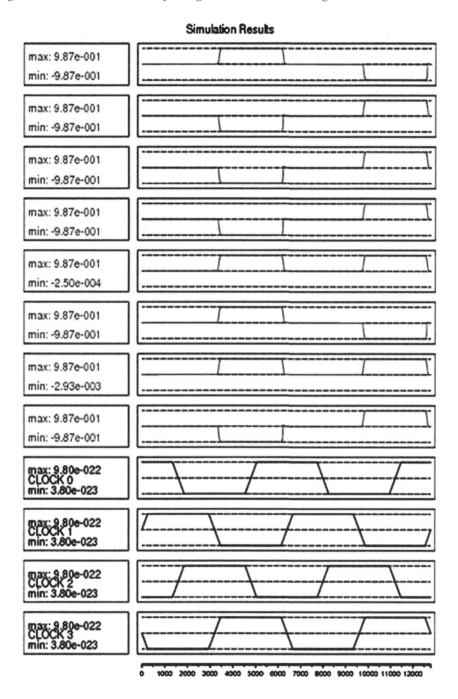

REFERENCES

Ahmad, F., Bhat, G. M., Khademolhosseini, H., Azimi, S., Angizi, S., & Navi, K. (2016). Towards single layer quantum-dot cellular automata adders based on explicit interaction of cells. *Journal of Computational Science*, *16*, 8–15. doi:10.1016/j. jocs.2016.02.005

Amiri, M. A., Mahdavi, M., & Mirzakuchaki, S. (2009). Logic-based QCA implementation of a 4. In Exhibition (pp. 1–5). IEEE. doi:10.1109/ IEEEGCC.2009.5734314

Angizi, S., Alkaldy, E., Bagherzadeh, N., & Navi, K. (2014). Novel Robust Single Layer Wire Crossing Approach for Exclusive OR Sum of Products Logic Design with Quantum-Dot Cellular Automata. *Journal of Low Power Electronics*, *10*(2), 259–271. doi:10.1166/jolpe.2014.1320

Cavin, R. K., Lugli, P., & Zhirnov, V. V. (2012). Science and Engineering Beyond Moore's Law. *Proceedings of the IEEE*, *100*, 1720–1749. doi:10.1109/ JPROC.2012.2190155

Das, J. C., & De, D. (2017). Nanocommunication network design using QCA reversible crossbar switch. *Nano Communication Networks*, *13*, 20–33. doi:10.1016/j. nancom.2017.06.003

Das, J. C., De, D., Mondal, S. P., Ahmadian, A., Ghaemi, F., & Senu, N. (2019). QCA Based Error Detection Circuit for Nano Communication Network. *IEEE Access*, *7*, 67355–67366. doi:10.1109/ACCESS.2019.2918025

Debnath, B., Das, J. C., & De, D. (2017). Reversible logic-based image steganography using quantum dot cellular automata for secure nanocommunication. *IET Circuits, Devices & Systems*, *11*(1), 58–67. doi:10.1049/iet-cds.2015.0245

Kelsey, J., Schneier, B., Wagner, D., & Hall, C. (n.d.). *Side Channel Cryptanalysis of Product Ciphers*. Retrieved from https://www.schneier.com/academic/paperfiles/ paper-side-channel2.pdf

Kianpour, M., & Sabbaghi-Nadooshan, R. (2014). A conventional design and simulation for CLB implementation of an FPGA quantum-dot cellular automata. *Microprocessors and Microsystems*, *38*(8), 1046–1062. doi:10.1016/j. micpro.2014.08.001

Kim, K., Wu, K., & Karri, R. (2006). Quantum-Dot Cellular Automata Design Guideline. *IEICE Transactions on Fundamentals of Electronics, Communications and Computer Sciences*, *E89-A*(6), 1607–1614. doi:10.1093/ietfec/e89-a.6.1607

Kocher, P. C. (1996). *Timing Attacks on Implementations of Diffie-Hellman, RSA, DSS, and Other Systems* (pp. 104–113). Berlin: Springer. doi:10.1007/3-540-68697-5_9

Lent, C. S., & Tougaw, P. D. (1997). A device architecture for computing with quantum dots. *Proceedings of the IEEE, 85*(4), 541–557. doi:10.1109/5.573740

Lent, C. S., Tougaw, P. D., Porod, W., & Bernstein, G. H. (1993). Quantum cellular automata. *Nanotechnology, 4*(1), 49–57. doi:10.1088/0957-4484/4/1/004 PMID:21727566

Liu, W., Srivastava, S., Lu, L., O'Neill, M., & Swartzlander, E. E. (2012). Are QCA cryptographic circuits resistant to power analysis attack? *IEEE Transactions on Nanotechnology, 11*(6), 1239–1251. doi:10.1109/TNANO.2012.2222663

Pain, P., Das, K., Sadhu, A., Kanjilal, M. R., & De, D. (2019). Novel True Random Number Generator Based Hardware Cryptographic Architecture Using Quantum-Dot Cellular Automata. *International Journal of Theoretical Physics*, 1–20. doi:10.100710773-019-04189-2

Sabbaghi-Nadooshan, R., & Kianpour, M. (2014). A novel QCA implementation of MUX-based universal shift register. *Journal of Computational Electronics, 13*(1), 198–210. doi:10.100710825-013-0500-9

Thapliyal, H., Ranganathan, N., & Kotiyal, S. (2013). Design of Testable Reversible Sequential Circuits. *IEEE Transactions on Very Large Scale Integration (VLSI) Systems, 21*(7), 1201–1209. doi:10.1109/TVLSI.2012.2209688

Vacca, M., Wang, J., Graziano, M., Roch, M. R., & Zamboni, M. (2015). Feedbacks in QCA: A Quantitative Approach. *IEEE Transactions on Very Large Scale Integration (VLSI) Systems, 23*(10), 2233–2243. doi:10.1109/TVLSI.2014.2358495

Walus, K., Dysart, T. J., Jullien, G. A., & Budiman, R. A. (2004). QCADesigner: A Rapid Design and Simulation Tool for Quantum-Dot Cellular Automata. *IEEE Transactions on Nanotechnology, 3*(1), 26–31. doi:10.1109/TNANO.2003.820815

Chapter 5

Quantum Cryptography Key Distribution:
Quantum Computing

Bhanu Chander

https://orcid.org/0000-0003-0057-7662
Pondicherry University, India

ABSTRACT

Quantum cryptography is actions to protect transactions through executing the circumstance of quantum physics. Up-to-the-minute cryptography builds security over the primitive ability of fragmenting enormous numbers into relevant primes; however, it features inconvenience with ever-increasing machine computing power along with current mathematical evolution. Among all the disputes, key distribution is the most important trouble in classical cryptography. Quantum cryptography endows with clandestine communication by means of offering a definitive protection statement with the rule of the atmosphere. Exploit quantum mechanics to cryptography can be enlarging unrestricted, unfailing information transmission. This chapter describes the contemporary state of classical cryptography along with the fundamentals of quantum cryptography, quantum protocol key distribution, implementation criteria, quantum protocol suite, quantum resistant cryptography, and large-scale quantum key challenges.

DOI: 10.4018/978-1-7998-2253-0.ch005

INTRODUCTION

Cryptography is learning process for transfer secret information or intelligence by using mathematical operations, only applying secret or specific key the intended receipts can read or gets the original message. The message which is revolved around a masquerading structure process is called encryption. Converting masquerading text messages to plain text is called decryption. The key which makes plain text to cipher text is called the encryption key, coming to the receiver's end the key which makes cipher text to plain text is called the decryption key. Our standing statement will be that any time a person sends a message, that person has to send it over an unrestricted medium, so that anybody who wishes can pick it up. So, the eavesdropper can take delivery of any message that A and B send to each other. The point, then, is to make it so that even though eavesdropper can see the message, it just looks like twaddle to her/him: she can't right to use the content of the message. Cryptography is the encounter among A and B on one track and eavesdropper on the other track. In a variety of times in the past, A and B have had the superior hand. At other times, the eavesdropper has been on top. At the current scenario, it seems that A and B are winning, but eavesdropper is inflexible at work trying to recapture her/his lead.

In cryptography, the procedures which are apply to shield information are achieved from mathematical theories and a set-of-rule based computations acknowledged as algorithms to translate messages in ways that create it tough to decode it. These algorithms are exploiting for cryptographic key generation, digital signing, and certification to protect data privacy, web browsing on internet and to shelter top secret dealings like credit and debit card dealings. The uncertainty law of quantum physics fabricates the most primitive fundamentals for quantum cryptography. Through quantum computers future being estimated to answer discrete logarithmic crisis as well as the commonly known cryptography schemes like AES, RSA, DES, quantum cryptography turn out to be the forecasted solution. In observation it is exploit to set-up a mutual, secret along with arbitrary sequence of bits to communicate among two arrangements, for instance take A and B. This set-up is acknowledged as Quantum Key Distribution. Subsequent to this key is shared among A and B, additional swapping of information can take place in the course of well-known cryptographic techniques.

In cryptography main role taken by keys, based on the chosen key cryptography split into two styles Symmetric or secret-key cryptography and Asymmetric key or public-key cryptography (Bennett and Brassard, 1987; Ekert 1991; Zhao and Qi, 2006; Padmavathi and Vishnu, 2016; NIST, 2016).

- **Secret Key Cryptosystem:** In secret-key cryptography, just a single key is shared within dispatcher as well as the recipient that key sustain for encryption as well as decryption which will keep as secret. That's the reason to call it a secret key or symmetric key cryptography. Security mainly established on problematical nonproven algorithms, most importantly it depends upon protected medium on behalf of key distribution.

- **Public Key Cryptosystem:** In asymmetric cryptography, two keys are used public and private keys, the private key is used to encrypt the messages and the public key is used to decrypt the encrypted message. Security is based on computational mathematical assumptions, most of the security algorithms found on non-proven mathematical assumptions.

CLASSICAL CRYPTOGRAPHY

Confidentiality is the topmost priority for cryptography. To accomplish this objective an innovation called cryptosystem is revealed. It used to join information along with some supplementary material or knowledge well-known as key and fabricate as a cryptogram. Sending secret messages is the principal application for cryptography. Most of the cryptosystems are depending on computational mathematical hypothesis; encryption and decryption are must equivalent by solving some computational difficult problems. The main problem is the distribution of keys or key distribution which can be solved by two methods one is mathematical assumptions known as classical cryptography and another method is Physics known as Quantum cryptography. Classical cryptography depends over computational difficulties of factoring large integer numbers but quantum cryptography depends over universal laws of Quantum Mechanics (Bennett and Brassard, 1987; Peev, 2009; Vasileios and Kamer, 2018; Alfred and Pal, 2018; Guru and Raghu, 2016; Diff, 1976).

Suppose that Alice and Bob communicating over insecure transmission medium and encryption, decryption is done with the best of accepted cryptography algorithm which is most probably intractable by any accepted computing structure. At this time imagine here an Eve as an intruder who continuously listening over the communicational channel where Alice and bob sending and receiving intelligence messages. Assume Alice and Bob use the factoring method then Eve also can make use of Factoring to break the key communication and steal the important data. The limitation of symmetric key cryptography is key sharing and it is the main reason since asymmetric cryptosystem gaining importance over symmetric one-time pad algorithm. Recent times Elliptic curve cryptography (ECC) acknowledged as state-of-the-art crypto and mostly handle for guaranteed financial transactions (Diff, 1976; Vasileios and Kamer, 2018; Alfred and Pal, 2018; Mateusz, 2018; Yin and Chen, 2016; Bennet and Brassard, 1982).

Because of computational complex calculations, public-key cryptography turns into as sluggish, mainly engaged toward swap keys. For instance, to distribute keys among two distant parties we may use most widely developed explanations such as RSA and Diffie-Hellman key formats. Nevertheless, asymmetric key is somewhat slower than symmetric key because of computation. Many people proposed hybrid models that combine the advantages of both cryptosystems to give better results in terms of security. These types of schemes exploit the speed of performance with speed of secret key design although power the adaptability of asymmetric cryptography. At the same time, existing asymmetric crypto methods are first-rate along with adequate on the way to provide confidentiality with integrity levels, but they may be exposed to a handful of risks. For example, the innovations in computer processing like quantum computing can proficient to decode the application like RSA, etc., in a timely manner so making public cryptosystems straight away out of fashion. Asymmetric cryptosystems like RSA plus Diffie-Hellman algorithms aren't more situated on mathematical testimonies. Above mentioned schemes reasonably measured as secured based on the elementary progression of factoring great integers into their primes. Thus the power of these algorithms is factoring of large prime numbers and till now there is no computer process that has the power of computing mathematical operation which can quickly compute the factoring of very large numbers. In a minute understanding take a look at DES symmetric key cryptography which was once considered as the first more secure algorithm, it contains 64-bit key length but mainly its key length is 56 bit remaining 8-bit keys are used to check error rate in data. But it is no longer secured as think; progression in machinery prepared it will inconsiderable to overthrow. But the reality is with the intention of modern mainframes can break the DES algorithm within a day or a few hours of time. After DES breakability Advanced Encryption Standard takes the position of Security. It has key lengths of 128,192,256 bits as we increase the key length security of algorithm increases but this public algorithm vulnerable to coming advancements in computing technologies. Another interesting fact is, breakable theorems might elaborate in upcoming or while back developed algorithms may modify to compute factors of enormous integers into respective primes in time comportment. Moreover, present no realizable witness is stated that it is impracticable to build up such a separating algorithm. From the above discussions asymmetric key crypto schemes are defenseless to insecurity concerning in future those type algorithms may be created (Johnson and Colin, 2002; Padmavati and Vishnu, 2016; Rosenberg and Harington, 2007; Shor, 1997; Vasileios and Kamer, 2018; Alfred and pal, 2018; Bennett and Brassard, 1982).

Modern Cryptography Key Distribution

Traditional cryptography key distribution is the main problem. In previous times people by sending through a physical medium (like a disk which contains the key) they believe that the problem is solved, but in the present digital world, this experiment is clearly impracticable. There is no possible way to check whether the medium is interrupted, whether its stuffing copied or not. To overcome this problem many researchers and scientists of the British invented a solution by using a padlock. For example, assume a scenario that two parties are communicating with each other before that communication the intended receiver sends one open padlock to the party which sends important information at the same time it keeps its own secret key. By using this open padlock sender will defend information, then the receiver is the solitary party who can undo information through the help of the key that he kept. Formally those padlocks are mathematical expressions known as "one-way function" because they can easily compute but hard to reverse (Brassard, 1998)

Many public-key algorithms are slow; the reason is complex computations. So the length of the key selection must be in a careful manner. In principle, the invaders who have indeed records of communication must have to wait for powerful computers enough to break communication. Classical cryptosystems are good for one to two years to keep valuable information keep secretly such as credit card numbers but when it comes the matter of information has to keep secret for a decade. Then three invertors came and propose RSA algorithm a new cryptography algorithm "which takes millions of years to break" and they are given the challenge to break the code for 100 dollars however this code is later broken by a group of scientists over the internet in 1994 (Bennett, 1982; Brassard, 1992). The second thing is public-key cryptography is vulnerable to progress against mathematical operations. There are many efforts are done on mathematics directed toward turnout that public crypto-system be secured. Till now notably no such algorithm is determined which can perform reversing one-way function for factors of primes. But the discovery of such algorithms can make difficult to public-key security to insecure. It has more interest and problematic to access the speed of a hypothetical process than that of scientific advances. Here is proof for this in the past of mathematics, where one person can capable to answer a dilemma, the same dilemma can be kept busy for years or decades. There are more possible chances for designing such an algorithm which can reverse the factor numbers one way function. Maybe the algorithm is already revealed but reserved in top secret. These all things basically mean that asymmetric cryptography is not more secure in future moreover can't guarantee future proof of key distribution (Omar and Shawkat, 2018; Alfred and pal, 2018; Guru and Raghupathy, 2016; Bennett and Brassard, 1982; Mullins and Justin, 2003).

One Time Pad Encryption Technique

Most of the symmetric and asymmetric cryptosystems are has combined the personality of the encryption algorithm (E) through plain text (P) is restored to cipher cryptosystem (C) which could openly well-known since such communications security mostly depends on Key (K). But which is secretly shared between sender and receiver and one more essential hypothesis of a cryptosystem is Kirchhoff's algorithm where privacy is necessity exist in key, not on the method. Alice produces cryptogram $C = Ek(P)$, throw it to Bob who decrypts it by $P = (E)$-$1k(C)$ to recovering the original plain text P. this entire process is run under the Eva eye surroundings. Numerous cryptography techniques are presented based on this simple principle some are secured and some can able to break depending on recent advancements in technology. But one algorithm invented in 1917 named "One-time pad" is provably unbreakable. In this both Alice as well as Bob detachment a magnitude of top-secret key objects consists of arbitrary characters like letters, bits, digits which is as large as a transmitted message. Take a look on the principle $Ci = Pi + Ki$ (modN) describe where Alice Sending message P (p1, p2..., pn) p will be in digits, bits, numbers and by using his own Key K (k1, k2..., kn) produce the cryptosystem C= (c1, c2, ..., cn) by applying interchangeable mathematics with base N. when bob receives cryptosystem C, using interchangeable mathematics subtracts key from C to recover the original message P. In 1949 Shannon with information hypothesis proves that this cryptosystem is protected and key material is truthfully unsystematic moreover exploited for only once, advantages like speed, left to right encipherment.

If the one-time pad is resistant then why it not at all utilizable why we are using factorial cryptosystems, reason is one-time pad involves key distribution, key management, and key management problems. At the beginning of crypto, Alice has to create accidental numbers that are not simple like appear. The system generated pseudo-random numbers will not give a secure secret key because it will generate the same sequence always. One key is generated by Alice to encrypt any message Alice should organize a replica for Bob to attain key, without giving any knowledge to Eve strictly a smooth fractional understanding of key. Possible chance is there if both Alice and Bob meet before communication and transfer key to each other, then key distribution is done securely but this does not happen every time. If they are not meet before and no secret key is shared and Alice can't simply send key substance to Bob since the foremost application in cryptosystems is broadcast which disposed to reactive eavesdroppers where Eve easily gets the key material. One easy way to avoid this one-time pad is, it requires encrypting with another one time pad. One time pad is indestructible, but in theory it is extremely tricky to utilize, through taking this motive public-key cryptosystems are complex but not impracticable to crack and simple to apply (Johnson and Colin, 2002; Omar and

Shawkat, 2018; Mateusz, 2018; Peev, 2009; Vasileios and Kamer, 2018; Bennett and Brassard, 1982; Seema, 2017).

QUANTUM CRYPTOGRAPHY

Quantum cryptography idea first programmed in the late 1970s now it is the field handles for information security. Quantum crypto mainly used to develop crypto protocols that are used to defend quantum circumstances that have material goods that can't imitative. One of the most important advantages of quantum cryptography is which gives a piece of faultless sheltered information transmits. The first successful quantum cryptographic machine transmits top-secret key over 30 centimeters with polarized light (Bennett and Brassard, 1982; Seema, 2017). Besides other cryptosystems that perform computational complication of factoring huge integers, quantum crypto performs on the basic, fixed ideology of quantum technicalities. Mainly quantum crypto takes a Break on top of two supporter mechanics Heisenberg uncertainty principle as well as the principle of photon polarization. Without disturbing the system it cannot achievable to determine any quantum classification position accordingly polarization of photon in other words a light particle can only be identified at the point when it is measured. The above-indicated approach shows the main function at eavesdropper to uncomfortable in quantum cryptosystems. Second thing the photon polarization principle illustrates how the light particle can polarize in particular directions. While filtering a photon acceptable polarization filter will only discover a polarized photon or else shattered. In 1984 with the help of these most attractive principles as part of physics and information, two scientists named Charles H. Bennet along with Gilles Brassard promote the theory of quantum cryptosystem. Both of them believe corresponds to the fact that light can behave light waves in addition to the characteristics of particles. Photons usually polarized in a variety of directions and these directions experience signify bits which corresponding to ones and zeros. These bits are utilized to generate secret keys for one time pad and some other public-key methods (Shor, 2000; Omar and Shawkat, 2018; Mateusz, 2018; Peev, 2009; Vasileios and Kamer, 2018; Bennett and Brassard, 1982; Seema, 2017; Bennett and Brassard, 1992).

Light is generally applied to interchange information in telecommunication networks. Where each and every bit of information is taken as pulse, a pulse is released and sent over optical fiber to the receiver here is registered and transferred backward as electronic signals each pulse typically contains millions of particles of light which pronounced as Photons. The same thing is followed in quantum cryptography, a single photon contains an extremely small amount of light which came from laws of quantum physics moreover it cannot divide into fractions; it means

Figure 1. Quantum cryptosystem model for solidly transmit arbitrary key

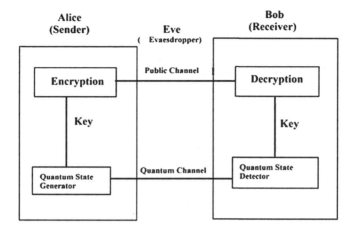

eavesdroppers cannot measure the value of bit with the help of half photon. If the eavesdroppers want to know the bit value, he must observe the photon completely then only he can interrupt and disturb the communication. Another intelligent strategy for eavesdroppers can spot the photons, record the rate of that photon and set up a cloned photon, propel it to the intended beneficiary. But in quantum cryptography, two parties co-operate each other to prevent eavesdroppers from doing such types of actions (Bennett, 1992; Tang and Chen, 2014; Yin and Chen, 2016; Seema, 2017; Shor, 2002).

Difference Between Classical and Q-Bits

Classical knowledge represented in classical bits as 0 and 1. Mentioned classical bits are mostly used in classical or traditional cryptosystems. Q-bits: quantum cryptography mechanism works with quantum bits additionally known as Q-bits. Q-bits are different from classical bits mostly take superposition values between zero and one and they can't be copied.

In BB84 Alice send Bob an arbitrary sequence of Q-bits, which are uniformly expected to be in one of four feasible statuses [see Table]. When Bobs receives a Q-bit he measures that on Z basis or X basis in a random manner and saves records for future use. Then Alice makes an announcement to Bob on which basis the state came from but didn't reveal what is the actual state was. Then bob announces the results on what substructure or basis he calculated. If Bob calculated the same substructure as Alice measured, then prepare sate to gets the value as shown in the table. Both Alice and Bob keep the value which is measured on the same basis and discard the other values, measured bits are used as to generate the private key. But

Table 1.

State	Basis	Value
$\lvert 0 \rangle$	Z	0
$\lvert 1 \rangle$	Z	1
$\lvert 0 \rangle + \lvert 1 \rangle$	X	0
$\lvert 0 \rangle - \lvert 1 \rangle$	X	1

if Eva is clever he can implement all possible chances to bamboozle both Alice and Bob (Seema 2017).

Polarization of Photons

Sender and receiver implement quantum protocol by exchanging photons, whose polarization states are used to encode bit values over fiber channel this fiber channel is called a Quantum channel. Here use four positions both concur for that. For suppose, a 1-bit assessment is able to encode whether vertical position or +45 degree diagonal, a 0-bit assessment be able to encode whether horizontal or -45 degree diagonal one. Basically, emission or polarization of luminous is the path of fluctuation of electromagnetic territory which is related to its field. Linear emission positions are definite in the direction of the fluctuation field. Linear polarization examples are Horizontal and vertical moreover diagonal states also considered as linear polarization. Photon can be able to polarize in whatever of the above-mentioned forms. Some filters subsist to discriminate horizontal states from vertical ones. When transient during similar filter, vertically polarized photon diverged to right, while horizontally polarized photon diverged to left. During this scenario rotate the filter to 45 degrees to organize differential among angular polarized photons. Suppose if a photon send in incorrect directed orientation like angular polarized photon through non-rotated filter, then it resolves accidentally diverged in one of the two indications so it's very difficult to recognize photon path prior to the filter (Poppe, 2004; Zhao and Qi, 2006; Peev, 2009; Pearson and David, 2004).

Figure 2. Quantum cryptosystem – polarization of photons

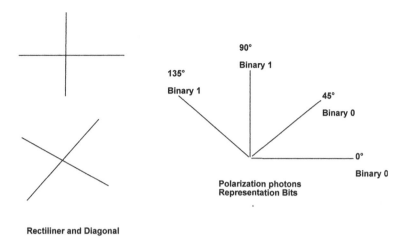

Quantum Key Distribution

Before concerning QKD we have to move forward over traditional key distribution, In cryptography where Alice/Bob send some quantity of key to Alice/Bob which have some negative aspects those we discuss above, to overcome those negative aspects we launch some supplementary practice where Alice/Bob create individual keys, arbitrary sequence number sets, enclose with more numbers share to each one which is more than there key material. Finally correlate the above-mentioned set of numbers to distill or purified mutual subset, whichever remodeled the mutual key. In this direction they are not preferred entire number sets or precise numbers to key material, essential key material numbers should be secret, undercover furthermore random. Alice constructs successive of signs, one fluctuation for "1" and disparate fluctuation for "0" for each bit in his sets send a sign for Bob. Bob also transfer with his set bit by bit examine Alice sign with his bits, and constitute acknowledgment to Alice whether the sign is similar or not. Both Alice and Bob notify the bits accepted, reserve those bits in memory for shape final key, in addition, wipe out every other bit. Quantum cryptography proved experimentally in 1989 carry out by Bennett and Brassard where the key was transmitted/exchanged over 30 cm air. In 1990 at the University of Geneva key exchanged over optical fiber, key distribution takes cms to several kilometers. B92 QKD protocol expressed in provisions of measurement states in two structural Hilbert space equivalents to ½ spin particles, spin operators $\alpha1, \alpha2, \alpha3$ comply with algebra (Brandao & Oppenheim, 2012; Bennett and Brassard, 1998; Elliott and Chip, 2003; Rajani and Girma, 2007; Zhao and Qi, 2006; Yin and Chen, 2016; Padamavathi and Vishnu 2017; NIST, 2018; Richard and Alde, 2001).

$[\alpha i, \alpha j] = 2i\epsilon ijk\alpha k;\ I, j, k = 1, 2, 3$

The starting point of position with spin-up as well as spin-down on ahead the Z-axis

$$\alpha_3 \left\{ \begin{matrix} |\uparrow\rangle \\ |\downarrow\rangle \end{matrix} \right\} = \left\{ \begin{matrix} +|\uparrow\rangle \\ -|\downarrow\rangle \end{matrix} \right\}$$

Fulfilling the ortho-normality affairs

$$\langle\uparrow|\uparrow\rangle = \langle\downarrow|\downarrow\rangle = 1$$

$$\langle\uparrow|\downarrow\rangle = 0$$

Starting point states with spin up and spin down on ahead X-axis

$$\alpha_1 \left\{ \begin{matrix} |\rightarrow\rangle \\ |\leftarrow\rangle \end{matrix} \right\} = \left\{ \begin{matrix} +|\rightarrow\rangle \\ -|\leftarrow\rangle \end{matrix} \right\}$$

Substitute $|\rightarrow\rangle = 2^{\frac{1}{2}}\left(|\uparrow\rangle + |\downarrow\rangle\right)$ and $|\leftarrow\rangle 2^{\frac{1}{2}}\left(|\uparrow\rangle | - |\downarrow\rangle\right)$

An analysis with quantum theory is projection operator in Hilbert space, an analysis on behalf of spin-down
Onwards Z-axis is revealed as

$$P_{|\downarrow\rangle} = |\downarrow\rangle\langle\downarrow|$$

Similarly spin up along X-axis is revealed as

$$P_{|\leftarrow\rangle} = |\leftarrow\rangle\langle\leftarrow|$$

In B92 protocol Alice postures a pair of non-orthogonal measures; Bob also constructs a pair of non-orthogonal measurements. Various possible probabilities for the pass are given below (see table below).

Table 2.

$P_{|\downarrow\rangle}$	0	0.5
$P_{|\leftarrow\rangle}$	0.5	0

Alice, as well as Bob, set up a self-sufficient set of random numbers, thereafter planed bit by bit synchronization. Alice formulates photon polarization for each bit [see table (1)], plus dispatch it to Bob over a quantum channel. Bob arranges an analysis of each bit state he entangled as reported by his photon polarization [see table (3)]. Assemble record as "pass" or "fail".

Bob will never record a "pass" if inherent bits are incomparable from Alice, moreover, Bob records a "pass" on at least 50% bits are familiar. In this direction we can't anticipate which one is "pass", nevertheless there are two achievable scopes one passes another one is fail there are no extra options. At last, Bob circulates entire bits over the public channel were the chance for eavesdroppers to plagiarize key material. Straightaway Alice, as well as Bob, considers just those bits in support of Bob's result is "Pass" the above-mentioned particular bits used for key material (Yin and Chen, 2016; Padamavathi and Vishnu, 2017).

Table 3.

Bit	State
0	$|\uparrow\rangle$
1	$|\rightarrow\rangle$

Table 4.

bit	Measurement
0	$P_{|\leftarrow\rangle}$
1	$P_{|\downarrow\rangle}$

Simple BB84 Quantum Key Distribution Protocol

- Alice sends a random sequence of photons polarized horizontal, vertical, right circular and left circular.
- Bob measures the photons polarization in a random sequence of basis rectilinear, circular.
- Bobs measures his results
- Bob notify Alice which basis he uses for each photon on received ones.
- Alice tells Bob whos bases are correct.
- Alice and Bob keep the data that was correct and leaves the remainder data which was not useful.
- This data is interrupted as a binary sequence according to the coding sequence.
- **B92 Protocol:** B92 considered as the customized protocol of BB84 by two states 0° and 45°. Photon polarization 0° in rectilinear basis symbolize binary value 0; polarization of photon 45° within diagonal basis symbolizes binary value 1.
- **Six State Protocols:** Six state protocols alike as BB84 protocol apart from it has three orthogonal bases to encode bits that intended to make broadcast among entities. As the name suggests it represents six states utilized to represent the bits.

Table 5. Process of quantum key distribution – BB84 protocol

Alice's bits	0	0	1	0	1	0	1	1	0	0	0	1
Alice's Basis	+	x	x	+	x	+	+	x	+	x	+	+
Alice's photon polarization	↖ ↗	↘	↗	↘	↙	→	←	↑	↑	←	←	
Bob's basis	+	+	x	+	+	x	+	x	+	x	x	+
Bob's Photon polarization	↘ ↗	↗	←	↘	↑	↘	→	↑	→	←		↘
Alice's Bob's sequence polarization	↖		↘			↑		←	↗			
Alice's and Bob's bit sequences	0		0			1		0	1			
Final key	0					1		0	1			

- **SARGO04 Protocol:** The first phase which was introduced in the BB84 protocol is the same as the first phase of the SARGO04 protocol. Coming to the second phase initiator broadcasts pair of non-orthogonal states, where initiator utilizes one of them to predetermine his own bits unlike announcing bases directly. Both initiator and sender verify which bits they contain subsequent bases. If the receiver can able to measure accurate state if he used a suitable basis or else not able to achieve the bit.

QUANTUM CRYPTOGRAPHY IMPLEMENTATION

Quantum cryptography provides the best suitable secure communications nevertheless entire prototype systems have pointed to point links moderately than networks that distribute associations. BOSTON, HARVARD University along with BBN technology scientists combined to build six node quantum key cryptography system which provides continuous secure key exchanges between HARVARD and BBN which are 8-10 Km away from each other. Soon after scientists move the nodes across the network. This six node cryptography network is flexibility set up because the breakdown of connection or node doesn't indicate vanished of quantum cryptography some node be capable of taking steps to bond two extra nodes. Around the world research labs are under work to implement quantum repeaters (Elliot and Chip, 2002; Yin and Chin, 2006; Vasileios and Kamer, 2018; Brandao & Oppenheim, 2012).

DARPA

Quantum cryptography work through internet protocols to protect internet protocols, in addition, construct one type of VPN which endows with secure communication over unsecured networks similar to the internet at large. The DARPA security model is a cryptographic security model called Cryptographic virtual private network. Both public and symmetric key cryptography are used in traditional VPN networks to achieve authentication, integrity, and confidentiality. Where symmetric mechanisms provide traffic confidentiality and integrity and Public cryptography support authentication of endpoints, supports key exchanges. In consequence, the VPN system provides confidentiality and authentication without trusting the public network. Where in DARPA network existing VPN keys replaced by quantum cryptography and construction structure of VPN are unchanged.

MagiQ

MagiQ is New-York based start-up technology develop solutions for quantum cryptography. MagiQ technologies said that quantum cryptosystem is not the exact alternate for long-established cryptography techniques, but they add another comment for security that traditional crypto models can use to generate hybrid models that will provide more security. They made a bond with Cavium's networks, Cavium's security chips are integrated within MagiQ servers as well as network boards. MagiQ claimed a quantum cryptographic box that compromises 40 pounds mountable in 9-inch rack that sells for 50000 dollars a unit. This box contains transmitter, receiver, electronics, and software's moreover it connects to remote parties via fiber optic cable links.

The SECOQC

Secure Communication based on Quantum Cryptography (SECOQC) is a collective research work designed and implemented by 41 industrial, research organizations under a European project. It suggests the system by QKD through importance on the prototype with the authenticated repeater. SECOQC introduced in the year 2003 and obtain popularity between 2004-2009. The SECOQC has a most important network-based agent named as SECOQC node module, which takes care of key distillation authentication for communications.

Hub and Spoke Network by Los Alamos National Laboratory

To route Quantum messages Los Alamos National Laboratory designed a focal pointed Hub as well as Spoke network in 2011. Basically, Hub used to receive quantum messages from respective nodes quantum transmitters. Here broadcast starts once every node points a one-time pad acknowledged via Hub, which was placed for protected broadcast over the conventional channel. As soon as the received message transmitted or routed to other nodes, the hub will initiate another one-time pad.

Tokyo QKD Network

Tokyo QKD initiated a conference held in Tokyo named Updating Quantum Cryptography and Communications (UQCC2010), it follows a star-based pattern connecting various centers. It has three phases namely the Quantum layer phase – generate keys with QKD functionality, Key management phase – gather and store QKD devices, Communication phase – allows secure allocation of keys.

QUANTUM CRYPTOGRAPHY PROTOCOL

Quantum cryptography entails a collection of dedicated protocols called Quantum protocols. New protocols are easy to implement or developed with help of these quantum protocols, this engine was premeditated by DARPA (Rivest, Shamir, and Adelman, 1978; Mullins and Justin, 2003; Tang and Chen, 2014; Yin and Chen, 2014; Shor, 2000; Zhao and Qi, 2006; Peev, 2009).

Sifting

Sifting is a mechanism where Alice, as well as Bob fenestration, moved out from complete failure q bits from a suite of pulses. This failure q bit includes those Q-bits where Bob's spotters didn't endeavor to uncover photons vanished in transportation that Alice laser never transmitted. They also include the above-mentioned photon indications wherever Alice selects one base for transference however Bob selects another base for receiving. Near to the end of this procedure, Alice as well as Bob abandons the entire worthless patterns from individual enclosed storage, takes off simply those patterns that Bob expected moreover compared with Bob's basis.

Error Correction

Error bits 1's and 0's whereas Alice transmits as 1 however Bob captured as 0 or vice versa. Error bits allow both Alice plus Bob to resolve the entire error bits they shared, sifted moreover appropriate them so that Alice and Bob share alike error-corrected bits. Most of these error bits produce as a result of noise or through eavesdropping. Mostly fault detection in quantum cryptography includes unexpected things like indication confess assume to be Eavesdropper. So, there is a need for planed error discovery with adjustment codes which reveals miniature feasible in individual public control transportation enclosed by Alice and Bob.

Figure 3. Protocol suite for quantum key distribution

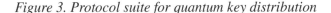
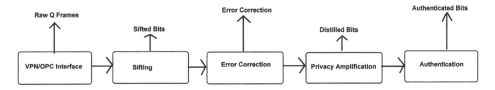

Key Distillation

The BB84 procedure pretended that the only resource for inaccuracy in a series swap over through transmitter and receiver was the achievement of Eavesdroppers. Every part of other sensible quantum cryptography assumed errors caused by environmental perturbations of quantum channel or component imperfections. In order to avoid errors, a post-processing step acknowledged as key distillation executed behind the sifting of the key. Key distillation process expressed by two steps. In the first step allows us to estimate the actual error rate with the help of these error rates it is probable to compute the quantity of advice on key. The Second stair is called privacy amplification with the appropriate factor rate it will reduce or compress the key which helps to reduce the information of the eavesdropper. In order to prevent man in the middle attack, key distillation is accompaniment with authentication step where the eavesdroppers cut announcement carriers and make-believe to the emitter that he is the recipient. The pre-established secret key in receiver and emitter used for authentication in the standard channel. These initial undercover keys used to validate in primary quantum cryptography following that every conference or session a piece of key is formed is used to substitute prior validation key.

Privacy Amplification

This method called advantage distillation, where both Alice as well as Bob decline Eva's understanding of their mutual bits. The region which commences the privacy amplification decides on one linear hash function above the Galois Field (GF) where n is a number of bits as participation input, curved up to multiple of 32. Then transmit 4 bits to another end –the number of m bits of the shortened end result, primitive polynomial of the Galois Field, a multiplier, an m bit polynomial to add by commodity. Every surface then presents equivalent hash and abbreviates results into m bits presents privacy enlargement.

Authentication

Authentication permits both Alice as well as Bob defender adjacent toward "man in the middle attacks" who permits Alice to make sure as long as she exchanges a few words with Bob. Eavesdroppers may itself insert into the discussion among Alice and Bob at any phase in there contact. BB84 described the authentication problem using universal hash functions. The temperament of general hashing, every party that does not recognize top undisclosed key would have identified the exceptionally slighter possibility of being proficient to fabricate the communication but limitless computational power. Fortunately, a comprehensive authentic exchange can authorize a big number of fresh shared secret bits from QKD.

QKD CHARACTERISTICS

QKD suggests a technique as an agreement where collective unsystematic sequences of fragments between two types of machinery and awfully small probability those eavesdroppers capable to formulate successful interference of those fragments. Those random sequence fragments are used as secret keys between two distinct devices (Bennett and Brassard, 1982; Padmavathi and Vishnu, 2016; Vasileios and Kamer, 2018; NIST, 2018; Yin and Chen, 2016; Alfred and Menezes, 2018; Brassard and Bernett, 1996; Buttler, 2003).

Key Delivery

QKD is clearly a key distribution technique. Normally key distribution center task is to deliver keys speedily; it makes encipher equipment do not overwork their contribution of key bits.QKD systems achieve key material throughput of 1000 bits/second but in realistic achievements, this speed may be low, based on the uses of certain keys also speed comes to low. One time pad, high secure algorithms speed of traffic flow is high. Low is acceptable to speed for reliable low (compare to one-time pad) secure algorithms such as AES.

Authentication

Authentication certifies that information approaching from authentic source; moreover, it should be certified that no unlawful third-party stand-in like an authorized user. QKD not directly provides authentication process but the QKD system provides a recommendation of secret keys at paired machinery. Secret keys must distribute before QKD begins with the help of human courier or some other techniques, but it is a challenging task.

Robustness

In the QKD key object, fundamental is safe communication; moreover, it is tremendously vital that the flow of key objects is not interrupted which may happen through adversary or else accidentally. Here QKD techniques employed with a point to point, if the point link is disrupted by any event instead via active probing otherwise any fiber cut the entire flowing key material would stop.

Confidentiality

Data confidentiality protects the data so any unauthorized user can't understand and examine it. Invaders should not know the regularity facts and content of facts broadcasted. Classical undisclosed key structures deteriorate from insider hazard or a logical load of keying objects distribution. Public key systems suffer from encryption and decryption is mathematically intractable, Diffie-Hellman may break at some point in the future. Privacy is the foremost justification for getting a concentration in QKD, it contributes to mechanical circulation of keys to provide safekeeping higher to its participants.

Traffic Analysis

In key distribution, traffic analysis such as the heavy flow of keying material between two parties which make eavesdroppers estimate that a large amount of useful information flows between them. In QKD most steps assumed dedicated, point to point links between communicating entities that clearly underlay key distribution techniques.

EAVESDROPPING

Eavesdropping is the process of someone who secretly listens, read messages and conversations by unintended recipients. Eavesdropping done in phone calls, email, instant messages and any other communications which considered private. Providing security services to these messages when data transmission over public channels. This security service is habitually executed by Encryption. Eve has unlimited power resources and has access to future technologies. In quantum cryptography, Eve can hide in noise, replace quantum channels with better instruments with lower-level noise, which makes the identification of Eve difficult. Eve also possesses all possible traditional attacking methods like attacking RING, spoofing, flooding, at a time attach one probe to Q-bit and accessing local storage of Alice or Bob, but measure several probes coherently. Individual attack attaches one q-bit at a time and measures one time. In a joint attack, Eve possesses several q-bits collectively (Richard and Alde, 2002).

LARGE SCALE QUANTUM KEY CHALLENGES

Quantum key distribution (QKD) along with a one-time pad produces a secure transportation base on quantum principles. Here the ultimate goal is to establish global Quantum key distribution for all over world appliances. Various researchers, scientists come up with dissimilar methods but still, it has faced some critical issues (Qiang, Feihu and Yu, 2018; Mateusz, 2018)

1. There is a huge breach among theory and practical approaches of QKD, QKD secure only when it deployed with ultimate devices like faultless distinct photon but that type devices are not more available.
2. Large scale key distribution which shows huge channel failure and no-stability. At present 440 km distance in fiber tunnel is recorded. But the problem in fiber tunnel is as the distance increases the key velocity significantly reduces. Quantum repeaters, satellite-based quantum transportation are some solution to avoiding these concerns.

(Y. Zhao and Qi, 2006) executed QKD through a 15 km fiber spool, (Rosenberg and Harrington, 2007) apply decoy-state QKD from end to end 100 km fiber, (Y, Zhao, Lo and Qiet, 2009) complete 144 km decoy-state QKD in free space, (Tang and Yin, 2014) attain MDI-QKE over 200 km fiber through enlarge the system clock rate from 1 – 75 MHz with help of solitary photon detectors. (Yin and Chen, 2016) complete the MDI-QKD space to 404 km low loss fiber via optimizing the limitation along with a low-loss fiber.

OUTLINE OF QUANTUM-RESISTANT CRYPTOGRAPHY

From past decades Public key cryptography (PKC) turns to be inseparable from our digital communications. Security concepts of these cryptosystems lean on the complexity of theoretic mathematical problems like discrete log problems and Factorization etc. the invention of quantum computers resolves the issues quicker than convolution computers. The foremost utilization of PKC in these days is digital signatures and the key establishment and the formation of a large-scale quantum computer would be rendering many of these PKCs insecure.

There is a huge requirement for strong cryptography computing levels in both classical and quantum cryptography techniques. To avoid security attacks in classical crypto techniques, NIST (National Institute of Standards and Technology) instructs to maintain algorithm key sizes from 80 bits to 112-128 bits. It is still undecided when scalable quantum computers accessible for everyone. Research groups seriously working on a quantum computer that can break or crack the security code of the RSA technique in a few hours of time. This is a super-serious threat to current cryptography systems. Earlier evolutions from weaker to stronger cryptography security determined based on the time-complexity of attacking through a classical computer. Unluckily bit-of-security methods not able to consider into account the security of algorithms against quantum cryptanalysis, hence it was insufficient to show evolution to quantum-resistant cryptography. Moreover, there is no conformity view on what key lengths endow with satisfactory levels of security next to quantum molests.

The progress for post-quantum cryptography needs major resources to analyze quantum-resistant schemes. In recent times importance in the areas of quantum computing and quantum-resistant cryptography enlarged because of various adversaries in the improvement of quantum computing hardware. NIST is working on the above-mentioned standardization endeavors in quantum cryptography. Moreover, it also draws strategies to specify a preliminary evolution criterion that contains security and performance requirements for quantum-resistant public-key cryptography standards.

Modern Quantum Resistant Cryptography Techniques

The imminent consciousness of adaptable quantum computers makes a tremendous shake on present security transportation. Powerful expansion of quantum computers, public key infrastructure based cryptographic methods turn vulnerable to the quantum algorithm. Quantum resistant cryptography is an energetic research area, that makes an effort to design innovative fresh quantum-resistant public cryptography protocol. Lattice-based cryptography is promising as one of the majority possible options. Because of it efficiently execution on software, hardware that has previously shown to calculate and even outshines the presentation of existing conventional protection public key proposals

Lattice-based cryptography: Lattice base key organization crypto techniques reasonably simple, parallelizable and well-organized. Moreover, the security of these techniques verified secure under a worst-case fighting hypothesis, moderately than on the adequate case. Code-based Cryptography: Early 1978, a well-known researcher proposed the McEliece crypto algorithm, it has not broken since. But it suffers from huge key sizes, with the addition of some pre-arranged structures algorithms key sizes able to reduce. Code-based digital signatures, Code-based-crypto techniques more useful in modern systems. Hash-based signature: Hash-based digital signatures produce tremendous security against all attacks, even against quantum attacks also. However, the negative aspect is that the signer must keep a record of the exact number of previous messages, and additionally, it produces a limited number of signatures.

Multivariate polynomial cryptography: Numerous multivariate crypto techniques presented base on the complexity of explaining multivariate polynomials in excess of finite fields. A few of them mostly unbeaten as an advance to signatures.

CONCLUSION

Assigning Quantum physics to cryptography opens a door for research in security and enhancement of modern cryptosystem troubles. Quantum cryptography modifies the security way of all modern cryptosystems using Q-bits. QKD in concern with one time pad encoding can produce intellectual-theoretical security for communication. At this time QKD has been extensively employed in numerous fiber networks, however, its employment in large scale remains experimentally exigent. Chapter provides QKD characteristics, key challenges and Modern Quantum resistance cryptography techniques are described briefly. Many researchers around the world find out innovative mechanisms for making quantum cryptography indestructible. We can glance frontward to the electrifying the outlook of quantum cryptography with countless potential hypothetical and investigational.

REFERENCES

Abood, O. G., & Guirguis, S. K. (2018). A Survey on Cryptography Algorithms. [IJSRP]. *International Journal of Scientific and Research Publications*, 8(7).

Bennett, C., & Brassard, G. (1984). Quantum cryptography Public key distribution and coin tossing. In *Proceedings of the International conference on computers, systems and signal processing*. Academic Press.

Bennett, C.H. (1985). Quantum public key distribution system. *IBM systems*.

Bennett, C.H. & Brassard. (1987). Quantum Public key distribution. *Seget news, 18*(4), 51-53.

Bennett, C. H. (1992). Quantum cryptography using two non orthogonal states. *Physical Review Letters*, 68(21), 3121–3124. doi:10.1103/PhysRevLett.68.3121 PMID:10045619

Bennett, C. H. (1992). Quantum cryptography using two non orthogonal states. *Physical Review Letters*, 68(21), 3121–3124. doi:10.1103/PhysRevLett.68.3121 PMID:10045619

Bennett, C. H., Brassard, G., Breidbart, S., & Wiesner, S. (1982). Quantum Cryptography, or Unforgeable Subway Tokens, Advances in Cryptology. In *Proceedings of Crypto '82*. Plenum Press.

Bennett, C. H., Brassard, G., Breidbart, S., & Wiesner, S. (1982). Quantum Cryptography, or Unforgeable Subway Tokens, Advances in Cryptology. In *Proceedings of Crypto '82*. Plenum Press.

Bennett, C. H., Brassard, G., & Mermin, N. D. (1992). Quantum cryptograph. *Physical Review Letters*, *68*(5), 557–559. doi:10.1103/PhysRevLett.68.557

Bennett, C. H., Brassard, G., & Mermin, N. D. (1992). Quantum cryptography without Bell's theorem. *Physical Review Letters*, *68*(5), 557.

Bennett, C.H. & Shor, P.W. (1998). Quantum information theory. *IEEE Information theory, 44*(6), 2724-2742.

Brandao, F. G., & Oppenheim, J. (2012). Quantum one-time pad in the presence of an eavesdropper. *Physical Review Letters*, *108*(4).

Brassard, G. (1988). *Modern Cryptology*. New York: Springer.

Brassard, G. (1996). Cryptography columns- 25 years of Quantum cryptography. *Sigact news, 27*(3), 13-24.

Buttler, W. T. (2003). Fast and Efficient error reconciliation for quantum cryptography. *Physical Review*, *76*, 5.

Curcic, T. (2004). Quantum networks: From Quantum cryptography to quantum architecture. *Computer Communication Review*, *34*(5), 3–8.

Elliott, C. (2002). Building the quantum network. *New Journal of Physics*, *4*(1), 46.

Elliott, C., Pearson, D., & Troxel, G. (2003). Quantum cryptography in practice. In *Proceedings of the conference on Applications, technologies, architectures, and protocols for computer communications*. ACM.

Goel, R., Garuba, M., & Girma, A. (2007, April). Research directions in quantum cryptography. In *Proceedings of the Fourth International Conference on Information Technology (ITNG'07)* (pp. 779-784). IEEE.

Hellman, D. (1976). New Directions in Cryptography. *IEEE Transactions Theory*, *22*(6), 644–654. doi:10.1109/TIT.1976.1055638

Hughes, R. J., Alde, D. M., Dyer, P., Luther, G. G., Morgan, G. L., & Schauer, M. (1995). Quantum cryptography. *Contemporary Physics*, *36*(3), 149–163.

Johnson, R. C. (2002). *MagiQ employs quantum technology for secure encryption.* EE Times.

Kumar, M. G. V., & Ragupathy, U. S. (2016, March). A Survey on current key issues and status in cryptography. In *Proceedings of the 2016 International Conference on Wireless Communications, Signal Processing and Networking (WiSPNET)* (pp. 205-210). IEEE.

Kute, S. S., & Desai, C. G. (2017). Quantum Cryptography: A Review. *Indian Journal of Science and Technology, 10*(3).

MagiQ Technologies. (2003). [Press Release].

Martinez-Mateo, J., Elkouss, D., & Martin, V. (2013). Key Reconciliation for High Performance Quantum Key Distribution. *Scientific Reports, 3*(1), 1576. doi:10.1038rep01576 PMID:23546440

Mavroeidis, V., Vishi, K., Zych, M. D., & Jøsang, A. (2018). The impact of quantum computing on present cryptography. *International Journal of Advanced Computer science and Applications, 9*(3).

Menezes, A. J., van Oorschot, P. C., & Vanstone, S. A. (2016). *A Handbook of Applied cryptography.* CRC press.

Mullins, J. (2003). *Quantum Cryptography's Reach Extended.* IEEE Spectrum Online.

NIST. (2016). Recommendation for Key Management Special Publication (SP) 800-57 Part 1 Revision 4. doi:10.6028/NIST.SP.800-57pt1r4

Padamvathi, V., Vardhan, B. V., & Krishna, A. V. N. (2016, February). Quantum Cryptography and Quantum Key Distribution Protocols: A Survey. In *Proceedings of the 2016 IEEE 6th International Conference on Advanced Computing (IACC)* (pp. 556-562). IEEE.

Pearson, D. (2004, November). High-speed QKD Reconciliation using Forward Error Correction. *AIP Conference Proceedings, 734*(1), 299–302.

Peev, M., Pacher, C., Alléaume, R., Barreiro, C., Bouda, J., Boxleitner, W., ... Zeilinger, A. (2009). The SECOQC quantum key distribution network in Vienna. *New Journal of Physics, 11*(7), 075001. doi:10.1088/1367-2630/11/7/075001

Poppe, A., Fedrizzi, A., Ursin, R., Böhm, H. R., Lorünser, T., Maurhardt, O., ... Jennewein, T. (2004). Practical quantum key distribution with polarization entangled photons. *Optics Express, 12*(16), 3865–3871.

Rivest, R. L., Shamir, A., & Adleman, L. (1978). A method for obtaining digital signatures and public-key cryptosystems. *Communications of the ACM, 21*(2), 120–126.

Rosenberg, D., Harrington, J. W., Rice, P. R., Hiskett, P. A., Peterson, C. G., Hughes, R. J., ... Nordholt, J. E. (2007). Long-distance decoy-state quantum key distribution in optica fiber. *Physical Review Letters, 98*(1), 010503. doi:10.1103/PhysRevLett.98.010503 PMID:17358462

Scarani, A., Acin, A., Ribordy, G., & Gisin, N. (2004). Quantum cryptography protocols robust against photon number splitting attacks. *Physical Review Letters, 92*(5), 057901. doi:10.1103/PhysRevLett.92.057901 PMID:14995344

Shor, P. W. (1999). Polynomial-time algorithms for prime factorization and discrete logarithms on a quantum computer. *SIAM Review, 41*(2), 303–332. doi:10.1137/S0097539795293172

Shor, P. W., & Preskill, J. (2002). Simple proof of security of the BB84 Quantum key distribution protocol. *Physical Review Letters, 85*(2), 441–449.

Tang, Y.-L., Yin, H.-L., Chen, S.-J., Liu, Y., Zhang, W.-J., Jiang, X., ... Pan, J. W. (2014). Measurement device-independent quantum key distribution over 200 km. *Physical Review Letters, 113*(19), 190501. doi:10.1103/PhysRevLett.113.190501 PMID:25415890

Yin, H.-L., Chen, T.-Y., Yu, Z.-W., Liu, H., You, L.-X., Zhou, Y.-H., ... Pan, J.-W. (2016). Measurement-device-independent quantum key distribution over a 404 km optical fiber. *Physical Review Letters, 117*(19), 190501. doi:10.1103/PhysRevLett.117.190501 PMID:27858431

Zhang, Q., Xu, F., Chen, Y. A., Peng, C. Z., & Pan, J. W. (2018). Large scale quantum key distribution: Challenges and solutions. *Optics Express, 26*(18), 24260–24273.

Zhao, Y., Qi, B., Ma, X., Lo, H.-K., & Qian, L. (2006). Experimental quantum key distribution with decoy states. *Physical Review Letters, 96*(7), 070502. doi:10.1103/PhysRevLett.96.070502 PMID:16606067

Zych, M. (2018). Quantum Safe Cryptography Based on Hash Functions: A Survey [Master's Thesis]. University of Oslo.

Chapter 6
Quantum Internet and E-Governance:
A Futuristic Perspective

Manan Dhaneshbhai Thakkar
U. V. Patel College of Engineering, Ganpat University, India

Rakesh D. Vanzara
ⓘD https://orcid.org/0000-0002-6629-350X
U. V. Patel College of Engineering, Ganpat University, India

ABSTRACT

We are leaving in the era where almost everyone in the world uses internet for the communication over social media site, shopping, E-commerce, online transaction and many more. The exponential growth in usage of internet resulted in security related challenges. Since last several years, traditional cryptography algorithms are found working well. Evolution of quantum computer and its high computing capability can break existing cryptography algorithms. To handle the security constraints, this chapter provides details on evolution of quantum cryptography, components involved to design network architecture for quantum internet, quantum key exchange mechanism and functionality wise stages for quantum internet. This chapter also includes challenges involved in evolution of quantum internet. Further, chapter also contains the details on e-governance, challenges in e-governance and solution using quantum cryptography.

DOI: 10.4018/978-1-7998-2253-0.ch006

INTRODUCTION

Quantum cryptography, is the way of encrypting messages by applying principles of quantum mechanism, in contrast with the traditional cryptography mechanism to encrypt the messages by applying the mathematical function over actual message (Maria Korolov, Doug Drinkwater, 2019). Main purpose of this quantum cryptography is to encrypt message in such a way that no outsider recipient can even read that message. Quantum communication is to be considered more secured than any existing information relay system. If quantum communications were like sending a letter, entangled photons are like the envelope, they carry the message and keep it secure. It is expected that by 2030 (Sophia Chen, 2017), quantum communications will spread almost in all countries and that would be an era of quantum Internet. It means, all kind of communications (i.e. multimedia, text, voice) would happen by means of quantum signals compared to traditional digital signal (i.e. 0 and 1).

Quantum Internet provides new Internet technologies to us to solve the tasks which are impossible to achieve over classical Internet (Kimble, H. Jeff, 2008). As it's a new technology which is yet to explore fully, thus we cannot expect all the sectors making its usage initially. But, it provides good enough applications containing security related concern over Internet, to justify its importance. Basic elements of quantum Internet do not look much different from a classical one (Vesna Monojlovic, 2017). The way classical Internet is having one of component as end node, this quantum Internet also needed end node. But, that end node should support quantum Internet. So, as a node we cannot use normal laptop, phone or computer, but we need to make use of quantum computer. The way we have switch type of component in classical Internet as an intermediate point to establish connection, for the quantum Internet we need kind of switch which is capable to transmit qubits. Table-I depicts the comparison of classical and quantum Internet.

Electronic governance (E-governance) playing an important role in integrating information, science and technology within the administrative and management

Table 1. Comparison between classical internet and quantum internet

Classical Internet	Quantum Internet
• End node: traditional computer, phone, laptop	• End node: Quantum system
• Switch	• Quantum switch
• Repeater	• Quantum repeater
• Data in the form of digital signal with combination of 0 and 1	• Data in the form of qubits
• Threat of cyber attack	• Secure

systems of an organization (Das, S. R., & Chandrashekhar, R., 2007). E-governance is the key to organize everything in public domain to increase the accessibility, efficiency, transparency and openness to the stakeholders. E-governance concept was basically designed to improve citizen's access to government information and services (Faraj, Sufyan T., M. Sagheer Ali, 2011). The concept of E-governance has found its wide range of applications by including several governmental domains like education, health care, security, power, citizen services and many more. In order to make information excessive and open for all, security threat is a major concern and information must be protected from unauthorized access (Faraj, Sufyan T., M. Sagheer Ali, 2011). Security is a major concern for successful implementation of E-Governance and transaction based services. Some of the security issues in E-Governance are: Authenticity, Confidentiality, Non-repudiation, Integrity. The important thing to understand is, how to solve security related challenges by using the concept of quantum cryptography and quantum key exchange. Many industries and government sectors are currently trying to build the quantum computer which will avoid many computing and security related problems (Faraj, Sufyan T., M. Sagheer Ali, 2011).

BACKGROUND

Due to more and more usage of technologies and user's seamless connectivity with Internet, it has become playground for hackers to perform malicious tasks (Anil Ananthaswamy, 2019). From data stored on cloud or any other storage device for communication, insecurity and vulnerability are everywhere. But, quantum physics have their own way to protect against these challenges. Classical computers work with traditional bit system with value 0 and 1 (Wehner, S., Elkouss, D., & Hanson, R., 2018), but with the help of qubits we can have more storage for information. In future, quantum network may replace classical network.

As per the classical policy of encryption, it highly depends on keys to encrypt the message. Based upon type of key used, there are two types of mechanisms: symmetric key cryptography and asymmetric key cryptography. Cryptography using symmetric key works using a single shared secret key (Wehner, S., Elkouss, D., & Hanson, R., 2018). To crack such type of key requires double the computing power after every increment in bit size of key. Thus, longer the size of key, more and more powerful computing system require and require larger amount of time to crack. On the other hand, cryptography using asymmetric key uses pair of public and private key that needs to be generated mathematically (Wehner, S., Elkouss, D., & Hanson, R., 2018). Though it's very tough to crack with asymmetric key, but it is not the impossible task and key can be cracked by applying mathematical formula or more computing power behind it. No matter which type of approach used for encryption, but it is necessary to keep some private information secret. One threat related to security is in key exchange step. In order to secretly exchange keys among users, one possible way is by using quantum cryptography. The mechanism of exchanging key secretly using quantum mechanism is known as Quantum Key Distribution (QKD) (Wehner, S., Elkouss, D., & Hanson, R., 2018).

The Internet has a revolutionary impression across the globe. The vision and mission behind quantum Internet is to bring future Internet technology by evolving quantum communication between any two nodes across the world. As with the rapid changes in technology, it is very hard to make everyone to use futuristic quantum Internet in replacement of a classical Internet. Due to its high range of secure environment, it finds application in various domains like quantum key exchange, secure identification, two party cryptography, position verification, secure access to quantum computers in cloud, secure exchange of information across the globe, clock synchronization, quantum sensor network and many more. Essence of all these applications is the ability of a quantum Internet to transmit qubits compared to bits in traditional Internet.

The biggest question to understand importance of quantum is: What makes the transmission of qubits so powerful than what we have today? One of the important feature of qubits is that, they cannot be copied, which makes them ideal for security applications. Anyone who tries to attempt this, can be easily identified. Qubits can be entangled among each other, that brings high level of and stronger correlations in contrast with that of classical information. This is the reason which makes qubits as one of the most suitable thing for security related applications. Though qubits are well suited but it also brings rapidly new concept in terms of technological components, which is also more challengeable. Early effort in development of quantum network, bring network with capacity to handle few qubits, But, as time elapsed, it evolved with more advanced network with more capacity and it also brings need of a unified framework for researchers.

Quantum Bits

There is a difference in a bit and a qubit. As per the traditional cryptography, we are used to transmit all the information in the 1s and 0s form. Whereas, qubits have a little different approach when we send and receive that. In case of traditional cryptography, the encryption-decryption key remains same, irrespective of how one read it (Nils Jacob Sand, 2018). Whereas, in case of quantum cryptography the value of key bit depends on how the value of qubit is measured. In case of quantum computer beam of photons transmitted and it gets represented in the form of 0s and 1s. Each of these particle is known as qubit.

Figure 1. Quantum bit transmission scenario
Source: *(Nils Jacob Sand, 2018)*

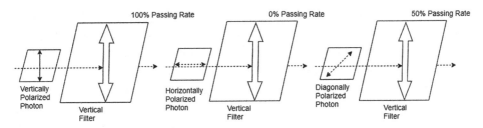

To send the qubits, we need to send photons via polarizer as shown in Figure 1. In this Figure, example of only vertical filter is included along with different types of polarized photons. At the receiver end, the value of received bit is determined based on the filter used (Nils Jacob Sand, 2018). In real world, qubits would have to be stored by atoms, ions (atoms with few or many electrons) or electrons and photons (Chris Woodford, 2019).

Quantum Cryptography: Overview

Quantum cryptography is the mechanism to allow users to interact or exchange information using safe and secure approach compared to traditional cryptography. The tern Quantum Cryptography was firstly mentioned by Stephen weisner in early 1970s as a part of their work 'conjugate coding' (Jorge Ortiz, Adam Sadovsky, and Olga Russakovsky, 2004). BB84 was very first quantum cryptography protocol developed in 1984. In 1991, very first experimental evaluation was carried out using quantum cryptography by operating it for a distance of 32 centimeters. Later, this experiment has been refined and executed for a distance of few kilometers.

The very first computer network using secure quantum cryptography approach for communication is up and running in Cambridge, Massachusetts. In 2003, entangled photons were transmitted at University of Vienna across the Danube river. As a part of real world application, first money transfer between two Austrian bank was carried out using quantum keys in April, 2004 (Jorge Ortiz, Adam Sadovsky, and Olga Russakovsky, 2004).

Purpose of quantum cryptography is not to replace traditional cryptography, but to provide more secure way of exchanging quantum keys useful for encryption and decryption purpose. The information transmitted through quantum cryptography is not large or fast, but it's very secure. To transmit data as quickly as possible, it is good to achieve key exchange mechanism by using quantum cryptography and then encrypting and sending the data using traditional methods.

In quantum cryptography, data is converted into 0s and 1s to transfer using polarized photons. Afterwards, sender put photons into specific quantum state and these photons are observed by the recipient. A photon can be in one of the four polarizations: 0, 45, -45 and 90 degrees. These photons can be measured by using three different polarizer: rectilinear (vertical or horizontal), diagonal and circular (left or right circular) (Jorge Ortiz, Adam Sadovsky, and Olga Russakovsky, 2004). The receiver can discriminate between a 0 and 90, or 45 and -45 degree polarization for each signal. As per the principle of physics, a measurement of photons must destroy it (Jorge Ortiz, Adam Sadovsky, and Olga Russakovsky, 2004). So, it is not at all possible to carry observation without affecting its state. To understand the mechanism of quantum cryptography, BB84 protocol for quantum cryptography is an important reference(Brilliant.org, 2019).

BB84 protocol was designed in 1984 for quantum cryptography and named after Charles Bennett and Gilles Brassard. When sender generates photons, receiver does not aware about the type of polarizer used by sender. So, receiver randomly pick any one type of beam splitter as shown in Figure 2 (Brilliant.org, 2019).

Whenever sender sends horizontal or vertical polarized photon, receiver does not aware about which splitter to use. Receiver can choose between '+' and '×' beam splitters and this result in choosing right beam splitter only 50% of time. If receiver select '+' beam splitter for horizontal or vertical polarized photon, then receiver detects 0 or 1. Whereas, if receiver select '×' beam splitter, then polarized photon will detect -45 or 45 degree which also corresponds to 0 or 1.

After receiving all the photons, receiver will be having key of bits also called raw bits. Afterwards, sender announces over insecure channel regarding sequence of beam splitters instead of 1s or 0s. After comparing beam splitters, sender and receiver discards the beam splitters which are not matching at both the side. As receiver randomly selected beam splitters, it has to generally discard half of the beam splitters used.

After shifting the set of bits, sender and receiver keeps only fraction of their key by comparing them on public channel to see if they have same value. The fraction

Figure 2. Types of polarization
Source: (Nils Jacob Sand, 2018)

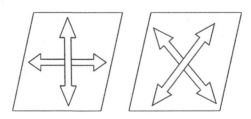

Figure 3. Photon transmission scenario
Source: *(Nils Jacob Sand, 2018)*

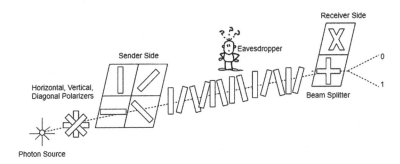

of keys having same value are selected as secure quantum key (Jorge Ortiz, Adam Sadovsky, and Olga Russakovsky, 2004). If the eavesdropper tries to detect or intercept while transmitting set of bits, eavesdropper may pick up correct beam transmitter half of the times as there is 50% chances of picking up right one. There is no way for interceptor to alter the beam as after reaching at receiver that would be altered. This can be determined at the end when sender and receiver compare it. If the result does not match the polarization of the photon, that means that someone might has observed the signal priori (Jorge Ortiz, Adam Sadovsky, and Olga Russakovsky, 2004).

Example: Step-by-Step Cryptography

Consider the step by step role of sender Alice, receiver Bob, Eve as an eavesdropper and error correction mechanism (Jorge Ortiz, Adam Sadovsky, and Olga Russakovsky, 2004).

- Alice needs to identify the polarization (rectilinear, diagonal or circular) of every single photon which Alice is looking to transfer towards Bob. Many information will get discarded at the receiver side, this polarization detection step needs to be done properly. The purpose of key exchange is to make both parties (sender and receiver) agree on a key.
- A light source from a LED or a laser is filtered to produce the desired photons.
- At the receiver side (Bob), it randomly generates multiple polarizer (rectilinear, diagonal or circular) and measures the polarization of each photon.
- Receiver publicly tells the sender regarding polarizer used at the receiver end without worrying about other people.
- Sender also publicly tells to receiver about which polarizer randomly chosen at sender side.
- Receiver discards all the incorrect observations received at the end.

- The remained observations need to be converted into binary code.
- To identify and resolve the error in the received bits, the strings of bits are partitioned into K blocks with each block of small size to minimize error in bits of block. If Alice's string is 110010 and Bob's string is 110111, the parity in both the case is same, though there are multiple bits in error.
- Alice and Bob exchange the computed parities of each block. This information also shared publicly but to avoid problem of Eve an eavesdropper, last bit of each block is then discarded. Reason to discard last bit is to make information meaningless for Eve.
- The above error corrected mechanism repeated for multiple number of times by increasing block size to discover multiple errors.
- At last, to detect any more errors, sender and receiver performs other random check. Alice and Bob publicly agree on a random assortment of half the bit positions in their string and compare parities. In this case also, they discard the last digit of string.
- If the strings are not same, both the parties do not agree on that.
- After repeating the above steps for r number of times, by agreeing on received strings always, both Alice and Bob can conclude that their strings disagree with r/2 probability.

HARDWARE COMPONENTS TO BUILD QUANTUM NETWORK

Figure 4 depicted the framework to establish quantum network with required network components. Each component of the framework is briefly explained in following subsections.

Link

As information needs to be transmitted in the form of qubits, it cannot be handled by traditional communication links. To transmit qubits between end nodes or node and repeater, photonic channels needed to be established. There are two types of photonic channels available: fiber based channels and free space channels. Both the types of available channels are having their own advantages and disadvantages. Thus, future Internet can be a combination of both the types of channels. Our ultimate need is to ensure kind of channel which exhibits minimal loss of qubits.

Figure 4. Framework to establish quantum network with network components
Source: *(Johan Dubbeldam, 2019)*

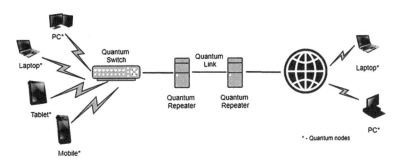

Quantum Nodes: Quantum Computer

Purpose of end node is to send and receive information. Quantum node for the purpose of quantum key distribution can be designed by using photodetector combined with telecommunication laser and parametric down-conversion. Sometimes these quantum nodes can be containing only beam splitters and photodetectors (Liam Critchley, 2018).

Before getting about quantum computer, it is necessary to define classical computer first. The essential part of classical computer is its integrated circuits. Over integrated circuits, we can find several transistors and these transistors can be used to construct classical bits. These bits are used to perform calculation with the nodes (ScienceDaily, 2019). Quantum mechanics can offer unique phenomena by including superposition, interference and entanglement. Quantum computer generates high computing power with its promise to outperform today's and tomorrow's supercomputer. In classical computer interpreted values are either a 0 or a 1, Whereas, in quantum computer quantum bit or qubit can take both the values together at a time. The secret behind ability of quantum computer is to generate multiple qubits. To generate and manage these qubits, is a challenging task. The challenge is to find suitable platform for these qubits and have all the electronics to perform operations with these qubits. Quantum mechanical efforts are usually associated with small energy scales. These qubit systems build in the very special fridges offering temperature around 0 kelvin (-273°C) (Mohammad Choucair, 2016). Though such types of care have been taken while building qubits, still it does not work correctly. As a one of the solution to handle error correction is by building one large physical qubit by combining multiple copies of qubits. We don't need many logical qubits to build a powerful quantum computer, since many quantum algorithms provide an exponential speedup as compared to their classical counterpart. The thing which we need is, many physical qubits to build logical qubits. Thus, quantum computer may contain millions of qubits.

In 2000, David P. DiVincenzo listed out five key criteria for quantum computer:

- It must be scalable.
- It must be possible to initialize the qubits.
- Good qubits are needed, so the quantum state cannot be lost.
- We need to have a universal set of quantum gates. Which means, one can do the operation needed to execute a quantum algorithm.
- We need to be able to measure all qubits.

Quantum Switch

Quantum computer enables quantum bits to get transmitted simultaneously among multiple space time trajectories. Now, whatever quantum information transmitted through carrier can travel through multiple communication channels and arrives in a different order (Caleffi, M., & Cacciapuoti, A. S., 2019). So, relative time order of communication channels becomes unfixed. This thing can be managed by the device called quantum switch. The proper utilization of a quantum switch provides numerous benefits for the purpose of quantum computation, quantum information processing and many more with different applications (Caleffi, M., & Cacciapuoti, A. S., 2019).

Quantum Repeater

In most of the communication medium including optical fibre, there could be a loss of signal whenever there is a long communication distance to travel for a message. In classical Internet, in order to boost the signal to travel long distance, amplifiers were used. But, these amplifiers cannot handle qubits as it cannot be copied as per the no cloning principle. Thus, to mimic the features of amplifier, complete flying qubit would be needed, which is not desirable and bit difficult (Lisa Zyga, 2018).

The quantum repeater can be found as an alternative to handle this challenge of end to end transmission of qubits (Lisa Zyga, 2018). In the transmission of a quantum key, one has to rely on intermediate trusted quantum repeater. After exchanging key with both the node, key distribution protocols can be used to test for the entanglement. Hence, while exchanging keys, the sender and receiver are secured even if they do not trust the quantum repeater.

QUANTUM KEY EXCHANGE

In order to protect important data from external user, encryption is an important mechanism. It protects confidential information by shielding from exposure of attacks. Before one should transmit data or file, or store that over cloud, security related mechanism must be applied. One of the most widely used approach to perform encryption is the symmetric key cryptography (Quantum-Safe Security Working Group, 2015). The main challenge that has been faced while working with symmetric key is the secure share of the keys among sender and receiver. In order to make secure communication between two parties, it is necessary to exchange cryptographic keys among both parties. In classical encryption and key exchange mechanism, the most commonly used algorithms are Diffie-Hellman key exchange algorithm, RSA, ECC etc. upon which all gets agree (Quantum-Safe Security Working Group, 2015). As these encryptions are based upon some mathematical formula, it requires some amount of mathematical function to decrypt that. Though, it is possible to decrypt by applying all possible combination of keys, but due to very large number of bits for the purpose of encryption key, it requires very high and infeasible computing power.

As it is possible to crack this encrypted message, which plays one big challenge as a security threat with powerful computing system. The emerging infrastructure in the form of a quantum computer will make classical encryption unsafe. Thus, the continuous growth of quantum information processing makes it necessary to think again on, how to exchange symmetric cryptographic key securely? One of the most powerful technique against any high computational power, quantum computer or any new algorithm, is Quantum Key Distribution (QKD) which tries to handle the secret key exchange related challenge (Quantum-Safe Security Working Group, 2015). QKD relies on generating a random key and securely transmitting it on a separate channel from where encrypted data transmitted. Key data is generated by quantum engine and transmitted as a stream of photons through optical fiber quantum link. The key is completely random which contains quantum information that can be successfully interpreted by the designated recipient (Quantum-Safe Security Working Group, 2015).

For example, consider the person 'A' transmitting confidential information over the Internet to the bank and their quantum engine generates a random key. Data on how to reconstruct the key is then transmitted through the quantum link to the bank. Figure 5 depicted the scenario of key and data.

The QKD end node (transmitter) at the source node end establishes a QKD link with the node at forthcoming end (receiver) by making use of QKD transmitter in the intermediate node (Yongli Zhao, Yuan Cao, Xiaosong Yu and Jie Zhang, 2018). These end nodes transmit or receive qubits that would have to be stored by atoms,

Figure 5. Exchange links for quantum key and encrypted data
Source: *(Yongli Zhao, Yuan Cao, Xiaosong Yu and Jie Zhang, 2018)*

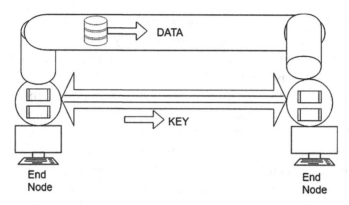

ions (atoms with few or many electrons) or electrons and photons (Chris Woodford, 2019). To transmit or receive qubits, there will be a need of quantum node. While transmitting data, it is possible that any interceptor person (hacker) can intercept the confidential information. But, interceptor cannot recreate the key to decrypt the confidential information. This is because, when the hacker tries to intercept the photons stream passed on a separate quantum channel, any interruption or change over photon channel will alert the system about the unauthorized access. The benefit of using secure fiber channel makes sense in all protected communications. However, photon transmission is limited to about 60 miles (Quantum XC[1], 2019). This problem of signal getting weakens is solved by creating a chain of QKD trusted nodes (including quantum repeaters) spread across the globe. These nodes allow us to share keys over long distances and among multiple users.

As this way of exchanging QKD comes out as one of the promising approach, there are two different types of quantum key distributions that have been emerged. The first variant is called Discrete Variable QKD (DV–QKD) (Josue Aaron Lopez-Leyva et al., 2018) This DV-QKD encodes the quantum information in discrete variables and make use of a single photon detectors to calculate the quantum states. The protocols emerged for this DV-QKD are the BB84 and the E91 protocol (Josue Aaron Lopez-Leyva et al., 2018). Another variant of QKD is Continuous Variable QKD (CV-QKD). In this CV-QKD type, quantum detail is encrypted onto the amplitude and phase quadrature of a coherent laser, and can then be measured by the receiver using homodyne detectors. The protocols arisen for this CV-QKD are the Silberhorn and the Grangier protocol (Quantum-Safe Security Working Group, 2015).

STAGES OF QUANTUM INTERNET DEVELOPMENT

In order to understand how quantum Internet works along with its application, it is necessary to understand the functionality wise stages of quantum Internet. There are total six stages and each stage is different from other based on amount of functionality. Here, every new stage not only improves the functionality of previous stage, but it brings new functionalities (Wehner, Stephanie, David Elkouss, Ronald Hanson, 2018). Figure 6 depicted six stages of Quantum Internet Development.

Apart from the challenge for newer infrastructure development, quantum Internet also brings challenge as well as research opportunity to for the quantum related software developer to design new protocols, understand and design functionality of all the associated stages. While understanding the functionality of each stage,

Figure 6. Functionalities of quantum network
Source: (Davide Castelvecchi, 2018)

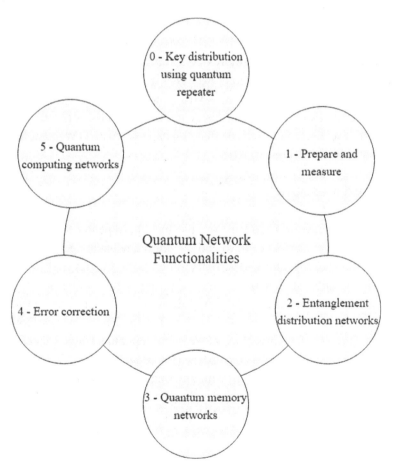

the need of hardware component including communication link, quantum node and quantum repeater can also be realized. Researchers have identified following six stages of futuristic quantum Internet at which it might reach with functionalities available for user at each level:

Key Distribution Using Quantum Repeater

This is the very first stage of quantum Internet which is different from others by not allowing end to end transmission of qubits. Quantum repeater came out as one of the trusted network component which allow securely exchange of quantum key. Generally, quantum repeater has at least two nodes directly connected with it with very short distance link connecting end node or any other intermediary quantum repeater (Wehner, Stephanie, David Elkouss, Ronald Hanson, 2018) (Davide Castelvecchi, 2018) (Johan Dubbeldam, 2019).

Consider the two end nodes M and N, and a trusted repeater R in between two nodes. Before M and N exchange quantum key KMN, initially M and R exchange quantum key KMR. Similarly, R and N exchange quantum key KRN. Now, M and N can exchange key KMN. M send KMN to R encrypted using the key KMR. R decrypts that to obtain quantum key KMN. Then after R re-encrypts quantum key KMN using the key KRN and sends it to N. Finally, N decrypts that encrypted key using KRN. This indicates that, KMN is not only known to M and N, but trusted repeater is also aware about this quantum key. Thus, it creates end to end communication securely until intermediate repeater is trusted (Wehner, Stephanie, David Elkouss, Ronald Hanson, 2018).

Prepare and Measure

In above stage we have to keep trust on intermediate repeater to ensure security. It is also sufficient to perform end to end quantum key exchange without keeping trust on intermediate repeater nodes. In the other word, this level allows any node to prepare a one qubit state and send that resulting state to other node. The node on the receiving end measure it. This level allows two or more end user to share a private key once they know each other and users can share their password or any confidential details without revealing it (Wehner, Stephanie, David Elkouss, Ronald Hanson, 2018) (Davide Castelvecchi, 2018) (Johan Dubbeldam, 2019).

Consider the two nodes p and q, with any one qubit state Ψ and any one qubit measurement M. Then, there exists a way for p to prepare Ψ, transfer it to q in such a way that q performs measurement M on Ψ or q can conclude that the qubit was lost (Wehner, Stephanie, David Elkouss, Ronald Hanson, 2018).

Entanglement Distribution Networks

This third level of quantum Internet development allows end to end creation of deterministic quantum entanglement and make user to get entangled states. The important thing to observe is, the end node does not need quantum memory for this level. The term deterministic quantum entanglement refers to the fact that the process succeeds with probability closure to one (Wehner, Stephanie, David Elkouss, Ronald Hanson, 2018) (Davide Castelvecchi, 2018) (Johan Dubbeldam, 2019).

Quantum Memory Networks

This fourth level justifies the capability of end nodes to have local quantum memory to get and store entangled qubits. This storage allows the implementation of complex protocols which sometimes needed to store quantum state for further communication (Wehner, Stephanie, David Elkouss, Ronald Hanson, 2018) (Davide Castelvecchi, 2018) (Johan Dubbeldam, 2019). For any two node m and n, the quantum network allows the entanglement generation and some additional tasks as specified below by using the quantum memory (Wehner, Stephanie, David Elkouss, Ronald Hanson, 2018):

- Preparation of a one qubits with qubits state generated Ψ by end node m and n
- As seen in level 2, at any node it permits measurements of any qubits
- It permits storage of qubits for minimum of k*ld*t time. Here, t is the amount of time needed to generate one ERP pair and transmit a classical message from node m to n, k is the number of rounds, d is the circuit depth, ld is the amount of time taken to execute depth d quantum circuit at the end node.

Error Correction

The next stage allows devices (quantum computers) on the network to handle error correction and provides fault tolerance on transferred data. Fault tolerance property is necessary for many quantum Internet protocols. Apart from this error correction related benefit, it also allows the execution of quantum computation of high circuit depth. As a cost of this benefit, it brings arbitrary extension of storage time to execute protocols with different rounds (Wehner, Stephanie, David Elkouss, Ronald Hanson, 2018) (Davide Castelvecchi, 2018) (Johan Dubbeldam, 2019).

Quantum Computing Networks

The problems that were identified with classical computers and for which it has no solution, can now be solved with quantum computing networks. This network provides facility to arbitrarily transfer quantum communication. It permits number of qubits to get efficiently transmitted through quantum computer (Wehner, Stephanie, David Elkouss, Ronald Hanson, 2018) (Davide Castelvecchi, 2018) (Johan Dubbeldam, 2019).

CHALLENGES WITH QUANTUM NETWORKS

For the globally acceptance of quantum Internet, it has to overcome several challenges alongside of its applications (Abhishek Sharma, 2018).

Quantum Signal Weakens After Certain Distance

In order to establish connection and communication at the global level, one of the biggest challenge is with long distance. Generally, photons get transmitted through the air or optical fiber. After travelling through these mediums for about 60 miles, majority of quantum signal dies. After a travel of about few hundred kilometers, 99.99% signal get vanished and signal becomes too weak to travel and communicate for a long distance. Variation of signal strength with distance is illustrated in Figure 7.

Figure 7. Unviable view of signal strength variation with distance

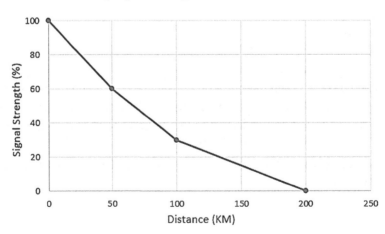

Network Infrastructure

In order to transit from classical network to quantum network, new technological infrastructure must be needed. Very first need in order to establish the communication over transmission medium (quantum channel) is support for transmission of qubits. As per the very first challenge where signal becomes weaker after travelling a long distance, classical network uses amplifier type of equipment to boost the signal strength. But, because of no cloning theorem used with qubits, it cannot be copied and ultimately amplifier cannot be used in quantum network. As per the theoretical proof, to overcome this long distance problem, quantum repeaters can be used in optical fiber at certain distance. One more and important network component of any network is end point host, i.e., quantum processor connected to quantum Internet. This node may vary with its processing capability from simple node with capability to measure single qubits to large and complex quantum computer.

Quantum Memory

As with the memory used for the storage purpose in classical computer, quantum memory is the need of quantum computer. For the storage and transmission of a single photon quantum, photonic quantum memories are available. But to handle more photon quantum, development of powerful quantum memory is still one big challenge as it requires perfectly matched photon-matter quantum interface. Few researchers already have worked and come up with more efficient memory compared to traditional one. The need of such powerful quantum memory is must there as single photon is too weak and can be easily mislaid.

E-Governance

The E-governance called as Electronic governance or Electronic government sometimes can be understood as a collection of new technology tools used to improve the current working scenario of government (Kumar, Manish, and Omesh Prasad Sinha, 2007). E-governance can be treated as publicly representation of the conclusion of governmental interactions, governmental policies, the public services, policy development, service delivery and many more. It is not only restricted towards openness of governmental dataset in front of public, but it also uses adoption of new Information and Communication Technology (ICT) to improve the services, enhance mode of service delivery and include better newer services for the betterment of citizen (Kumar, Manish, and Omesh Prasad Sinha, 2007). This E-governance concept can also be referred to as smart governance, online governance or digital governance.

Figure 8. E-Governance model
Source: (E-SPIN, 2017)

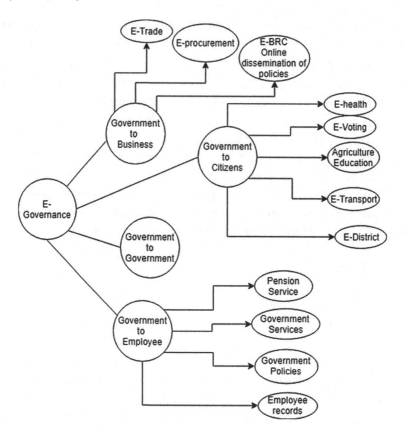

The E-governance can be applied by governmental administrative, legislative or judiciary departments to improve the current process and efficiency. Based upon the bodies who are connected with governmental dataset, E-governance model can be classified into 4 categories: Government to Government (G2G), Government to Business (G2B), Government to Customer (G2C) and Government to Employees (G2E) (Kumar, Manish, and Omesh Prasad Sinha, 2007). As our aim is to discuss Internet based governmental services, but before that consider the list of some of non-internet (offline) governmental services and technologies as, Fax, SMS (Short Message Service), MMS (Multimedia Messaging Service), Telephone, Biometric, Identity cards, voting system, CCTV (Closed Circuit Television), RFID (Radio Frequency Identification), Smart cards, Bluetooth, email, Tracking system, radio, newsgroups and many more (Kumar, manish, and omesh prasad sinha, 2007). there is a strong need to implement these services in some better way to fulfil the dream of e-governance.

There is a one important subset of e-governance and that is m-governance (kumar, manish, and omesh prasad sinha, 2007). in case of m-governance, the use of governmental services is restricted with mobile phones or wireless cellular devices instead of ict. with the advent of usage of mobile phone devices, m-governance found its wide spread popularity by helping general public by providing governmental services and information available anywhere and anytime. the citizens will be benefitted as their energy and valuable time will get saved by accessing the needed service using the device connected with internet. consider the example set by developing country malaysia by adopting e-governance and m-governance (kumar, manish, and omesh prasad sinha, 2007). in malaysia, citizens can verify their voting card related details including parliament and place where they have to vote by sitting at a very long distance by using ict or sms service. their citizens are also permitted to access a real time information or any latest governmental figures with the one click. in california also, their government had designed service for their users, where after registering, their users can get traffic updates, lottery result details, any governmental notification, any new services, any governmental articles etc (kumar, manish, and omesh prasad sinha, 2007). e-governance not only came as blessing to get efficient service, but it also makes active citizens by their continuous involvement into governmental policies. in philippines also, one can take benefit by using anti-pollution service to complaint against person smoking in public transport, to avoid illegal drugs, to fight against crime etc (kumar, manish, and omesh prasad sinha, 2007).

Critical Issues With E-Governance

As everyone trying to inject traffic over internet, there is a threat of inception. some unethical persons (hackers) may try to spy over wireless networks to scan e-mail contents, documents and any other confidential information (kumar, manish, and omesh prasad sinha, 2007). as wireless networks use public airways to transmit the signals, which are vulnerable. to transmit confidential data over network, it must be strongly encrypted and key to decrypt that message must also be securely exchanged. even though classical encryption technique is already available and worked satisfactorily till date. but, because of the development of powerful computing platform capable of resolving mathematical based encryption using classical encryption, that strategy becomes vulnerable. quantum compute with its tremendous computing power, can resolve decryption key quickly by applying all possible combination of keys. in order to get access over 802.11b networks, specific type of programs have been developed and available, working using the wired equivalent privacy (wep) encryption system (kumar, manish, and omesh prasad sinha, 2007). there are also tools namely wepcrack and airsnort are available that are used to grab the password and other confidential information.

Quantum Cryptography – The Solution

Quantum cryptography is the mechanism of using properties of quantum mechanics to perform encryption tasks. the best thing to justify secureness of quantum cryptography is its quantum key distribution (qkd) which offers secure solution to the classical key exchange problem (paolo comi, 2018). the advantage of quantum cryptography can be understood by the fact that the security related solutions which are possible by using quantum cryptography that are proven impossible by using classical cryptography (paolo comi, 2018). because of qubits instead of numerical bit and due to entanglement, no cloning principle and qkd, quantum cryptography recognized to be secured. quantum cryptography, by extension, simply uses the principles of quantum mechanics to encrypt data and transmit it in a way that cannot be hacked. figure 9 depicted difference between classical encryption and quantum encryption.

Though at a very first glance, definition looks simpler, but the complex parts that have to be taken care behind the principle of quantum cryptography are as (Quantum XC, 2019):

- The particle through which data gets transmitted called as qubits makes the universe uncertain by being in more than one state simultaneously and can also be transmitted simultaneously.
- Photons are generated randomly in one of two quantum states.

Figure 9. Classical encryption vs quantum encryption
Source: (Nils Jacob Sand, 2018)

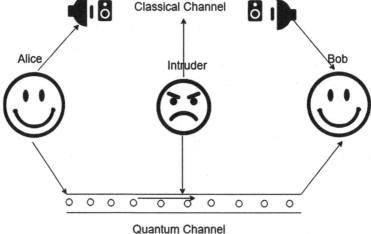

- Nobody is permitted to change or read the property of quantum bits without affecting or altering it.
- It is possible to clone some quantum property, but cloning the entire quantum is not possible.

The mathematical equation and large size of key requires larger amount of time like months or years to break and determine the actual message. However, because if powerful Shor's algorithm running behind quantum computer make it to break that encryption in moments. Instead of using encryption by applying mathematical formula, quantum cryptography uses quantum mechanics which makes them non vulnerable and secured from hackers. Quantum cryptography along with quantum key distribution (QKD), makes use of photons to transmit the data from one location to another over a fiber optic cable. In order to understand this process in better way, it is good to break it down in smaller steps (Quantum XC, 2019):

- After transmitting photons randomly through filter, it can provide one of four divergences and bit designations including Vertical (One bit), Horizontal (Zero bit), 45 degrees right (One bit), or 45 degrees left (Zero bit).
- While travelling to a receiver, the photons uses either horizontal/vertical and diagonal beam splitters, to read the polarization of every photon. But, as the receiver does not know from that two beam splitters, which one to use. Thus, it has to guess from available two which is to be used.
- After receiving the beam splitters, the receiver tells the sender which beam splitter was used for every single photon sent in the sequence by sender. Then after sender compares that received information with the sequence of polarization used to transmit the key. After comparison, the photons which found with wrong beam splitter are discarded. The remaining sequence of bits can be treated as key.
- The eavesdropper who tries to read or copy the photon, that photon's state will get changed. This changes will get immediately detected by the endpoint. In other words, without getting detected, one will not be able to read or copy the photon.

CONCLUSION AND FURTHER RESEARCH DIRECTIONS

The evolution of quantum computer brings high computing power which will be capable enough to compute any key of classical cryptography algorithms. As a part of this challenge, quantum cryptography brings revolutionary approach in cryptography. It solves the key exchange issue as with classical cryptography, by using quantum key exchange mechanism. Our government is also turning into e-governance by keeping records of every governmental department. The security issues associated with e-governance can also be resolved by using quantum cryptography. This quantum cryptography can be considered as pioneer of new and secure network architecture. Chapter presented all the components required for quantum internet and cryptography approaches and challenges to overcome. In future, it would be interesting to create test-bed of quantum networks and test all the mechanisms of cryptography for the challenges posed in the Chapter. Further, it would pave the way to have quantum cryptography in all IT based systems to have robust mechanisms as far as the security is concerned.

REFERENCES

Ananthaswamy, A. (2019). *The Quantum Internet Is Emerging, One Experiment at a Time.* Scientific American. Retrieved from https://www.scientificamerican.com/article/the-quantum-internet-is-emerging-one-experiment-at-a-time/

Caleffi, M., & Cacciapuoti, A. S. (2019). Quantum Switch for the Quantum Internet: Noiseless Communications through Noisy Channels.

Castelvecchi, D. (2018). *Here's what the quantum internet has in store.* Nature. Retrieved from https://www.nature.com/articles/d41586-018-07129-y

Chen, S. (2017). *Quantum Internet Is 13 Years Away. Wait, What's Quantum Internet?* Wired; Retrieved from wired.com/story/quantum-internet-is-13-years-away-wait-whats-quantum-internet/

Choucair, M. (2016). *All you need for quantum computing at room temperature is some mothballs.* Phys.org. Retrieved from https://phys.org/news/2016-07-quantum-room-temperature-mothballs.html

Comi, P. (2018). *Integration of classic cryptography with QKD.* Italtel. Retrieved from https://www.italtel.com/focus-integration-of-classic-cryptography-with-qkd/

Critchley, L. (2018). *What are Quantum Networks?* AZO Quantum. Retrieved from https://www.azoquantum.com/Article.aspx?ArticleID=96

Das, S. R., & Chandrashekhar, R. (2007). Capacity-Building for e-Governance in India. *Regional Development Dialogue*, 27(2), 75.

Dubbeldam, J. (2019). *The quantum Internet - A glimpse into the future.* Network Pages. Retrieved from https://www.networkpages.nl/the-quantum-internet-a-glimpse-into-the-future/

E-SPIN. (2017). *Definition and type of E-government.* Retrieved from https://www.e-spincorp.com/definition-and-type-of-e-government/

Faraj, S. T., & Ali, M. S. (2011). Enhancement of E-Government Security Based on Quantum Cryptography. In *Proceeding of the International Arab Conference on Information Technology (ACIT'2011)* (pp. 11-14). Academic Press.

Kimble, H.J. (2008). The quantum internet. *Nature, 453*(7198), 1023–1030. doi:10.1038/nature07127 PMID:18563153

Korolov, M. & Drinkwater, D. (2019). *What is quantum cryptography? It's no silver bullet, but could improve security.* CSO Online. Retrieved from https://www.csoonline.com/article/3235970/what-is-quantum-cryptography-it-s-no-silver-bullet-but-could-improve-security.html

Kumar, M., & Sinha, O. P. (2007). M-government–mobile technology for e-government. In *Proceedings of the International conference on e-government* (pp. 294-301). Academic Press.

Lopez-Leyva, J., Talamantes-Alvarez, A., Ponce-Camacho, M., Garcia, E., & Alvarez-Guzman, E. (2018). *Free-Space-Optical Quantum Key Distribution Systems: Challenges and Trends. In Quantum Cryptography.* IntechOpen. Retrieved September 30, 2019 from https://www.intechopen.com/books/quantum-cryptography-in-advanced-networks/free-space-optical-quantum-key-distribution-systems-challenges-and-trends

Monojlovic, V. (2017). *Introduction to the Quantum Internet.* Retrieved from https://labs.ripe.net/Members/becha/introduction-to-the-quantum-internet

Ortiz, J., Sadovsky, A., & Russakovsky, O. (2004). *Modern Cryptography: Theory and Applications.* Retrieved from https://cs.stanford.edu/people/eroberts/courses/soco/projects/2004-05/cryptography/quantum.html

Quantum XC. (2019). *What is Trusted Node Technology, and Why Does It Matter?* Retrieved from https://quantumxc.com/what-is-trusted-node-technology-and-why-does-it-matter/

Quantum XC. (2019). *Quantum Cryptography, Explained.* Retrieved from https://quantumxc.com/quantum-cryptography-explained/

Quantum Cryptography by Brilliant.org (2019). *Quantum Cryptography.* Retrieved from https://brilliant.org/wiki/quantum-cryptography/

Quantum-Safe Security Working Group. (2015). *What is Quantum Key Distribution?* Retrieved from https://www.quintessencelabs.com/wp-content/uploads/2015/08/CSA-What-is-Quantum-Key-Distribution-QKD-1.pdf

Sand, N.J. (2018). *Introduction to Quantum Cryptography.* Norwegian Creations. Retrieved from https://www.norwegiancreations.com/2018/11/introduction-to-quantum-cryptography/

ScienceDaily. (2019). *Quantum Computer.* Retrieved from https://www.sciencedaily.com/terms/quantum_computer.htm

Sharma, A. (2018). *The Quantum Internet Is Still A Futuristic Dream, At Least A Decade Away.* Analytics India Mag. Retrieved from https://www.analyticsindiamag.com/the-quantum-internet-is-still-a-futuristic-dream-at-least-a-decade-away/

Wehner, S., Elkouss, D., & Hanson, R. (2018). Quantum internet: A vision for the road ahead. *Science, 362*(6412).

Woodford, C. (2019). *Quantum computing.* Explain That Stuff. Retrieved from https://www.explainthatstuff.com/quantum-computing.html

Zhao, Y., Cao, Y., Yu, X., & Zhang, J. (2018). *Quantum Key Distribution (QKD) over Software-Defined Optical Networks.* IntechOpen. Retrieved from https://www.intechopen.com/books/quantum-cryptography-in-advanced-networks/quantum-key-distribution-qkd-over-software-defined-optical-networks

Zyga, L. (2018). *New quantum repeater paves the way for long-distance big quantum data transmission.* Phys.org. Retrieved from https://phys.org/news/2018-02-quantum-paves-long-distance-big-transmission.html

Section 2
Cyber Security

Chapter 7

Critical Infrastructure Security:
Cyber–Physical Attack Prevention, Detection, and Countermeasures

Ayush Sinha
Indian Institute of Information Technology, Allahabad, India

Ranjana Vyas
Indian Institute of Information Technology, Allahabad, India

Venkatesan Subramanian
Indian Institute of Information Technology, Allahabad, India

O. P. Vyas
Indian Institute of Information Technology, Allahabad, India

ABSTRACT

Cyber-physical security applied to the domain of critical infrastructure (CI) poses different challenges. To acknowledge the security concern of CI from a cyber-physical perspective becomes imperative since the failure of any one of the CI's components may not only lead to cascading effects, but also the overall services may shutdown state. The energy infrastructure is becoming the backbone in CI due to the complexity of environment, heterogeneous communication technologies, and different configurations of the energy infrastructure, so securing the communication among these devices and control centers becomes a central issue. Many significant works in the related domain has been done. The main focus of the chapter is identification of the attack vector formulation with prevention and detection mechanisms for different components, providing countermeasures cohesively against security threats.

DOI: 10.4018/978-1-7998-2253-0.ch007

INTRODUCTION

Energy infrastructures, assisted by the adoption of modern information and communication technology (ICT), are the main critical infrastructures (CIs) which are essential to maintain essential societal functions. Any harm of these infrastructures by cyber-attacks, natural disasters and criminal activity may have bad consequences for the security and safety of modern Smart Cities and society at large. Emerging cyber, physical and combined cyber-physical threats, as well as non-traditional attacks to CIs have exposed the limitation of risk assessment done traditionally, as well as those of protection solutions. Inevitably, the energy production and distribution systems, which comprise a vital economic and social infrastructure, are exposed to: (a) security threats inherited from the ICT sector, (b) physical attacks like bombing, fires and floods, and (c) combinations of cyber and physical threats. Considering that a potential attack to an energy installation may lead to cascading failures, these threats can lead to disruptions with severe consequences like destruction of other interconnected CIs (e.g., water, communications and transportation), loss of human lives and environmental impact. The context of Energy Infrastructure is mainly discussed through Smart grid domain and it is very essential to adequately address the cyber and physical security of the energy infrastructure and its underlying smart grid setup.

The smart grid (SG) is the term seen as the combination of legacy and existing electrical infrastructure for the power distribution domain along with distributed set of control and networking devices for the effective data and control communication. The various important constituents of SG are the electrical infrastructure which work as a backbone for the power generation, transmission and distribution domain and geographically distributed smart devices that work concurrently and in individual to make the system stable and configurable using supervisory software like supervisory control and data acquisition (SCADA) as suggested by D. Yang, A. Usynin, and J.W. Hines (2008).

Cyber Physical Attack and Solution: NIST Framework

Furthermore, despite the wide palette of currently available security mechanisms, the protection of the energy infrastructures requires an integrated solution that can efficiently and jointly deal with the major challenges stemming from the multiple threat scenarios. This chapter analyses the attack vector formulation for the cyber, physical and cyber-physical threats, discusses the present state of the art for the Cyber Physical attack and to the end presents the comprehensive and systemic approach combining cyber and physical security solutions to protect Energy infrastructure installations of smart environment system. The approach to address the above-mentioned cases is structured around the National Institute of Standards and Technology (2014) cyber security framework as shown in the figure.

So, in the subsequent sections of this chapter, the cyber physical security attacks, detection and prevention techniques will be addressed under the umbrella of NIST framework and guidelines. The brief of the five verticals of NIST framework is as below:

- **Identify:** This module is focused on the formulation of attack vector that would address the cyber and physical attack as a whole. The task like risk assessment are considered here.
- **Protect:** Nab et al. proposed securing the cyber-physical system as a whole is very crucial phenomenon and this module handles the key management framework for the secure authentication and presents communication protocols for wired or wireless communication among different smart devices.
- **Detect:** Even though after taking the necessary precautionary techniques for securing the communication channel, there might be some chances that adversary might successfully attack the system. Thus, it is very critical to define the detection mechanism that will consider the multivariate and multidimensional nature of the critical infrastructure into account. Most of the existing methods focus on a single parameter or a reduced set of them (e.g., network packet payloads, network flows, process variables) mainly at the cyber level, without relating to the rest of existing parameters at physical level, leading to false negatives. So, this module covers state-of-art for the cyber physical threat and attacks as well as coordinated attack on the critical infrastructure.
- **Respond:** Broadly covers how the system respond once the attack happens and detected successfully. Broadly, there are two prevalent methodologies in

Figure 1. NIST framework for the cyber physical systems

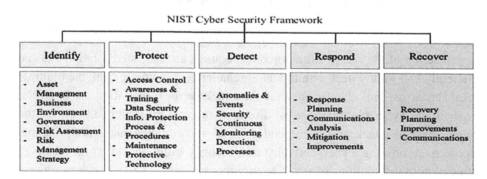

this direction: (i) the use of fault tolerant control approaches together with graph-based traffic engineering strategies as proposed by S.X. Ding, Ping Zhang, Shen Yin, and E.L. Ding (2013) and (ii) the adoption of an emerging paradigm in traditional IP networks (i.e., Software-Defined Networks), where the by global routing decision software replaces the local router-based decisions.

- **Recover:** The recovery mechanism is based on QoS routing mechanism as proposed by H. Li and W. Zhang, (2010) for the communication system in smart grid or based on wireless mesh network that focused on time critical communications integrated with the power system protections.

Cyber Physical Security

Mo et al. (2012) shows that challenges for the smart grid cyber physical security is on the rise. K. Morison, L. Wang, and P. Kundur (2004) demonstrated that due to inherent physical vulnerabilities of the power system, even the small contingencies may lead to severe blackout. The integration of the cyber domain has increased the significant security threats, as it will increase the attacker's capability to launch simultaneous, remote, intrigue and/or cyber-physical coordinated attacks. H. He and J. Yan (2016) presented a survey for the study of cyber, physical and cyber-physical security prospects and challenges. It is shown by S. Sridhar, A. Hahn, and M. Govindarasu (2012) that the research on the CPS of the critical energy infrastructure is the frontier of the CPS system and mainly aimed at the junction of the physical security of the critical infrastructure and cyber security of the communication, information and computational part of the system.

Physical Security

The protection of the physical security of the power system is purely depends upon the assessment and continuous screening of the contingencies. Morison et al. (2004) showed that the power system security is evaluated by contingency analysis (CA) once the selection of operating points and credible inadvertent contingencies is applied on it. Typically, the CA covers faults occurred, planned outages and disturbances. CA establishes the security constraints related to contingency to ensure the best survival state of the critical infrastructure with a minimum outage of power delivery.

However, the interconnected power system in the form of the micro grids and the emerging CPS imposes challenges for the analysis of physical security features. So when the system scales, the CA cast has been increased dramatically, making it difficult to work with multi-CA. Due to heterogeneous and complex nature of the software, hardware and different operation in the power systems, it becomes very difficult to accurately evaluate the contingencies which are remotely located but the impact of that is propagated with the speed of electromagnetic waveform.

Moreover, the integration of cyber component imposes new set of challenges. Devices deployed on fields and systems are not capable enough and equipped with sufficient security attributes against mischievous events, particularly from the cyber world as stated by He et al. (2016).

Cyber Security

For the cyber security framework, the National Institute of Standards and Technology, (2014) established the CIA triad through the Principles of confidentiality, integrity, and availability for the information security framework. To defend the field devices and control centre against the external intrusion, the IDS and firewall have been deployed. Secure protocols like TLS and IPSec are used to secure the SCADA system for within and for outside communication with the control centre.

Meanwhile the cyber security for the energy infrastructure has to include physical component also in order to completely address the requirements and dependencies of the power sector. For example, it is very natural step in cyber space to block an account after certain number of invalid login attempt but attacker may take the advantage of this situation to intentionally block the control centre operator account and this may lead to catastrophic consequences. Smart grid network is flooded with real time data and this also pose a big challenge to security analysis for the network. So similar to acknowledging the physical aspect of the security, the cyber-security also needs to incorporate the physical security component into it.

Cyber Physical Security

As per He et al. (2016), a security aware smart grid is incidental on the cohesive security that combines the stability in both physical and cyber security analysis against the involuntary and hostile events. There should be broader spectrum to investigate the vulnerable points and contingencies arise from them. The identification, detection and consequence measurement across the cyber physical spaces shall be systematically analysed keeping intact the interoperability and interdependence therein. The deep dive into the critical infrastructure security has exhibited a notable number of attack plans that could be used to exploit censorious vulnerabilities with most severe upsetting and damages. The full understanding of these attack schemes is crucial to grasp and further enhance the Cyber Physical security of the energy infrastructure network as a whole and the underlying technologies within it. Analysing the critical infrastructure as a combine cyber physical system would streamline the effort to identify new vulnerabilities and thus possible solutions for the modern emerging CPS in the critical infrastructure.

State Estimation Attack Models

In this section, authors present two cyber-attack models for the correct state estimation scenario. The existing bad data detector module deployed at the control centre is not capable enough to identify the sophisticated cyber-attack. Cyber-attack targeted for the state estimation is classified in to different type like DoS attack where the due to the missing or unavailable data, the certain state cannot be observed, eavesdroppers which analyse the network traffic to access some private information and thus raise privacy concern (Mo, Kim, Brancik, Dickinson, Lee, Perrig, & Sinopoli, 2012), and integrity or FDI attacks where the message that is being communicated is modified by a "MITM" where attackers are nothing but the intermediate nodes in the communication network. So bad data detector embedded in the energy management system module is escaped and FDI attack becomes invisible and thus raising a lot of concern, so the subsection is concentrated for this type of attack.

FDI Attacks Targeting the Grid Topology

The connectivity of the power system has been represented by its topology and it is constantly updated over the certain interval inside the topology processor of the smart grid. The circuit breaker sends the binary reading corresponding to transmission lines to the control centre. An attacker may modify these reading as well as the SCADA measurements. Such attack facilitates the topology update in malicious manner and it's undetected by bad data detector configured at control centre (Kim & Tong, 2013). So, for the topological modification of the smart grid, attacker only needs to know the SCADA analog measurements communicated to the control centre and the circuit breaker states. Researchers discuss the vulnerabilities that may cause by stealthy cyber-attack on topology of the grid (Chakhchoukh & Ishii, 2015) and also evaluated and compared robust state estimation methods in the presence of different configurations of attacks possibilities through Monte Carlo simulations using IEEE 14- and 30-bus test beds.

State Estimation Based on PMU

Phase measurement units are group of devices that has the reporting rate (30 to 120 measurements per second) and consisting of better synchronising mechanism than SCADA because of the use of GPS clocks (Kezunovic, Meliopoulos, & Venkatasubramanian, 2014). Since PMU is of having higher cost with compare to usual state estimation devise, power companies have shown vested interest for combining their in use old SCADAs and the newly installed and working PMUs for the estimation of the system state using the approach known as hybrid state estimator. Since PMUs measure the states, i.e., phase angles and magnitudes of the voltage directly, so to monitor the smart grid with PMUs that have the capability of delivering large amount of RT data imposes cyber vulnerability. Thus, it is demonstrated by researchers in (Abur & Rouhani, 2016: Wang & Chakrabortty, 2016) that PMUs are vulnerable to cyber-attack as well random bad data both.

ATTACK CATEGORISATION

Cyber physical attack categorisation can be done either on the basis of access level of the adversary or on the basis of location of the adversary. Further depending upon the adversary access level, attacks is classified as active or passive in nature and on the basis of location the categorisation is done as internal or external attack. The brief description of these two major categories and some other important common type of attack is as:

Active Attacks

It is done by an intruder either through theft and modification of data, or through the fulfilment of some operation to damage the confidentiality, availability and integrity of data. Some common types active attacks may be packet modification, false data injection, capturing of node, wormhole, resource exhaustion, jamming, spoofing, Denial of Service and sinkhole.

Passive Attacks

It is performed by an adversary with basic aim of compromising the confidentiality of the network through an observation of network activities. Some common types of passive attacks are information capture, traffic analysis and vulnerable data encryption.

Internal Attacks

This is a kind of attack in which the adversary plans and launches its attack residing within the range of the communication network. This type of attacks requires a competent skills level such as revelation of confidential information and physical tampering of the node itself.

External Attacks

This is a kind of attack in which the intruder remains outside from the range of the intended communication network and that includes both i.e. the physical and the virtual networks. Most common attacks fall under this category for examples such as network jamming, resource exhaustion, Denial of service and Distributed Denial of service.

In the subsequent section of the attack categorisation authors give the brief introduction of various attack types and their present state-of-the-art.

DoS (Denial of Service)

This is most widely type of attack and can be categorised under active attack category with types as jamming, flooding, blackhole, worm and sink attack (Butun I., Morgera S.D. & Sankar R., 2014). The perpetrator willing to target a network resource to make it unavailable for its potential users by partially or indefinitely interrupting services of a host machine connected to the Internet. The task of DoS is achieved by flooding the intended resource with requests that are superfluous in nature and thus making an attempt to overload system and prevent few or all the legitimate requests from being fulfilled. More in detail, threats oriented from DoS can be further explained as:

- **Physical Devastation/Node Capture:** In which the device is physically damaged, along with hardware and software alteration activity with the objective to mutate the availability of the device itself.
- **Network Resources Flooding:** An attacker exploits resource shortage making them partially/completely unavailable for other devices.
- **Alteration in the Network Configurations:** Here an attacker wants to falsify the network characteristics, thus the network becomes unapproachable even for the genuine devices that is connected through it (e.g. network jamming, physical attacks, ambiance camouflaging).

One possible solution to make all of above applications less vulnerable and more resilient to the Dos attack is to switch its implementation from centralized to distributed fashion. So, the appropriate use suitable technologies like cryptography, key management, etc. facilitates to protect a PLC network from unintended integrity, disclosure and DoS threats (Davoli, Belli, Veltri, & Ferrari, 2017).

False Data Injection (FDI) Attack

In case the adversary has the knowledge of the complete system model, then he can plan a stealthier attack even without come in notice. This is a class of deception attack and comes under the category of FDI attack. One of the common FDI attack on the critical infrastructure is attack on the state estimation vector. State estimation is known to be a very crucial function for the smart grid infrastructure as it is used to calculate load forecasting, contingency analysis and locational marginal price calculation for the power markets (Liang, Zhao, Luo, Weller, & Dong, 2016). The planning of FDI attack can be done on the information layer or the physical layer of the communication network and the brief about both of them is as below:

FDIA for the Information Layer

The possible option for the invasion in the power sector is through the control devices, backbone communication networks and measuring units. Since the control devices are thoroughly protective the invasion can be achieved in two possible manners:

- Destroying the data stored in the measurement units like remote terminal units (RTUs) and phase measurement units (PMUs). The attacker accomplishes this by exploiting the inherent vulnerabilities of the encryption and authentication mechanisms (Yi, Wang, Tai, & Ni, 2018).
- By invading the communication network, DoS or MITM attack can be targeted between measurement units and the control centres in order to temper the control information through the communication channel. Researchers introduced a new addressing mechanism in (Pal, Sikdar, & Chow, 2016) to address the grey-hole attack to handle the scenario where the data packets belonging to PMUs devices are being dropped while transmission and as a result, the loss of observability and incorrect control decisions are made subsequently.

FDIA for the Physical Layer

Once the information layer is invaded, the capability of modification in measurement is obtained by attacker. Through modifying the load, power flow information and real-time price which are capable enough to be overlooked by the bad data detection module, it is possible for attacker to obstruct with the subsequent control services (Yang, Chang, & Yu, 2013).

The state estimating function is represented by

$z = h(x) + e$

Here z stands for readings including generator output, branch active, bus voltage and reactive power flows. x is for the state vector that includes the phase angle and amplitude of the node voltage. Here, h(x) is the relation matrix for the state variables and the measurement variables that represents the system topology. So, in general, the total measured variables are more than the number of state variables. This resulting redundancy is considered to improvise the estimation accuracy.

Man-in-the-Middle

Man-in-the-middle attack (MITM) is strategy where an attacker secretly relays and tries to make some alteration/modification in the communications among the two parties and each of them believe that they are directly communicating with each other. One of the famous examples of this attack category is active eavesdropping where attacker deliberately makes a connection with the victims and starts relaying messages with them in a way that would make them believe that they are talking to each other. So, to accomplish this task, the attacker must be efficient enough to intercept the messages between parties and as a consequence injecting new ones. Unencrypted wireless access point is the most vulnerable point to be the victim of such attack.

In context of smart grid, the MITM attack can be embedded through the communication between RTUs and the utility if the attacker has prior knowledge about topology of system. In this case, the attacker can change the state estimate which means that attack is sly to the bad data detector on the basis of analysing the residual. Since attacker knows the whole topology of the smart grid, it does not need to target all sensors and only few vulnerable points is sufficient enough and the operator will not come to know because he obtains a modified result that does not reflect the actual state of the grid (Liu, Ning, & Reiter, 2011).

Another example of MITM is the case of an HTTPS connection, where two independent socket secure layer connections are established on the top of each TCP connection. By taking advantage of the network communication protocol vulnerabilities, MITM convinces the victim to make changes in the traffic route via the attacker instead of normal router and this phenomenon is generally known as ARP spoofing.

Eavesdropping

This is categorised as passive attack and the attacker will temper the node and demolishing the operation by traffic analysis. So eavesdropping is the interception of an en-route communication in an unauthorized fashion without the permission taken from the communicating stakeholders. So while the transmission of the data from smart grid instruments to the Energy Management System (EMS), this kind of attack by an adversary could result in leaking of valuable data, which can be processed by them to infer inside about a customer's way of living (Komninos, Philippou, & Pitsillides, 2014).

Under this attack category, the attacker gets in to customer privacy and highlights the communication protocols used, and as a consequence of this, it could help the adversary to plan injection of false traffic in the grid and its consequence is meter impersonation attack, with already known consequences (Grochocki, Ho Huh, Berthier, Bobba, Sanders, Cardenas, & Jetcheva, 2012).

Spoofing

Spoofing is classified as an active attack category. For the smart grid perspective, spoofing can be termed as malicious imitation of a trusted device installed in the system, which is used to capture and gives fake time stamps to the phase measurement units (PMUs) (Zhang, Gong, Dimitrovski, & Li, 2012). So, for the correct estate estimation task, the accuracy and the utility of the measured unit may be undermine and altered if the GPS is spoofed or jammed. Since the GPS signals do not have any mechanism for authorisation or encryption, attackers may become capable of generating the counterfeit GPS signals and that is unable to differentiate from the original data by the receivers (Yi, Wang, Tai, & Ni, 2018).

Another major effect of this attack is the alteration of the receiving PMU's clock offset and the effect of this is to enhance the false alarms indications and false negatives results in voltage stability monitoring systems (Fan, Zhang, Trinkle, Dimitrovski, Song, & Li, 2014; Jiang, Zhang, Harding, Makela, & Dominguez-Garcia, 2013). So researchers demonstrated the spoofing attack as an optimization problem and the objective function is to maximize the difference of the PMU's receiver clock offset (in accordance to the GPS time that is measured through the satellite clocks) taken before and after the attack (Jiang, Zhang, Harding, Makela, & Dominguez-Garcia, 2013). Since the PMU computes a synchronized time stamp for its measurements using this clock offset, even a miniscule error possibility in the receiver clock offset will introduce a proportional phase error for current phase or voltage measurements provided by the PMUs.

Replay (Playback)

A replay also known as playback attack is a category of attack where a valid message during its transmission is maliciously repeated or delayed. This can be done either by the data originator or by an attacker who maliciously intercepts the message and further retransmits it by IP packet substitution. So this attack is treated as a breach of secure communication between parties that destroys the very intent of the protocols designed for authentication and key distribution (Singh, Arun, & Misra, 2012). The figure below is the mechanism through which replay attack may happen.

In order to formulate the attack model for the replay attack (Miao, Pajic, & Pappas, 2013), it is assumed that the attacker can read the sensor measurements, select and chose the window size for replay as T, and take decision at each time-step whether either to send the correct measurement or intentionally delayed plant outputs. So, data y'_k (k $\geq$ 0) that will be received at estimator and detector is explained as:

$$y'_k = \begin{cases} Yk, & sensor\ output\ is\ not\ changed\ at\ k \\ Yk - T, T > 0, & sensor\ output\ is\ changed\ at\ k \end{cases}$$

ATTACK AGAINST THE SMART GRID

For the critical infrastructure network, the main vulnerable points, potential risk and threat are (Saponara & Tony, 2012; Tourani, Misra, Mick, Brahma, Biswal, & Ameme, 2016):

- The grid is too complex, it may lead to vulnerable multiple points and unforced error.
- With the emerging new technologies, new issues can come to the network.
- Grid based on multi-agent model, the intelligent node can contribute to DoS attack.

Figure 2. Illustration of the replay attack, a) wants to send its hashed password to, b) E sniffs the hash and replays it.

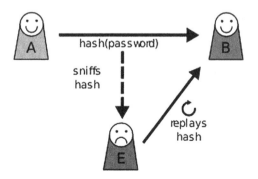

- Interference from the utility telecommunication network that can make alteration in the transmission, distribution and generation system.
- Manipulation in the bill.
- Week protection scheme at customer end device may lead to unauthorized access.
- Human made error.
- Equipment failure.
- Natural disaster threats.

To achieve the attack objective, four step processes may be adopted by the attacker:

- Investigation
- Discovery
- Vulnerability identification
- Infiltration

Categorization of attack on smart grid depends upon the layers, technological stack being used and platform etc. So the aspects to consider for the attack categorization is: attack aimed at smart grid security objective, attack aiming for the utility companies and attack aimed for customer at home area network component.

Attacks on Smart Grid Security Objectives

As the three level security objectives defined for the smart grid are confidentiality, availability, and integrity, and the brief description of the attack on these objectives are as follows:

Attacks that aims confidentiality – The attacker's main aim is to gather unauthorized data and information from the communication framework of the intelligent grid.

Attacker that aims availability – DoS is the best example for this type of attack like jamming in control centres and substations, flooding in traffic and buffer, etc., and this attack is contemplate to partially or totally block, corrupt or inserting delay in the smart grid communication framework.

Attacker that aims integrity – FDI and smart meter data manipulation are the example under this attack category. Here attackers are intended to modify or to disrupt traffic inside the smart grid network.

Attacks Against the Utility Companies

While planning attack on utility companies and organization, hackers use multiple attack methods in the form of coordinated attack on the several sections and resources critical to the organization to achieve their objective (Flick & Morehouse, 2011). Furthermore, the attack against the utility units can be categorised as: Physical attacks, Attacks on communication network, Application attacks and Social engineering attacks.

Utility companies install thousands of smart meters to their customer premises but too little effort while protecting them from physical tempering and to disturb the transmission lines attached with smart meter. The most prevalent practices that must be tackled are:

- Obtain the physical access without the permission like access badge.
- Eavesdropping and shoulder-suffering.
- Stealing the unattended or not properly locked mobile/computer device attached with a machine.

The core of the smart grid is its information network infrastructure that is always in process to transmit the data in order to improve the efficiency and availability of the grid itself. Since the smart grid implementation is not simple and it involve multiple network altogether, the attacker plans to attack from many different location. The attack can be the IP based or on the vulnerable points for the existing protocol like WLAN, ZigBee, RF mesh, WiMax and Wi-Fi that is being used for the communication network of smart grid and mostly based on IEEE 802.11, IEEE 802.1.4 and IEEE 802.16 (Pandey, R. & Misra, M., 2016).

In order to automate the traditional way of inefficient working for manual business process and to provide relatively better customer experience, utility company are rolling out the web application-based processing. With the current advancement of migrating the traditional web application from thin client to thick client-based application, the security threats increase as the attacker may attack on listening to socket calls, stealing data base connecting parameters, etc.

Social engineering attack is aimed to test the knowledge about security awareness of a particular utility company. An attacker may use some trick to revel the information from the company employee.

Attacks Against the Customers

Attack planned for the customer surroundings is mainly focused on the home area network (HAN) defined for it. The main attack categories that are targeted for HAN are:

- Attacks through network
- Wireless attacks

- Attacks planned for the smart meters
- Attacks planned for the management devices

CPS ATTACK MODEL

To exactly measure the result of the cyber physical attack on the critical infrastructure system, a proper impact analysis and attack vector formulation is an important step towards achieving this goal. Kundur et al. (2011) have proposed solution in this regard as synthesis of modeling the cyber physical system relationship as a graph. In this graph structure, every node contains it's associated state information which is being directed by the some dynamical state equation that model the interaction between the physical component (electrical system) and the cyber component(for cyber grid element).

Graph Structure for Cyber Physical Attack

In early stage of the attack impact analysis, the associated risk for the CPS is defined by:

$R(F) = L(F) \times I(F)$

Where $R(F)$, $I(F)$ and $L(F)$ represent the risk, impact and likelihood of a given failure F due to a cyber-attack. Researchers further propose to break this likelihood into the product of the vulnerabilities and likelihood of threats for evaluating risk by a three-dimensional method.

$R(F) = L(F) \times I(F) = T(F) \times V (F) \times I(F)$

In case of attack, it is necessary to relate the cyber-attack to the corresponding physical consequence in smart grid network. So, a mathematical formulization of state $\dot{s}$ that is the time-evolution of state s can be represented functionally as:

$$\dot{s} = f\left(s, u\right)$$

Where $\dot{s}$ is the time derivative of s and u is the input vector. Researchers proposes that graph based dynamic state system formulation is effective as a cause effect relationship can be expressed easily and it enables a tight coupling between cyber and physical system in terms of nodes and edges. Step to produce graph from the grid component is as below:

Step to Produce Graph

1. Cyber and electrical graph is formed where each node represents its associated grid element.
2. Nodes can be transformers, generators, plug-in hybrids or loads, electric circuit-breakers, switches and control centers, sensors.
3. Cyber component can be used to represents breaker actuator controls.
4. Edges are drawn to represent the state dependency among the various components.

Cyber-attack is attempted for tampering the sensor s3 effecting control centre's load management decisions.

The corresponding graph of the above figure is as below.

Attack A is targeting the sensor s3.

Figure 3. Diagram for the elementary power system

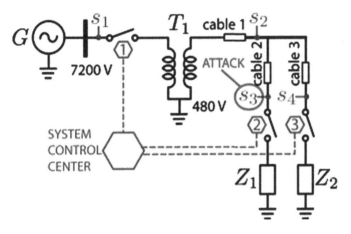

Figure 4. Nodes are combination of a cables, a transformer T, circuit breakers Bi, generator G and loads Zi of the power network and a sensors si, control centre cc and actuator controls ci of the cyber-space network. The cyber graph is distinguishable with dashed edges and shaded nodes

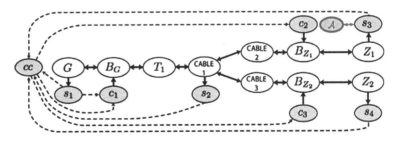

3M ARCHITECTURE FOR CYBER PHYSICAL SYSTEMS - AN INTRODUCTION

Since the cyber physical systems is envisioned as a combination of public services, transportation and communication systems and energy and all are interlinked with each other. The interdependency among these systems may impose the basis of influence on estimating and analysing the post effect of coordinated attack on the cyber physical system and thus is becomes essential to understand the operation of the heterogeneous infrastructures as a single combined unit. So, Xing et al. (2019) proposed a novel 3M architectural i.e. multi-level, multi-layer, multi-agent approach is adduced to enable flexible modelling of the interconnected components of the system. Using this 3M architecture, the energy, transportation and communication system can be studied as a whole and the interdependencies can be cyber, physical or logical, and both internal and external in nature.

In the energy domain, the various components will communicate among themselves to achieve stable and most economic operations of the smart grid. While in the transportation area, various components will interact with each other to accomplish a good traffic condition. Communication domain works as a backbone infrastructure to facilitate the communication among these areas. Since the post effect of the attack may be cascading in nature and thus lead to severe blackout so the interdependency of different domain represented by this model can be used while estimating the consequence arises. So the interdependency can be understood with modelling of system agent model (energy, transport, communication), block layer (that reflects the communication interface of the different system agents in a block) and community layer (connects different numbers of blocks. According to the 3M approach, various blocks are connected through the power lines and the communicative roads).

Cyber Security Countermeasures

In this section, authors present some widely accepted countermeasures that could be taken against the various attacks as stated in the previous section. As the smart grid security goals is identified as confidentiality, integrity, availability, authenticity, authorization, and non-repudiation. The different scenario for the security threat can be classified as security threat for smart grid or the smart home, security threat for smart home to the smart grid and security threat from smart grid to the smart home communication link. The below table would state the categorical representation of these defined security domains:

Figure 5. Energy, Transportation and communication system using 3M architecture representation

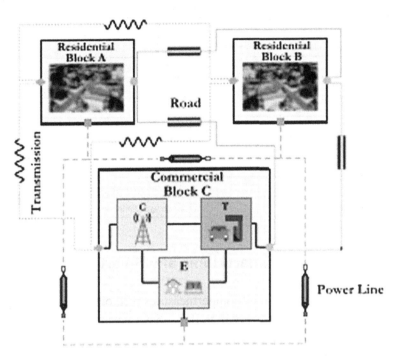

Table 1. Smart home security issues

Smart Home Security Issues	
Possible threat	Security Goal compromised
Eavesdropping	confidentiality
Traffic analysis	Integrity
Modification of message	Authenticity
Replay Attack	Authenticity
Tempering/Reversal/Metcr removal/	Authenticity
Modification of Illegal software /updates	Integrity
Customer Imitation	Integrity
Device Imitation	Integrity
Interception	Authenticity

Table 2. Smart grid security issues

Smart Grid Security Issues	
Publicly Available Information	confidentiality
Configuration of Weaker platform	Integrity
Malware	Authorization
Attack from inside	Authenticity
Message fabrication	Authenticity
Reply attack	Authenticity
Fiddling with system files	Authenticity
Man in the Middle	Availability
Denial of Service	Authenticity, Authorization
False data injection attack	Integrity, Availability

Countermeasures for Smart Home and Smart Grid

The authors suggest analysing the countermeasures methods for the smart grid and smart home cyber physical security in to three major category and those are:

1. Ensuring authenticity, integrity, and Non-repudiation
2. Ensuring privacy and confidentiality
3. Ensuring availability

The detail description of each of the above stated methodology is as follows:

Ensuring Authenticity, Integrity and Non-Repudiation

Ensuring the data integrity and authenticity of the user's data for the smart grid/ smart home is very crucial phenomenon regardless of the degree of the privacy for a particular device. This section covers the techniques to ensure these objectives.

- **Ensuring Integrity**: Commonly in use methods to ensure integrity like cryptographic hashing formulated for the assurance of high integrity for the communication system may also be enforced for the smart grid also provide they are less computationally expensive in practicality and do not introduce restrictive delays. With this legacy method, sender uses the hash function to calculate checksum and attach it to originally generated message and the same hash function is applied by receiver to the message and compares the resulting hash to attach in the original message and thus ensuring the integrity of the message.

From the Smart Grid perspective, the attack on the integrity is not only confined to message modification but also covers the areas like false data injection attack, replay attack and device impersonation attack. Another low-cost technique called lightweight digital watermarking is a simple and effective way to ensure the False Data Injection attack. This technique will embed the digital data within the real smart meter reading with the watermark holding the unique knowledge about the originator of the reading. Watermark also serves the purpose of validating the integrity of the data. The smart meter sends the watermarked data to the utility company that have already store the watermark with them. So, they could track the FDI attack and validate the integrity of the data too.

- **Ensuring the Non-Repudiation and Authenticity***:* Authenticity always ensures that no compromise is made against the transaction within the smart grid. Authors already discussed about using the hash key cryptographic method to ensure this feature and not limited to this there are some other alternative ways too for this challenging objective. Physically un-cloneable function (PUF) is a module within hardware for achieving the very strong hardware-based authentication of smart meter and effective key management. M. Nabeel, S. Kerr, and E. Bertino, (2012) proposes the PUF that is inexpensive in nature for the manufacturer and to replicate it becomes impossible even though having the exact manufacturing process. Author uses this PUF along with the zero knowledge proof of knowledge protocol (ZKPK) and Pedersen commitment scheme not only to ensure integrity, authenticity and confidentiality but also used it for protecting the Smart Meters secret keys. Using this scheme, non-repudiation can also be verified and targeted if the sender asks an acknowledgement endorsed from the receiver, verifying it actually received the message.

Ensuring Privacy and Confidentiality

Since the inception of smart grid, deployment of multivendor and different IoT devices impose numerous concerns for being potentially privacy invasive. For example, by analysing the consumed data collected from smart meters can disclose a lot about the activities, habits and behaviour of the consumers within a locality, thus become the cause of the customers fear. There are various options to ensure the privacy of the customers and some of these techniques are introduced as is:

- **Trusted Aggregators:** To manage the collection of metering data and its safe forwarding mechanism to the utility company, a trusted third party. Utility company in such scenario can use only the aggregation of data and cannot access the individual consumption data of users.
- **Anonymization:** This process is to remove the linkage between the data and its originator. So, the utility company can see the data for computation but can't see the mapping between data and its originated meter.
- **Homomorphic Encryption:** This is an encryption technique where specific computation is applied on the cipher text and obtains the result in encrypted form while decryption process matches the result of the operation performed on the plain text. By adopting this mechanism, the utility company can decrypt the cipher text of the metering data in aggregated form but not the individual meter data of plain text.
- **Verifiable Computation Models:** Under this scheme, the aggregator gives the substantial evidence with the aggregate reading of the metering data for the calculation that has been performed with the metering data. The mechanism of providing the proof is through zero knowledge proof system, with the system where smart meter being worked as the prover and the utility as the verifier. In such mechanism the verifier only certify that the prover has the information that it claims and nothing else.

Ensuring Availability

Security requirement of the day to day communication network is based on the Confidentiality, Integrity and Availability triad and of course the order of it has not any specific meaning. But when it applies to the smart grid cyber physical security perspective, major stakeholders view and recommendation is that the triad should be given priority as Availability, Integrity, Confidentiality (AIC) so that this ordering clearly shows that availability is the most important outcome to achieve followed by integrity and confidentiality. Potential attack categorization under this category is the DoS, FDI and Jamming attack. FDI attack countermeasure has been already discussed by authors in the first section i.e. ensuring Integrity.

DEFENCE AGAINST CP ATTACK

After the extensive investigations based on the potential cyber-physical attack schemes, smart grid operators would establish appropriate defence mechanism those are majorly orchestrated in to three consecutive stages such as protection, detection and mitigation. The section presents the authors review on generic attack mechanism against cyber-physical attack.

Protection

To protect the critical infrastructure against the vulnerabilities, it is essential to define new mechanism and security techniques that may disdain (Kim, Kwon, Kim, Cheon, Ju, Lim, & Choi, 2011):

- Key generation mechanism and device provisioning without being exposed.
- Device sync up and bootstrap process to make them authenticate through the network as well as key sharing mechanism among the devices before they start the data exchange.
- Securing sharing and data transmission.
- To handle the discarded and obsolete devices, key revocation mechanism used to prevent points of failure and thus reducing the scope of DoS attack against central control points.

Researchers proposed (Vukovic, Sou, Dán, & Sandberg, 2012) a mathematical foundation in accordance with topologies and different electrical parameter of the smart grid in case of coordinated cyber physical attack. A bi-level model is proposed to investigate the relation between adversary and the control centre with an objective function to maximize the number of overloaded transmission lines. Based on the output investigation given by this bi-level model, researchers proposed the countermeasure to protect the smart grid against coordinated attack in tri level model with one leader with its multiple followers.

Detection

Proposing a countermeasure for the attack is purely depends on how effective the detection mechanism is applied on the system so that even the most sophisticated attacks do not go unnoticed. This section explains the latest attack detection techniques for the attack like cyber-physical coordinated attack, DoS attack and reply attack.

Cyber-Physical Coordinated Attack

The most damaging coordinated cyber physical attack can be investigated by transforming the bi level model, as explained in section 12.1, to the single mixed-integer linear programming problem with the use of Karush-Kuhn-Tucker conditions (Vukovic, Sou, Dán, & Sandberg, 2012). The step for the bi-level programming model is as:

- Identify the injected data into the measurement.
- Identify the topology and reactance parameter of the smart grid.
- Formulate the relationship between injected data and parameter under coordinated cyber physical attack.
- A bi-level programming model is developed to find the most critical attack corresponding to a particular transmission line.
- Karush-Kuhn-Tucker conditions are being used for the transformation of the bi-level model to single mixed-integer linear programming problem.

DoS Attack

DoS is considered as a single source of attacks in the smart grid distributed environment. For applying the appropriate countermeasure, the detection of DoS is necessary. So, from the IT security perspective, detection methods like flow entropy, signal strength, sensing time measurement, counting the transmission failure etc. have been explored to identify the DoS attack. So, for the countermeasure techniques proposed accordingly are pushback, rate-limiting, filter, reconfiguration, and clean centre approach (Shapsough, Qatan, Aburukba, Aloul, & Al Ali, 2015).

Replay Attack

Researchers proposed in (Miao, Pajic, & Pappas, 2013) an optimized control policy for selection between secure (but cost-suboptimal) controllers and control-cost optimal (but non secure) in presence of replay attacks and thus demonstrated a zero-sum,, finite horizon, non-stationary stochastic game theory paradigm to minimize the worst-case control and cost consumed for the detection. By combining the finite horizon stationary stochastic game algorithm and robust game techniques, a suboptimal algorithm is proposed and is utilized to calculate the system's strategy. So, in accordance with the system dynamic manner, the security overhead and control performance for the replay attack is balanced.

Mitigation

After the clear attack signal detected, the mitigation plan immediate comes in to effect to minimise the potential damage done to the system. In case the attack is successfully cleared from the system, the existing restoration and mitigation strategies is sufficient enough to resume the power system completely. However, in case the threat caused by attack is not resolved, the control centre has to make persistent malicious effort in the system. This is considered as an interactive scenario where the mitigation strategy is modelled as game theoretic approach or bi-level optimization problem.

(Chen, Dong, & Hill, 2011) developed an attacker defender game against the generic attack on the different component of the power infrastructure. (Chen, Cheng, & Chen, 2012) proposed a zero sum game between a system operator and an informed cyber-attacker under the condition of different network configurations. (Ma, Yau, Lou, & Rao, 2013a) proposed a strategy based on zero-sum Markov game and is used to cheat an attacker through a kind of misinformation to reduce the damage caused by attack. Later on based on this theory (Ma, Yau, Lou, & Rao, 2013b) worked and proposed a scalable solution to effectively induce the mitigation plan on the system.

CONNECTING THE GAP: CYBER-PHYSICAL SYSTEM SECURITY

The section deals with "Connecting the gap: cyber-physical system security" that states that in spite of significant work for the cyber physical security, this field as a whole is often addressed in disjoint fashion. A framework needed to counter such situation should be efficient enough to handle the situation such as by making changes in the security property of either cyber of physical subcomponent will change the affects the security parameter of whole system and its component. Due to lack of expert who is well versed with cyber and system both, this is of utmost important to have a unified framework that have a common language to address the problems for the cyber and physical system security. So, a common framework that takes the accountability theory for the control and computational system for the information flow will give the generic foundation to evolve a theory that encapsulate the elements from cyber and physical system simultaneously.

CONCLUSION

Smart grid, Smart sensors and IoT technologies have produced enormous amount of big data that lead to new challenges and opportunities to the critical infrastructure and energy systems (Perez, Zeadally, & Pear, 2017) introduced a new formal protection model for data privacy called l-diversity that can shield against attacks and studied the scenario where there is very little diversity in sensitive attributes and less background knowledge of attackers is available. The Machine learning models have become popular to deal with big data in the constructive use for attack estimation, informed decision-making and efficient modeling for the critical infrastructure resilience in case of contingency reported.

Machine learning models presented by Mosavi et al. (2019) in critical infrastructure as the state of the art of identified 10 different groups of most popular machine learning algorithms for model building in critical infrastructure, i.e., MLP ANN, ANFIS, ELM, SVM, WNN, decision trees, ensembles, deep learning, and advanced hybrid ML models. Diverse applications of each ML models have been analyzed showing the popularity and effectiveness of ML models almost in security handling scenario of energy domain. (Handa, Sharma, & Shukla, 2019) demonstrate that how Machine learning algorithms provide a solution to various cyber-attack detection problems like detection of intrusions, malware detection, and most importantly addressing the security issues pertaining to Critical Infrastructure like intrusion detection in SCADA systems, power system security, intrusion detection for VANET, industrial control systems, etc. The solution strategies for security issues involve effective and efficient training and as a consequence, classification of data in huge volumes. Though the existence of potential adversarial attacker who can play and evade such tools by manipulating the classifiers is a very growing concern. In this chapter some approaches that have been used by adversaries to threat current defense procedure against cyber-attacks is presented and the overall goal of the chapter is to create awareness on latest technological techniques in cyber security for Critical Infrastructure.

REFERENCES

Flick, T. & Morehouse, J. (2011). Attacking the utility companies in securing the Smart Grid. In Securing the smart grid: next generation power grid security (pp. 109-142). EPDF. doi:10.1016/B978-1-59749-570-7.00007-8

Butun, I., Morgera, S. D., & Sankar, R. (2014). A survey of intrusion detection systems in wireless sensor networks. *IEEE Communications Surveys and Tutorials*, *16*(1), 266–282. doi:10.1109/SURV.2013.050113.00191

Chakhchoukh, Y., & Ishii, H. (2014). Coordinated cyber-attacks on the measurement function in hybrid state estimation. IEEE transactions on power systems, 30(5), 2487-2497. doi:10.1109/TPWRS.2014.2357182

Chen, G., Dong, Z. Y., Hill, D. J., & Xue, Y. S. (2010). Exploring reliable strategies for defending power systems against targeted attacks. *IEEE Transactions on Power Systems*, *26*(3), 1000–1009. doi:10.1109/TPWRS.2010.2078524

Chen, P. Y., Cheng, S. M., & Chen, K. C. (2012). Smart attacks in smart grid communication networks. *IEEE Communications Magazine*, *50*(8), 24–29. doi:10.1109/MCOM.2012.6257523

Davoli, L., Belli, L., Veltri, L. & Ferrari, G. (2017). THORIN: an Efficient Module for Federated Access and Threat Mitigation in Big Stream Cloud Architectures. *IEEE Cloud Computing*. doi:. doi:10.1109/MCC.2017.455155318

Fan, Y., Zhang, Z., Trinkle, M., Dimitrovski, A. D., Song, J. B., & Li, H. (2014). A cross-layer defense mechanism against GPS spoofing attacks on PMUs in smart grids. *IEEE Transactions on Smart Grid*, *6*(6), 2659–2668. doi:10.1109/TSG.2014.2346088

Grochocki, D., Ho Huh, J., Berthier, R., Bobba, R., Sanders, W., Cardenas, A., & Jetcheva, G. (2012). AMI threats, intrusion detection requirements and deployment recommendations. In *Proceedings of the 2012 IEEE 3rd International Conference on Smart Grid Communications, SmartGridComm 2012* (pp. 395-400). IEEE Press. doi:10.1109/SmartGridComm.2012.6486016

Handa, A., Sharma, A., & Shukla, S. K. (2019). Machine learning in cybersecurity: A review. *Wiley Interdisciplinary Reviews. Data Mining and Knowledge Discovery*, *9*(4).

He, H., & Yan, J. (2016). Cyber-physical attacks and defences in the smart grid: a survey. IET Cyber-Physical Systems: Theory & Applications, 1(1), 13-27.

Jiang, X., Zhang, J., Harding, B. J., Makela, J. J., & Domı, A. D. (2013). Spoofing GPS receiver clock offset of phasor measurement units. *IEEE Transactions on Power Systems*, *28*(3), 3253–3262. doi:10.1109/TPWRS.2013.2240706

Kezunovic, M., Meliopoulos, S., Venkatasubramanian, V., & Vittal, V. (2014). *Application of time-synchronized measurements in power system transmission networks*. Springer; doi:10.1007/978-3-319-06218-1

Kim, J., & Tong, L. (2013). On topology attack of a smart grid: Undetectable attacks and countermeasures. *IEEE Journal on Selected Areas in Communications*, *31*(7), 1294–1305. doi:10.1109/JSAC.2013.130712

Kim, S., Young Kwon, E., Kim, M., Hee Cheon, J., Ju, S. H., Lim, Y. H., & Choi, M.-S. (2011). A Secure Smart-Metering Protocol Over Power-Line Communication. *IEEE Transactions on Power Delivery*, *26*(4), 2370–2379. doi:10.1109/TPWRD.2011.2158671

Komninos, N., Philippou, E., & Pitsillides, A. (2014). Survey in Smart Grid and Smart Home Security: Issues, Challenges and Countermeasures. *IEEE Communications Surveys and Tutorials*, *16*(4), 1933–1954. doi:10.1109/COMST.2014.2320093

D. Kundur, X. Feng, S. Mashayekh, S. Liu, T. Zourntos, K.L. Butler-Purry.(2011). Towards modeling the impact of cyber attack on a smart grid. *International Journal of Security and Networks (USN) special issue on security and privacy in smart grids, 6*(1), 2-13.

Li, H., & Zhang, W. (2010, December). QoS routing in smart grid. In *Proceedings of the 2010 IEEE Global Telecommunications Conference GLOBECOM 2010* (pp. 1-6). IEEE.

Liang, G., Zhao, J., Luo, F., Weller, S. R., & Dong, Z. Y. (2016). A review of false data injection attacks against modern power systems. *IEEE Transactions on Smart Grid, 8*(4), 1630–1638. doi:10.1109/TSG.2015.2495133

Liu, Y., Ning, P., & Reiter, M. (2011). False data injection attacks against state estimation in electric power grids. *ACM Transactions on Information and System Security, 14*(1), 13. doi:10.1145/1952982.1952995

Lu, X., Hinkelman, K., Fu, Y., Wang, J., Zuo, W., Zhang, Q., & Saad, W. (2019). An Open Source Modeling Framework for Interdependent Energy-Transportation-Communication Infrastructure in Smart and Connected Communities. *IEEE Access : Practical Innovations, Open Solutions, 7*, 55458–55476. doi:10.1109/ACCESS.2019.2913630

Ma, C. Y., Yau, D. K., Lou, X., & Rao, N. S. (2012). Markov game analysis for attack-defense of power networks under possible misinformation. *IEEE Transactions on Power Systems, 28*(2), 1676–1686. doi:10.1109/TPWRS.2012.2226480

Ma, C. Y., Yau, D. K., & Rao, N. S. (2013). Scalable solutions of Markov games for smart-grid infrastructure protection. *IEEE Transactions on Smart Grid, 4*(1), 47–55. doi:10.1109/TSG.2012.2223243

Meng, T., Cui, M., Dong, Z., Wang, X., Yin, G., & Zhao, L. (2019). Multilevel Programming-Based Coordinated Cyber Physical Attacks and Countermeasures in Smart Grid. *IEEE Access : Practical Innovations, Open Solutions*. doi:10.1109/ACCESS.2018.2890604

Miao, F., Pajic, M., & Pappas, G. J. (2013, December). Stochastic game approach for replay attack detection. In *Proceedings of the 52nd IEEE conference on decision and control* (pp. 1854-1859). IEEE. doi:10.1109/CDC.2013.6760152

Mo, Y., Kim, T. H. J., Brancik, K., Dickinson, D., Lee, H., Perrig, A., & Sinopoli, B. (2011). Cyber–physical security of a smart grid infrastructure. *Proceedings of the IEEE, 100*(1), 195–209. doi:10.1109/JPROC.2011.2161428

Morison, K., Wang, L., & Kundur, P. (2004). Power system security assessment. *IEEE Power & Energy Magazine, 2*(5), 30–39. doi:10.1109/MPAE.2004.1338120

Mosavi, A., Salimi, M., Faizollahzadeh Ardabili, S., Rabczuk, T., Shamshirband, S., & Varkonyi-Koczy, A. R. (2019). State of the art of machine learning models in energy systems, a systematic review. *Energies, 12*(7), 1301. doi:10.3390/en12071301

Nabeel, M., Kerr, S., & Bertino, E. (2012). Authentication and key management for advanced metering infrastructures utilizing physically unclonable functions. In *Proc. IEEE Third Int. Conf. SmartGridComm* (pp. 324–329). IEEE Press. 10.1109/SmartGridComm.2012.6486004

National Institute of Standards and Technology. (2014). Framework for Improving Critical Infrastructure Cybersecurity, Version 1.0.

Pal, S., Sikdar, B., & Chow, J. H. (2016). An online mechanism for detection of gray-hole attacks on PMU data. *IEEE Transactions on Smart Grid, 9*(4), 2498–2507. doi:10.1109/TSG.2016.2614327

Pandey, R. K., & Misra, M. (2016, December). Cyber security threats—Smart grid infrastructure. In *Proceedings of the 2016 National Power Systems Conference (NPSC)* (pp. 1-6). IEEE. doi:10.1109/NPSC.2016.7858950

Perez, A. J., & Zeadally, S. PEAR: A privacy-enabled architecture for crowdsensing. In *Proceedings of the International Conference on Research in Adaptive and Convergent Systems* (pp. 166–171). Academic Press. 10.1145/3129676.3129685

Rouhani, A., & Abur, A. (2016). Linear phasor estimator assisted dynamic state estimation. *IEEE Transactions on Smart Grid, 9*(1), 211–219. doi:10.1109/TSG.2016.2548244

Saponara, S., & Tony, B. (2012). Network architecture, security issues, and hardware implementation of a home area network for Smart Grid. *Journal of Computer Networks and Communications*, 1–19. doi:10.1155/2012/534512

Shapsough, S., Qatan, F., Aburukba, R., Aloul, F., & Al Ali, A. R. (2015, October). Smart grid cyber security: Challenges and solutions. In *Proceedings of the 2015 international conference on smart grid and clean energy technologies (ICSGCE)* (pp. 170-175). IEEE. 10.1109/ICSGCE.2015.7454291

Singh, A. K., & Misra, A. K. (2012). Analysis of Cryptographically Replay Attacks and Its Mitigation Mechanism. In *Proceedings of the International Conference on Information Systems Design and Intelligent Applications 2012 (INDIA 2012)* (pp. 787-794). Springer, Berlin, Heidelberg. doi:10.1007/978-3-642-27443-5_90

Sridhar, S., Hahn, A., & Govindarasu, M. (2012). Cyber–physical system security for the electric power grid. *Proceedings of the IEEE, 100*(1), 210–224. doi:10.1109/JPROC.2011.2165269

Tourani, R., Misra, S., Mick, T., Brahma, S., Biswal, M., & Ameme, D. (2016, November). iCenS: An information-centric smart grid network architecture. In *Proceedings of the 2016 IEEE International Conference on Smart Grid Communications (SmartGridComm)* (pp. 417-422). IEEE Press. doi:10.1109/SmartGridComm.2016.7778797

Vukovic, O., Sou, K. C., Dan, G., & Sandberg, H. (2012). Network-aware mitigation of data integrity attacks on power system state estimation. *IEEE Journal on Selected Areas in Communications, 30*(6), 1108–1118. doi:10.1109/JSAC.2012.120709

Wang, Y., & Chakrabortty, A. (2016, July). Distributed monitoring of wide-area oscillations in the presence of GPS spoofing attacks. In *Proceedings of the 2016 IEEE Power and Energy Society General Meeting (PESGM)* (pp. 1-5). IEEE. doi:10.1109/PESGM.2016.7741175

Yang, D., Usynin, A., & Hines, J. W. (2006, November). Anomaly-based intrusion detection for SCADA systems. In *Proceedings of the 5th intl. topical meeting on nuclear plant instrumentation, control and human machine interface technologies* (NPIC&HMIT 05) (pp. 12-16). Academic Press. doi:10.1109/GLOCOM.2010.5683884

Yang, Q., Chang, L., & Yu, W. (2013). On false data injection attacks against Kalman filtering in power system dynamic state estimation. *Security and Communication Networks, 9*(9), 833–849. doi:10.1002ec.835

Yi, T., Wang, Q., Tai, W., Ni, M. (2018). A Review of the False Data Injection Attack Against the Cyber Physical Power System. *IET Cyber-Physical Systems: Theory & Applications*. doi:10.1049/iet-cps.2018.5022

Zhang, Z., Gong, S., Dimitrovski, A., & Li, H. (2012). Time Synchronization Attack in Smart Grid: Impact and Analysis. *IEEE Transactions on Smart Grid, 4(1)*. doi:10.1109/TSG.2012.2227342

Chapter 8

Cryptography in the Healthcare Sector With Modernized Cyber Security

Prisilla Jayanthi
 https://orcid.org/0000-0002-4961-9010
K. G. Reddy College of Engineering and Technology, Hyderabad, India

Muralikrishna Iyyanki
Defence Research and Development Organisation, India

ABSTRACT

Cryptography is an indispensable tool used to protect information in any organization; providing secure transmission over the Internet. The major challenge faced by health-sector is data security, and to overcome this several advancements in medicine and biomedical research have proven to increase computer processing in data security. The study focuses on cryptography, the most emerging field in computer industries. Both artificial intelligence and quantum technology are both transforming the health sector in regard to cybersecurity. In this study, the AES algorithm is a cryptographic cipher used. One such application is implemented and is responsible for handling a large amount of the information in the health sector. An application with a double Hashing algorithm is accomplished to can maintain the data in a secure fashion.

DOI: 10.4018/978-1-7998-2253-0.ch008

INTRODUCTION

Grand View Research Inc. in a statement announced by that "the global healthcare biometric market is expected to reach USD 14.5 billion by 2025." In this regard, an insistent for Electronic Health Records (EHR) was raised by health system and hospitals. Hence the need to computerize the health databases drives an insistent for healthcare biometrics over the prognosis term of the patient. The concern is over protecting the data from intruders and reduces fraud for providers and financiers by payment collection through automated process, and increases patient contentment.

The science of shielding confidential information from unauthorized access, by making sure about data integrity and authentication is cryptography. The technique of hashing makes it more indispensable for ensuring that the transmitted messages will not be tampered. The concept of fingerprints, facial recognition and iris recognition are techniques derived from Artificial Intelligence. In this chapter Advanced Encryption Standard (AES) algorithm and blockchain (BC) are discussed to understand the need to safeguard and protect the electronic health data in more secure manner.

The protection of data is required at every phase; the three phases of data shown in figure 1 are: 1. data in action; 2. data in use; and 3. data at rest. The data in action is the one which moves across the various networks, from system to system placed at various locations. The data in use is frequently updated and altered on usage.

Figure 1. Data in three phases

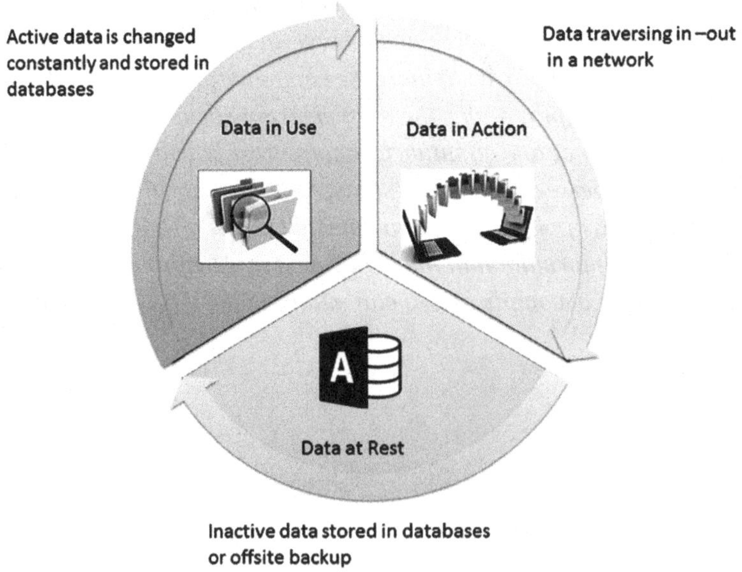

Active data is changed constantly and stored in databases

Data traversing in –out in a network

Data in Use

Data in Action

Data at Rest

Inactive data stored in databases or offsite backup

The data at rest is the huge one with volume increasing day-to-day and becomes a concern to businesses, government agencies and any other organization. The data is kept unused and inactive for longer time. Most of theft takes place on the data stored as backup. Hence, encrypting the data in every phase is essential.

NECESSITY OF CRYPTOGRAPHY IN HEALTHCARE

For any database which contains digital data, the need for data security is very essential for protecting data from any unauthorized users. Data stored on disk for longer period of time must be protected using disk encryption method known as on-the-fly encryption. Implementing hardware device security to such long-time data storage prevent malicious users or a data breach. One such application of hardware security is biometric technique which prevents malicious users from logging in, logging out and/ or tampering the privileges and is implemented in this chapter.

Authentication is verifying the user's identity. It has two phases - identification and actual authentication. In identification phase, any individual's identity is provided in the scheme of a user ID to the security system. The security system examines all the abstract objects and maps the actual user, and grants permission. This is carried out when the user provides indication to prove the specification to the system. The authentication phase involves claiming of user identity by checking user-provided evidence.

Encryption is the technique of encoding a message or information in which only approved parties can access it. The algorithm generates pseudo-random encryption key. The two encryptions used are symmetric and asymmetric encryption. In symmetric, the encryption and decryption keys are the same. Communicating groups use the same key for secure communication. In asymmetric, the encryption key is published for anyone (publicly) and receiving team has the access to read the messages using the decryption key known as private key.

The encryption of data at rest uses AES or RSA (Rivest–Shamir–Adleman) algorithms. Cryptography will be implemented on the database housing the data on the physical storage. In this case study, AES is implemented on the Electronic Health Record databases.

Biometric in Industries

Biometric is a part of security in any industries as it gives the measurement and numerical analysis of person's unique physical and behavioral characteristics. For identifying any individual, biometric can be used for proof of identity and right of control, the one under surveillance. One can find it difficult for breaking into a system with biometrics. The device measures unique features of a person, such as voice pattern, the iris, or fingerprint patterns. The biometric is broadly classified into two categories such as physiological and behavioral where face recognition, fingerprints, hand / palm, iris identification, DNA falls into the physiological categories. The keystroke, signature, and voice pattern fall under behavioral categories shown in figure 2.

Voice Print

As the growing population needs a secure means for settling the disbursement, in and around the workplace, people found more comfortable with biometrics. One such biometric is voice authentication, which discovers wider expansion across trading activity, including healthcare, financing companies, and educational system. Voice recognition systems monitor the rhythm and accent, in addition indicates the structure of the larynx, nostril passage, and person's vocal tract, to identify and validate an individual.

(Chinnaswamy, 2018) discusses about the voice recognition system capturing the voices by sound tracking the name, age, address, and a set of secret sound notes and analyzes the speech and breathing patterns and stores it. Further the voice print is encrypted and stored in the Active Directory in user's authentication data, along with

Figure 2. Types of biometric for human identification

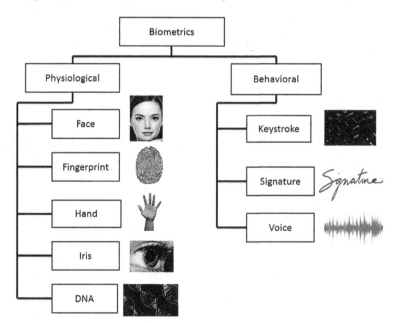

added authentication credentials. When a person signs up for voice authentication calls, the voice is coordinated with the voice print stored in the Active Directory, ensuing in speedy and unified verification. This voiceprint recognition system is referred as a Speaker Recognition System (SRS).

In a case study on voice prints suggested that each individual's voice will be different because the structure of the vocal cords, vocal cavity, oral and nostril cavities is unique to every individual. Later the comparison of two recorded speeches is carried out by spectrogram or the voice prints for the identification purpose are called as voice fingerprinting. The person's voice changes over time of the individual aging; at time due to stress, illness and alcoholism. The person's accent may also vary as they move from one region to another. The best saying "garbage in, garbage out" - garbage may come from various background similar to the sounds such as trouble-some voices, music, or any machine noise that adds to the internal voice while recording. If data received are unclear, analyzer produces conclusions that are incorrect as described (Parmar & Udhayabanu, 2012).

Fingerprints and Facial Recognition

The biometric inputs for fingerprints and face identity results proved their results accurately on the image quality received. Figure 3 represents how the fingerprints are scanned for the biometric and later stored in the form of matrix of 1's and 0's. This matrix is stored for further use of the security need which is implemented on regular source. The data captured is encrypted using Advanced Encryption Standard algorithm in figure 4 and then stored in the database.

Face recognition is a three-step process. Initiating with the subject picture and making an effort to identify a person in the given image. The system locates the individual's head and eyes. A face signature is developed in matrix form centered on the individual's face characteristics. Comparing this matrix with the database in figure 5 and generating a similar score for each comparison in figure 6.

The biometric system works on two types of comparisons namely verification and identification. The automated facial image quality evaluation software (AFQES) module captures real-time facial image and automated fingerprint identification

Figure 3. The representation of fingerprints in form of 1's and 0's

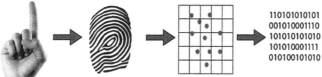

systems (AFIS) module for obtaining fingerprints as discussed (Ko & Krishnan, 2003). The database of the faces of a person is collected in different angles with different moods in figure 5. In this study as only one pose of photo was given, the photos in different angles are shown in the database. The database will consist of doctors, surgeons, and clinicians and other staff of health care center.

(Ablayev et al., 2016) introduced the quantum fingerprinting computational aspects and clarifies the properties of cryptographically quantum hashing, and thereby the possible use of quantum hashing for quantum hash-based message authentication codes is done. (Buhrman et al., 2001) describes about quantum fingerprints in a case study where the entire group analyzed fingerprints using without shared key and shared key. In without shared key requires fingerprints of Θ ($\sqrt{n}$) are sufficient whereas for shared key requires a fingerprints of length (n). Next, the scheme with a shared quantum key of $O(\log n)$ that requires fingerprints of length $O(\log n)$ bits. The condition was relaxed to the error probability of O ($1= n^c$) (where c is constant) with classical keys and fingerprints of length $O(\log n)$.

(ElDahshan et al., 2017) proposed a quantum face authentication method. This method is for face boundaries detection, image resizing, and removal of any noise, feature extraction, matching and decision. Also the method used QFWT (Quantum Fast Wavelet Transform) and QFT (Quantum Fourier Transform) in extraction phase.

In this study, the doctor's photos were taken for face recognition and are authenticated for accessing the electronic health records. The faces and eyes in the photos are identified by the square block using the software python code on Spyder, a cross-platform shown in figure 7 and figure 8.

Figure 4. Implementation of AES algorithm for fingerprints

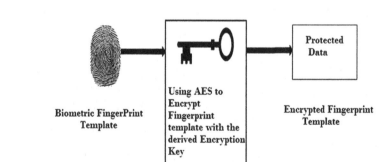

Figure 5. Sample set of facial database

Figure 6. Cipher facial recognition database

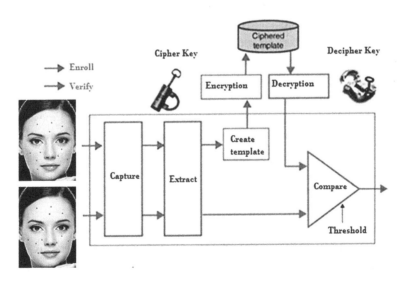

Figure 7. Authenticated doctors after face recognition

Figure 8. Iris detection

CRYPTOGRAPHY: QUANTUM TECHNOLOGY- QUANTUM KEY

Cryptography is a technique for secure communication with the third party. The aim of cryptography is that the sender and receiver will communicate with the unintelligible with third parties. This gives an authentication of messages to demonstrate that the data were not altered while in transit. Both the sender and receiver share the secret key which is a random sequence number, a valuable strength for both. Quantum communications makes the secret key distribution possible. The key distribution process is accomplished by quantum cryptography and encrypted message is not transmitted. This is known as quantum key distribution, proposed by (Hughes et al., 1995). The emerging field of physics and engineering is termed as quantum technology, which creates practical applications - such as quantum computing, quantum sensors, quantum cryptography, and quantum simulation. The quantum technology is paving its way in keeping data secure.

Health Sector is the largest source of repository as it consists of all the patients complete information and this huge data is stored on electronic device. This data can be easily attacked by any active attacker, lost, stolen or data breaches. The health records have family name, addresses, state and ZIP code, social security number / Aadhaar card number/ pan card number, email addresses, phone numbers and insurance policy ID numbers, among the general information provided by the patients shown in figure 9.

Figure 9. Electronic health record for patient entries

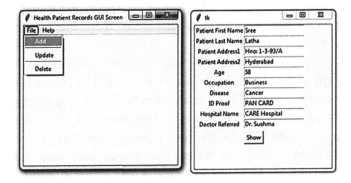

Figure 10. Health Records in encrypted form

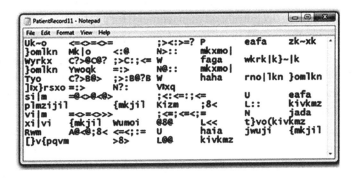

The figure 10 shows the encrypted data of the health record at healthcare center. This healthcare data is a precious and is prey for the ransomware, spear phishing attacks or any other attacks.

BLOCKCHAIN – INDUSTRIES – HEALTHCARE

An increasing list of records, named as blocks are interconnected using cryptography is known as blockchain (BC). Every individual block comprises of the following: a cryptographic hash of the preceding block, a timestamp, and transaction data. As the number of applications of BC technology is increasing rapidly, the knowledge in realization of the technology and its potentials is accordingly extreme. The potential for dramatic change in the society with the developments and implementation of BC includes improvements in the healthcare information exchange. BC characteristics are its nature of de-centralization, openness and lesser privilege for permission that offer a unique solution for any industry but here in this context it is healthcare. The development of cryptocurrencies drives current usage by reaching global greater than 20 million users; in the other areas, the use of BC is growing was discussed (Prokofieva & Miah, 2019).

Several BC facilities in integrating and encrypting digital assets comprising of health records or dispensation claims on a ledger. The ledger ensures patient confidentiality and protection of relevant data thereby ensuring regulatory compliance, e.g. HIPAA - Health Insurance Portability and Accountability Act. Medical chain is operational engaged with EHR Blockchain Company, in enabling several healthcare agents, such as doctors, hospitals, testing laboratories, pharmacists, and insurers, for requesting permission to access and interact with patients' medical records.

(Dimitrov, 2019) discusses the personal health records (PHR) service trajectory has an appreciated data source for BC service providers and BCs are good alignment with General Data Protection Regulation (GDPR). As stated earlier, BC have the potentiality for enabling decentralized management; for applications where healthcare stakeholders (e.g., hospitals, patients, and payers) cooperating with one another without the need of an intermediary central management. They provide immutable audit trails; that are suitable for recording unvarying databases for insurance claim. They enable data source and manage patient digital resources. Only the owner has the rights to change. They provide robustness and data availability; preservation and continuous EHR availability. Finally, they enhance the data security and privacy; data is encrypted in BCs and can be decrypted with the patient's private key. Thou the network are infiltrated by a malicious party, there is no concrete way to access the patient data.

The applications of healthcare are redefining data modeling in BC technology. The adaptability and abilities to segment secure and share medical data and services. Many developing industries with BC technology are at the center of healthcare. The blockchain-based healthcare system is organized into four layers that include data sources, BC technology, healthcare applications, and stakeholders.

Figure 11. Block chain healthcare data management

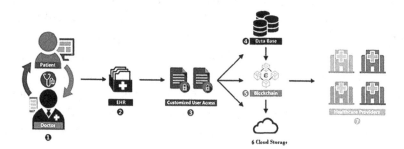

In figure 11, initially the data is generated between the patient and their concerned doctors. The health data comprises of medical history, existing issue/ problem and other related biological information. This medical information is gathered from nursing care, medical imaging, and medication history and pathological investigation to be mentioned in EHR. The patient who has the ownership of EHR, and customized access control is given the ownership. Parties who would like to access any valuable information must seek permission which is advanced to the EHR owner, and the owner will decide to whom access should be granted. The whole healthcare process includes database, BC, and cloud storage shown in the steps 4, 5 and 6.

(Khezr et al., 2019) used database and cloud storage for storing the records in a distributed fashion and BC provides privacy for ensuring customized authentic user access. Healthcare providers such as ad-hoc clinic, community care center, hospitals are the end user who gets access for a safe and sound care delivery which will be authorized by the owner.

(Vora et al., 2018) used the framework based on BC for providing efficient storage and maintenance of EHRs. This provides secure and efficient access of medical data to patients, providers, and third parties, while preserving the patient confidential information. The aim of this study was to analyze how the proposed framework fulfills the patients' needs between the providers and third parties, and thereby understand the framework maintenance regarding the privacy and security concerns in the healthcare 4.0.

In figure 12, a block consists of all the related information of patient is gathered in database as in figure 13 and the transactions are addition, updating and deletion that take place in every patient health record are shown in table 1. This information is further hashed and maintained in the block and again the information is hashed to get a unique and unobtainable number shown in table 2. Such a hashing value cannot be easily broken by any intruders.

The patients details are entered as shown in table 1, and table 2 represents the outcome of the hashing python code. The hashing value will be different for each record entered. And when hashing is carried out the second time, a new random number is generated as shown in table 2. The figure 13 is generated, when the first

Figure 12. The structure of block chain

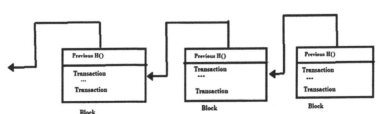

Figure 13. Patient details in a database while hashing

hash is executed. The hashing value will not be the same, each time the code is executed. A new random number is generated, hence this random number cannot be broken that easily by intruders. By using this method, one can save the database of the patient's details in very secure manner and confidential.

Each time a patient record gets added or updated. Then, the record is said to have a transaction when it is finalized. The chaining of blocks is achieved through a cryptographic way that involves the use of hash functions. A hash function takes a message of arbitrary length and crunches it into a hash output of a fixed length, known as a message digest or a digital fingerprint shown in annexure 1 and table 2.

(Knezevic, 2018) stated for any financial transaction, the records will be tracked by BC and can serve to keep confidential information issued and controlled by government agencies. The digital ID through BC is much safer in any technology. The BC- ID permits any person to verify their personal identity, helps in connecting to their families, and exchange money without the need for intermediary banks. While a person's fingerprint is taken with all the related information is linked through BC with other information about the individual (name, gender, nationality). If in case of any verification of the person's identity, the fingerprint unlocks the BC-ID.

Nowadays, in several organizations, Quantum Key Distribution is making a big wave and making it possible. Any two-level quantum system would be used to implement Quantum Cryptography (QC), which is also called quantum encryption. It relates to the quantum mechanics to encrypt messages in a way it is read by anyone outside of the intended recipient. The Shor's algorithm is used in QC and the algorithm is a quantum computer algorithm for integer factorization. If an integer is given the prime factors are found. The algorithm's efficiency is due to the efficiency of the quantum Fourier transform (Nam, 2011 & Fang).

In this approach, a quantum circuit is used for quantum computation which has a sequence of quantum gates, which does reversible transformations on a quantum mechanical analog of an *n*-bit register referred to as an *n*-qubit register (Beauregard, 2003; Wikipedia, n.d.). Shor's algorithm has basically two parts namely classical and

Table 1. Patients details

```
Name: Jyotsna
Age: 40
Weight: 80
Address: Kurnool
Disease: Thyroid Cancer
Enter more data? (y/n): y
Name: Bringanzo
Age: 42
Weight: 87
Address: Hyderabad
Disease: Stomach Ulcer
Enter more data? (y/n): y
Name: Sudheer Kumar
Age: 52
Weight: 67
Address: Secunderabad
Disease: Throat Cancer
Enter more data? (y/n): y
Name: Susheela
Age: 45
Weight: 88
Address: Medak
Disease: Heart Disease
Enter more data? (y/n): y
Name: Sweety
Age: 77
Weight: 80
Address: Bangalore
Disease: Brain Tumor
Enter more data? (y/n): y
Name: Helen
Age: 20
Weight: 70
Address: Karimnagar
Disease: Shoulder Cancer
```

quantum period finding part. The implementation of Shor's algorithm and quantum circuit is carried out to show the secret key generated. This quantum period finding' results are based on the quantum circuit and are shown in figures 14, 15, 16 and 17.

The figure 15 shows the quantum circuit generated and the corresponding GridQubit is shown in figure 14. The circuit can be generated based on the requirement of the length, be it 4, 6, 8 or more. Different combinations are generated and result is produced using a python code shown in figure 15.

Table 2. Patient details with hash values

Name: Jyotsna
Age: 40
Weight: 80
Address: Kurnool
Disease: Thyroid Cancer
dict_keys(['name', 'age', 'weight', 'address', 'disease'])
Keys hash values -8177344308388891750
patient values {FH} → 7017358820209295784
{SH} -> 99829792568213931
Name: Bringanzo
Age: 43
Weight: 87
Address: Hyderabad
Disease: Stomach Ulcer
dict_keys(['name', 'age', 'weight', 'address', 'disease'])
Keys hash values -8177344308388891750
patient values {FH} → -7684213949946050628
{SH}-> -766684922304968775
Name: Sudheer Kumar
Age: 52
Weight: 78
Address: Secunderabad
Disease: Throat Cancer
dict_keys(['name', 'age', 'weight', 'address', 'disease'])
Keys hash values -8177344308388891750
patient values {FH} → -8942438013081472235
{SH} → -2024908985440390382
Name: Sheela Marimam
Age: 45
Weight: 88
Address: Medak
Disease: Heart Disease
dict_keys(['name', 'age', 'weight', 'address', 'disease'])
Keys hash values 8177344308388891750
patient values { FH } → 2487048830996786795
{SH} →2349367120759344459
Name: Sweety
Age: 78
Weight: 80
Address: Bangalore
Disease: Brain Tumor
dict_keys(['name', 'age', 'weight', 'address', 'disease'])
Keys hash values 8177344308388891750
patient values {FH}→ 6140692638140212949
{SH} → 1529006619712825047
Name: Ellen Sushma
Age: 20
Weight: 55
Address: Karimnagar
Disease: Shoulder Cancer
dict_keys(['name', 'age', 'weight', 'address', 'disease'])
Keys hash values 8177344308388891750
patient values {FH}→ 5230373201553129828
{SH} →618687183125741926
All_ dict_keys([]) {HV} 133156838395276
All_values:{HV} 8754152354750935598

*{FH} indicates first hash and {SH} is 2nd hash value, {HV} represents hash value

Figure 14. Defining Qubit values of length = 8

```
[cirq.GridQubit(0, 0), cirq.GridQubit(0, 1), cirq.GridQubit(0, 2), cirq.GridQubit(0, 3), cirq.GridQubit(0, 4), cirq.GridQub
it(0, 5), cirq.GridQubit(0, 6), cirq.GridQubit(0, 7), cirq.GridQubit(1, 0), cirq.GridQubit(1, 1), cirq.GridQubit(1, 2), cir
q.GridQubit(1, 3), cirq.GridQubit(1, 4), cirq.GridQubit(1, 5), cirq.GridQubit(1, 6), cirq.GridQubit(1, 7), cirq.GridQubit
(2, 0), cirq.GridQubit(2, 1), cirq.GridQubit(2, 2), cirq.GridQubit(2, 3), cirq.GridQubit(2, 4), cirq.GridQubit(2, 5), cirq.
GridQubit(2, 6), cirq.GridQubit(2, 7), cirq.GridQubit(3, 0), cirq.GridQubit(3, 1), cirq.GridQubit(3, 2), cirq.GridQubit(3,
3), cirq.GridQubit(3, 4), cirq.GridQubit(3, 5), cirq.GridQubit(3, 6), cirq.GridQubit(3, 7), cirq.GridQubit(4, 0), cirq.Grid
Qubit(4, 1), cirq.GridQubit(4, 2), cirq.GridQubit(4, 3), cirq.GridQubit(4, 4), cirq.GridQubit(4, 5), cirq.GridQubit(4, 6),
cirq.GridQubit(4, 7), cirq.GridQubit(5, 0), cirq.GridQubit(5, 1), cirq.GridQubit(5, 2), cirq.GridQubit(5, 3), cirq.GridQubi
t(5, 4), cirq.GridQubit(5, 5), cirq.GridQubit(5, 6), cirq.GridQubit(5, 7), cirq.GridQubit(6, 0), cirq.GridQubit(6, 1), cir
q.GridQubit(6, 2), cirq.GridQubit(6, 3), cirq.GridQubit(6, 4), cirq.GridQubit(6, 5), cirq.GridQubit(6, 6), cirq.GridQubit
(6, 7), cirq.GridQubit(7, 0), cirq.GridQubit(7, 1), cirq.GridQubit(7, 2), cirq.GridQubit(7, 3), cirq.GridQubit(7, 4), cirq.
GridQubit(7, 5), cirq.GridQubit(7, 6), cirq.GridQubit(7, 7)]
```

Figure 15. Quantum circuit

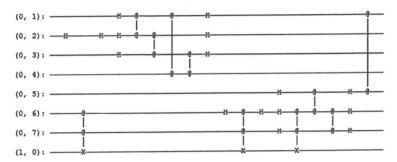

Figure 16 is the key length generated on executing python code. The figure 16 shows the randomly generated key of length equal to 40 for different input values (4, 8) and (8, 10). Figure 17 displays the factors of the Shor's algorithm when N = 4, the factors are 1.0 and 1.0 and for N = 6, the factors are 3.0 and 1.0. The results show that quantum technology is advancing with qubits values. Thereby the quantum cryptography or quantum communication system signifies that they offer virtually unbreakable encryption.

CONCLUSION

In the world of networks, the cryptography plays a significant part for all the data transmitted over the wireless network and how it is stored on any electronic device. In this study the complete implementation of the Advanced Encryption Standard algorithm and hashing technique are used to carry out for handling the security of the electronic health database. But the safety measures should be emphasised for storing and preserving the data for the employees of any industries, as the data can be stolen through malicious programs. To avoid such cases, the implementation of Artificial Intelligence techniques are used. Facial recognition and eye detection are deep learning techniques of AI that helps to verify the authentication of right person

Figure 16a. Outputs of circuit with 40 length key for different input values

```
Circuit:
(4, 8): ——X^0.5——M('m')——
Results:
m=01100000000000100000111001000010100111100
```

Figure 16b. Outputs of circuit with 40 length key for different input values

```
Circuit:
(8, 10): ——X^0.5——M('m')——
Results:
m=001001101010000100011111000000011110101
```

Figure 17a. Shor's algorithm results for N=4 and N=6

```
Enter N4
2 is a trivial factor
gcd 1
r 81
gcd 1
r 81
gcd 1
r 81
gcd 1
r 1
gcd 1
r 81
gcd 1
r 1
gcd 2
r 16
p1 1.0
p2 1.0
N = 1.0 * 1.0

Out[18]: (1.0, 1.0)
```

Figure 17b. Shor's algorithm results for N=4 and N=6

```
Enter N6
2 is a trivial factor
gcd 1
r 1
gcd 3
r 729
gcd 1
r 1
gcd 1
r 1
gcd 1
r 1
gcd 2
r 64
p1 3.0
p2 1.0
N = 3.0 * 1.0

Out[23]:  (3.0, 1.0)
```

to access the database, in this case study doctors of the healthcare sector can only access the data. Hence, the health database is secured with cryptographic cipher, a concept of quantum cryptography is used from being tampered or stolen.

ACKNOWLEDGMENT

The authors would like to thank all the doctors for sharing their photos for the face recognition work to be carried out in this study.

1. Dr. Veena Acharya is a senior Gynecologist at Jaipur Hospital and is associated with NARCHI.
2. Dr. Priya Yenebere is Nephrologist at Chicago.
3. Dr. Sadhana Agrawal is Cancer Immunologist at AIIMS, New Delhi.
4. Dr. Chandana Gandam is Physiotherapist at New Jersey.

REFERENCES

Ablayev, F., Ablayev, M., Vasiliev, A., & Ziatdinov, M. (2016). Quantum Fingerprinting and Quantum Hashing Computational and Cryptographical Aspects. *Baltic J. Modern Computing.*, *4*(4), 860–875.

Beauregard, S. (2003). Circuit for Shor's algorithm using 2n+3 qubits. *Quantum Information & Computation*, *3*(2), 175–185.

Buhrman, H. Cleve, R. Watrous, J. & Wolf, R. (2001), Quantum Fingerprinting. doi:10.1103/PhysRevLett.87.167902

Chinnaswamy, S. (2018). The Future is Calling: Using Voice Recognition for Authentication. TCS. Retrieved from https://www.tcs.com/blogs/using-voice-recognition-for-authentication

Wikipedia. (n.d.a). Cirq Documentation. Retrieved from https://en.wikipedia.org

Dimitrov, D. V. (2019). Blockchain Applications for Healthcare Data Management. *Healthcare Informatics Research*, *25*(1), 51–56.

ElDahshan, K. A., Elsayed, E. K., Aboshoha, A., & Ebeid, A. E. (2017). Applying Quantum Algorithms for Enhancing Face Authentication. *Al Azhar Bulletin of Science*, *9*, 83–93.

Hughes, R. J., Alde, D. M., Dyer, P., Luther, G. G., Morgan, G. L., & Schauer, M. (1995). Quantum cryptography. *Contemporary Physics*, *36*(3), 149–163.

Khezr, S., Moniruzzaman, M., Yassine, A., & Benlamri, R. (2019). Blockchain Technology in Healthcare: A Comprehensive Review and Directions for Future Research. Applied Sciences, 9(9), 1736. doi:10.3390/app9091736

Knezevic, D. (2018). Impact of Blockchain Technology Platform in Changing the Financial Sector and Other Industries. *Montenegrin Journal of Economics*, *14*(1), 109–120. doi:10.14254/1800-5845/2018.14-1.8

Ko, T., & Krishnan, R. (2003). Fingerprint and Face Identification for Large User Population. *Systemic. Cybernetics and Informatics*, *1*(3), 87–92.

Korolov, M., & Doug, D. (2019). What is quantum cryptography? It's no silver bullet, but could improve security. CSO Online. Retrieved from https://www.csoonline.com/article/3235970/what-is-quantum-cryptography-it-s-no-silver-bullet-but-could-improve-security.html

Lin, F. X. (2014). Shor's Algorithm and the Quantum Fourier Transform. McGill University. Retrieved from www.math.mcgill.ca/darmon/courses/12-13/nt/projects/Fangxi-Lin.pdf

Nam, Y.S. (2012). Running Shor's Algorithm on a complete, gate-by-gate implementation of a virtual, universal quantum computer. Retrieved from http://citeseerx.ist.psu.edu

Parmar, P., & Udhayabanu, R. (2012), Voice Fingerprinting: A Very Important Tool against Crime. *J. Indian Acad. Forensic Med.*, *34*(1).

Prokofieva, M., & Miah, S. J. (2019). Blockchain in healthcare. *AJIS. Australasian Journal of Information Systems*, *vol*, 23.

Vora, J., Nayyar, A., Tanwar, S., Tyagi, S., Kumar, N., Obaidat, M. S., & Rodrigues, J. J. (2018, December). BHEEM: A Blockchain-Based Framework for Securing Electronic Health Records. In *Proceedings of the 2018 IEEE Globecom Workshops (GC Wkshps)* (pp. 1-6). IEEE.

Wikipedia. (n.d.b). Shor's algorithm. Retrieved from https://en.wikipedia.org

APPENDIX 1

The transactions in blocks are chained to form a block chain as figure 18.

Figure 18.

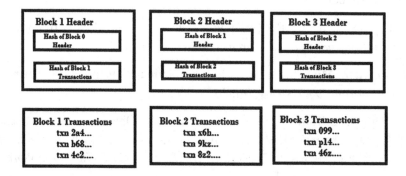

APPENDIX 2

1. Face and IRIS Recognition Partial Source Code

Step 1: Import the Libraries

```
import numpy as np
import cv2
```

Step 2: read the face

```
face_cascade = cv2.CascadeClassifier('haarcascade_frontalface_
default.xml')
eye_cascade = cv2.CascadeClassifier('haarcascade_eye.xml')
img = cv2.imread('1303786.jpg')
for (x,y,w,h) in faces:
    img = cv2.rectangle(img,(x,y),(x+w,y+h),(255,0,0),2)
    roi_gray = gray[y:y+h, x:x+w]
    roi_color = img[y:y+h, x:x+w]
    eyes = eye_cascade.detectMultiScale(roi_gray)
    for (ex,ey,ew,eh) in eyes:
        cv2.rectangle(roi_color,(ex,ey),(ex+ew,ey+
eh),(0,255,0),2)
```

Step 3: Print the Image

```
cv2.imshow('imgc',img)
```

Step 4: Close all windows

```
cv2.waitKey(0)
cv2.destroyAllWindows()
```

2. Hashing Algorithm

Step 1: Read the required inputs, in this case study- patient name, age, weight, address and disease and so on.
Step 2: Write / Store the details in a database.
Step 3: Apply hash ()
Step 4: Repeat Step 3 i.e. Hash function is applied twice. And store the details in database.

3. Advanced Standard Encryption Algorithm

Step 1: Read the patient details
Step 2: Encrypt the details and store them
Step 3: Decrypt the details from the database and print the details
Step 4: The Algorithm is implemented for addition, updating and deletion of the patient record.

Chapter 9
Improved Methodology to Detect Advanced Persistent Threat Attacks

Ambika N.
SSMRV College, India

ABSTRACT

Cybersecurity is essentials in today's era. An increase in cyberattacks has driven caution to safeguard data. An advanced persistent attack is an attack where the intellectual property of an organization is attempted to be misused. The attacker stays on the network for a long-time intruding into confidential files. The attacker switches into sleep mode, masking himself. Hence, the attacker is quite difficult to trace. The proposed work is suggested to tackle the problem. Public key cryptography is used to encrypt the data. The hash code is affixed to the transmitted message to provide reliability to the transmitted data. The work proves to be 4.9% stronger in authenticating the received packets, provides 4.42% greater data reliability, and decreases the load of the server by 43.5% compared to work.

INTRODUCTION

We are into an era where gaining access to information has to be in seconds. The internet has bought answers where the user can access data anytime/anywhere. The Internet has become an essential part of today's technology era. The technology has become a part-parcel of human life. Innumerable people across the globe are using technology to a very large extent. This technology is the backbone of many organizations ranging from small scale industries to global giants. A large amount

DOI: 10.4018/978-1-7998-2253-0.ch009

of data in various forms are exchanged and shared by the organizations. To provide a store and transfer of a large amount of data cloud (Wan, Zhang, Sun, Lin, Zou, & Cai, 2014) is being introduced. The system is capable of availing service anywhere/anytime. The merge of the two (Bhagat, 2012) has increased production to a large extent. As the demand for the same is increasing the threats are also increasing. Many kinds of cyberattacks (Kim, Kim, & Park, 2014; He & Yan., 2016) are introduced into the system.

Advanced persistent threats (APT) (Lemay, Calvet, Menet, & Fernandez, 2018; Chen, Su, Yeh, & Yung, 2018) is one such attack. It is characterized to work for long periods. They use encrypted connections and forge normal behavior. These attacks are human-driven infiltrations. The attacks are usually customized to target an organization especially open resources are targeted. Though the attacks are unique, the same follows a pattern. It commences with initial reconnaissance. After initial compromise, it starts elevating its privileges. It moves towards the destination file using the privileges. Once it reaches its destination it extracts the required data. The companies are aimed at their reputation or any monetary gain.

APT has left many traces. The sequence of attacks was launched on Google, adobe systems, Jupiter networks in 2009. Operation Aurora (Varma, 2010) was able to gain access to Google's intellectual property. The attack originated in China. Stuxnet (Langner, 2011) is one of its kinds. This was a worm discovered in 2010. A USB thumb drive spread the infection into the system. The attack exploited the vulnerabilities of windows OS. It destroyed Iran's uranium facilities.

Another kind of attack that started in 2006 and is still in existence is the Shady RATS attack (Gross, 2011; Amorosi, 2011). The adversary utilizes encrypted HTML to introduce the attack into the system. This is one of the high potential damaging acts of cyber espionage. The attack has pilfered intellectual property from more than 70 public/private sectors around the globe. Cyber espionage in the year 2009 targeted around 100 countries. The attacker (Deibert, Rohozinski, Manchanda, Villeneuve, & Walton, 2009) used phishing and remote administrative tools to harm the intellectual property of the organization. Another attack (Li, Huang, Wang, Fan, & Li., 2016) that targets the guest using wireless networks were discovered from August 2010 and continued to 2013. The attack misuses the check-in data of the respective. The users are lured with offers. The packages provided as offers are loaded with Trojan and key loggers.

The main contributions of the chapter include-

- One-way authentication is done when the terminal joins the network or the terminal gets active. The terminals generate hash code to identify it. The Markov-chain process is used to generate a unique hash code for every session.
- Public key encryption is used to encrypt the data.

- Hash code is affixed to the transmitted data.
- Early detection of illegitimate node is proposed.

The proposal is written using 7 sections. Following the introduction, the literature survey is detailed in section 2. The characteristics of the advanced persistent attack are explained in section 3. The proposed work is detailed in section 4. The security analysis for the work is described in section 5. The work is simulated in NS2, the details of the same are provided in section 6. The Proposal is concluded in Section 7.

LITERATURE SURVEY

Advanced Persistent attack is introduced into cyberspace aiming at a particular organization. The attack usually intents to destroy the reputation of an organization/ gain momentary profit. This section provides various contributions provided by the authors to tackle the attack.

An innovative approach is adopted (Marchetti, Pierazzi, Colajanni, & Guido, 2016) to tackle APT attacks (Au, Liang, Liu, Lu, & Ning, 2018). The author has considered analyzing APT, botnet and insider threat detection. High volumes of data are scrutinized in the proposed work to reveal weak signals. Suspicious activity is tracked with their positions. Only the outgoing traffic is taken into consideration. Five phases are proposed in the framework. The initial phase commences with the collection of flow records. The information is extracted from the packet by filtering source and destination IP header. Data exfiltration happens in the second phase. This procedure is repeated for a time interval. The comparing attributes are normalized (Duffield & Presti, 2000) in the third phase. The suspiciousness scores are computed considering magnitude and direction. The last phase provides ranking to the suspiciousness score.

The authors (Pawlick, Farhang, & Zhu, 2015) have designed a framework to secure cloud-based systems. The system is used in a wide range of applications including traffic control, drone delivery, design of smart homes, etc. The procedure used guides the respective when it has to trust the cloud. The proposal has considered the methodology as a game between three players. The cloud, attacker and the device are considered as players in the game. FlipIt game is considered in the proposal. The platform provides flexibility for dynamic interactions. One player is provisioned to operate based on the belief about private information of the other. The signaling and FlipIt are coupled. The attacker and defender are chosen with a prior commitment. Gestalt equilibrium is considered in the work. A case study is considered, to which Gestalt equilibrium is applied.

In (Ahn, Sung-Hwan, Kim, & Chung, 2014) the authors have provided a solution for unknown attacks in the network. The model developed is based on big data analysis technology. It aids in preventing and detecting advanced persistent threat (APT) attacks (Sood & Enbody, 2012). APT attacks penetrate the system with many advanced methodologies. They use social engineering to accomplish their tasks. They aim to penetrate the system and collect valuable information. These kinds of attacks aim at damaging national agencies and large enterprises. Some of the popular attacks of this kind are Stuxnet (Langner, 2011), an intelligent malware that aimed at intruding Iran's nuclear facilities and created failure. Other attacks include RSA secure ID hacking and Night Dragon. The attack is done in three stages. The first stage is known as intrusion where the hacker learns about the target system doings and prepares itself for an attack. The system aims in searching for high access privileges to get complete control of the system. The accounts of these high personnel are attacked using various methodologies. SQL injection, phishing, farming, and social engineering are some of the commonly used methodologies to hack the personnel account. Important files are searched like a System log to gain access to valuable information. The malware is installed that gain access to these important data sets.

A new big data analysis model is suggested in (Ahn, Sung-Hwan, Kim, & Chung, 2014). The model is divided into four stages. Event-related data from firewalls and logs, behavior and status information are collected in the first stage. This data set is stored in a big data appliance. The second stage is known as the data processing stage where the key-value pair is created. The third stage is known as the data analysis stage. Prediction, classification, association analysis, and unstructured data analysis are applied to the collected data. This aids in deciding the user behavior, system status, packet integrity and misuse of the system. Dashboard and management tools are provided to monitor the results. Using these tools abnormal behaviors are detected. The system also incorporates configuration update, rule manipulation, and deletion, analysis pattern update mechanism in its system. The proposed model provides better security management aiming to detect the abnormalities at an early stage.

A methodology named as TerminAPTor is suggested in (Brogi & Tong, 2016). The algorithm is an APT detector. The traces left by the attackers are scrutinized during the attack campaign. The proposed system works as an intrusion detection system (Lunt, 1993), recording the information flow. The IDS outputs the events in chronological order. The event list consists of event type, timestamp, list of references of input objects and list of references to output objects as its contents. The output also includes the alerts. Utilizing the output list, the attack is traced. Using the traces left by the similar attacks, the tools used by them are tracked.

A Novel graph analytic metric is used to measure the threats in (Johnson & Hogan, 2013). The algorithm analyses the potential of the threat. The proposal suggests controlling the level of exposure after authenticating. The cyber is considered as graph having systems represented as vertices and connections represented as edges. A reachability graph is constructed. A metric is computed by summating the number of vertices lying on the path towards the selected vertex. The methodology is a quantitative measure of compromised nodes. Utilizing the methodology, the administrator can evaluate the compromised nodes number during various instances. If the measure increases beyond threshold the system opts for appropriate action.

The flow-based analysis is used to detect APT (Vance, 2014). The methodology aggregates the network traffic and analyses the same. The adopted technology provides a high rate of detection of anomalies, low false positives, and provides in-depth incident reporting. The method reduces the amount of data to be analyzed. The proposal includes network gateways that capture flow packets. The analysis is performed without the need for a signature or deep packet inspection (DPI). The system calculates and creates standards of statistical measurements for normal and abnormal traffic. It enables sketch-based projections for the collected traffic. The model examines the change detection. The model is created using the history and the change of behavior is searched against the baseline. The methodology enhances better detection of anomalies.

The adversary is assumed to maintain a path in the graph and tends to move towards the inner part of the graph. A dynamic game framework model is proposed in (Rass & Zhu, 2016) to minimize advanced persistent threats. The methodology is based on two-person zero-sum games. The sub-game is designed to capture the attack. The directed acyclic graph is considered. At each level, the concrete game structure is defined by the node. The vulnerabilities are examined and counteraction can be formulated. The distance in the game is determined by having a count of access control between the controller nodes and attackers.

A framework combining different methodologies based on bid data analysis and security intelligence is proposed in (Marchetti, Pierazzi, Colajanni, & Guido, 2016). The system adopts a network-centric approach. The methodology aids in collecting and analyzing the data. The compromise score is calculated for the set of indicators. The proposal adopts to prioritize internal clients. Three levels are analyzed in the protocol. In the maintenance access phase, the adversary deploys the Remote administrative tool which contacts the external servers. The system overcomes this attack by analyzing the traffic between the external and internal hosts. The system builds a bipartite undirected graph corresponding to several flows. It calculates the compromise indicator for each client.

A Framework is proposed in (Saud & Islam, 2015) that uses honeypots and network-based intrusion detection systems to provide security to the network. An alert is created and posted to the administrator when the detection system finds some traces of the threat. The system will be able to identify the attacker without any testimony and correlation of the events. Honeypots are incorporated in the network to deceive the attackers.

Sensor outputs are designed that tackle APT (Sayin & Basar, 2017). Markov-Gaussian is used in the proposed work. The sensors supervise the state of the system. The information is shared with the controller. A common finite horizon quadratic loss function is created for the agents in the stochastic control scenario. Sensor strategies are characterized. They usually show properties of memory-less and linear in the underlying state. This procedure leads to equilibrium. The algorithms used are numerically computed.

Fixing the insecure host under an APT attack is suggested in (Yang, Li, Yang, & Tang, 2018). Based on derived organization potential loss, the APT response model is derived. The response strategy remains the same over time in the proposal. The greedy algorithm NE-GREEDY algorithm is used in the proposed work. The procedure starts by creating attack-response pair. If the pair is within the proximity of another region, the created is exchanged with the other. The same procedure is continued. The algorithm proves to be optimal w.r.t Nash equilibrium considering small-world network, scale-free network, and E-mail network.

One-class classification anomaly detection is addressed in (Demertzis, Iliadis, & Spartalis, 2017). Evolving spiking neural network algorithm (Pavlidis, Plagianakos, Nikiforidis, & Vrahatis, 2005) is used to tackle OCC anomaly detection. Data sets including the data logs are collected. The topology of the proposed work is strictly feed-forward and organized systematically into many layers. The weight modifications are made on the connections. The structure is well-organized in a continuous manner. The adaptive and interactive approach is adopted for incoming information. The data sets are classified into a sequence of spikes. Rank order population encoding (Soltic & Kasabov, 2010) methodology is used to classify them. In the encoding methodology adopted, the connections are organized into maps. The connections of the same weight come in together. The modification is reflected in the map. During the commencement of the transmission, all the activities are initially set to zero.

ADVANCED PERSISTENT ATTACK CHARACTERISTICS

Advanced persistent attacks (Vukalović & Delija, 2015) are stealthy attacks introduced into the system targeting government, companies or military groups. These are a group of attackers who possess an abundance of knowledge and resources. Usually, the group is funded to damage the intended. The attackers use phishing and malware tools to accomplish the same. In some cases, they also build their own tools to accomplish the task. The group persistently attacks the target until they gain access to the required information. They usually aim for the intellectual property of the target.

Once the attacker gains access to the system, they indulge in creating backdoors (Yamada, Morinaga, Unno, Torii, & Takenaka., 2015). Using this methodology, they extract sensitive information and also try accessing the other parts of the system.

The guilty can be detected through a high level of knowledge of the host. Advanced tools and competent personnel have to work along to track the attacker. The life cycle of the APT are:

- **Reconnaissance:** The attacker initially makes a thorough survey of the organization of interest. He finds it to locate the weak points of the same. Usually, the attacker searches the public resources available on the target. The personnel information of the executives of the companies is searched. Company related websites and social network profiles are inspected to gain information on the target. After gaining ample information on the target the attacker moves to the next phase.

- **Preparation:** In this phase the attacker prepares himself for an attack on the targeted system. The specific information of the target is extracted in this phase. The test methods and tools to be used to extract the required information are organized. The tools include malware, phishing tools. Some of the methodologies adopted include scanning the network, ports. Infrastructure to be used to control the flow of attack is set up. To accomplish the act fake domains and email accounts are created. The servers are also taken into control and Domain Network Service (DNS) (Hacherl, Garg, Satagopan, & Reichel., 1007) entries are modified.

- **Execution:** In this phase, the attacker launches his first attack on his target. The task is usually accomplished using phishing emails (Fette, Sadeh, & Tomasic., 2007). The mail contains a Uniform Resource Locator (URL) (Chasin, 2005) or document as an attachment (Largman, More, & Blair., 2011) sent to the addressee. The mail may impersonate any trusted party of the target. Other methodologies include zero-day vulnerabilities (Bilge & Dumitraş, 2012) and spreading malware infections (Gu, Porras, Yegneswaran, Fong, & Lee, 2007). The attacker waits for the signal of a successful breach after intruding into the system.

- **Gaining Access:** After gaining access to the system, the attacker tries installing additional malware and backdoors (Maier, 2001). The adversary tries to gain administrative privileges. The attacker tries to gain control of the terminals making an easy way to the information it requires. The attackers try launching visible/known attacks into the system making the system administrators busy sorting it out. This methodology gives them the opportunity to gain access to the required information.

- **Conceal Itself:** The goal of the attacker is to gain continuous access to the system. To accomplish the goal, it tries concealing itself. The rootkits are installed to provide the false illusion of the system. The attacker modifies the event and the log entries. It deletes its traces on the system. It periodically enters the sleep state.
- **Gather Information:** After enough exploring the system, if the attacker is able to gain access to the required information it uses different methodologies to hide. The encryption methodology is used to resemble legal traffic. It encrypts the captured data. This encrypted data is slowly extracted from the system.
- **Connection Maintenance:** To gain access to all the required information the attacker has to make a prolonged search on the target system. The guilty has to keep a check on the backdoors and the control infrastructure. The attacker in many instances launches new malware to exploit the weakness of the system.

Measures that can be used to tackle the attack-

- **Creating Awareness:** The working professionals have to be made aware (Bass, 2000) of the attack. Different attack vectors have to be considered. The system administrators and the users have to possess some knowledge to aid them in tackling the same.
- **Implement Security Policies:** The system has to adhere to some security policies to tackle the attack. The users of the system should provide their authentication to gain access to the required information. Some encryption methodology (Goldwasser & Micali, 1984) has to be applied to the stored data. The security implemented has to be updated from time-time.
- **Usage of Software Intrusion Detection System Tools:** Strong IDS software (Skowyra, Bahargam, & Bestavros, 2013) is to be implemented to trace the attacker in the system.

PROPOSED MODEL

Notations Used in the Study

Table 1 describes the notations used in the study.

Assumptions Made in the Study

- The system is assumed to be free from any attack until the network is set up.

Table 1. Notations used in the study

Notations	Description
N	Network under study
S	Server used in the study
T_i	i^{th} Terminal of the network
P_k	Public key transmitted by the server
P_r	Private key generated by the server
H_i	Hash code generated by the ith terminal
ID_i	Unique identity of ith terminal
$P_{<null>}$	Null public-key transmitted

- The adversary is capable of introducing Advanced Persistent attack into the system.
- All the terminals are provided with a unique identity.

Authentication of the Terminal with the Main Server

For the intranet network, the terminals are provisioned to gain access to a particular section of the server. They also have given access to the internet. The server uses public-key cryptography to safeguard information (Paillier & Naccache, 2003; Beth, Thomas, & Gollmann, 1989). In this methodology, the source will generate two keys. Private key generated is used to decrypt the message. The Public-key is used to encrypt the message. In the notation (1) server S is transmitting public key P_k to the network N.

$$S \rightarrow N : P_k \tag{1}$$

For every session, the terminal uses the unique identity of itself to generate the hash code. The hash code generated differs for every session. The terminal encodes the generated hash code using the public key. From the notation (2) terminal T_i generates the hash code H_i and encrypts the same using the public key P_k. This generated data is transmitted to the server S.

$$T_i \rightarrow S : Alg\left(H_i, P_k\right) \tag{2}$$

Table 2. Algorithm used to generate the hash code

Algorithm to generate hash code
Begin

If session == 1 then
Hash_code=algorithm(ID$_i$)
Else
Hash_code(0)=prev_code(0)
For i=1 to length(prev_code) − 1
Hash_code(i)=prev_code(i-1) ⊕ prev_code(i)
End for
End if
End

Figure 1. Illustration of generation of hash code

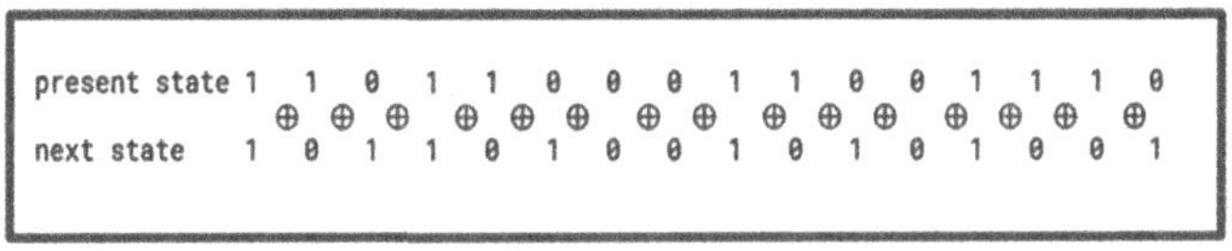

For every transmission made by the terminal, the hash code is attached to the transmitted message. The data to be transmitted is also encrypted using public key and transmitted. The server makes a verification check on all the messages transmitted. It uses the private key to decrypt the message and cross-verify against the registered users of the system. It takes appropriate action on finding the inappropriate message. To trace the exact terminal early, the server transmits a null public key. The normal terminals will be to identify and will not transmit the packets during that session. The attacker unknowing will transmit the packets and will get caught. In the notation (3) the server S is dispatching P$_{<null>}$ packet to the network N. fig 2, represents the flow of methodology of the proposed work.

$$S \rightarrow N : P_{\langle null \rangle} \tag{3}$$

Security Analysis

The proposed work tackles APT threats in the network. These threats showcase many characteristics. To detect the illegitimate terminal among the terminals attached to the server, the server evaluates the received packets. in case of inappropriateness, appropriate steps are taken.

Figure 2. Flow chart of the proposal

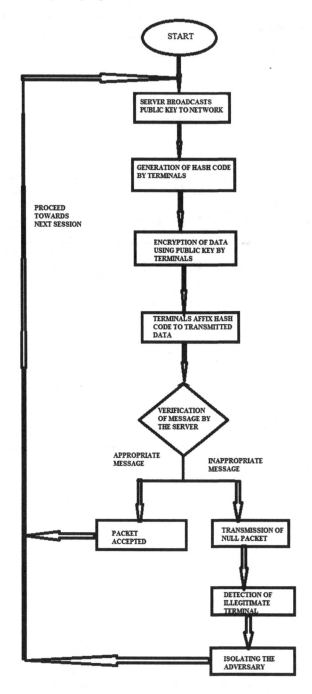

The work is compared with (Marchetti, Pierazzi, Colajanni, & Guido, 2016). The author in this work has considered analyzing APT, botnet and insider threat detection. High volumes of data are scrutinized in the proposed work to reveal weak signals. Suspicious activity is tracked with their positions. Only the outgoing traffic is taken into consideration. Five phases are proposed in the framework. The initial phase commences with the collection of flow records. The information is extracted from the packet by filtering source and destination IP header. Data exfiltration happens in the second phase. This procedure is repeated for a time interval. The comparing attributes are normalized (Duffield & Presti, 2000) in the third phase. The suspiciousness scores are computed considering magnitude and direction. The last phase provides ranking to the suspiciousness score.

The proposed work uses the hash code as its IP header. This hash code is generated for every session and will vary for every session. The public key is used to encrypt the hash code and the message sent. The server verifies the hash code for its identity. If the terminal is the compromised or is the attacker, the attacker –

- **Transmit the Packets:** After receiving the <null> public key, the guilty may unknowingly transmit its packets. The server will be able to track the attacker and take appropriate action.
- **The Attacker Enters the Sleep State:** The attacker may enter sleep state after it receives the <<null>> public key. After a time interval T, the server again transmits the << null>> public key if it is not able to trace the attacker by that time.

Experimental Results

The work is simulated using NS2. Table 3 provides the description of the simulated work.

Table 3. Representation of the simulated work

Description	Details
Area considered	200m * 200m
Number of terminals used	10
Number of attackers used	1
Time duration	60s
Length of public key	24 bits
Length of hash code	16 bits
Length of the transmitted message (actual message)	80 bits

Security Against APT

Advanced persistent attacks is an attack launched by a group of attackers. The attacker aims the organization for momentary gain or harms the reputation. The attacker for a long time tries to gain access to the system. Once the attacker gains access to the required data he tries to transmit the packets by coinciding with the same.

The work is compared with (Marchetti, Pierazzi, Colajanni, & Guido, 2016). The author in this work has considered analyzing APT, botnet and insider threat detection. High volumes of data are scrutinized in the proposed work to reveal weak signals. Suspicious activity is tracked with their positions. Only the outgoing traffic is taken into consideration. Five phases are proposed in the framework. The initial phase commences with the collection of flow records. The information is extracted from the packet by filtering source and destination IP header. Data exfiltration happens in the second phase. This procedure is repeated for a time interval. The comparing attributes are normalized (Duffield & Presti, 2000) in the third phase. The suspiciousness scores are computed considering magnitude and direction. The last phase provides ranking to the suspiciousness score.

The proposed work generates the hash code using the unique identity. It uses the previous hash code to generate the new one. This methodology provides better security to the network. The hash code along with the transmitted message is encrypted with the public key. The server ensures that the public key is transmitted for every session. The approach brings in better security than (Marchetti, Pierazzi, Guido, & Colajanni, 2016). The proposed work proves to be 4.42% more reliable than (Marchetti, Pierazzi, Colajanni, & Guido, 2016). The same is represented in the form of a graph in fig 3.

Figure 3. Graphical representation of data reliability

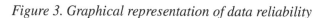
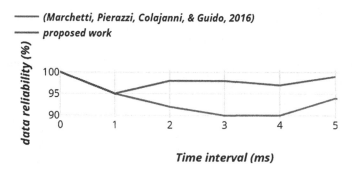

Load on the Server

In (Marchetti, Pierazzi, Colajanni, & Guido, 2016) the server is given the following responsibilities:

- It has to track Suspicious activity with their positions
- It extracts information from the packet by filtering source and destination IP header.
- Data exfiltration is to be done.
- The suspiciousness scores are computed considering magnitude and direction.
- It ranks the suspiciousness score.

In the proposed work the server has the following responsibilities-

- Generating a public key for every session and broadcasting them.
- Generating <<null>> public key in case of suspicion.
- Decrypting the received packets using the private key and checking its authentication.

Comparing (Marchetti, Pierazzi, Colajanni, & Guido, 2016) to proposed work, the server responsibilities increase with the amount of data communicating in the network. The proposed work has 43.5% less workload compared to (Marchetti, Pierazzi, Colajanni, & Guido, 2016). The same is represented in fig. 4

Authentication

The terminals transmit their packets affixing the hash code to them. The hash code varies for every session. This hash code is encrypted using the public-key broadcasted

Figure 4. Comparison of the load on the server

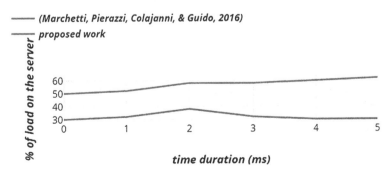

by the server. As the public-key and hash code change for every session, security is increased to a larger extent. The authentication has increased by 4.9% compared to (Marchetti, Pierazzi, Colajanni, & Guido, 2016). The same is represented in fig 5.

CONCLUSION

Usage of the internet has increased by 34.4% since 2000. A huge amount of work irrespective of the sector they are working in using huge bandwidth. It has become a necessity for big giants. The industry set up is based on the internet. As technology has advanced to a great extent, the hazards for them has also increased. Hence cybersecurity is in limelight. Securing the companies data becomes very essential. The proposed work is suggested to tackle Advanced persistent attack in the network. It is based on Markov-chain property. The terminal has a unique identity. Using this identity and Markov-chain property the hash code is derived. The server is given the responsibility to broadcast the public key for every session. The terminal generates a unique hash code for every session and encrypts the code and transmitted the message with the key. This methodology aids in authenticating the packets. The proposed work aids in minimizing the load on the server by 43.5% and increases reliability by 4.42% compared to previous work.

Figure 5. Graphical representation of authentication

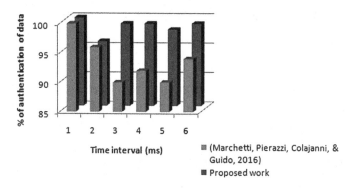

Table 4. Provides the efficiency of the proposed methodology w.r.t

Measured Parameters	Effectiveness of the Proposed Methodology
Security	Increased by 4.42%
Load on the server	Decreased by 43.5%
authentication	Increased by 4.9%

(Marchetti, Pierazzi, Colajanni, & Guido, 2016)

REFERENCES

Ahn, S.-H., Kim, N.-U., & Chung, T.-M. (2014). Big data analysis system concept for detecting unknown attacks. In *Proceedings of the 16th International Conference on Advanced Communication Technology* (pp. 269-272). IEEE. 10.1109/ICACT.2014.6778962

Amorosi, D. (2011). *You Dirty RAT.* Elsevier. doi:10.1016/S1754-4548(11)70061-4

Au, M. H., Liang, K., Liu, J. K., Lu, R., & Ning, J. (2018). Privacy-preserving personal data operation on mobile cloud—Chances and challenges over advanced persistent threat. *Future Generation Computer Systems, 79,* 337–349. doi:10.1016/j.future.2017.06.021

Bass, T. (2000). Intrusion detection systems and multisensor data fusion: Creating cyberspace situational awareness. *Communications of the ACM, 43*(4), 99–105. doi:10.1145/332051.332079

Beth, T., & Gollman, D. (1989). Algorithm engineering for public key algorithms. *IEEE Journal on Selected Areas in Communications, 7*(4), 458–466. doi:10.1109/49.17708

Bhagat, B. C. (2012). Patent No. 13/016,999. U.S.

Bilge, L., & Dumitraş, T. (2012). *Before we knew it: an empirical study of zero-day attacks in the real world. In Proceedings of the ACM conference on Computer and communications security* (pp. 833–844). ACM. doi:10.1145/2382196.2382284

Brogi, G., & Tong, V. V. (2016). TerminAPTor: Highlighting Advanced Persistent Threats through Information Flow Tracking. *In Proceedings of the 8th IFIP International Conference on New Technologies, Mobility and Security (NTMS)* (pp. 1-5). IEEE. 10.1109/NTMS.2016.7792480

Chasin, C. (2005). Patent No. 10/888,370. U.S.

Chen, J., Su, C., Yeh, K.-H., & Yung, M. (2018). Special Issue on Advanced Persistent Threat. *Future Generation Computer Systems, 79,* 243–246. doi:10.1016/j.future.2017.11.005

Deibert, R. J., Rohozinski, R., Manchanda, A., Villeneuve, N., & Walton, G. M. (2009). *Tracking ghostnet: Investigating a cyber espionage network.* Oxford: oxford university research archive.

Demertzis, K., Iliadis, L., & Spartalis, S. (2017). A Spiking One-Class Anomaly Detection Framework for Cyber-Security on Industrial Control Systems. *In* Proceedings of the *International Conference on Engineering Applications of Neural Networks* (pp. 122-134). Springer.

Duffield, N. G., & Presti, F. L. (2000, March). Multicast inference of packet delay variance at interior network links. In *Proceedings IEEE INFOCOM 2000* (Vol. 3, pp. 1351–1360). IEEE.

Fette, I., Sadeh, N., & Tomasic, A. (2007). Learning to detect phishing emails. *In* Proceedings of the *16th international conference on World Wide Web* (pp. 649-656). ACM.

Goldwasser, S., & Micali, S. (1984). Probabilistic encryption. *Journal of Computer and System Sciences*, *28*(2), 270–299. doi:10.1016/0022-0000(84)90070-9

Gross, M. J. (2011). *Exclusive: Operation shady rat—unprecedented cyber-espionage campaign and intellectual-property bonanza. Vanity Fair.*

Gu, G., Porras, P. A., Yegneswaran, V., Fong, M. W., & Lee, W. (2007). Bothunter: Detecting malware infection through ids-driven dialog correlation. *In* Proceedings of the *USENIX Security Symposium* (pp. 1-16). Usenix.

Hacherl, D. J., Garg, P., & Satagopan, M. D. & Reichel., R. P. (2007). Patent No. 7,200,869. U.S.

He, H., & Yan, J. (2016). Cyber-physical attacks and defences in the smart grid: A survey. *IET Cyber-Physical Systems: Theory & Applications*, *1*(1), 13–27.

Johnson, J. R., & Hogan, E. A. (2013). A Graph Analytic Metric for Mitigating Advanced Persistent Threat. *In Proceedings of the IEEE International Conference on Intelligence and Security Informatics* (pp. 129-133). IEEE. 10.1109/ISI.2013.6578801

Kim, Y., Kim, I., & Park, N. (2014). Analysis of cyber attacks and security intelligence. In Mobile, Ubiquitous, and Intelligent Computing (pp. 489-494). Springer. doi:10.1007/978-3-642-40675-1_73

Langner, R. (2011). Stuxnet: Dissecting a cyberwarfare weapon. *IEEE Security and Privacy*, *9*(3), 49–51. doi:10.1109/MSP.2011.67

Largman, K., More, A.B., & Blair, E. (2011). Patent No. 12/868,611. U.S.

Lemay, A., Calvet, J., Menet, F., & Fernandez, J. M. (2018). Survey of publicly available reports on advanced persistent threat actors. *Computers & Security*, *72*, 26–59. doi:10.1016/j.cose.2017.08.005

Li, M., Huang, W., Wang, Y., Fan, W., & Li, J. (2016). The study of APT attack stage model. *In* Proceedings of the *IEEE/ACIS 15th International Conference on Computer and Information Science (ICIS)* (pp. 1-5). Okayama, Japan: IEEE.

Lunt, T. F. (1993). A survey of intrusion detection techniques. *Computers & Security*, *12*(4), 405–418. doi:10.1016/0167-4048(93)90029-5

Maier, M. J. (2001). Backdoor liability from Internet telecommuters. *Computer L. Rev. & Tech. J.*, *6*, 27.

Marchetti, M., Pierazzi, F., Colajanni, M., & Guido, A. (2016). Analysis of high volumes of network traffic for Advanced Persistent Threat detection. *Computer Networks*, 1–15.

Marchetti, M., Pierazzi, F., Guido, A., & Colajanni, M. (2016). Countering Advanced Persistent Threats through Security Intelligence and Big Data Analytics. *In* Proceedings of the *8th International Conference on Cyber Conflict* (pp. 243-261). NATO CCD COE Publications. 10.1109/CYCON.2016.7529438

Paillier, P., & Naccache, D. (2003). Public Key Cryptography. *In* Proceedings of the *5th International Workshop on Practice and Theory in Public Key Cryptosystems*. Springer.

Pavlidis, N. G., Plagianakos, V. P., Nikiforidis, G., & Vrahatis, M. N. (2005). Spiking neural network training using evolutionary algorithms. *In Proceedings of the IEEE International Joint Conference on Neural Networks (Vol. 4*, pp. 2190-2194). IEEE. 10.1109/IJCNN.2005.1556240

Pawlick, J., Farhang, S., & Zhu, Q. (2015). Flip the Cloud: Cyber-physical Signaling Games in the Presence of Advanced Persistent Threats. *In Proceedings of the International Conference on Decision and Game Theory for Security* (pp. 289-308). Springer. 10.1007/978-3-319-25594-1_16

Rass, S., & Zhu, Q. (2016). GADAPT: A Sequential Game-Theoretic Framework for Designing Defense-in-Depth Strategies Against Advanced Persistent Threats. *In Proceedings of the International Conference on Decision and Game Theory for Security* (pp. 314-326). Springer. 10.1007/978-3-319-47413-7_18

Saud, Z., & Islam, M. H. (2015). Towards Proactive Detection of Advanced Persistent Threat (APT) Attacks using Honeypots. *In Proceedings of the 8th International Conference on Security of Information and Networks* (pp. 154-157). ACM. 10.1145/2799979.2800042

Sayin, M. O., & Basar, T. (2017). Secure Sensor Design for Cyber-Physical Systems Against Advanced Persistent Threats. *In Proceedings of the International Conference on Decision and Game Theory for Security* (pp. 91-111). Springer. 10.1007/978-3-319-68711-7_6

Skowyra, R., Bahargam, S., & Bestavros, A. (2013). Software-defined ids for securing embedded mobile devices. *In Proceedings of the IEEE High Performance Extreme Computing Conference (HPEC)* (pp. 1-7). IEEE. 10.1109/HPEC.2013.6670325

Soltic, S., & Kasabov, N. (2010). Knowledge extraction from evolving spiking neural networks with rank order population coding. *International Journal of Neural Systems*, *20*(6), 437–445. doi:10.1142/S012906571000253X PMID:21117268

Sood, K. A., & Enbody, R. J. (2012). Targeted cyberattacks: A superset of advanced persistent threats. *IEEE Security and Privacy*, *11*(1), 54–61.

Vance, A. (2014). Flow based analysis of Advanced Persistent Threats detecting targeted attacks in cloud computing. *In Proceedings of the First International Scientific-Practical Conference Problems of Infocommunications Science and Technology* (pp. 173-176). IEEE. 10.1109/INFOCOMMST.2014.6992342

Varma, R. (2010). *McAfee Labs: combating aurora.* Retrieved from https://paper.seebug.org/papers/APT/APT_CyberCriminal_Campagin/2010/Combating%20Threats%20-%20Operation%20Aurora.pdf

Vukalović, J., & Delija, D. (2015). Advanced Persistent Threats – Detection and Defense. *In Proceedings of the 38th International Convention on Information and Communication Technology, Electronics and Microelectronics (MIPRO)* (pp. 1324-1330). IEEE. 10.1109/MIPRO.2015.7160480

Wan, J., Zhang, D., Sun, Y., Lin, K., Zou, C., & Cai, H. (2014). VCMIA: A novel architecture for integrating vehicular cyber-physical systems and mobile cloud computing. *Mobile Networks and Applications*, *19*(2), 153–160. doi:10.100711036-014-0499-6

Yamada, M., Morinaga, M., Unno, Y., Torii, S., & Takenaka, M. (2015). RAT-based malicious activities detection on enterprise internal networks. *In Proceedings of the 10th International Conference for Internet Technology and Secured Transactions (ICITST)* (pp. 321-325). IEEE. 10.1109/ICITST.2015.7412113

Yang, L.-X., Li, P., Yang, X., & Tang, Y. Y. (2018). A risk management approach to defending against the advanced persistent threat. *IEEE Transactions on Dependable and Secure Computing*.

Chapter 10

IoT and Cyber Security:
Introduction, Attacks, and Preventive Steps

Keyurbhai Arvindbhai Jani
ⓘ https://orcid.org/0000-0002-6050-9365
U. V. Patel College of Engineering, Ganpat University, India

Nirbhay Chaubey
Acharya Motibhai Patel Institute of Computer Studies, Ganpat University, India

ABSTRACT

The Internet of Things (IoT) connects different IoT smart objects around people to make their life easier by connecting them with the internet, which leads IoT environments vulnerable to many attacks. This chapter has few main objectives: to understand basics of IoT; different types of attacks possible in IoT; and prevention steps to secure IoT environment at some extent. Therefore, this chapter is mainly divided into three parts. In first part discusses IoT devices and application of it; the second part is about cyber-attacks possible on IoT environments; and in the third part is discussed prevention and recommendation steps to avoid damage from different attacks.

INTRODUCTION

Nowadays technology changing rapidly day by day and affect our lives in many ways. Internet connectivity easily available everywhere. Many devices like computers, laptops, network devices, smartphones etc. connected with internet around us.

DOI: 10.4018/978-1-7998-2253-0.ch010

Popularity of the Internet of Things (IoT) has increase in last few years and number of applications for introduced in market for different IoT domain such as traffic controlling, home automation, transportation management, manufacturing management, environmental monitoring, defense system, medical industries, smart farming, etc. In different applications of IoT many sensors, actuators, Gateway, Circuits, hardware and routers communicate with each other via wired/wireless communication technologies are known as IoT devices. More than 50 billion IoT devices will connect with internet by 2020 as per Cisco white paper.

There are many communication technologies and way to connect anything(IoT devices) such as radio frequency identification (RFID), ZigBee, Bluetooth, Bluetooth low energy (BLE), wireless fidelity (Wi-Fi), worldwide interoperability for microwave access (WiMAX), wireless personal area network (WPAN), near field communication (NFC),Ethernet cables, coaxial cable, mobile communication technology (1G/2G/3G/4G/5G/GSM/CDMA) and many more that depends on existing infrastructure whether wired or wireless.

There are various protocols used in IoT such as advanced message queuing protocol (AMQP), constrained application protocol (CoAP), message queuing telemetry transport (MQTT), multicast domain name system (mDNS), domain name system service discovery (DNS-SD), extensible messaging presence protocol (XMPP), representational state transfer (RESTFUL) services, IPv6 over low-power wireless personal area networks (6LowPAN), internet protocol version 4 (IPv4)/ internet protocol version 6 (IPv6), routing protocol for low-power and lossy networks (RPL), HyperText transfer protocol (HTTP), web sockets and many more protocols being used at the different layers.

Security play vital role when these devices are near to us and send their data over network. IoT devices are also widely used in industries. Therefore, it is important to consider risk of cyber vulnerabilities & attacks in IoT environment and implementing recommendation steps to secure IoT environment to some extent.

Introduction to IoT

Many people and organizations gave different definitions of IoT. IoT is not a new concept. In previous era internet connect people so it has called "the Internet of People." Few years ago, the internet was not widely available in industries, research institutes, and in the government sector. The concept of M2M, machine-to-machine, was introduced so machines can talk to each other with some wired or wireless technologies to take some collaborative decisions and perform some tasks. It is also famous as Sensor Network. Nowadays internet widely available to every person at low cost, therefore these IoT objects (cloud/web server/node/sensor/machine/ app) has direct connectivity to the internet and send their data via internet to other objects and all these IoT objects considered as Things, so it is called "the Internet of Things." Cisco gave its name as "Internet of Everything". Bruce Schneier gave it the name "World Size Web." In the *Terminator* movie, "Skynet," was the name given to the IoT concept.

Now, let us discuss more about things in IoT. Things are mainly identified as physical world objects and information world (virtual) objects. Things have unique identities and able to communicate with each other via communication layer. Physical things are surrounding environment, sensors, electrical-electronics equipment, actuators etc. whereas IoT applications (web/mobile app), Twitter, Facebook, Thingspeak, Blynk, etc., are virtual things, its capable of being stored, processed, and accessed.

Therefore, The IoT is a connected network of physical and virtual objects (Devices, vehicles, Buildings and other items embedded with electronics, software, web application, mobile application, sensors, and network connectivity, etc.) that enables these objects to collect and exchange data as per description given in (Wikipedia, n.d.). Therefore, as shown in Figure 1, IoT is environment, which connect people & process with physical/virtual objects (sensors) via some connectivity technologies.

In IoT by accessing IoT web/mobile applications like CRM system, remote monitoring/maintenance /supply chain management, location tracking, and many more people can take part as shown in Figure 2. E.g.: In location tracking applications, at some interval GPS sensors send its location data to its configured server, on server that data processed and stored in database, Mobile application & web app provide interface to user to access that data & do necessary action/decision based on application requirement.

Figure 1. IoT Environment components

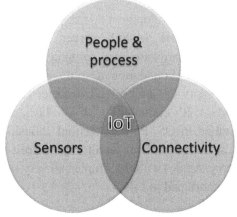

Figure 2. People & Process in IoT
Source: (Postscapes, n.d.)

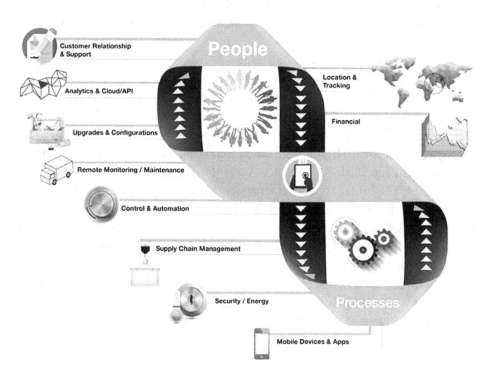

Sensors and actuators are core of IoT. There are many known sensors which are easily available in the market and widely used by people, government and industries as per application requirements as shown in Figure 3.

Few Sensors, Actuators, Development Boards and Power Supplies are described as below for reference:

- **Raspberry Pi:** Use it as development board, web server and gateway. Install Raspbian OS, Apache, PHP, MySQL server, FTP server and many more software. To develop a hardware level computer skill of school students in the UK, the Raspberry Pi Foundation, develops single-board computers with I/O pins. The University of Cambridge Computer Laboratory and tech firm Broadcom supports it. It's come with C, C++, Java, Scratch, and Ruby like software pre-installed in OS. Purpose behind choosing this name was the combination of the desire to create an alternative fruit-based computer (like Apricot, Blackberry, Apple) with the simple and very powerful programming language Python (shortened to Pi).

Figure 3. Sensors in IoT
Source: *(Postscapes, n.d.)*

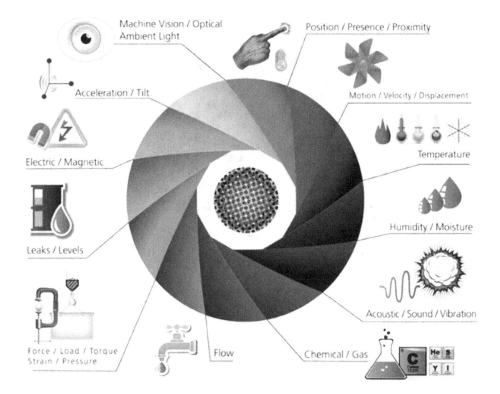

- **Arduino:** With this development board, we can attach different sensors, actuators and communication devices. Developer can implement their logic with Arduino IDE, which uses C language type of syntax. Its open source project so there is strong developer communities and tutorials like resources easily available on the internet.
- **NodeMCU:** NodeMCU is an open source IoT platform. It is low cost development board based on ESP8266 with GPIO, PWM, IIC, 1-Wire and ADC all in one board which easily powered by your mobile charger (5v DC). The default firmware uses the Lua as a scripting language. It provides Arduino-like hardware IO, Nodejs style network API and lowest cost WI-FI. We can develop program in Arduino IDE also. In new NodeMCU, people can get advantages of WI-FI and Bluetooth also.
- **Bluetooth Module:** This communication device use for data transfer from Arduino, Raspberry Pi like board or microcontroller.

Figure 4. Raspberry Pi

Figure 5. Arduino

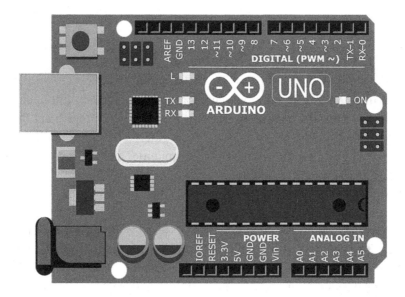

Figure 6. NodeMCU

Figure 7. Bluetooth Module (HC-05)

- **Solenoid Valve:** Used for automated water valve open close, here you can choose four type of water valve
  - 12v DC high pressure electric solenoid valve
  - 12v DC low pressure solenoid valve
  - 24v DC solenoid valve
  - 5v DC Modified brass ball valve for regulated water flow using servo motor
- **Water Flow Sensor:** These sensors are used to track information of water usages and leakages.
- **Ultrasonic Sensor:** Used as object distance detection sensor.
- **DHT (Digital Humidity Temperature):** These sensors use for measure temperature and humidity and give output in digital format.
- **Soil Moisture Sensor:** This sensor will give moisture level in soil.
- **Relay Module:** Use for AC/DC power switching.

Figure 8. Solenoid Valves

Figure 9. Water Flow Sensors

Figure 10. Ultrasonic Sensor

Figure 11. DHT 11 Sensor

Figure 12. Soil Moisture Level Sensor

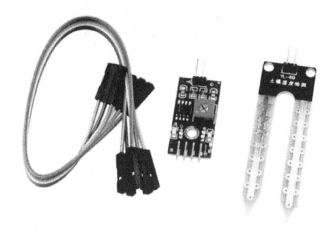

Figure 13. Relay Modules

- **Breadboard Power Supply:** Some devices use 5V and some use 3.3V power for working. This will act as power source for Arduino and many sensors.
- **Step Up/Down DC-DC adjustable voltage regulator, SMPS, Power Adaptor, etc.**

Figure 14. Breadboard power supply Module

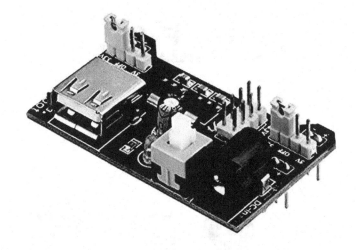

- **Working with Sensors:** Most of sensors are not able to transfer data directly on internet or able to do process on sensed data. So, controller or development boards that have capability to do process on sensed data and transfer it to the server via internet are used in IoT application. To collect, process and store data, developers create web server or use cloud services. So, before discussing IoT architecture and all, let us take one example to understand simple IoT application with Thingspeak.com server (Website for storing, processing, analyzing and visualizing sensors data).
- **Experiment-1:** To sense environment temperature and humidity using DHT-11 sensor and upload data on thingspeak.com using NodeMCU.
- **Connection Diagram:** See Figure 15.

Steps to upload DHT data on thingspeak.com using NodeMCU:

1. Sign Up on www.thingspeak.com using your email id
2. Make sure to click the checkbox saying "By signing up, you agree to the Terms of Use and Privacy Policy
3. Goto Channels and Create a New Channel
4. Fill the following Details
   a. Any Name for the channel
   b. Description: if you have any description like "Monitoring temp and humanity"
   c. Field 1 Label as 'temp' and field2 label as humanity since we are going to upload temperature and humanity

Figure 15. NodeMCU-DHT11 Connection

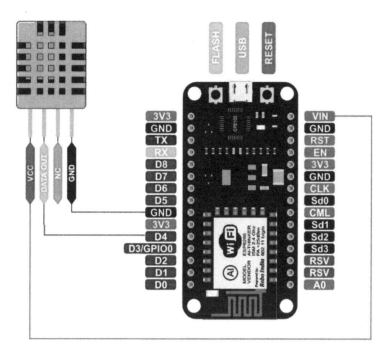

5. Save Channel
6. Saving Process might take a while.
7. Please select your channel
8. You would see tabs Like
    a. Private View
    b. Public View
    c. Channel Settings
    d. API Keys
    e. Data Import/Export
9. Click API Keys Tab
10. You will find Write API Key similar to this "OHYNG8WWGHXXXXXX"
11. Please copy paste the API Key in your Project Code (NodeMCU, Arduino)
12. Once the Code is uploaded and the Arduino/NodeMCU starts running, Arduino/ NodeMCU will upload the Temperature and Humidity value in few second gaps
13. Open Serial Monitor to see the process running in Arduino/NodeMCU
14. Click Private View Tab to see the graph.

NodeMCU Code:

```
// Hardware: NodeMCU,DHT11
#include <DHT.h>  // this Include library for all known DHT
sensors
#include <Adafruit_Sensor.h>
#include <ESP8266WiFi.h>
String apiKey = "OHYNG8WWGHXXXXXX"; //replace your ThingSpeak
channel's //Write API key here
const char *wifi_ssid = "Your Wi-Fi Router/hotspot name";
const char *wifi_pwd = "Your Wi-Fi Router/hotspot password";
const char* server = "api.thingspeak.com";
#define DHTPIN 2          //pin where the dht11 is connected D4
nodemcu
DHT dht(DHTPIN, DHT11);
WiFiClient client;
void setup()
{
      Serial.begin(9600);
      delay(100);
      dht.begin();
      Serial.println("Trying to Connect with ");
      Serial.println(wifi_ssid);
      WiFi.begin(wifi_ssid, wifi_pwd);
     while (WiFi.status() != WL_CONNECTED)
     {
          delay(5000);
          Serial.print("#");
     }
      Serial.println("");
      Serial.println("WiFi connected sucessfully");
}
void loop()
{
     float h = dht.readHumidity();
     float t = dht.readTemperature();
             if (isnan(h) || isnan(t))
                {
                    Serial.println("Failed to read from DHT
sensor!");
```

```
                        return;
                }
            if (client.connect(server,80))
            {
                    String postStr = apiKey;
                    postStr +="&field1=";
                    postStr += String(t);
                    postStr +="&field2=";
                    postStr += String(h);
                    postStr += "\r\n\r\n";
                    client.print("POST /update HTTP/1.1\n");
                    client.print("Host: api.thingspeak.
com\n");
                    client.print("Connection: close\n");
                    client.print("X-THINGSPEAKAPIKEY:
"+apiKey+"\n");
                    client.print("Content-Type:application/
x-www-form-urlencoded\n");
                    client.print("Content-Length: ");
                    client.print(postStr.length());
                    client.print("\n\n");
                    client.print(postStr);
                    Serial.print("Temperature: ");
                    Serial.print(t);
                    Serial.print(" degrees Celcius,
Humidity: ");
                    Serial.print(h);
                    Serial.println("%. Send to
Thingspeak.");
                }
        client.stop();
        Serial.println("Waiting...");
  // thingspeak needs minimum 15 sec delay between updates,
i've set it          to 30 seconds
  delay(30000);
      }
```

- **Output:** See Figure 16.

Figure 16. Temperature & Humidity data on Thingspeak.com

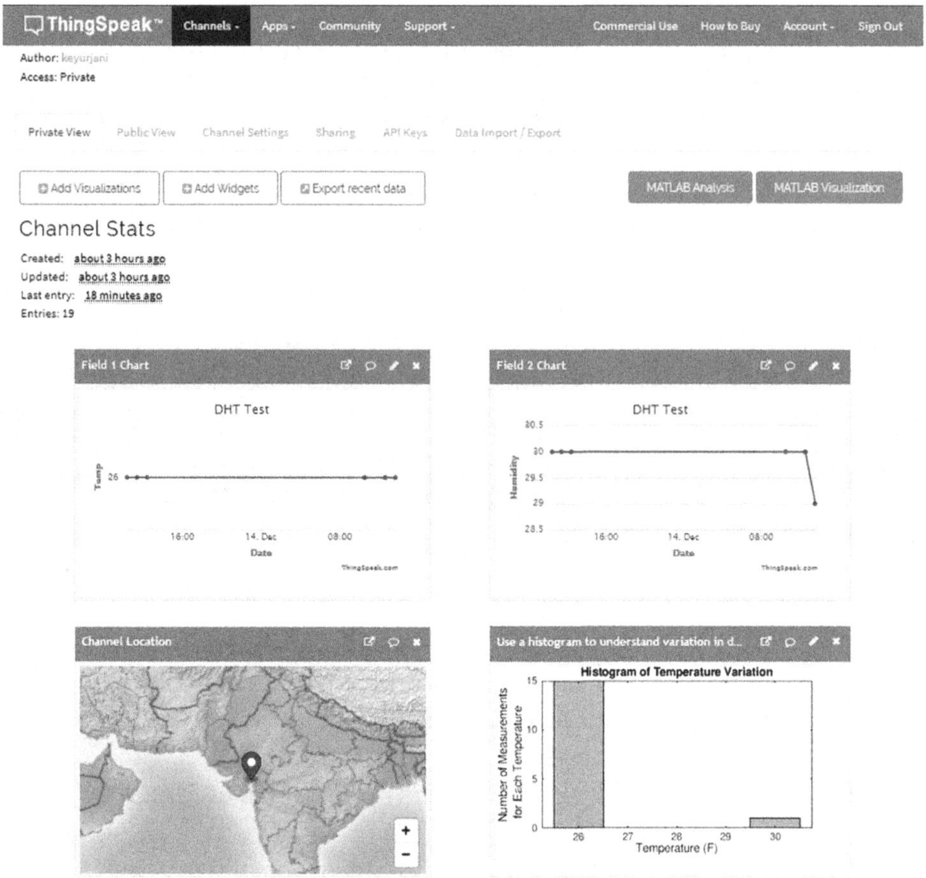

IoT Architecture

Different people describe IoT Architecture with different layers. Different researchers proposed different IoT Reference Models (RM) like: Three-level model (Abdul-Ghani & Konstantas, 2019), A Four-level model (Abdul-Ghan et al., 2018), a Five-level model (Atzori, Iera, & Morabito, 2010) and a Seven-level model (Cisco, 2014). Figure 17 shows few well-known IoT architectures layers as below:

Each layer provides some functionalities to upper and lower layer. To achieve interoperability, Industries people use standards of each layer. (Lee, 2016) Discussed each layer from seven layers architecture very well:

Figure 17. IoT Reference Models: 3/4/5/7 layers architecture

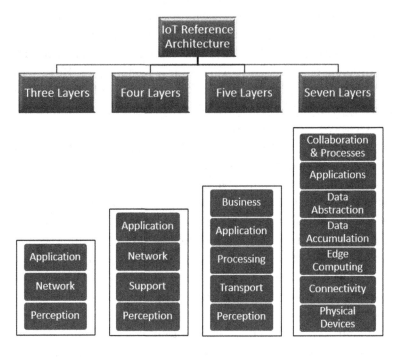

1. **Physical Devices:** This layer is 'T' (Things in IoT), alternatively called edge devices. It contains sensors, actuators, embedded systems, microcontrollers, cameras, RFID, Communication devices, hardware, power supplies, etc. Most of these physical devices has constrained resources (i.e., power source, processing, storage and communication interface) and use battery as the power source. However, based on the application requirement main power supply or battery power used. Power will be a limited resource, so most of the IoT Applications try to reduce power consumption of the nodes. In addition to numerous techniques to scale back the power consumption, IoT devices use low-power microcontrollers as we as low-power communication technologies. Most of the objects in IoT network has low-end microcontroller that has RAM, ROM and processing unit in it. Devices within the Perception Layer will be either static or mobile, however the proportion of mobile devices are smaller than the static ones (Arış, Oktuğ, & Voigt, 2018).

2. **Connectivity:** This layer provides an interface between physical layer and upper layers. It mainly consists communication related interface and protocols like (i.e., 6LoWPAN, Bluetooth Low Energy (BLE), LoRa and LoRaWAN, WiFi, Ethernet, Cellular, ZigBee, RF and Thread) which are used for the in-network communication. Most of them are open technologies, whereas a number of

them are (e.g., ZigBee, LoRa, Cellular) proprietary. These communication technologies give varied knowledge rates and transmission ranges reciprocally of various power consumptions and prices. Hence, depending on the several design constraints, the nodes in the Perception Layer can form IoT networks with different characteristics. Among these technologies, BLE, Wi-Fi, LoRa and Cellular offer star-based topologies. However, 6LoWPAN, ZigBee and Thread support mesh topologies, where elements of the network can forward others' packets. Some of them are projected for specific application areas (i.e., Thread was projected for smart-home environments). Most of these technologies require a gateway or border router, which used to connect the nodes in IoT network to the Internet (Arış, Oktuğ, & Voigt, 2018).

3. **Edge Computing:** The main objective of this layer is to perform simple data processing, which in turn decreases the computation load in the higher layers and offers a quick response. It is wise for real-time applications to process data closer to the edge of the network, rather than to process data in the cloud. Many factors (e.g., service providers and computing nodes) can be used to define the amount of data processing at this layer (Abdul-Ghani & Konstantas, 2019).

4. **Data Accumulation:** This layer given the Velocity, Volume and Variety that IoT systems can provide it is essential to provide incoming data storage for subsequent processing, normalization, integration, and preparation for upstream applications. While a part of the general "data lake" design, this layer of the design serves the intermediate storage of incoming storage and outgoing traffic queued for delivery to lower layers. This layer may be implemented in simple SQL or may require more sophisticated Hadoop & Hadoop File System, Mongo, Cassandra, Spark or other NoSQL solutions.

5. **Data Abstraction:** in this layer we have a tendency to "make sense" of the data, assembling "like" data from multiple IoT sensors or measurements, expedite high priority traffic or alarms, and organize incoming data from the information lake into acceptable schema and flows for upstream process. Similarly, application information destined for downstream layers is reformatted fittingly for device interaction and queued for process. A key design part for larger high-performance deployments could be a publish / subscribe or data distribution service (DDS) software package to modify data movement between Edge Computing, Data Accumulation, Application Layer, and User Processes (Lee, 2016). In general, this layer provides several functions such as normalization/renormalization, indexing, and access control to different data centers.

6. **Application:** In this layer, people see applications in various deployment areas, which make use of the meaningful information obtained from lower Layers. Applications of IoT can be in home, building, industry, urban or rural

environment Monitoring, process optimization, alarm management, statistical analysis, control logic, logistics, consumer patterns, are just a few examples of IoT applications (Arış, Oktuğ, & Voigt, 2018) (Lee, 2016).

7. **Collaboration and Processes:** At this layer, application processing is presented to users, and data processed at lower layers is integrated into business applications. This layer is concerning human interaction with all of the layers of the IoT system and wherever quantity is delivered. The challenge at this layer is to effectively leverage the worth of IoT and also the layers of infrastructure and services below and leverage this into economic process, business improvement and/or social good.

Table 1. Few IoT protocols

Protocols	Purpose
CoAP	CoAP is designed in such a way that it enables the low-power sensors to make usage of restful services It is built upon the UDP instead of the TCP that is commonly used in HTTP.
DDS	It provides an excellent quality of service levels and reliability that suits the IoT and M2M communication.
MQTT	It facilities the embedded connectivity between applications and the middleware at one side and networks and communications on the other
SMQTT	In this, one message is encrypted but delivered to multiple other nodes.
AMQP	In this, the broker is divided into two main components that are exchange and queues.
6LoWPAN	6LoWPAN is designed to work with variant length addresses, various network topologies including mesh and star, low bandwidth, scalable networks, mobility, and low cost
RPL	Routing Protocol for Low-Power and Lossy Networks (RPL) supports data link protocol
CORPL	An extension of RPL is CORPL or cognitive RPL, which is designed for the cognitive networks and uses DODAG topology generation.
CARP	A distributed routing protocol is designed for the underwater Communication. It has lightweight packets.
6TiSCH	A 6TiSCH working group in IETF is developing standards to allow IPv6 to pass through Time- Slotted Channel Hopping (TSCH) mode of IEEE 802.15.4e data links.
LTE-A	LTE-A is a scalable, lower- cost protocol as compared to other cellular protocols
Z-WAVE	Z-Wave is a low-power MAC protocol that is designed for home automation
IEEE 802.11 AH	IEEE 802.11ah is a low energy version of the original IEEE 802.11 wireless medium access standard.
Zigbee Smart Energy	It is designed for a broad range of IoT applications including Smart homes, remote controls, and healthcare systems. It supports a wide star, peer-to-peer or cluster-tree topologies.

Source: (Masoodi, Alam, Siddiqui, & Liz, 2019)

IoT Protocols

Table 1 shows a few protocols that are discuss by (Masoodi, Alam, Siddiqui, & Liz, 2019) at different layers of IoT architecture.

IoT Characteristics

IoT is a complex system with a number of characteristics. Characteristics vary from one domain to another in IoT. Few general and key characteristics are described by (Chandrashekhar, 2016) as follows:

1. **Sensing:** IoT would not be possible without sensors, which will detect or measure any changes in the environment to generate data that can report on their status or even interact with the environment. Sensing technologies give the means that to make capabilities that replicate a real awareness of the physical world and the folks in it. The sensing information is simply the analogue input from the physical world, but it can provide a rich understanding of our complex world.

Figure 18. IoT characteristics

2. **Connectivity:** It empowers Internet of Things by bringing together everyday objects. Connectivity of those objects is crucial as a result of straightforward object level interactions contribute towards collective intelligence in IoT network. It allows network accessibility and compatibility within the things. With this connectivity, the networking of smart things and applications can create new market opportunities for Internet of things.

3. **Intelligence:** IoT comes with the combination of algorithms and computation, software & hardware that makes it smart. Ambient intelligence in IoT enhances its capabilities that facilitate IoT Objects to retort in an intelligent way to a specific scenario and supports them in completing specific tasks. In spite of all the popularity of smart technologies, intelligence in IoT is only concerned as a means of interaction between devices, while user and device interaction is achieved by standard input methods and graphical user interface.

4. **Dynamic Nature:** The primary activity of Internet of Things is to gather information from its surroundings, this is often achieved with the dynamic changes that turn up nearer to the devices. The state of those devices change dynamically, for instance sleeping and awakening, connected and/ or disconnected in addition because the context of devices change together with temperature, location and speed. In addition to the state of the device, the quantity of devices additionally changes dynamically with an individual, place and time.

5. **Enormous Scale:** The quantity of devices that require to be managed which communicate with one another are abundant larger than the devices connected to the present internet. The management of information generated from these devices and their interpretation for application functions becomes a lot of essential. Gartner (2015) confirms the big scale of IoT within the estimated report wherever it explicit that 5.5 million new things can get connected each day and 6.4 billion connected things are in use worldwide in 2016, that is up by 30% from 2015. The report conjointly forecasts that the quantity of connected devices can reach 20.8 billion by 2020.

6. Heterogeneity: Heterogeneity in IoT as one of the key characteristics. Devices in IoT are supported completely different hardware platforms and networks and may move with different devices or service platforms through different networks. IoT design ought to support direct network connectivity between heterogeneous networks. The key style needs for heterogeneous things and their environments in IoT are interoperability, scalabilities, modularity and extensibility.

7. **Security:** IoT devices are naturally vulnerable to security threats. As we tend to gain efficiencies, novel experiences, and alternative edges from the IoT, it would be an error to ignore security issues related to it. There is a high level

of transparency and privacy problems with IoT. It is necessary to secure the endpoints, the networks, and also the information that's transferred across all of it suggests that making a security paradigm.

IoT Applications

IoT has several applications. In Figure.19 Application divided domain wise. IoT applications connects billions of smart objects every day in different domain. Few key applications from every domain as below:

In Consumer domain Smart Home, Smart Cities, Smart building, Elder care, Wearables, Smart Gym & Museum type of applications are there. Even Smart Home contains lot of small application in it, which includes smart lighting, smart heating and air conditioning, smart media and smart security systems. Therefore, by implementing Smart Home we can make our life easy, secure and most important we can save valuable energy by smartly controlling it. However, if it can introduce significant risk to security and privacy. Attackers can directly compromise home devices, thereby undermining the user's security and privacy (Kumar & Patel, 2014). In many existing SmartApps, its communication with the device is accomplished by event. Due to the lack of sufficient protection, attackers can easily obtain sensitive information of users. Moreover, many of the existing development frameworks of SmartApps have vulnerabilities, and attackers can use these vulnerabilities to achieve a variety of attacks (Arias, Ly, & Jin, 2017) (Fernandes, Jung, & Prakash, 2016). Smart Cities also include Smart Parking, Smart lighting, Smart Traffic monitoring, Smart Road, Structural Health Monitoring etc.

In Utilities domain, also IoT has many applications like Smart Metering, smart grid, workforce Tracking, Asset and inventory management etc. Smart Grid integrated with electrical energy field. It collect electricity generation, Consumption, Storage & equipment's health status data. This data can be used for smart power distribution, faultfinding and prediction of usages. IoT also used for tracking asset and workforce for better management of it.

In Transportation & logistics domain IoT applied in Assisted Driving, Mobile Ticketing, Fleet Management & goods Tracking, Smart Traffic control, Smart parking, Electronic Toll Collection System, Remote Vehicle Control etc. Using IoT authorized person can track their asset as well as vehicle. Even in case of theft case they can control vehicle functionalities. In case of traffic system can find alternate route and suggest it for on time delivery in supply chain management system. In toll both there are RFID reader connected with software which detect smart tag (RFID tag) on vehicle and automatically debit money from account.

Figure 19. IoT applications

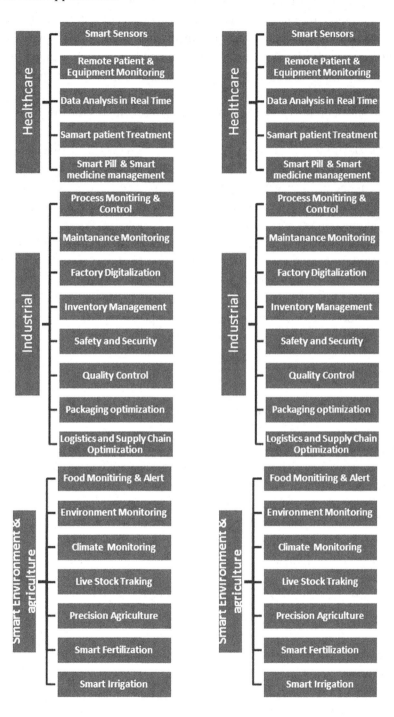

In healthcare domain IoT used with Smart Sensors, Remote patient monitoring, Medical equipment monitoring, Real time data analysis and alert system, Wearable devices, Smart patient treatment, Telemedicine, Smart pill, Smart medicine management system etc. To diagnose patient condition many sensors like: body temperature, blood pressure, electrocardiogram (ECG), heart rate, pulse oximeter oxygen saturation (SPO$_2$), patient movement, bed occupancy, etc., continuously sense data and send it to patient monitoring system which show history as well as alert in case of an any emergency.

In Industrial IoT application Process monitoring and control, equipment monitoring and maintenance, Quality control system, Safety and Security, Supply chain management and inventory management and many more are there. Using different sensors, actuators and devices most of industrial requirement can be manageable by IoT implementation.

Smart environment and agriculture applications are food monitoring and alert, air pollution monitoring, weather monitoring, noise pollution monitoring, forest fire detection, river flood detection, agriculture products livestock tracking, precision agriculture, smart irrigation, smart fertilization, etc., so with help of IoT implementation in above application we can improve quality of environment and agriculture product, take appropriate decision and able to save valuable resources.

IoT Stakeholders

In IoT development many stakeholders play important roles. Below are few of them:

- **Hardware:** The hardware manufacturer is one of the key stakeholders who builds devices which used for developing IoT application. Different sensors, microcontroller, development board electronic actuators, etc., manufacture companies are key player and responsible for improving quality and security of IoT. It is duty of manufacturers to disclose their security support commitment to users prior to purchase.
- **Connectivity Provider:** Connectivity play major role in IoT. Without internet service providers (ISPs) the IoT applications can work just like WSN network. To work at its full potential ISPs provide infrastructure for it. To provide secure IoT environment they also play important role by securing their services. Ex: To prevent Botnet attack, several countries including Australia and Germany, ISPs block botnets emanating from residential IP addresses.
- **Software Platform:** Companies who provide software platform for developing IoT software, cloud services, server platform, etc., are also stakeholder of IoT. Many attacks done from vulnerabilities in this software platform so it is duty

of software platform companies to take care of it and provide solution to protect its product.

- **Service Provider:** Many Companies Provide different IoT services (hardware, software, server, Cloud etc.). Some time there are some security hole in their service so it duty of them to check frequently for security hole in their service and provide patch to protect IoT environment.

- **Standard Bodies:** Various organizations develop or approve standards for IoT platforms. Other IoT stakeholders follow standards for interoperability and secure environments.

- **Academia:** Universities and research organization are also one of the stakeholders for IoT development. They invent new technology or improve existing IoT technologies for efficient and secure IoT environment.

Figure 20. IoT stakeholders

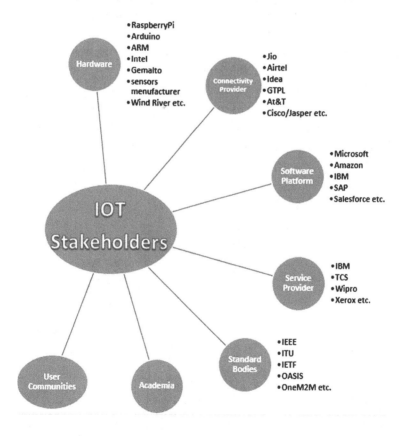

- **User Communities:** Users are the basic stakeholder for IoT platform development. Due to user requirements, IoT applications develop. There are many attacks possible due to users careless, so users have to follow some recommendation to secure their IoT platform and if there are some vulnerabilities in IoT application its duty of user to give feedback to developer or authorities.

IoT Security Goals

To make IoT environment secure (Abdul-Ghani & Konstantas, 2019) discuss, all IoT components must try to achieve below security goals:

- **Confidentiality:** Is about keeping data private, so that only authorized users (both humans and machines) can access that data. Cryptography is a key technology for achieving confidentiality (Lin & W. Bergmann, 2016).
- **Integrity:** Is the process in which data completeness, and accuracy is preserved (Abdul-Ghani & Konstantas, 2019).
- **Non-Repudiation:** Is the process in which an IoT system can validate the incident or non-incident of an event
- **Availability:** Is an ability of an IoT system to make sure its services are accessible, when demanded by authorized objects or users.
- **Privacy:** Is the process in which an IoT system follows privacy rules or policies and allowing users to control their sensitive data.

Figure 21. IoT security goals

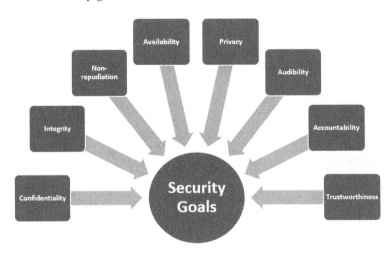

- **Audibility:** Is ensuring the ability of an IoT system to perform firm monitoring on its actions.

- **Accountability:** Is the process in which an IoT system holds users taking charge of their actions.

- **Trustworthiness:** Is ensuring the ability of an IoT system to prove identity and confirm trust in third party.

Possible Attacks

The Internet of things applications are used by many users but at the same time can expose the users to unprecedented security threats and challenges. Most of the IoT Devices directly connected with internet and share its data with some level of trust without performing any security tests. So most of attacks which are there in cyber space are also possible in IoT. IoT use Wireless Sensor Network as base so attacks of WSN are also there in IoT environment. Below are few attacks possible at different layers of IoT architecture discuss by (Abdul-Ghani & Konstantas, 2019) and (Chen et al., 2018).

Few of above attacks describe below to understand nature of attacks, which do damage at different layers of IoT environment:

- **Hardware Trojan**: One of the major security issues for ICs is hardware Trojans. They maliciously modify ICs to allow attackers to exploit their functionalities and gain access to software operating on them.

Table 2. Possible attacks at IoT architecture layers

Layer	Possible Attacks
Edge / Physical	Hardware Trojan, Node Replication, DoS Attacks (Sleep Deprivation, Battery Draining, Outage Attack), Physical Attack, Malicious Node, Side Channel Attack, Eavesdropping, Sniffing Attacks, Noise in data, Replay attack, etc.
Communication/ Network	Side Channel Attack, Collision Attack, Fragmentation Attack, Routing Attacks (Hello packet flood, Gray Hole, Sybil Attack, Worm Hole, Selective Forwarding, Black Hole, etc.), Eavesdropping, Inject Malicious Packets, Unauthorized Conversation, DoS attacks, Desynchronized attack, etc.
Middle layers	Web Browser attack, Signature Wrapping attack, Cloud Malware Injection, Flooding attack on cloud/server, SQL Injection, etc.
Application, Collaboration and Processes	Code Injection, Buffer Overflows, Phishing Attack, Authentication & Authorization, Private data Hijacking, Tampering with Node-based application, Application Security hole, Remote configuration, etc.

- **Node Replication:** The main goal of such an attack is to add maliciously an object by duplicating one object's identification number to a current set of objects. A remarkable drop in network performance can happen because of this attack. Furthermore, upon arrival of packets at a replica, it may not only corrupt the packets, but also misdirect them, causing serious damage to IoT systems by allowing an attacker to gain access to security parameters (e.g., shared keys). It is also capable of revoking authorized nodes, since it can carry out an object-revocation protocol (Parno, Perrig, & Gligor, 2005).

- **Denial of Service (DoS) Attacks:** DoS attacks in computing nodes can be classified into three categories: sleep deprivation, outage, and battery draining attacks at edge layer. In sleep deprivation, battery-operated node may receive a huge number of requests, which look like legitimate ones, sent by an attacker. Some IoT device work on battery. Battery draining attack are extremely powerful, leading to harmful impacts, such as a power outage. Outage attacks takes place when an IoT object stops carrying out its essential functions. This might have happened due to undesired error in the manufacturing phase, sleep deprivation, and code injection (Chaubey, Akshai Aggarwal, & Jani, 2015) (Chaubey, 2016).

- **Physical Attack:** In some IoT Application objects deployed in hostile environments, such objects are vulnerable to physical access, which may lead to hardware/firmware attacks. With physical access to an object, an attacker can derive precious cryptographic information, alter operating system, and vandalize circuit, all of which may result in long-term destruction.

- **Malicious Node:** In IoT environment, some node obtaining unauthorized access of an IoT network and other objects, and disturb functionalities and security of environment (Aggarwal, Chaubey, & Jani, 2013), (Chaubey, Aggarwal, Gandhi, & Jani, 2015).

- **Side Channel Attacks:** It is a strong attack against encryption techniques, which may affect their security and reliability. In Side-channel attack at edge node level objects perform their normal operations, there is a possibility that such objects might disclose critical information, side-channel attacks at communication level are not invasive, since they only elicit intentionally leaked information.

- **Collision Attacks:** This type of attacks can be launched on the link layer. One way is by adding noise in communication channel, which lead to retransmission of packets and drainage of limited power resources.

- **Fragmentation Attacks:** Although 6LoWPAN lacks any security mechanisms, its security is offered by underlying layers (e.g., an IEEE 802.15.4). The IEEE 802.15.4 has Maximum Transmission Unit (MTU) of 127 bytes, whereas IPv6 has a minimum MTU of 1280 bytes. Being developed with fragmentation technique, 6loWPAN provides the transfer of IPv6 packets over IEEE 802.15.4. In this case, an attacker can insert a malicious packet among other fragments, as 6loWPAN has designed without authentication techniques given by (Tomic & McCann, 2017).

- **Routing Attacks:** To transfer data in IoT environment many routing protocols used in network. Malicious node modified packet, generate fake packets, modify route. As per literature study, there are Sybil, Gray Hole, Wormhole, Hello flood, and Selective-forwarding types of attacks are possible in it (Aggarwal, Chaubey, & Jani, 2013), (Patel, Aggarwal, & Chaubey, Analysis of Wormhole Attacks in Wireless Sensor Networks, 2018) and (Patel, Aggarwal, & Chaubey, 2017).

- **Unauthorized Conversation:** To share and access data, each IoT object requires to communicate with other objects. That said, each object must only interact with a set of objects, which need its data. This kind of restricted interactions will prevent unauthorized access to IoT objects that is a fundamental security requirement of IoT. For instance, a thermostat, in a smart home, depends heavily on a smoke detector's data to turn a heating system off in case of danger. Nevertheless, insecurely sharing data with other objects by the smoke detector may put the entire smart home at risk (Mosenia & Jha, 2017).

- **Flooding Attack in Cloud**: This is one form of denial-of-service attacks in the cloud. Here, attackers constantly send requests to a service in the cloud, which depletes the resources in the cloud, thereby affecting the quality of service. When the cloud system finds that the current service instance cannot meet the requirements; it will transfer the affected service to other servers. This will lead to increased work pressure on other servers (Chen et al., 2018).

- **Cloud Malware Injection:** The attacker can modify the data, obtain control, and execute malicious code by injecting malicious service instance or virtual machine into the cloud.

- **Signature Wrapping Attack:** Cloud system uses XML signature to ensure the integrity of the service. The attacker modifies the eavesdropped messages without invalidating the signature. Some cloud use SOAP Attackers exploit vulnerabilities in SOAP to modify eavesdropped messages (Chen, et al., 2018).

- **SQL Injection Attack:** Attackers use web or mobile application interface to fire SQL statements for reading, writing, and deleting operations. This kind of attack can not only obtain the user's private data but also threaten the entire database system. When Web applications are attacked by SQL injection, the current page shows different outcomes compared to the true information discussed by (Chen et al., 2018) and (Dorai, 2011).

The attacks in the application layer mainly target (unauthorized) access of sensitive data of the user. Attackers typically exploit the vulnerabilities of programs and application (e.g., code injection, buffer overflow), or unauthorized access to attack. One approach for an unauthorized agent to obtain the same permission as legitimate users is through counterfeiting identity. In addition to these attacks, viruses, worms, and Trojans also threaten the application layer. Furthermore, other malicious programs (Rootkit, spyware, adware, etc.) also undermine the privacy of users.

Preventive Steps

Most of the above attacks are possible due to improper configuration & not following certain standards in IoT environment. Many organizations work for assessing security and providing guidelines for secure setup of IoT environment. The OWASP (Open Web Application Security Project) work on some security issue and come with Internet of Things Project which is designed to help manufacturers, developers, and consumers better understand the security issues associated with the Internet of Things, and to enable users in any context to make better security decisions when building, deploying, or assessing IoT technologies. OWASP and (Pal, n.d.) suggested some common issues in IoT applications and countermeasure steps to secure it.

FUTURE RESEARCH DIRECTIONS

As seen above in this chapter, there are various applications of IoT in market with different functionalities. Many applications have their own vulnerabilities and lack of following standards at each layer. In addition, IoT environment connected with internet so all threats related to cyber can be also applicable to IoT, therefore continuous software and firmware patch shall be produced for IoT applications are necessary to protect it. Many new technologies, protocols, hardware and communication devices research require to develop and secure IoT environment.

CONCLUSION

In this chapter, author discuss about IoT, which is fastest growing technology now days and much research is going on in this domain. IoT makes people's lives easier with its variety of applications. To do this task most of IoT objects use internet so they are directly vulnerable with internet threats. Therefore, to make IoT environment secure all IoT stakeholders have to do collaborative efforts by following standards and have to work towards improvement of standards and security for IoT environment.

Table 3. Common issues, reasons and prevention steps

Issue	Reasons for Issue	Prevention Steps
Poor Physical Security Weaknesses are present when an attacker can disassemble a device to easily access the storage medium and any data stored on that medium. Weaknesses are also present when USB ports or other external ports can be used to access the device using features intended for configuration or maintenance. This could lead to easy unauthorised access to the device or the data.	• Access to Software via USB Ports • Removal of Storage Media.	Ensure following • Data storage medium cannot be easily removed • Stored data is encrypted at rest • Device cannot be easily disassembled • USB ports or other external ports cannot be used to maliciously access the device • Only required external ports such as USB are required for the product to function • The product has the ability to limit administrative capabilities.
Insecure Software/Firmware Devices should have the ability to be updated when vulnerabilities are discovered and software/ firmware updates can be insecure when the updated files themselves and the network connection they are delivered on are not protected. Software/ Firmware can also be insecure if they contain hardcoded sensitive data such as credentials. The inability of software/ firmware being updated means that the devices remain vulnerable indefinitely to the security issue that the update is meant to address. Further, if the devices have hardcoded sensitive credentials, if these credentials are exposed, then they remain so for an indefinite period.	• Encryption Not Used to Fetch Updates • Update Not Verified before Upload • Update File not Encrypted • Firmware Contains Sensitive Information • No Update functionality or OTA option	Ensure following • The device has the ability to update • Update file is encrypted using accepted encryption methods • Update file is transmitted via an encrypted connection • Update file does not expose sensitive data • Update is signed and verified before allowing the update to be uploaded and applied • Update server is secure.
Insecure Network Services This relates to vulnerabilities in the network services that are used to access the IoT device that might allow an intruder to gain unauthorized access to the device or associated data.	• Vulnerable Services • Buffer Overflow • Open Ports via UPnP • xploitable UDP Services • Denial-of-Service • DoS via Network Device Fuzzing	Ensure following • Services are not vulnerable to buffer overflow and fuzzing attacks • Only necessary ports are exposed and available • Services are not vulnerable to DoS attacks which can affect the device itself or other devices and/or users on the local network or other networks • Network ports or services are not exposed to the internet via UPnP for example
Lack of Transport Encryption This deals with data being exchanged with the IoT device in an unencrypted format. This could easily lead to an intruder sniffing the data and either capturing this data for later use or compromising the device itself.	• Unencrypted Services via the Internet • Unencrypted Services via the Local Network • Poorly Implemented SSL/TLS • Misconfigured SSL/TLS	Ensure following • Data is encrypted using protocols such as SSL and TLS while transiting networks • Other industry standard encryption techniques are utilised to protect data during transport if SSL or TLS are not available • only accepted encryption standards are used and avoid using proprietary encryption protocols
Insufficient Authentication/ Authorization Its due to ineffective mechanisms being in place to authenticate to the IoT user interface and/or poor authorization mechanisms whereby a user can gain higher levels of access then allowed	• Lack of Password Complexity • Poorly Protected Credentials • Lack of Two Factor Authentication • Insecure Password Recovery • Privilege Escalation • Lack of Role Based Access Control	Ensure following • The strong passwords are required • Granular access control is in place when necessary • Credentials are properly protected • Implement two factor authentication where possible • Password recovery mechanisms are secure • Re-authentication is required for sensitive features • Options are available for configuring password controls

continued on following page

231

Table 3. Continued

Issue	Reasons for Issue	Prevention Steps
Insecure Web Interface Web interfaces built into IoT devices that allows a user to interact with the device, but at the same time could allow an attacker to gain unauthorized access to the device.	• Weak Default Credentials • Account Enumeration • Credentials Exposed in Network Traffic • Cross-site Scripting (XSS) • SQL-Injection • Session Management • Weak Account Lockout Settings	Ensure following • Default passwords and ideally default usernames to be changed during initial setup • Password recovery mechanisms are robust and do not supply an attacker with information indicating a valid account • Web interface is not susceptible to XSS, SQLi or CSRF • Credentials are not exposed in internal or external network traffic • Weak passwords are not allowed • Account lockout after 3 -5 failed login attempts
Privacy Concerns It generated by the collection of personal data in addition to the lack of proper protection of that data. Privacy concerns are easy to discover by simply reviewing the data that is being collected as the user sets up and activates the device. Automated tools can also look for specific patterns of data that may indicate collection of personal data or other sensitive data.	• Collection of Unnecessary Personal Information	Ensure following • only data critical to the functionality of the device is collected • Any data collected is of a less sensitive nature • Any data collected is de-identified or anonymized • any data collected is properly protected with encryption • Device and all of its components properly protect personal information • Authorized individuals have access to collected personal information • Retention limits are set for collected data • End-users are provided with "Notice and Choice" if data collected is more than what would be expected from the product.
Insufficient Security Configurability It is present when users of the device have limited or no ability to alter its security controls. Insufficient security configurability is apparent when the web interface of the device has no options for creating granular user permissions or for example, forcing the use of strong passwords. The risk with this is that the IoT device could be easier to attack allowing unauthorised access to the device or the data	• Lack of Granular Permission Model • Lack of Password Security Options • No Security Monitoring • No Security Logging	Ensure the ability to as following • Separate normal users from administrative users • Encrypt data at rest or in transit • Force strong password policies • Enable logging of security events • Notify end users of security events.
Insecure Cloud Interface Related to the cloud interface used to interact with the IoT device. Typically this would imply poor authentication controls or data traveling in an unencrypted format allowing an attacker access to the device or the underlying data	• Account Enumeration • No Account Lockout • Credentials Exposed in Network Traffic	Ensure following • At the first time setup, default usernames and password must be changed. • Password reset mechanisms should not be vulnerable. • There must be some mechanism to lockout account after few failed unauthorized access attempts • Cloud-based web interface is not susceptible to XSS, SQLi or CSRF • In wireless networks connection, IoT object must send their sensitive information in secure way. • Implement multi factor authentication.
Insecure Mobile Interface Similar to the Cloud Interface, weak authentication or unencrypted data channels can allow an attacker access to the device or underlying data of an IoT device that uses a vulnerable mobile interface for user interaction	• Account Enumeration • No Account Lockout • Credentials Exposed in Network Traffic	Ensure following • At the first time setup, default usernames and password must be changed. • Password reset mechanisms should not be vulnerable. • There must be some mechanism to lockout account after few failed unauthorized access attempts • In wireless networks connection, IoT object must send their sensitive information in secure way. • Implement multi factor authentication.

REFERENCES

Abdul-Ghani, H. A., & Konstantas, D. (2019). A Comprehensive Study of Security and Privacy Guidelines, Threats, and Countermeasures: An IoT Perspective. *Journal of Sensor and Actuator Networks*, *8*(2), 22. doi:10.3390/jsan8020022

Abdul-Ghani, H. A., Konstantas, D., & Mahyoub, M. (2018). A Comprehensive IoT Attacks Survey based on a Building-blocked Reference Model. *International Journal of Advanced Computer Science and Applications*, *9*. doi:10.14569/ IJACSA.2018.090349

Aggarwal, A., Chaubey, N., & Jani, K. A. (2013). A simulation study of malicious activities under various scenarios in Mobile Ad hoc Networks (MANETs). In Proceedings of the 2013 International Mutli-Conference on Automation, Computing, Communication, Control and Compressed Sensing (iMac4s) (pp. 827-834). IEEE.

Arias, O., Ly, K., & Jin, Y. (2017). Security and Privacy in IoT Era. In H. Yasuura, C.-M. Kyung, Y. Liu, & Y.-L. Lin (Eds.), *Smart Sensors at the IoT Frontier* (pp. 351–378). Cham: Springer International Publishing; doi:10.1007/978-3-319-55345-0_14

Arış, A., Oktuğ, S. F., & Voigt, T. (2018). Security of Internet of Things for a Reliable Internet of Services. In I. Ganchev, R. D. van der Mei, & H. van den Berg (Eds.), *Autonomous Control for a Reliable Internet of Services: Methods, Models, Approaches, Techniques, Algorithms, and Tools* (pp. 337–370). Cham: Springer International Publishing; doi:10.1007/978-3-319-90415-3_13

Atzori, L., Iera, A., & Morabito, G. (2010). The Internet of Things: A survey. *Computer Networks*, *54*(15), 2787–2805. doi:10.1016/j.comnet.2010.05.010

Chandrashekhar, K. (2016, September 19). *Internet of Things (IoT) Characteristics*. Retrieved from [REMOVED HYPERLINK FIELD]https://www.linkedin.com/pulse/ internet-things-iot-characteristics-kavyashree-g-c

Chaubey, N., Aggarwal, A., Gandhi, S., & Jani, K. A. (2015). Performance analysis of TSDRP and AODV routing protocol under black hole attacks in manets by varying network size. In *Proceedings of the 2015 Fifth International Conference on Advanced Computing & Communication Technologies* (pp. 320-324). IEEE. 10.1109/ACCT.2015.62

Chaubey, N., Akshai Aggarwal, S. G., & Jani, K. A. (2015). Effect of pause time on AODV and TSDRP routing protocols under black hole attack and DoS attacks in MANETs. In *Proceedings of the 2015 2nd International Conference on Computing for Sustainable Global Development (INDIACom)* (pp. 1807-1812). IEEE.

Chaubey, N. K. (2016). Security analysis of vehicular ad hoc networks (VANETs): A comprehensive study. *International Journal of Security and Its Applications*, *10*(5), 261–274. doi:10.14257/ijsia.2016.10.5.25

Chen, K., Zhang, S., Li, Z., Zhang, Y., Deng, Q., Ray, S., & Jin, Y. (2018). Internet-of-Things Security and Vulnerabilities: Taxonomy, Challenges, and Practice. *Journal of Hardware and Systems Security*, *2*(2), 97–110. doi:10.100741635-017-0029-7

Cisco. (2014). The Internet of Things Reference Model. In *Proceedings of the Internet of Things World Forum*. Academic Press.

Dorai, R. K. V. (2011). SQL injection—database attack revolution and prevention. *J. Int. Commercial Law Technol.*, *6*, 224.

Fernandes, E., Jung, J., & Prakash, A. (2016, May). Security analysis of emerging smart home applications. In *Proceedings of the 2016 IEEE Symposium on Security and Privacy (SP)* (pp. 636-654). IEEE. doi:10.1109/SP.2016.44

Gubbi, J., Buyya, R., Marusic, S., & Palaniswami, M. (2013). Internet of Things (IoT): A vision, architectural elements, and future directions. *Future Generation Computer Systems*, *29*(7), 1645–1660. doi:10.1016/j.future.2013.01.010

Ishino, M., Koizumi, Y., & Hasegawa, T. (2014). A Study on a Routing-Based Mobility Management Architecture for IoT Devices. In *Proceedings of the 2014 IEEE 22nd International Conference on Network Protocols* (pp. 498-500). doi:10.1109/ICNP.2014.78

Kumar, J. S., & Patel, D. R. (2014). A Survey on Internet of Things: Security and Privacy Issues. *International Journal of Computers and Applications*, *90*, 20–26. doi:10.5120/15579-4304

Lee, H. (2016). *IoT: Architecture*. Juxtology. Retrieved from https://juxtology.com/iot-transformation/iot-world-forum/

Lin, H., & W. Bergmann, N. (2016). IoT Privacy and Security Challenges for Smart Home Environments. *Information, 7*, 44. doi:10.3390/info7030044

Masoodi, F., Alam, S., Siddiqui, S., & Liz, L. (2019). 3). Security & Privacy Threats, Attacks and Countermeasures in Internet of Things. *International Journal of Network Security & Its Applications*, *11*(02), 67–77. doi:10.5121/ijnsa.2019.11205

Mosenia, A., & Jha, N. K. (2017). A Comprehensive Study of Security of Internet-of-Things. *IEEE Transactions on Emerging Topics in Computing*, *5*(4), 586–602. doi:10.1109/TETC.2016.2606384

Pal, A. (n.d.). *The Internet of Things (IoT) – Threats and Countermeasures*. CSO. Retrieved from [REMOVED HYPERLINK FIELD]https://www.cso.com.au/article/575407/internet-things-iot-threats-countermeasures/

Parno, B., Perrig, A., & Gligor, V. (2005). Distributed Detection of Node Replication Attacks in Sensor Networks. In *Proceedings of the 2005 IEEE Symposium on Security and Privacy* (pp. 49-63). IEEE Computer Society. 10.1109/SP.2005.8

Patel, M., Aggarwal, A., & Chaubey, N. (2017). Wormhole attacks and countermeasures in wireless sensor networks: A survey. *IACSIT International Journal of Engineering and Technology*, *9*(2), 1049–1060. doi:10.21817/ijet/2017/v9i2/170902126

Patel, M., Aggarwal, A., & Chaubey, N. (2018). Analysis of Wormhole Attacks in Wireless Sensor Networks. In *Recent Findings in Intelligent Computing Techniques* (pp. 33–42). Springer Singapore.

Patel, M., Aggarwal, A., & Chaubey, N. (2018). Variants of wormhole attacks and their impact in wireless sensor networks. In Progress in Computing, Analytics and Networking (pp. 637-642). Springer Singapore.

Postscapes. (n.d.). *Internet of Things Infographic*. Retrieved from [REMOVED HYPERLINK FIELD]https://www.postscapes.com/what-exactly-is-the-internet-of-things-infographic/

Tomić, I., & McCann, J. A. (2017). A survey of potential security issues in existing wireless sensor network protocols. *IEEE Internet of Things Journal*, *4*(6), 1910–1923. doi:10.1109/JIOT.2017.2749883

Wikipedia. (n.d.). Internet of things. Retrieved from https://en.wikipedia.org/wiki/Internet_of_Things

Chapter 11

Security and Privacy in Big Data Computing:
Concepts, Techniques, and Research Challenges

Kiritkumar J. Modi
 https://orcid.org/0000-0001-6462-059X
Parul University, India

Prachi Devangbhai Shah
U. V. Patel College of Engineering, Ganpat University, India

Zalak Prajapati
U. V. Patel College of Engineering, Ganpat University, India

ABSTRACT

The rapid growth of digitization in the present era leads to an exponential increase of information which demands the need of a Big Data paradigm. Big Data denotes complex, unstructured, massive, heterogeneous type data. The Big Data is essential to the success in many applications; however, it has a major setback regarding security and privacy issues. These issues arise because the Big Data is scattered over a distributed system by various users. The security of Big Data relates to all the solutions and measures to prevent the data from threats and malicious activities. Privacy prevails when it comes to processing personal data, while security means protecting information assets from unauthorized access. The existence of cloud computing and cloud data storage have been predecessor and conciliator of emergence of Big Data computing. This article highlights open issues related to traditional techniques of Big Data privacy and security. Moreover, it also illustrates a comprehensive overview of possible security techniques and future directions addressing Big Data privacy and security issues.

DOI: 10.4018/978-1-7998-2253-0.ch011

INTRODUCTION

In the era of distributed computing data are scattered among different machine. The rapid and exponential growth of data has increased the storage size where we can store huge pile amount of data. As per the Google report, 2.5 quintillion units of data are generated per day and this data is coming from different sources like social media, banking sector, Internet of Things, mobile generated data, etc. Data is very crucial part in any sector for communication and Information. This all data in form of structured, unstructured and semi structured type so we need to provide security on this data to achieve confidentiality. There are four basic attributes that defines Big Data, which are known as four V's: volume, variety, velocity, and veracity. The main trait that makes data "big" is its sheer volume. Due to digitization, continuous feeding of unstructured data flows from various sources and thus variety of data increases. In this era structured data is easily augmented by unstructured data. Veracity refers to the reliability of the data. Accuracy and trustworthiness of data is measured through veracity factor. Velocity is the rate at which the huge amount of data that is generated and needs to be processed.

The security of big data relates to all the solutions and measures to prevent the data from threats and malicious activities. Security refers to personal freedom from external forces. The main objective of security are confidentiality, integrity, and availability. Moreover, privacy is one's right to freedom from intrusion. Privacy prevails when it comes to processing personal data, while security means protecting information assets from unauthorized access (Mahmood & Afzal, 2013).

Higher Integrity and confidentiality can be achieved by providing security on three levels. First level is data storage level where crucial and important information stored e.g., credit card information, customer information. The Second level is built as a strong big data security tool e.g. a firewall, which can prevent unauthorized user to access information by filtering traffic. Third level is Implementing Access control method, which can access data by centralized key management. By developing policies, procedures and security software, it is possible to protect data at every level by against malware and unauthorized access (Gahi, Guennoun & Mouftah, 2016).

Cloud computing is the commodification of computing and data storage by means of globally accepted techniques. The advantages of having big data on cloud are cost cutting, availability of instant infrastructure and faster access of data. The integration of big data with cloud storage also leads to many privacy breaches. One of the reasons for these breaches is that no appropriate security application is available to achieve privacy goals for such massive data. The shifting towards big data in the cloud has many benefits; it can bring powerful data analytics and boost decision making in data driven approaches. Cloud-based data analytics requires high-level, easy-to-use design tools for dealing with huge, distributed data sources.

The 2018 Thales Data Threat Report (DTR) (Mahmood & Afzal, 2013) surveyed 99% organization uses big data with security techniques e.g. Stronger authentication and access controls, Improved monitoring and reporting tools (Jain, Gyanchandani, & Khare, 2016), Encryption and access controls for underlying platforms (Jain, Gyanchandani, & Khare, 2016).

In this chapter we are going to discuss different Encryption technique and Key management technique and compare it. These two techniques are used to provide security at Storage level and Access Control level to protect system from Ransomware, Distributed Denial of service attack threats which can crash server or leak sensitive information. We elaborate different security techniques with their pros and cons.

Recently, many organizations works on Big Data security e.g. Thales working on encryption, access control, and key management which audit and report for governance purposes. CLOUDWICK (Jain, Gyanchandani, & Khare, 2016) include technology is Cloudera's Hadoop distribution and data analytics tool is used for managing data security. IBM Security Guardium (Jain, Gyanchandani, & Khare, 2016) monitor big data environment to protect the vulnerability of data.

Blockchain can be a successful venture for security of large amount of data because of its distributed and decentralized structure of storing data without having any third-party application. Distributed consensus algorithms and asymmetric cryptography have been implemented for ledger consistency and data security. Blockchain over cloud computing will largely saves cost and time due to its characteristics like consistency, decentralization and anonymity (Zheng, Zibin, Shaoan, Hongning, Xiangping, & Huaimin, 2015).

The remainder of this chapter is organized as follows. In Section 2, presents the literature reviews on existing technology and their contribution regarding algorithm. In Section 3, briefly explain the core features and functions different algorithm of key management and Encryption techniques. In Section 4, provide detailed survey and analysis of big data with block chain technology as future direction. Finally, in Section 6, conclude the chapter after discussing the challenges, open problems, and future directions of Big data security.

RELATED WORK

In this section, we present the research work done related to security and privacy of big data with emphasizing their key contribution and methodology/techniques incorporated.

Table 1. Related work

Title	Study Description	Contribution	Methodology	Remarks
Protection Of big data Privacy (Zhang, 2018)	Provide Overview of privacy preservation technique and give future research challenges for existing mechanisms.	Provide comparison on different Integrity verification scheme	IDE, ABE, PRE, Homomorphic Encryption, Anonymization Technique.	They find security challenges in each phase of Big Data also discussed the pros and cons of different privacy preservation technique.
Security Analytics: Big Data Analytics for CyberSecurity (Mahmood, & Afzal, 2013)	Security techniques and tools for Security Analytics can monitor real time network stream and detect malicious pattern	They identify different cyber-attacks and big data sources for security Analytics and their solutions.	IBM Security Intelligence, Actian Data Rush	They discuss real time network streams using traditional techniques and provide analytics solutions for cyber security with their futures.
Big Data analytics: Security and privacy challenges (Gahi, Guennoun, & Mouftah, 2016)	Present some existing protection techniques and propose some tracking techniques to enable security and privacy in the context of big data.	The authors proposed following tracks for security. 1. Rule and legality 2. Encryption on storage, computation and communication. 3. Authentication 4. Metadata and tag data 5. Unstructured distribution. 6. Tracing activity.	Reducing node authority by de-privileged users, CL-PRE, Holomorphic encryption and blind processing, cryptographic based transformation scheme	They highlighted solutions to implement privacy techniques for an open source and distributed analytic tool.
Towards efficient and privacy preserving computing in big data era (Lu, Zhu, Liu, & Shao, 2014)	Identified privacy requirement and introduces Cosine similarity computing protocol for privacy of Big Data.	Author invented an efficient technique for Preserving privacy named "Cosine similarity computing protocol"	1. Privacy Preserving aggregation 2. Operations over encrypted Data 3. De-identification.	Author analyzed security challenges in big data analytics.
The security of Big Data in Fog-enabled IOT Application Including Blockchain: A survey (Tariq, Asim, Al-Obeidat, Zubair, Baker & Ghafi, 2019)	Presented security requirement in fog enabled system. Block chain is solution for many security related issues.	They find threats in IoT based application and solve using fog-based computing system and contribute their work for security challenges in fog computing.	Block chain and anonymity solutions for security and privacy problems in IOT.	Main goal is to provide security to data generated by fog enabled IOT application.
A survey on security and privacy issues in big data (Terzi & Sagiroglu, 2015)	In spite of conventional techniques authors highlighted security & privacy techniques for big data as different categories.	Authors described various security and privacy techniques, purpose & data sets for different categories like hadoop & client security, monitoring & auditing of big data, anonymization, and encryption key management.	1. Identity based encryption 2. Maliciousness likelihood matrices 3. k-anonymity based metrics 4. Adaptive utility-based anonymization model.	Better understanding of ecosystem of big data for developing new tools, solutions and techniques (Terzi & Sagiroglu, 2015)
Survey of Various Homomorphic Encryption algorithms and Schemes (Vormetric Encryption Architecture Overview Protecting Enterprise Data at Rest with Encryption, Access Controls and Auditing)	Homomorphic Encryption can be applied in system by using public key. When information is stored on server and provide privacy on stored data that time homomorphic technique is used.	Author Study on various principle and properties of homomorphic encryption techniques	Algebra homomorphic encryption scheme based on updated ElGamal (AHEE), Non-interactive exponential homomorphic encryption algorithm (NEHE), homomorphic Cryptosystem (EHC), Brakerski-Gentry-Vaikuntanathan (BGV)	They define additive and multiplicative homomorphic encryption technique using mathematical operation.

continued on following page

Table 1. Continued

Title	Study Description	Contribution	Methodology	Remarks
CL-PRE: a Certificateless Proxy Re-Encryption Scheme for Secure Data Sharing with Public Cloud (Xu, Wu & Zhang, 2012)	This technique provide privacy on shared data which are stored on cloud.	Author presented implementation of CL-PRE technique and evaluate security and performance.	1. CL-PRE 2. Multi proxy CL-PRE 3. Randomized CL-PRE	CL-PRE satisfied security requirements for big data and information shared in cloud. Multi-proxy CL-PRE improves robustness of system.
Main Issues in Big Data Security (Moreno, Serrano, & Fernández-Medin, 2016)	G-hadoop check user's authentication and protect from traditional attacks. Differential privacy which increase the analysis of large data and reduce the user's identifications from others	Author focus on problems and challenges related to Big data security and how researchers are dealing with these problems. So they presented methodology and mapping which helps in finding paper related to our goal	G-Hadoop, Differential privacy (Moreno, Serrano, & Fernández-Medina, 2016)	They focus on Four big data challenges such as, Infrastructure security, Data management, data privacy, integrity and reactive security
Big Data Classification: Problems and Challenges in Network Intrusion Prediction with Machine Learning (Suthaharan, 2014)	MDRL technique includes feature variable learning, feature extraction learning and distance-metric learning	Adopting machine lifelong learning framework for solving the problems associated with the continuity parameter. It also discussed the problems and challenges that the Big Data classification system for network intrusion prediction have to experience during the Big Data analytics	1. Machine lifelong Learning 2. Multi domain representation learning (Suthaharan, 2014)	This paper discusses the problems and challenges in handling Big Data classification using geometric representation-learning techniques and the modern Big Data networking technologies
Attribute Relationship Evaluation Methodology for Big Data Security (Kim & Chung, 2013)	Proposed technique useful for extracting information from relevance attribute and protecting information.	They presented technique which selects specific attributes for protecting value of big data	Attribute Relationship evaluation methodology (Kim & Chung, 2013)	Proposed techniques protect object of attributes which applicable to big data with multiple attributes
Information Security in Big Data: Privacy and Data Mining	They achieve security by utilizing security tool, by developing privacy preserving model, by choosing proper mining algorithm to secure sensitive information of users.	They provide security mechanism for four types of users such as data miner, decision maker, data provider and data collector	Privacy-Preserving Data Mining (PPDM) (Pilkington, 2016)	Goal of this technique is to modify data without compromising the security of data which contain sensitive information
Multi-key privacy-preserving deep learning in cloud computing	Using MKFHE technique multiple user send their data to untrusted party. Data owner extracts result from encrypted result set.	Authors proposed advance scheme which combine double decryption algorithm and fully homomorphic encryption.	Multi-Key Fully Homomorphic Encryption (MKFHE) (Xu, Jiang, Wang, Yuan & Ren, 2014)	Both proposed schemes are used to tackle security problems with multiple public keys. They also used deep learning cypher texts.

OBSERVATIONS

A literature survey based on research conducted on big data computing related to preserving security and privacy of data is discussed in the following section. We have observed that most of the authors focus on Encryption techniques, which applied on incoming data from various sources as well as Key management techniques which are used to restrict unauthorized access of data.

TECHNIQUES

In this section, we briefly discussed major techniques used for data encryption and key management over cloud platform. Furthermore, discussion breaks down into parts about identifying different methodology features, applications, merits and demerits.

HOMOMORPHIC ENCRYPTION TECHNIQUE

It is a category of encryption in which the encryption procedure will be conducted on cipher text. Basically, results are obtained by performing computing on encrypted data without performing decryption on encrypted data. Homomorphic encryption provides a secure environment in which data can be encrypted over and overusing a function and still can be decrypted to original state easily. There are many techniques having homomorphic properties are RSA and ELGAMAL. The crucial property of homomorphic encryption is that if an operation performed on plain text or operated text then the result obtained will be the same. (Zhang,2018) Currently homomorphic encryption exists in two flavors: partial and full. Anyone can encrypt a particular data, but it can be decrypted using a private function only. Therefore, no attacker can decrypt particular data without knowing private function f(m). The procedure of homomorphic encryption categorized into four parts naming: Key generation, Encryption, Evaluation and decryption. Partial homomorphic techniques allow simple operations while fully a homomorphic technique allows all operations to be performed on encrypted data. (Jin, Wah, Cheng, & Wang, 2015)

Homomorphic encryption is malleable in terms of anyone can intercept encrypted data, apply function and generate new encrypted data. This new encrypted data can be decrypted into meaning full data, but it loses its original value. As there are huge amount of unstructured data that are flowing across cloud platforms needs to be secured. Homomorphic encryption is very useful in terms of preserving privacy for

Figure 1. Homomorphic encryption procedure
Source: (Acar, Abbas, Hidayet, Uluagac, & Mauro, 2018)

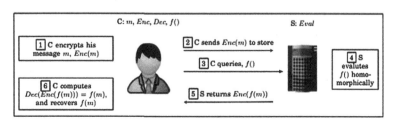

many emerging domains like big data stored on cloud and blockchain. Homomorphic encryption has great significance on many client server applications.

Based on number of operations that can be performed on encrypted data, following homomorphic encryption types are derived: Partial Homomorphic Encryption (PHE), SomeWhat Homomorphic Encryption (SWHE) and Fully Homomorphic Encryption (FHE). The PHE is designed to perform only single types of operation can be performed multiple times on data. The SWHE scheme limits the number of times any operation can be performed on data. Although it allows a greater number of operations than PHE. Partial Homomorphic Encryption allows either multiplicative or additive homomorphism but not both. But we could also do multiplication in additive HE by doing repeated addition on that particular value. (Acar, Abbas, Aksu, Uluagac, & Mauro, 2018)

PHE technique is used in some real-life applications such as Private Information Retrieval (PIR) (Kushilevitz and Ostrovsky, 1997) or e-voting (Benaloh, 1987). RSA algorithm exhibits multiplicative homomorphic encryption. Although one could also perform multiplication operation in additive homomorphic encryption by doing repeated addition on that particular data. (Chandhiny & Vairamuthu, 2018)

However, limitations of these implementations were types of homomorphic evaluation operations allowed. Nonetheless, in SWHE schemes that are proposed before the first FHE scheme, the size of the encrypted data grows with every homomorphic operation performed and hence the maximum number of allowed homomorphic operations is limited. This problem leads limited of use of SWHE and PHE in real-life applications. Furthermore, the vast usage of cloud-based services accelerated the design of HE schemes, which supports an arbitrary number of homomorphic operations with random functions. (Acar, Abbas, Aksu, Uluagac, & Mauro, 2018)

CERTIFICATELESS PROXY RE-ENCRYPTION SCHEME (CL-PRE)

This technique is basically used for secure data sharing between users, where data is stored, transformed, accessed publicly on cloud. Data owner initially encrypts data with private encryption key, then cloud itself applies transformation using its own encryption scheme and that encrypted data will be transferred to legitimate users according to their privileges. This scheme is used for many cloud-based applications like social network service (SNS) (Gahi, Guennoun, & Mouftah, 2016). In this technique, the cloud based encryption key will be calculated from private key of data owner as well as public key of recipients. Privacy of data and key will be preserved by the cloud resources only and leads to lesser computation cost to the data owner. Basically CL-PRE will give advantage of minimal computation at data owner's side. But cloud is semi-trusted platform for storing, transforming and sharing data. Thus, one should not trust completely on cloud for accession data and encryption key. So, to overcome these challenges CL-PRE uses different methodology. Initially data owner encrypts data with its symmetric private key and then this encrypted data will be stored on cloud. The private key (KY) is also encrypted with public key and stored in the cloud along with all generated proxy re-encryption keys. Here cloud will provide proxy resident service to data owner. Thus, the cloud will use this encrypted KY to compute data on cloud and send it to appropriate recipients for accessing. The recipient uses their respective public keys to use those data. In this manner, cloud will never be able to see actual data or KY, such data privacy and key confidentiality will be maintained. The major disadvantage of using CL-PRE is re-encryption computation cost and overhead. The computation cost increases as the number of recipients. As well as, the cloud is working as proxy provides to users leads to higher communication and storage requirements. However, it eliminates key escrow problem and also the requirement of certificates for authentication. (Xu, Wu, & Zhang, 2012)

Figure 2. Overview of CL-PRE scheme
(Xu, Wu, & Zhang, 2012)

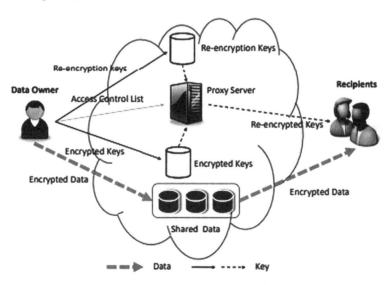

ATTRIBUTE BASED ACCESS CONTROL

ABAC techniques works on principle of Access control mechanism. The purpose of ACM is to protect different object such as data services, network devices and other sensitive information from unauthorised users. The unauthorised user performs malicious activity like deleting, reading, editing and discovering objects. Owner of Object have authority to establish a policy in which they describe who can perform those operations. If the user satisfies ACM policy which created by author then they authorised to perform an operation on objects. ABAC is a combination of ACm policy and Rule based Access control (RBAC). In this model person access object based on role they have assigned. Access requests is granted if role assigned to the user is authorised. In RBAC if Access control is changed then difficult to identify updatable places which will removed in ABAC. ABAC avoids access of particular users before they made a request. This method makes access control decision based on assigned attributes of objects, assigned attribute of requester.

Above figure describe ABAC mechanism in which if Organisation A's user wants to access Organisation B's resources they have to create repository in Organisation B's, then they can access resources.

Attribute based access control (ABAC) (Hu, Ferraiolo, Kuhn, Friedman, Lang, Cogdell, & Scarfone, 2013): This method is based on access control mechanism in which subject requests to object and they can permit if assigned attribute of object, subject, policy and environment condition is satisfied.

As more data is shared on the internet and stored in the cloud, we need to encrypt this sensitive data from threats and unauthorised access. But Encryption techniques is working on fine gain level, in which we have to share the secret key to other users which make data leaked by unauthorized person. So another approaches comes to resolve this problem is Attributed based access control. Attribute based access control helps to achieve effective cloud services, transparency and integrity.

Figure 3. Attribute based access control
Source: (Hu, Ferraiolo, Kuhn, Friedman, Lang, Cogdell, & Scarfone, 2013)

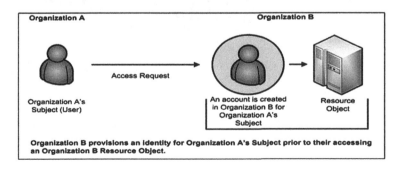

Attribute based access control is new cryptosystem which working at a fine grain level. It required set of attributes and private key to decrypt the original data. ABAC (Hu, Kuhn, Ferraiolo, & Voas, 2015) give privileges to authorised users by using policy and attributes. Policy used in ABAC can use different types of attributes e.g. user attribute which associated with application to access the system. For example, ABAC would allow access only those employees who are working in HR department. In (Hu, Kuhn, Ferraiolo, & Voas,2015), they implemented Fine grained access control, secret sharing scheme, Identity based encryption. ABAC consist key-value pairs to describe all entities with authorized value. This can be implemented by structured languages which is called the eXtensible Access Control Markup Language (XACML) (Goyal, Vipul, Omkant Pandey, Amit Sahai, & Brent Waters,2006), which is as easy to read or write as a natural language. (Hu, Kuhn, Ferraiolo, & Voas, 2015)

BLOCKCHAIN ACCESS CONTROL SCHEME

Block chain access control method provides protection against data breaches on large data sets. Block chain technology is stored data in distributed, secure, and cryptographic form which also used hash function for validation of data which are stored in block. Every block in block chain keep replicas of data therefore there is highly available data and no single point of failure. All nodes in block chain contain history of all transactions made between clients. Block chain technology uses Asymmetric cryptographic which ensure that all exchanges made between users is highly secured. Digital currencies, Networking data, supply chain management, medical science uses Block chain. This technique has been obtained by merging two of the existing techniques: Role-Based Access Control (RBAC) and Identity-based access control (IBAC) (Uchibeke, Ugobame, Schneider, Hosseinzadeh, & Ralph, 2018). Using identity based access control method user have to request to the owner of the data and they are verified by user's identity, If user gets successfully verified then they can view the particular requested data. Access control mechanisms rely on four different parameters, such as data owners, data storage provider, data retriever, block chain infrastructure. With combination of blockchain, a hyper ledger will be maintained for granting and revoking permissions to each and every user. Every user will be allocated a key to access a particular resource which can be stored on block chain hyper ledger. When new users join in block chain network, the issues key with identity to submitting processes in block chain. Using this key, they are able to see all history about submitted transaction and control the access of data which provide highly security. While in other techniques individual users will be allotted a role and based on roles certain permissions to access data can be given. Once a privilege, has been provided to users all the roles and privileges data can be stored in ledger in block chain. This technique has advantages of conventional algorithms as well as blockchain (Uchibeke, Ugobame, Schneider, Sara Hosseinzadeh, & Ralph, 2018). Block chain authentication and identification done by block chain ID. This block ID is associated with each and every block of data and verified by third party of by ECDSA (elliptic curve digital signature algorithm).

Aim of the above framework is to provide access rights for each data resources such as directory, images, file and delete these rights if required. Rights are defined by Data Retriever (DR) and register in smart contract as weight list which specify details description about access control with data retrievers. Data owner (DO) is responsible for creating smart contractor, adding and removing rights is whilte list. When Data receiver (DR) try to access data from Data storage (DS) they have to first authorized their accessess rights in contract through block chain controller infrastructure. Data owner first save file in data storage then create and add accesses right in smart contract (C). Then DO sends updated address of SC to DSP. DO send newly address of SC to DR. DO recover address of all authorized DR and update SC's whilte list.

DE-IDENTIFICATION SCHEME

De-identification is a conventional technique for privacy preserving technique which uses sanitization and suppression techniques. Basically, this technique will change data in such a way that key attributes will be protected from direct identification. In this technique data is first generalized by replacing quasi-identifiers with semantically

Figure 4. Block chain based access control framework
Source: (Acar, Abbas, Hidayet, Selcuk, & Mauro,2018)

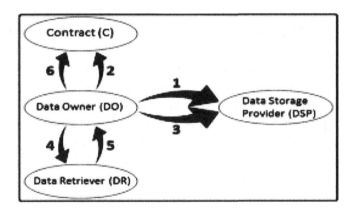

consistent values. Suppression includes limiting the values that are being released. Obviously de-identification is crucial technique for preserving privacy for big data. To mitigate the threats to getting data by applying re-identification, more privacy preserving techniques are associated with de-identification scheme. The k-anonymity, l-diversity and t-closeness schemes are associated with de-identification for enhancing feasibility and efficiency. (Abouelmehdi, Abderrahim, Hayat & Mostafa, 2017)

- **K-Anonymity:** To lower the probability of re-identification, higher value of k needs to be selected. However, it may lead to information loss. For example, a data set is called k-anonymized, if for a particular record there are K-1 other records that can be fetched. In K-anonymity, to identify individual data quasi-identifier associate it with publically available data. Thus, some sensitive information may get leaked. K-anonymization is still at risk of attacks like temporal attack, unsorted matching attack, and complementary release attack. Various schemes can be applied to prevent the attribute loss. (Abouelmehdi, Abderrahim, Hayat, & Mostafa, 2017)
- **L-Diversity:** By diminishing the granularity of data representation, L-diversity applies group-based anonymization. L-diversity is basically an improved version of k-anonymization, which helps in reducing the granularity of data representation by utilizing the generalization and suppression methods. This technique guarantees that each equivalence class of quasi identifiers has minimum L diverse set of data for sensitive entity. The protected entities to level of k-anonymization is not the same as securing respected sensitive entities on which suppression or generalization has applied. This flaw has been improved in L-diversity method. For making sensitive data more diverse, we can add some fabricated data along with sensitive data. Although applying L-diversity makes data secure, but leads to problems while analyzing the data. (Abouelmehdi, Abderrahim, Hayat, & Mostafa, 2017)
- **T-Closeness:** This is more advanced version of L-diversity. Instead of applying group-based anonymization, it focuses on the distribution of data values for an attribute. The major advantage of this technique is that it mitigates the chances of the attribute disclosure. We are increasing the diversity and volume of data at a large scale, such that reidentification of data also becomes quite costly. (Abouelmehdi, Abderrahim, Hayat & Mostafa, 2017)

PRIVACY AND SECURITY PRESERVATION IN BLOCKCHAIN

Based on several researches there are four basic characteristics of blockchain, which are Autonomous, Distributed, Immutability and Contractual. One remarkable property of blockchain is it is completely decentralized thus no single entity is governing the whole network. Secondly, blockchain's architecture is based on peer-to-peer (P2P) network, where every single signed transaction will be broadcasted to all nodes eventually. Whole global ledger and valid blocks will be synchronized such that any user can be assured of confidentiality and integrity of original data. The Consensus of contract is achieved by executing code-defined rules by each node without any central entity or human intervention (Feng, Zeadally, Khan, & Kumar, 2018).

Privacy preservation in blockchain basically means protecting links between transactions as well as protecting contents of transaction. Transaction privacy means not disclosing transaction data to only specific users. Identity privacy means intractability between identification of transaction contributors and actual transaction script. By applying some behavioral analysis schemes, user information may get revealed while traversing through public blockchain. Thus, it provides limited identity privacy. (Feng, Zeadally, Khan, & Kumar, 2018) A transaction holds items like identification of the previous transaction, trade values, the addresses of its participants, timestamp and signature of its sender. There are various attacks that can compromise with user's identity. Attackers can obtain user's information by performing Network analysis (due to P2P architecture), address clustering, transaction fingerprinting, Sybil attacks and DoS attacks. Three different methodologies are frequently used for identity preservation known as ring signature, mixing services and zero knowledge proof. (Swan, 2015)

ADAPTIVE UTILITY BASED ANONYMIZATION MODEL

Data anonymization secure individual user's data and increase quality of data. It will remove the identifier of user such as personal ID and name from others to protect persons information. Adaptive utility-based anonymization is intelligent model which disclose the risk. This model is worked as two part.in first, they associate entire data set with attribute and second they classify that attribute as frequent and infrequent data, From this iterative process they give results according to users' needs. Anonymization is often used for data mining and analysis. For data analysis different attribute has different utility such as data set about healthcare i n which patients has many attributes for data analysis. Privacy is become more serious issues in big data so we need good anonymization techniques. Utility based model boost quality of data but still it has some problems such as if many records are given in database and every record has its own privacy preserving requirement then this anonymization scheme not giving security for those records. Utility based anonymization is more important in many applications (Panackal, & Pillai, 2016).

FUTURE DIRECTIONS

After discussing various techniques, Block chain technology will give better solution for preserving privacy & security of data. For storing and transmitting information, Block chain technology secures cryptographically distributed data. This technology prevents data leak, enhances data analysis and Improvises Fraud Detection. Block chain technology allows banking institute to detect threats and detect search patterns in real time. Block chain is storage of secure trustful, authenticated, replicated non-erasable set of big data. Block chain with big data Analytics adds another data level which makes data secure and valuable. This data cannot be forged by threats and make complete and abundant source for further analysis.

CONCLUSION

Security and privacy are a crucial characteristic that needs to be achieved for storing, transforming and accessing data stored over cloud platform. We have presented the major characteristics of big data and issues with reference to preserving security and privacy of data along with the challenges regarding storing data on cloud platforms. We surveyed various data encryption techniques, key management methodology proposed by the researchers with comparative study. It has been observed from the study that major existing techniques involve higher computation overhead and storage costs. As an emerging concept, blockchain technology can be more efficient technique, if combined with conventional techniques which can turn into practical solution for achieving security and privacy of data. Blockchain basically provides you secure transaction of data without being dependent on any third party application.

REFERENCES

Abinesh, K. K., & Shiju, S. (2017). Intrusion Detection System Using Big Data Framework. *Journal of Engineering and Applied Sciences*, *12*(12).

Abouelmehdi, K., Beni-Hssane, A., Khaloufi, H., & Saadi, M. (2017). Big data security and privacy in healthcare: A Review. *Procedia Computer Science*, *113*, 73–80. doi:10.1016/j.procs.2017.08.292

Acar, A., Aksu, H., Uluagac, A. S., & Conti, M. (2018). A survey on homomorphic encryption schemes: Theory and implementation. *ACM Computing Surveys*, *51*(4), 79. doi:10.1145/3214303

Al Omar, A., Rahman, M. S., Basu, A., & Kiyomoto, S. (2017, December). Medibchain: A blockchain based privacy preserving platform for healthcare data. In *Proceedings of the International conference on security, privacy and anonymity in computation, communication and storage* (pp. 534-543). Springer. 10.1007/978-3-319-72395-2_49

Azaria, A., Ekblaw, A., Vieira, T., & Lippman, A. (2016, August). Medrec: Using blockchain for medical data access and permission management. In *Proceedings of the 2016 2nd International Conference on Open and Big Data (OBD)* (pp. 25-30). IEEE.

Bacon, J., Evans, D., Eyers, D. M., Migliavacca, M., Pietzuch, P., & Shand, B. (2010, November). Enforcing end-to-end application security in the cloud (big ideas paper). In *Proceedings of the ACM/IFIP/USENIX 11th International Conference on Middleware* (pp. 293-312). Springer-Verlag.

Cárdenas, A. A., Manadhata, P. K., & Rajan, S. P. (2013). Big data analytics for security. *IEEE Security and Privacy*, *11*(6), 74–76. doi:10.1109/MSP.2013.138

Chang, V. (2015). Towards a Big Data system disaster recovery in a Private Cloud. *Ad Hoc Networks*, *35*, 65–82. doi:10.1016/j.adhoc.2015.07.012

Crawford, K., & Schultz, J. (2014). Big data and due process: Toward a framework to redress predictive privacy harms. *BCL Rev.*, *55*, 93.

De Busser, E. (2002). Big Data: The Conflict Between Protecting Privacy and Securing Nations. *Policy*, *9*, 330.

Du, W., & Zhan, Z. (2003, August). Using randomized response techniques for privacy-preserving data mining. In *Proceedings of the ninth ACM SIGKDD international conference on Knowledge discovery and data mining* (pp. 505-510). ACM. 10.1145/956750.956810

Dwivedi, A. D., Srivastava, G., Dhar, S., & Singh, R. (2019). A decentralized privacy-preserving healthcare blockchain for iot. *Sensors (Basel)*, *19*(2), 326. doi:10.339019020326 PMID:30650612

Esposito, C., De Santis, A., Tortora, G., Chang, H., & Choo, K. K. R. (2018). Blockchain: A panacea for healthcare cloud-based data security and privacy? *IEEE Cloud Computing*, *5*(1), 31–37. doi:10.1109/MCC.2018.011791712

Feng, Q., He, D., Zeadally, S., Khan, M. K., & Kumar, N. (2019). A survey on privacy protection in blockchain system. *Journal of Network and Computer Applications*, *126*, 45–58. doi:10.1016/j.jnca.2018.10.020

Ferraiolo, D., Chandramouli, R., Kuhn, R., & Hu, V. (2016, March). Extensible access control markup language (XACML) and next generation access control (NGAC). In *Proceedings of the 2016 ACM International Workshop on Attribute Based Access Control* (pp. 13-24). ACM. 10.1145/2875491.2875496

Gahi, Y., Guennoun, M., & Mouftah, H. T. (2016, June). Big data analytics: Security and privacy challenges. In *Proceedings of the 2016 IEEE Symposium on Computers and Communication (ISCC)* (pp. 952-957). IEEE. 10.1109/ISCC.2016.7543859

Gentry, C. (2010). Computing arbitrary functions of encrypted data. *Communications of the ACM*, *53*(3), 97–105. doi:10.1145/1666420.1666444

Goyal, V., Pandey, O., Sahai, A., & Waters, B. (2006, October). Attribute-based encryption for fine-grained access control of encrypted data. In *Proceedings of the 13th ACM conference on Computer and communications security* (pp. 89-98). ACM. 10.1145/1180405.1180418

Habeeb, R. A. A., Nasaruddin, F., Gani, A., Hashem, I. A. T., Ahmed, E., & Imran, M. (2019). Real-time big data processing for anomaly detection: A Survey. *International Journal of Information Management*, *45*, 289–307. doi:10.1016/j.ijinfomgt.2018.08.006

Hu, V. C., Ferraiolo, D., Kuhn, R., Friedman, A. R., Lang, A. J., Cogdell, M. M., ... Scarfone, K. (2013). Guide to attribute based access control (ABAC) definition and considerations (draft). *NIST*.

Hu, V. C., Kuhn, D. R., & Ferraiolo, D. F. (2018). Access Control for Emerging Distributed Systems. *Computer*, *51*(10), 100–103. doi:10.1109/MC.2018.3971347 PMID:31092952

Hur, J., & Noh, D. K. (2010). Attribute-based access control with efficient revocation in data outsourcing systems. *IEEE Transactions on Parallel and Distributed Systems*, *22*(7), 1214–1221. doi:10.1109/TPDS.2010.203

Jain, P., Gyanchandani, M., & Khare, N. (2016). Big data privacy: A technological perspective and review. *Journal of Big Data*, *3*(1), 25. doi:10.118640537-016-0059-y

Jain, P., Pathak, N., Tapashetti, P., & Umesh, A. S. (2013, December). Privacy preserving processing of data decision tree based on sample selection and singular value decomposition. In *Proceedings of the 2013 9th international conference on information assurance and security (IAS)* (pp. 91-95). IEEE. 10.1109/ISIAS.2013.6947739

Jin, X., Krishnan, R., & Sandhu, R. (2012, July). A unified attribute-based access control model covering DAC, MAC and RBAC. In *Proceedings of the IFIP Annual Conference on Data and Applications Security and Privacy* (pp. 41-55). Springer. 10.1007/978-3-642-31540-4_4

Jin, X., Wah, B. W., Cheng, X., & Wang, Y. (2015). Significance and challenges of big data research. *Big Data Research*, 2(2), 59–64. doi:10.1016/j.bdr.2015.01.006

Joshi, A. P., Han, M., & Wang, Y. (2018). A survey on security and privacy issues of blockchain technology. *Mathematical Foundations of Computing*, 1(2), 121–147. doi:10.3934/mfc.2018007

Kim, H. K., So, W. H., & Je, S. M. (2019). A big data framework for network security of small and medium enterprises for future computing. *The Journal of Supercomputing*, 75(6), 3334–3367. doi:10.100711227-019-02815-8

Kim, S. H., Kim, N. U., & Chung, T. M. (2013, December). Attribute relationship evaluation methodology for big data security. In *Proceedings of the 2013 International conference on IT convergence and security (ICITCS)* (pp. 1-4). IEEE. 10.1109/ICITCS.2013.6717808

Labrinidis, A., & Jagadish, H. V. (2012). Challenges and opportunities with big data. *Proceedings of the VLDB Endowment International Conference on Very Large Data Bases*, 5(12), 2032–2033. doi:10.14778/2367502.2367572

Lee, J., Moon, D., Kim, I., & Lee, Y. (2019). A semantic approach to improving machine readability of a large-scale attack graph. *The Journal of Supercomputing*, 75(6), 3028–3045. doi:10.100711227-018-2394-6

Li, J., Chen, X., Li, J., Jia, C., Ma, J., & Lou, W. (2013, September). Fine-grained access control system based on outsourced attribute-based encryption. In *Proceedings of the European Symposium on Research in Computer Security* (pp. 592-609). Springer. 10.1007/978-3-642-40203-6_33

Li, P., Li, J., Huang, Z., Li, T., Gao, C. Z., Yiu, S. M., & Chen, K. (2017). Multi-key privacy-preserving deep learning in cloud computing. *Future Generation Computer Systems*, 74, 76–85. doi:10.1016/j.future.2017.02.006

Liang, X., Zhao, J., Shetty, S., Liu, J., & Li, D. (2017, October). Integrating blockchain for data sharing and collaboration in mobile healthcare applications. In *Proceedings of the 2017 IEEE 28th Annual International Symposium on Personal, Indoor, and Mobile Radio Communications (PIMRC)* (pp. 1-5). IEEE. 10.1109/PIMRC.2017.8292361

Longstaff, J., & Noble, J. (2016, March). Attribute based access control for big data applications by query modification. In *Proceedings of the 2016 IEEE Second International Conference on Big Data Computing Service and Applications (BigDataService)* (pp. 58-65). IEEE. 10.1109/BigDataService.2016.35

Lu, R., Zhu, H., Liu, X., Liu, J. K., & Shao, J. (2014). Toward efficient and privacy-preserving computing in big data era. *IEEE Network*, *28*(4), 46–50. doi:10.1109/MNET.2014.6863131

Mahalakshmi, S., Saiashwini, C., & Meghana, S. (2001). Research study of big data clustering techniques. *Int. J. Innov. Res. Sci. Eng*, 80-84.

Mahmood, T., & Afzal, U. (2013, December). Security analytics: Big data analytics for cybersecurity: A review of trends, techniques and tools. In *Proceedings of the 2013 2nd national conference on Information assurance (NCIA)* (pp. 129-134). IEEE.

Moreno, J., Serrano, M., & Fernández-Medina, E. (2016). Main issues in big data security. *Future Internet*, *8*(3), 44. doi:10.3390/fi8030044

Naik, N., Jenkins, P., Savage, N., & Katos, V. (2016, December). Big data security analysis approach using computational intelligence techniques in R for desktop users. In *Proceedings of the 2016 IEEE Symposium Series on Computational Intelligence (SSCI)* (pp. 1-8). IEEE. 10.1109/SSCI.2016.7849907

Panackal, J. J., & Pillai, A. S. (2015). Adaptive utility-based anonymization model: Performance evaluation on big data sets. *Procedia Computer Science*, *50*, 347–352. doi:10.1016/j.procs.2015.04.037

Parmar, P. V., Padhar, S. B., Patel, S. N., Bhatt, N. I., & Jhaveri, R. H. (2014). Survey of various homomorphic encryption algorithms and schemes. *International Journal of Computers and Applications*, *91*(8).

Pham, D., Le Nguyen, T., Zhang, P. P., & Lo, M. (2005). U.S. Patent No. 6,931,530. Washington, DC: U.S. Patent and Trademark Office.

Pilkington, M. (2016). 11 Blockchain technology: principles and applications. In *Research handbook on digital transformations* (p. 225). Academic Press.

Qi, H., Luo, X., Di, X., Li, J., Yang, H., & Jiang, Z. (2016, October). Access control model based on role and attribute and its implementation. In *Proceedings of the 2016 International Conference on Cyber-Enabled Distributed Computing and Knowledge Discovery (CyberC)* (pp. 66-71). IEEE. 10.1109/CyberC.2016.21

Riad, K., Yan, Z., Hu, H., & Ahn, G. J. (2015, October). AR-ABAC: a new attribute based access control model supporting attribute-rules for cloud computing. In *Proceedings of the 2015 IEEE Conference on Collaboration and Internet Computing (CIC)* (pp. 28-35). IEEE. 10.1109/CIC.2015.38

Richards, N. M., & King, J. H. (2013). Three paradoxes of big data. *Stan. L. Rev. Online*, *66*, 41.

Sarowar, M. G., Kamal, M. S., & Dey, N. (2019). Internet of Things and Its Impacts in Computing Intelligence: A Comprehensive Review–IoT Application for Big Data. In Big Data Analytics for Smart and Connected Cities (pp. 103–136). Hershey, PA: IGI Global. doi:10.4018/978-1-5225-6207-8.ch005

Suthaharan, S. (2014). Big data classification: Problems and challenges in network intrusion prediction with machine learning. *Performance Evaluation Review*, *41*(4), 70–73. doi:10.1145/2627534.2627557

Swan, M. (2015). *Blockchain: Blueprint for a new economy*. O'Reilly Media, Inc.

Takabi, H., Joshi, J. B., & Ahn, G. J. (2010). Security and privacy challenges in cloud computing environments. *IEEE Security and Privacy*, *8*(6), 24–31. doi:10.1109/MSP.2010.186

Tariq, N., Asim, M., Al-Obeidat, F., Zubair Farooqi, M., Baker, T., Hammoudeh, M., & Ghafir, I. (2019). The security of big data in fog-enabled IoT applications including blockchain: A survey. *Sensors (Basel)*, *19*(8), 1788. doi:10.339019081788 PMID:31013993

Tene, O., & Polonetsky, J. (2012). Big data for all: Privacy and user control in the age of analytics. *Nw. J. Tech. & Intell. Prop.*, *11*, xxvii.

Terzi, D. S., Terzi, R., & Sagiroglu, S. (2015, December). A survey on security and privacy issues in big data. In *Proceedings of the 2015 10th International Conference for Internet Technology and Secured Transactions (ICITST)* (pp. 202-207). IEEE. 10.1109/ICITST.2015.7412089

Uchibeke, U. U., Schneider, K. A., Kassani, S. H., & Deters, R. (2018, July). Blockchain access control Ecosystem for Big Data security. In *Proceedings of the 2018 IEEE International Conference on Internet of Things (iThings) and IEEE Green Computing and Communications (GreenCom) and IEEE Cyber, Physical and Social Computing (CPSCom) and IEEE Smart Data (SmartData)* (pp. 1373-1378). IEEE. Retrieved from https://www.infosecurityeurope.com/__novadocuments/21994

Wang, L., Wijesekera, D., & Jajodia, S. (2004, October). A logic-based framework for attribute based access control. In *Proceedings of the 2004 ACM workshop on Formal methods in security engineering* (pp. 45-55). ACM. 10.1145/1029133.1029140

Wang, S., Zhang, Y., & Zhang, Y. (2018). A blockchain-based framework for data sharing with fine-grained access control in decentralized storage systems. *IEEE Access, 6,* 38437–38450. doi:10.1109/ACCESS.2018.2851611

Wang, Z., Cao, C., Yang, N., & Chang, V. (2017). ABE with improved auxiliary input for big data security. *Journal of Computer and System Sciences, 89,* 41–50. doi:10.1016/j.jcss.2016.12.006

Ward, J. S., & Barker, A. (2013). Undefined by data: a survey of big data definitions.

Wolfert, S., Ge, L., Verdouw, C., & Bogaardt, M. J. (2017). Big data in smart farming–a review. *Agricultural Systems, 153,* 69–80. doi:10.1016/j.agsy.2017.01.023

Xia, Q., Sifah, E., Smahi, A., Amofa, S., & Zhang, X. (2017). BBDS: Blockchain-based data sharing for electronic medical records in cloud environments. *Information, 8*(2), 44. doi:10.3390/info8020044

Xia, Q. I., Sifah, E. B., Asamoah, K. O., Gao, J., Du, X., & Guizani, M. (2017). MeDShare: Trust-less medical data sharing among cloud service providers via blockchain. *IEEE Access, 5,* 14757–14767. doi:10.1109/ACCESS.2017.2730843

Xu, J., Wang, W., Pei, J., Wang, X., Shi, B., & Fu, A. W. C. (2006, August). Utility-based anonymization using local recoding. In *Proceedings of the 12th ACM SIGKDD international conference on Knowledge discovery and data mining* (pp. 785-790). ACM.

Xu, L., Jiang, C., Wang, J., Yuan, J., & Ren, Y. (2014). Information security in big data: Privacy and data mining. *IEEE Access, 2,* 1149–1176. doi:10.1109/ACCESS.2014.2362522

Xu, L., Wu, X., & Zhang, X. (2012, May). CL-PRE: a certificateless proxy re-encryption scheme for secure data sharing with public cloud. In *Proceedings of the 7th ACM symposium on information, computer and communications security* (pp. 87-88). ACM. 10.1145/2414456.2414507

Yang, Q., & Wu, X. (2006). 10 challenging problems in data mining research. *International Journal of Information Technology & Decision Making, 5*(04), 597–604. doi:10.1142/S0219622006002258

Zhang, D. (2018, October). Big data security and privacy protection. In *Proceedings of the 8th International Conference on Management and Computer Science (ICMCS 2018)*. Atlantis Press.

Zheng, Z., Xie, S., Dai, H., Chen, X., & Wang, H. An overview of blockchain technology: Architecture, consensus, and future trends. In *Proceedings of the 2017 IEEE International Congress on Big Data (BigData Congress)* (pp. 557-564). IEEE. 10.1109/BigDataCongress.2017.85

Zyskind, G., & Nathan, O. (2015, May). Decentralizing privacy: Using blockchain to protect personal data. In Proceedings of the 2015 IEEE Security and Privacy Workshops (pp. 180-184). IEEE.

Chapter 12
Cyber Security Techniques for Internet of Things (IoT)

Binod Kumar

iD https://orcid.org/0000-0002-6172-7938
Jayawant Institute of Computer Applications, Pune, India

Sheetal B. Prasad
SRM Institute of Science and Technology, Chennai, India

ABSTRACT

The purpose of the cyber security policy is to provide guidelines on how to secure public and private resources from cyberattacks. IoT devices are having challenges managing the personal information they collect and helps to people understand that information is managed by a system. Digital twins enhance development by allowing developers to directly manipulate the device's abstract version using programming instructions. It is required to think about possible attack vectors when tuning cyber security for the IoT environment concerns. So, a security administrator is required to think the about possible vulnerabilities of the environment. Supervision and protocols must also be developed for suppliers, manufacturers, vendors, etc. The deployment of consumer understanding to make best use of "smart" strategy, using their own "smart" minds is required. There is a need for a framework or other types of guidance for assessing IoT cyber security to provide an informed approach to securing devices and the ecosystems in which they are set up.

DOI: 10.4018/978-1-7998-2253-0.ch012

INTRODUCTION

All devices in the world today are primarily network-connected. In homes, offices, cars and services there are several devices available and various tasks are carried out to support everyday activities. When new internet connected technologies are available regularly to help users in their regular lives and create new digital opportunities, the number of connected devices is growing steadily. Existing and new internet-based systems include smart home appliances, smart cities, smart power plants, automobiles, health care, retail stores and transportation. For example, house monitoring cameras and refrigerators, intelligent city apps to help people find a vacant parking space and personal training equipment for the healthcare sector (Sulkamo, 2018).

The main features of all these systems and devices are that they are connected to the Internet in order to improve quality of life through digital experiences. Such instruments provide distinct knowledge, raw data and other software and information-sharing programs. For a variety of reasons, data produced by internet-connected devices may be stored and used. An example may be the tool or device wearable in the healthcare industry which indicates the medical condition of the person. The cooler can alert the food owner for shortages that need to be ordered. The data is then shared through a network of health experts (Sulkamo, 2018).

The security of IoT systems has to be incorporated with extensive checks of validity, authentication, data verification and encryption of all data. Software development companies at the application level need to be better able to write codes that are reliable, functional and have developed codes design practices, training, evaluation and testing. When systems communicate, an accepted interoperability standard is necessary, which is stable and accurate. Without a stable bottom-top framework, with each system introduced to the IoT, we will generate more risks. We need a safe and secure IoT, secured by confidentiality, hard to deal but not impossible (Banafa, 2019).

There are many different instances for different areas of life. Industrial production with Internet connected machinery is a significant area. The manufacturing business employs a variety of sensors and tracking tools to collect important data from the machinery and its conditions; the manufacturing process is tailored to make this data effective. Industrial production with Internet-connected devices is a significant field of activity. Different kinds of sensors and tracking instruments are used to gather important data from manufacturing machines. Another very significant field is the proactive compilation of machine maintenance information; maintenance breaks can therefore be scheduled with the shortest possible delays, depending on that information. The world of connected equipment covers all aspects of life, as can be seen.

INTERNET OF THINGS

The Internet of Things is a network of physical objects that contain embedded software to communicate and sensor, or to interact with its internal or outside environment. IoT is a forward-looking Internet architecture that integrates objects and devices into sensor and computer energy to communicate with one another. While the initial IoT idea excessively emphasizes machine-to-machine communication, the real change that underlies this is an increasingly indirect diversification of people-to-people communication. Machines can interact ultimately, but until now, this phenomenon has neither become universal nor includes all kinds of networks; even if machines can connect to one another, they stay as human communication tools (Miller, 2016).

The increasing networking capability of home, mobile and portable technology, cars and supply chains and even urban infrastructure machines and daily devices provides a wide array of business and customer satisfaction possibilities. Most IoT devices are using sensor-based technologies in which the sensors identify, measure or transfer data to a given device or server to analyze the data in order to generate the "Information" for the user and so on. The sensors also function as information collectors in company terms: cloud computing is a data storage and analysis platform, and Big Data Analytics converts this raw information into information or insights (Kessel, 2015).

The Internet of Things (IoT) provides numerous advantages to users and is likely to fundamentally change the way in which customers communicate with technology. In the future, the Internet of Things would potentially combine the virtual and physical environments in order to attempt to understand at present. The predicted widespread introduction of sensors and devices into sensitive areas today, such as home, smart watches and even the body, presents specific challenges from a perspective of security and privacy. When physical objects identify and communicate information about us more and more in our everyday life, consumer protection is also likely to continue (Banafa, 2019).

Within three groups, we may list the risks of IoT: privacy, security and safety. Experts say that Internet of Things security threats are wide and possibly even paralyzing systems. Since IoT will have critical parts of infrastructure, it is a good target for domestic and industrial surveillance and phishing and other attacks. The main concern is the security of personal privacy, which could also be a target for cyber-criminals, if any, in networks. It must be noted that IoT still has an ongoing work to do in determining security needs. Several objects are now connected to the Internet and we will experience an increase in this and the advent of contextual data sharing, the IoT allowance of a virtual presence to a physical object when creating, these virtual event activities will start interacting and exchanging contextual information, the devices will take decisions based on. This leads to highly physical challenges, including domestic infrastructure, environmental possessions, electricity, water and food, etc. (Banafa, 2019). Via IoT security tools, such as data encryption, reliable user authentication, secure coding, standardized and tested APIs, which respond in a predictable way, the protection of IoT environments is always being improved as threats are constantly occurring.

IoT employment business models can differ for every organization, whether it is key operations, production or services / technologies. The retail and retail industry, for instance, could in future advantage from IoT technologies: the measuring devices could measure their foot sizes if a fresh client joins a shoe business; information could be sent over to the cloud regarding accessibility of the stock.

OPPORTUNITIES DOES IOT OFFER

In the digital world, IoT is leading changes – and is quickly becoming the key component in commercial engineering. Some of the main forces that lead to IoT acceptance are (Kessel., 2015):

- **New Business Opportunities**: Many industries are given company possibilities through the Web of linked machines, individuals and information. Organizations can use IoT information to better understand the demands of their clients, and can enhance procedures such as coordination of the supply chain and inventory, investments and public security.
- **Growth Potential for Company Income**: There are numerous untapped financial impact possibilities to find new methods to use IoT technology to boost top-of - the-line development in income and value generation through cost reductions and improved asset productivity.
- **Enhanced Decision-Making**: Intelligent personal computing systems have increased and lead to a broader selection, updates in real time, improved equipment, more precise findings of facts, etc.
- **Cost Reductions**: IoT expenses, such as cloud services, sensors, GPS devices and microchips, have decreased, making IoT expenses more affordable every day.
- **Security and Safety**: Using cameras and sensors, there is the chance of guarding against, or avoiding, physical threats that may happen at work or at home. In moment, IoT will assist even disaster management or recovery systems.
- **Better Infrastructure**: IoT could assist convert infrastructure into a living organism, particularly when significant megacities transform into smart towns. Large population inflows into urban regions and depleted non-

renewable energy sources make resource management a challenge, but smart infrastructure and interconnected networks are beginning to provide alternatives to ideas such as smart grids, smart waste management (Kessel., 2015).

The Fundamental Theory and the Main IoT Modules

If anything is connected to the Internet, data, or both, may be sent or received. Sending and/or getting information makes things 'smart.' All web-related items can be put on the internet of things in three different types (Leverege LLC, 2018).

- **Things that Collect Information and Then Send it**: Temperature sensors, vibration sensors, humidity sensors, air quality sensors and light sensors could be detectors. This sensor and a link allow us to acquire information automatically from an installation that makes smarter decisions. On a farm, when watering their crops, farmers can automatically learn about soil moisture. Instead of watering too much (which can be a expensive overuse of irrigation systems) or watering too little (which could cause a expensive crop loss), the farmer can make sure crops receive the exact right amount of water. This enables farmers to increase crop yield while reducing associated expenses.
- **Things Which Receive and Act on Information**: We are all much acquainted with informing and then acting machines. Printer gets and prints a document. When the above things can do, the true strength of the internet of things emerges. Things which collect and communicate data but also receive and act on it.
- **Things That do Both**: We discuss again the case of agriculture. Soil moisture data can be gathered from detectors to let the farmer know how much water crops are available, but the farmer does not really need them. Instead, depending on how much moisture there is in the soil, the irrigation system can switch on automatically as needed.

We can take a move further. If the irrigation system receives climate data from its web connection, it can also understand when it will rain and decide not to water the plants today because they will still be affected by the rain. All this data about the soil moisture, how much the irrigation system watering the plants, and how well the crops actually grow can be gathered and sent to supercomputers operating incredible algorithms that are relevant to all this data.

Function of IoT System

Applications for IoT cover a wide range of application instances and verticals. But all IoT devices are identical in that they integrate four different parts: sensors / devices, connectivity, processing information and user interface (Leverege LLC, 2018).

- **Sensors/Devices**: The first to obtain information from their environment are sensors or machines. It can be as simple to read the temperature or as complex as a full video feed. We use sensors / devices because there are various sensors that can be combined or sensors that can be component of a delicate device. Telephone, for example, is a multi-sensor device, but it is not just a sensor because it can perform many tasks, so we need a camera, an accelerometer, and a GPS.
- **Connectivity**: Next, the information is being sent to the cloud and for this a wide range of ways can be used to connect sensors / devices to the cloud including: mobile, satellite, Wi-Fi, Bluetooth, low-power wide-scope networks, gateways and routers or the Internet via Ethernet.
- **Data Processing**: When the information is accessed by the cloud software, some processing takes place there. This could be very easy, for example to check that temperature reading is acceptable. Or it could also be very complicated to define items by using computer views on the video (such as property intruders).
- **User Interface**: The data is then somehow rendered helpful to the end user. This might happen via the user's e-mail alert, text, message, etc. For example, if the temperature in company cold storage is too high a text alert. An interface can be used by a user to verify the system proactively. For instance, a user could wish to monitor the video feed via a telephone app or web browser on multiple characteristics. It is not a one-way street, however. The user can also conduct an intervention and influence the system depending on the IoT implementation. For instance, the user can remotely adjust cold storage temperatures on the phone using an app.

IoT Architecture Basics: IoT Hardware, Software Architecture

IoT has been divided into two categories, namely people referred to as C2B (Customer to Business) and items referred to as M2M to things or machine to machine. People to things include IoT equipment, wearables, fitness equipment, linked products etc. M2M includes all aspects linked to production and automation.

Sensors, network connectivity and data storage applications are three primary components of the IoT scheme. The same was shown in Figure 1. Sensors in IoT systems, as shown in the figure, either interact directly with the main data storage server or interact through gateway systems.

For multiple IoT devices like temperature, energy, moisture, proximity, power and other applications sensors can be used in multiple applications. Gateway includes the installation of numerous standard wireless devices, which allows gateways to manage multiple software and sensors. The standard wireless technologies widely used are 6LoWPAN, Zigbee, Zwave, RFID, NFC etc. Gateway cloud interfaces using wireless or wired backbone technologies like WiFi, Mobile, DSL or Fiber.

As shown, IoT supports protocols IPv4 and IPv6. Due to IPv6 support, which has an IP address duration of about 128-bit, there are sufficient addresses available to increase the demand for IoT devices. IoT is the special feature of DTN (Delay Tolerant Networks) which manages a wide range of IoT-based network delays, compared to traditional computer networks. As shown, IoT service providers provide a range of QoS with distinct pricing and design specifications for memory, CPU and battery use.

Figure 1. IoT Architecture
(Leverege LLC, 2018)

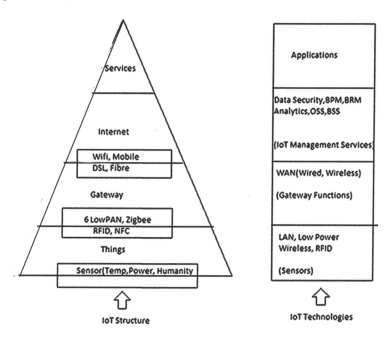

Hardware Architecture of IoT

The upper protocol stack and physical and RF layers make up the IoT system. MCU (Micro-Controller Units) can be used to build the system. MCU's choice relies on chip resources, energy requirements and interfaces as required by distinct sensors. IoT hardware memory specifications also required to be studied closely.

To finalize the IoT hardware architecture, which can be used to carry out the ideal IoT hardware model and the costs of necessary IoT hardware components, the following aspects must be compiled.

- Sensor Type
- Interface type of communications
- Data to be processed and transmitted
- Data transportation frequency

IoT Software Architecture

The IoT software architecture is based on open source components. The IoT architecture used by most applications is shown in Figure 2. As shown, Linux is widely used; as it does not have to wait until the target hardware is completed, then software development can go along with it. Several organizations are now working to ensure

Figure 2. IoT Software Architecture
(Leverege LLC, 2018)

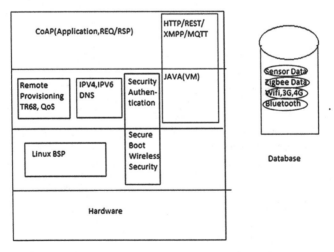

IoT Things Architecture

that IoT frames are ready for various IoT applications. The use of CoAP is unique to IoT and provides a common mechanism for communication with IoT devices.

IoT Frameworks Vendors

Following Table 1 mentions IoT Frameworks providers, developers or suppliers.

ISSUES DRIVING INDUSTRY OF THE IOT

IoT is considered to be affected by security and reliability issues (Olamide, Augustine, Kelvin, Bamidele, Mohammad, Haris, & Georgina, 2018). The entire IoT sector faces enormous difficulties that are increasing in severity as their acceptance rises and evolves. IoT device vulnerabilities provide simple access to attackers, resulting in additional malicious assaults, data theft, information destruction, hardware harm. Below are some of the significant problems influencing IoT.

Security

IoT involves cellular, RFID and Machine-to-Machine (M2 M), sensor and other wireless communications. Nevertheless, the IoT industry remains unregulated, with broader implications for security and privacy. Across nearly every market, including health and military, the adoption of unsecured IoT devices and their increasing popularity among end-users have created an all-inclusive brand-new vehicle. The easy way to hack IoT devices and to change unsecured software is troubling.

The risk of financial, personal and physical damage from hacked IoT equipment also has increased exponentially in recent years, due to its use of vital national

Table 1. IoT frameworks providers, developers or suppliers

IoT System Functions Providers, Developers
Zigbee and 6LoWPAN-based Thread Framework from Thread Group. In order to communicate with the server, this system includes gateway.
Open IoT Eclipse
IoT activity known as the Free Interconnect Consortium
Linear Systems Engineering
Microsoft
Oracle

The fundamentals of IoT technology include IoT hardware, IoT application architecture, IoT platform provider and IoT design.

infrastructure, such as in the healthcare sector, rail, traffic, power grids (Jogunola, Ikpehai, Anoh, Adebisi, Hammoudeh, Son, & Harris., 2017; Jerkins, 2017) and smart cities (Katz, 2019).

Interoperability

Due to the excess of components, information layers, languages and hardware support, interoperability between IoT systems is severely restricted and therefore the ware engaged in the production of an IoT network. In an ideal world, the systems mentioned above should easily fit together to facilitate connectivity and exchange of information. Nonetheless, interaction interoperability in the IoT sector is particularly challenging due to the wide range of available techniques, which makes communicating seamlessly between multi-vendor devices a challenge. In the industry, efforts have been made, such as Apple's HomeKit, to ensure that multi-IoT solutions can be merged into one user interface by different manufacturers, which means that standards for interoperability are urgently needed.

Governance Policy

An important consideration is efficient governance of the IoT industry. With the introduction of IoT in nearly all sectors, malicious rear door passage left by delicate devices may not immediately become apparent, but it opens up new opportunities for cyberattacks at a much larger scale (Hammoudeh and Arioua, 2018). Global regulation is in the IoT sector as a result of the lack of overall IoT regulations, such as rules, systems, protocols, inspections, accountability and reliability. These rates in business, domestic and global legislation can be very useful in helping companies with increased performance and quality of the process, as well as in reducing the likelihood of potential errors. The presence of heterogeneous systems and the broad range of services used to sustain IoT are more difficult but not impossible to accomplish.

IOT STRATEGIC PRINCIPLES

The guidelines were designed to improve the security of IoT throughout the scope of building, development and activities. The systematic use of these tactical concepts and associated protocols would dramatically improve the IoT security situation. Nonetheless, to mitigate IoT security risks, there is no single fit-all approach. Such concepts must be adapted and applied using a risk-based approach that represents appropriate business conditions and specific threats and consequences resulting from network-based devices, systems or services.

Design Phase Integrated Security

Exemptions may be found but economic drivers or a lack of awareness of risk contributes to businesses putting their consumer products in a low level of respect for their overall security.

Creating security during the design phase eliminates potential problems and avoids a much longer and more costly task during development and implementation to try to add security to goods. Focusing on security as a feature of network-connected devices often allows suppliers and service providers the ability to vary from the industry. The following are some of the most efficient ways of maintaining security at the earliest stages of development and growth.

- Enable default security with unique usernames and passwords that are hard to break. The industrial consumer should be intentionally disabled rather than intentionally allowed to maintain strong security controls.
- By using the current operating system, it is possible to reduce the known vulnerabilities.
- By using hardware with security features enhance device protection and integrity.
- Knowing what impacts the failure could have on developers, manufacturers and service providers in terms of more informed risk-based decisions on safety.

Encourage Security Updates and Risk Management

Even in the design phase, security problems may be found after implementation. Such mistakes can be mitigated by patching, software testing and vulnerabilities mitigation steps.

- Patches would be automatically implemented to tackle vulnerability and leverage cryptographic integrity and authenticity protections quicker.
- Coordination of third-party vendor software updates to tackle vulnerabilities and security improvements to secure the complete set of current protection systems for consumer devices.
- The development of automated vulnerability mechanisms: software engineering, for example, has mechanisms to capture the information

produced in real time by research and hacker communities from critical vulnerability reports.

- Developers should take into consideration issues related to product sunset in advance and inform manufacturers and consumers about the device's expectations and risks after its usability.

Draw on Established Standards of Security

A range of validated techniques used to locate bugs, detect irregularity, fix viable accidents and recover from IoT devices disruption or intrusion can be used in the conventional IT and network security.

- Commence with basic software and cyber security activities and use them in the IoT environment flexibly, adaptively and innovatively.
- Developers and manufacturers should adopt a comprehensive security approach including layers of defenses, including tools at user level, as probable entry points for malicious actors.
- Participate in the data-sharing network to document vulnerabilities and to gather information about emerging cyber threats and vulnerabilities from public and private stakeholders.

Prioritize Security Measures in Line With Possible Impact

Risk models differ considerably in the IoT ecosystem, and the impact of security breakdowns on different customers varies considerably.

- This know-how allows designers and manufacturers to take into account the technological features of an IoT product and how it operates, as well as the security measures required for it.
- A re-teaming activity where programmers deliberately try to avoid the necessary security steps for use, network, information or physical layers.
- With respect to known devices and services, the use of encryption mechanisms enables industrial customers to monitor these devices and services within their organization.

Promote Transparency Across IoT

The many affordable software and hardware solutions used in IoT can be used to address this challenge. Because developers and manufacturers utilize external sources of low-cost, readily available software and hardware alternatives the amount of security embedded into the components of networked device development and deployment may not be properly assessed.

- Conducting end-to-end risk evaluations where necessary to tackle the risks both internally and externally. Developers and suppliers will engage in the risk assessment phase through vendors and distributors, increase visibility and understanding of third-party possible risks and promote confidence and accountability.
- Consider developing an openly revealed vulnerability reporting mechanism. Identify vulnerabilities that the internal security teams of companies themselves cannot capture.
- Consider developing and using a product package program for building shared trust between suppliers and manufacturers. A database may be used to identify, manage and fix any vulnerabilities for other IoT ecosystems immediately after an incident.

Connect Carefully and Deliberately

IoT designers, suppliers and customers should understand how the interruption impacts upon the main role and business operation of the IoT system following the interruption. The IoT system may also be intrusion in the current networked world.

- There may also be no need for direct internet links in order to function critically in an IoT device, especially in the manufacturing environment. Consumer choices could inform information on the nature and intent of connections.
- In some cases, it is in the consumer's interest not directly to the internet, but to a local network which can add up critical information and evaluate it.
- The provision of guidance and control over final implementation can, according to the aim of the IoT device, be a good practice

Stakeholders need to be conscious of the risks of IoT, so that they can deal with them. Policymakers, legislators and stakeholders must look at how to enhance IoT security efforts. IoT is part of a global ecosystem, and many of these same security considerations are being evaluated by other countries and international organizations. It is important not to separate IoT-related activities into inconsistent standards or rules.

IOT CYBERSECURITY CHALLENGES AND SOLUTIONS

The Internet of Things (IoT) is normally an interconnected set of electronic devices that have an Internet connection and transmission of data. The initial "thing" was a Coca Cola sales machine that could report back to the HQ just how much soda was left in and whether it was ice-cold. But, since that time the IoT world has come with the Internet for a long time. The IoT activity is now becoming increasingly popular and can be separated into two main areas: customer and business (Zavalkovsky, 2017):

- **IoT Consumer**: Intelligent home equipment like coolers, door locks, light bulbs, IoT consumer/lifestyle surveillance and devices such as gymnastics, smart watches and drones.
- **IoT Enterprise/Business**: This consists mostly of power, gas and water meters, communications devices, distribution, medically sound, maritime and agricultural equipment and is divided into verticals.

The IoT spectrum hit a major milestone this year when the number of IoT devices exceeded the population of the world.

Increasing Security Concerns Around IoT Applications

In recent years, IoT security problems have evolved because IoT devices have become more increasingly obvious that their very existence is unsafe. The RFID journal, called IoT Technology, "The Doomsday Scenario Waiting to Unfold." This is mainly because these phones tend to be cheap, waste items that would not be as popular if they were more expensive. Little-to— no investment to make them safe is among the things that keeps down their value. In 2015, Kaspersky called IoT the "Low quality Things Internet," highlighting the fact that lo-tech, consumable artifacts would be the majority of the 20 billion IoT devices that are expected to exist by 2020. In January 2015, Wind River Systems of California published a report on "Internet security," which addressed many primary security issues in IoT. The study reported the previous findings of IoT security (Zavalkovsky, 2017):

- Setting IoT safety standards should be a keystone of IoT system development.
- The 25-year advancement of security into modern IoT systems is impractical.
- No IoT risk mitigation perfect solution exists.

Safety and Retention Risks IoT

The Web is not secure, but IoT systems can be even safer and a number of high-profile events have occurred, including the use of IoT devices as nodes in wider botnet attacks showing the vulnerability of IoT. IoT is the latest "kid on the block" Internet. Mirai malware, which struck networked computers running Linux operating systems in 2016, was the most infamous attack to date. Mirai targeted IoT devices for online consumers such as home routers and cameras connected to the Internet. The Mirai malware was used in the biggest ever DDoS attack on the French cloud computing site OVH on September 20, 2016, and the United States DNS provider Dyn later that year.

Security is likely to become a market differentiator with the increasing maturity of IoT devices. A business that sells Internet cameras offering lifetime safety upgrades will collect more revenues than a non-rival business (Zavalkovsky, 2017).

The following non-exhaustive list includes additional risks connected with both home and corporate IoT:

- Issues about data security.
- Physical safety threats to people and publics.
- Privacy issues. Data storage management has exponentially increased after IoT devices.

In order to reduce IoT risk, IoT OEMs are able to take many steps in their products. IoT device companies, for example, should make security a major concern in every step of device development. New features to the life cycle system may also be issued. Nevertheless, these and similar proposals are unlikely to occur. Our old friend, price, is the real problem. The recommendations above are all right and good and would be helpful to the consumer. "IoT Security Desires a Multi-Layered Approach," Frost, and Sullivan, released in October 2018, said that the best way to protect your CSP against IoT attacks is "to link up our IoT devices, but also to continuously mitigate the threats to cyber security that these IoT links create." (Zavalkovsky, 2017).

Protecting against IoT attacks on both companies and customers in the network itself brings important advantages, including:

- Centrally controlled system / endpoint autonomous solution.
- Activation of the Mass IoT security market for all phones.
- Use of worldwide intelligence and the capacity to use distinct types of databases and techniques in real time.
- CSP specialists provide protection accountability, removing this liability from the customer.

- Block the danger before entering the machine or home.

SAFE BUILD A SECURE FUTURE FOR THE INCORPORATE DIGITAL TWIN

Digital twin software has exceeded growth, artificial intelligence and analytics in the merging worlds and the Web. Using digital alternatives, software analysts and other IT personnel may simplify high efficiency implementations and create certain situations where the ability to produce knowledge is more complicated. Digital twins are digital replicas, which data scientists and IT professionals can use to model until they create and launch actual computers. (Heath & Rolington, 2018).

For IoT devices evolving which offer additional value to companies, digital-twin situations will include smaller and less complicated products. Digital Twins can often optimize an IoT application with additional software or data analysis to enhance their usefulness and allow designers to figure out where things are to go or how they function before they really incorporate themselves. The more reliability and other benefits can be identified the more the actual entity can be duplicated with Digital Twin. Yet digital twinning would require additional know-how such as machine learning, artificial intelligence, predictive analytics and other information science capabilities. (Heath & Rolington, 2018).

Cyber security as a practice mainly seeks to build processes and methods to defend any IOT system / application against cyberattacks. It is not always the target of a cyberattack that is malicious (e.g. businesses carry on hacking to find weak points on their Internet assets). Ransomware attacks, for example, are one of the most common cyberattacks in industries of any scale. The main objective of this cyber assault is to collect sensitive information that is necessary to maintain a company for the sake of efficiency evaluation by a criminal (hacker) (Miskinis, 2018).

When this happens, the cyber criminals can now ask the company that was attacked for cash to release the sensitive information. Most organizations not ready for such activities estimate that they can do better to cooperate with the hacker and fulfill his requirements than to lose the sensitive information they collect and release to the public.

Digital Security Improvement With Digital Twin Simulation

The ability to create future simulations about the way in which the digital mechanism or a variety of code executions operate under special conditions is based on a simulated model is one of the main advantages of this technology. For example, the cyber security algorithm of an anti-virus software can be replicated by replicating its algorithm once there is a cyberattack. Instead of recruiting in-house or outsourced capacities for the purpose of constantly breaking down asset defenses, the digital twin simulation designer will generate various virus and cyberattack scenario types. That would allow developers to expand the security ability of an anti-virus software and to plan a counterattack for every single cyberattack context that the virus would effectively try to violate. The more information and testing activities a digital twin will create, by registering a virtual registry, to generate a very powerful multi-faceted protection algorithm that protects information from potential attack by viruses (Miskinis, 2018).

Implementation of Digital Twin Technology for Virus Protection and Security

The more information and simulated experiments are put into it, the more digital twin software will be able to make better, faster and more effective decisions while having the ability to produce virus attack simulations. It ensures that the digital double-interface will be able to respond with severe speed and accuracy by making measured choices on its own by conducting enough testing and brainstorming of any situation in which a hacker could attempt to break into a useful online resource (Miskinis, 2018).

Explanations of the Impact on Cyber Attack Processes of Simulation Learning

The simulation principle will be based on system automation software named IFTTT (If This Then That). Essentially, when incorporating specific actions to activate code, it must integrate the IFTTT principle so that the algorithm can know when a sequence of actions is needed to produce the desired outcome. But a digital twin of code learns thousands of times quicker rather than manually applying IFTTT concepts. It is important to use the same strategy to explain why Digital Twin improves cyber security. In other words, while the developer has to manually develop the first few virus attack scenarios using prototypes, the digital twin software will be able to create simulations and accurately predict the conduct cyber-criminals will execute in the future prior to the hacker's success (Miskinis, 2018).

Naturally, the emergence in IoT sensors calls for digital twins, and as IoT systems become optimized, smaller and less complex products can be included in digital twins, offering additional benefits for companies. Based on differing data, digital twins can be used to predict different results. Digital twins can often automate IoT delivery by providing additional code and data analysis and engineers may figure out where items should go or how things work until physical implementation. When a digital twin is able to duplicate the physical item, efficiencies and other advantages are more likely to be discovered (Shaw & Fruhlinger, 2019).

MAKING IOT SECURE: A HOLISTIC APPROACH

The IoT (Internet of Things) has altered our way of interacting with many types of computers. It has affected our manner of living and working, and developments led by IoT like smart cities have enhanced our standard of life and the surroundings we reside in. However, as the IoT has expanded, its security has become one of the security community's most common issues (Heath & Rolington, 2018).

A new US business survey has shown that almost one-half of U.S. companies using an IoT network have suffered a security violation that can cost up to 13% of bigger businesses' annual earnings. Close to half of bigger companies with annual revenues of more than 2 trillion dollars reported a possible IoT infringement cost in excess of 20 million dollars. However, 70% of participants said IoT safety failures are much more expensive than conventional offences or cases.

Integrated IoT Vulnerabilities

As IoT came out, the goal of the industry was to quickly develop, sell and communicate equipment. The main factors that were accessible (cheap), connected, and manageable for equipment manufacturers, IoT networking providers, IoT application providers, and network operators. It was not a significant consideration to protect IoT devices from external attacks. It was just a reminder. Often devices had built-in default safety settings that were easily breached. They did not have any safety measures at all in many instances (Heath & Rolington, 2018).

Today IoT and mobile operators are more in-depth into the problem. Their two main issues are how to offer a safe IoT product or a security value-added service in relation to IoT communication. Both general goals and dedicated providers of IoT services were tasked with protecting their own networks from IoT network attacks.

Current Risks and Issues

Basically, all IoT devices/products are either Human Machines (M2H) or Machines to Machines (M2 M). These share a same network infrastructure with any other local devices, including non-IT-related equipment. M2H instruments included home-based products (coolers, laundry machines, amazon echo), as well as products put on a company network. Such systems are at risk. (Heath & Rolington, 2018):

- Committed and able to prevent their primary function from functioning properly or fully.
- It is in the botnet and can affect other network computers.
- A link on the local network for invasion. Always had to access private data and allow leakage of information.
- Also had to launch domestic and external infrastructure DDoS attacks.
- Make a significant contribution to the network congestion leading to a massive data change.

Machine to Machine devices (M2M) are usually used as independent remote systems and they communicate with the IoT service backend via mobile networks or a dedicated gateway. The following examples are fuel pressure meters for gas pipes, power control units for generators, energy meters, engine health check automated motor system and accident avoidance systems. Machine to Machine (or Industrial) IoT grows fast with far-reaching consequences. These devices risk, for example:

- If they are worried with critical workloads (such as gas piping or moving vehicles) or loss of income, failure can cause serious harm.
- Interaction pathway quality tolerance (e.g. insurance control equipment).
- Becoming used as component of shared botnet.
- Experience impaired lines of communication or the officer or server's impersonation.
- Failure resulting from the unauthorized use or dependence on an unauthorized source of the legitimate command (e.g. "controlling turbine spin").

So while IoT offers major advantages that require modern technologies, such as self-driving cars, intelligent grid and smart cities, the benefits are more risky.

A Comprehensive IoT Security Approach

The comprehensive strategy of integration of preventive and reactive security measures (including prevention and reactivity) between different components of the IoT services supply chain, including:

- Devices in IoT
- Gateways to IoT
- Network core IP (e.g. CSP core network)
- The cloud of communications and applications provider

Policy end Legislation

The primary principle of end-to-end regulation checks (E2E) is synchronized activity monitoring, anomaly detection and reactions in all critical components of the IoT infrastructure supply chains (Heath & Rolington, 2018):

- Behavior control
- Anomaly detection
- Security response

Behavior Control

Because most IoT services have a definite and predicted behavioral pattern, a behavior profile can be related or unique to a particular IoT application with several kinds of IOT-based services. Behavior monitoring is focused on each component in the chain's relevant security capacities and is particular to the element's feature and position (Heath & Rolington, 2018). See Table 2.

The use case (e.g. sales machine procedures or storage system restrictions for vehicles), for example, defines some of the security features, while others are unique to the individual IoT provider (e.g. IP addresses).

In any case, the standard actions of the individual IoT systems must be understood to attempt to enforce safe strategies. Instead, naturally, we can decide what to do and identify easily when incidents arise, so that the necessary security steps can be taken.

Table 2. Behavior control elements

Environment Function Element	Capacity for Security
Devices in IoT	Capability to remotely "Reset" the system, including business logician separation and infrastructure (Kaspersky OS, Android Things / Brillo, Windows 10 IoT Core). Automatic recording of acts carried out
Gateways to IoT	Protocol restriction, contact laws implementations of firewall, bandwidth restrictions, ports and networks available
Network core IP	FW rules, protocol and device use restrictions, link establishment speeds, contact time and volume
The cloud of communications and applications provider	Authenticating, approving and confidential E2E Legitimate acts plot (device-reported actions taken)

Anomaly Detection

Anomaly detection is based on predefined rules that explain deviation from the IoT behavioral implementation profile. Depending on a use case generalization, they can be comprehensive and unique to an IoT implementation or generally defined. Some of the rules for a very specific application can be built dynamically or precisely (Heath & Rolington, 2018).

Security Response

Some key components of the environment that detect an abnormality may trigger a coordinated response to security the same entity or other element(s) can take action, depending on the type of offense. In the case of the IP Core network identifying bot activity and re-establishing malicious databases and control lines, and advising a security operations center, for instance, network law compliance can do something. Likewise, certain network activities should be removed from the cloud system if an IoT Network senses unusual storage uses (Heath & Rolington, 2018).

In order to facilitate preventive action, such as the download of fresh malware signatures to the IP Core security component, or the fixing of devices for applications to solve vulnerabilities, or the close of communication ports used by new threats, fresh data on new threats and malware must be communicated worldwide through threat intelligence services.

Table 3. Baseline for Anomaly Detection

Environment Function Element	Features of the Personality Profile
Devices in IoT	Unintentional systems call CPU load KPIs, memory use, I/O frequency and volume Communication pattern deflection IoT device bot activities: port/IP scans, etc.
Gateways to IoT	Open ports / services IoT system bot activities: port/IP inspection, etc. Communication command and control
Network core IP	Bot operations, C&C interaction, uncommon protocol/application size. Certain activity anomalies in a network, FW exploitation rules, IPS / AV hits (based on feeds from the cloud)
The cloud of communications and applications provider	Operations and maintenance (O&M) information pattern anomalies, System operations (taken actions) Authentication attempts failed, etc. Predictive Analytic.

End-to-end anomalies would lead to coordinated, widespread security responses among key ecosystem components.

The Biggest Security Problems With IoT Devices

Privacy is not just an important concern for the IoT but for all apps that share information or require remote access. Hackers and intruders can use wireless Internet links or other sophisticated methods in such systems with unparalleled complexity–from public networks, private origin. These are some of the biggest problems about cyber security that must first be overcome:

Application Interface Insecure

If no suitable approach is used, hackers can use plain text passwords, SQL injection, phishing and other such old- or advanced-level methods to access the IoT-enabled solution.

Solutions

- See that XSS, SQL, and CSRF vulnerabilities have been tested on the web interface.
- A powerful code or other mechanism for locking.
- An integrated solution for the detection of unauthorized accesses.
- Encoding algorithms efficiently.
- No certificates should be sent in plain text.
- Detection and notification of irregularities by third parties when it happened.

Authentication or Permission Inadequate

Inadequate authorization can lead to loss of information, lack of accountability, or neglect of service. It is imperative for control hierarchy to be allowed and retained.

Solutions

- IoT enterprises need to ensure that all users, apps, applications and processes possess a unique identity and that there is an effective means of identifying them.
- Authentication of 2-factor
- All networks need to be encrypted and authenticated collectively

Network Vulnerable Infrastructure

Such attacks could be rendered by internally or externally users of a network. DDoS attacks might also be growing. Enterprises and businesses should be aware of such circumstances in particular.

Solutions

- Ensure that neither the outsiders nor their intruders have any required ports exposed.
- For filtering internet traffic on VPNs and intranets a good networking mechanism is needed.
- Knowledge web threats to staff.
- Restrict business equipment to a specific network rather than allow workers to expose them to any public / insecure networking network.

Failure to Encrypt Transport

The security of transport layers is inadequate because of those applications installed that take no effective measures in network traffic.

Solutions

- Implementing higher levels for authentication.
- Check applications and access them via the IoT device.
- Good communication limitations have been imposed.

Issues on Privacy

Data protection is an important issue in privacy which anyone can be put at risk when deploying and managing linked IoT products. He will not like the leakage of the video information that his has installed in his children's room to help keep track of it. But the worse is likely because of poor algorithms and smart hackers.

Solutions

- Devices must have checked OS enabled.
- The mounted applications on a computer must be properly fixed
- The devices need to be able to guard against attacks through intrusion and remote code execution.

Unconfident Interface With the Cloud and Mobile

Cloud and mobile services are easy to attract buyers, but these are not as safe as we feel. Cloud-based advances are getting efficient with every day, but they are not perfect yet.

Solutions

- Proper web, cloud or mobile interfaces should be tested to prevent any SQL, XSS or CSRF treatments.
- There must be a good authentication, encryption, identification of vulnerabilities and anomaly detection.

Today, cyber security solutions are not as mature for IoT applications as they should be. Thus, each 'smart' company or home needs to take account of IoT threats, along with the benefits it utilizes.

CONCLUSION AND DISCUSSION

We studied cyber security methods in this section with the objective of informing the design of future Things devices Internet. In order to protect the environment from the point of view of cyber security, the level of cyber security provided by the IoT setting is not sufficient. Because different objects are part of an inter interconnected system, we must take into account the physical safety of such devices, as they will be placed in uncomfortable locations, which the individual most likely to exploit the controls will easily use to identify them and to potentially intercept, read or alter information.

Management stakeholders should define the organization's cyber security policies and procedures and guarantee that security controls are implemented in practice. When defining security controls, consideration should be given to monetary value and market values. Because it may not be essential to invest a lot of resources in low-level IoT applications, but on the other hand market share loss and reputation are key elements for a profit-making organization. IoT devices are as critical as any other Internet-connected computer system for security. It protects not only the computer itself, but also other internet users as protection. The organization should consider the stakeholders responsible for each change and each stakeholder's capacity to implement it. The organization should develop its roadmap in order to improve its overall safety maturity and move towards its target state. As a result of the implementation of IoT, the security needs of enterprises must be discussed with a focus on the interactions between the organization and its environment, along with supporting cloud infrastructure and mobile devices-based technologies and services. Organizations need to adapt and look forward to and beyond the current business. With the awareness that attacks can never be completely avoided, businesses need to advance their ability to detect cyber threats so that they can react properly and intelligently.

More broadly, the design vulnerabilities that we discovered and the defenses that we proposed can help improve the security of IoT devices while maintaining the new features that they provide.

REFERENCES

Banafa, A. (2019). Internet of Things (IoT): Security, Privacy and Safety. Datafloq. Retrieved from https://datafloq.com/read/internet-of-things-iot-security-privacy-safety/948

Hammoudeh, M., & Arioua, M. (2018). Sensors and Actuators in Smart Cities. *Journal of Sensor and Actuator Networks*, *7*(1), 1. doi:10.3390/jsan7010008

Heath, T., & Rolington, A. (2018, July 30). News-News Analysis, Business-Services-IT & Telecoms. Cybersecurity Intelligence. Retrieved from https://www.cybersecurityintelligence.com/blog/what-is-digital-twin-technology-3564.html

Jerkins, J.A. (2017). Motivating a market or regulatory solution to IoT insecurity with the Mirai botnet code. doi:.2017.7868464 doi:10.1109/CCWC

Jing, Q., Vasilakos, A. V., Wan, J., Lu, J., & Qiu, D. (2014, November). Security of the Internet of things: Perspectives and Challenges. *Wireless Networks*, *20*(8), 2481–2501. doi:10.100711276-014-0761-7

Jogunola, O., Ikpehai, A., Anoh, K., Adebisi, B., Hammoudeh, M., Gacanin, H., & Harris, G. (2018). Comparative Analysis of P2P Architectures for Energy Trading and Sharing. *Energies*, *11*, 1.

Jogunola, O., Ikpehai, A., Anoh, K., Adebisi, B., Hammoudeh, M., Son, S.-Y., & Harris, G. (2017). State-Of-e-Art and Prospects for Peer-To-Peer Transaction-Based Energy System. *Energies*, *10*(12), 12. doi:10.3390/en10122106

Katz, H. (2019, January 8). IoT Cybersecurity Challenges and Solutions. Allot. Retrieved from https://www.allot.com/blog/iot_cybersecurity_challenges_and_solutions/

Leverage LLC. (2018). An Introduction to Internet of Things. Retrieved from https://www.leverege.com/iot-intro-ebook

Miller, L. (2016). IoT Security For Dummies, INSIDE Secure Edition. Learn ARM. Retrieved from https://learn.arm.com/iot-solutions-for-dummies.html

Miskinis, C. (2018, May). Incorporating digital twin into internet cyber security – creating a safer future. Challenge.org. Retrieved from https://www.challenge.org/insights/digital-twin-cyber-security/

U.S. Department of Homeland Security. (2014). Strategic principles For Securing The Internet of Things (IoT). Government of the USA. Retrieved from https://www.dhs.gov/sites/default/files/publications/Strategic_Principles_for_Securing_the_Internet_of_Things-2016-1115-FINAL_v2-dg11.pdf

Shaw, K., & Fruhlinger, J. (2019, January). What is a digital twin? [And how it's changing IoT, AI and more]. Network World. Retrieved from https://www.networkworld.com/article/3280225/what-is-digital-twin-technology-and-why-it-matters.html

Sulkamo, V. (2018). IoT from cyber security perspective. Theseus. Retrieved from https://www.theseus.fi/bitstream/handle/10024/151498/IoT%20from%20cyber%20security%20perspective.pdf?sequence=1&isAllowed=y

Techechelons Infosolutioms Pvt Ltd. (2019). Cyber security in IoT: Why is it critical to understand and implement? Retrieved from https://www.techechelons.com/blog/cyber-security-in-iot-why-is-it-critical-to-understand-and-implement

van Kessel, P. (2015, March). EYGM Limited, Cyber Security and the Internet of Things. EY. Retrieved from https://www.ey.com/Publication/vwLUAssets/EY-cybersecurity-and-the-internet-of-things/%24FILE/EY-cybersecurity-and-the-internet-of-things.pdf

RF Wireless World. (2012). IoT Architecture Basis- IoT Hardware Software Architecture. Retrieved from https://www.rfwireless-world.com/IoT/IoT-architecture.html

Zavalkovsky, A. (2017, July 25). Making IoT Secure: A Holistic Approach. Allot. Retrieved from https://www.allot.com/blog/making-iot-secure-a-holistic-approach/

Chapter 13
Cyber Security Aspects of Virtualization in Cloud Computing Environments:
Analyzing Virtualization-Specific Cyber Security Risks

Darshan Mansukhbhai Tank
 https://orcid.org/0000-0002-5138-8979
Gujarat Technological University, Ahmedabad, India

Akshai Aggarwal
School of Computer Science, University of Windsor, Canada

Nirbhay Kumar Chaubey
 https://orcid.org/0000-0001-6575-7723
Gujarat Technological University, India

ABSTRACT

Cybercrime continues to emerge, with new threats surfacing every year. Every business, regardless of its size, is a potential target of cyber-attack. Cybersecurity in today's connected world is a key component of any establishment. Amidst known security threats in a virtualization environment, side-channel attacks (SCA) target most impressionable data and computations. SCA is flattering major security interests that need to be inspected from a new point of view. As a part of cybersecurity aspects,

DOI: 10.4018/978-1-7998-2253-0.ch013

secured implementation of virtualization infrastructure is very much essential to ensure the overall security of the cloud computing environment. We require the most effective tools for threat detection, response, and reporting to safeguard business and customers from cyber-attacks. The objective of this chapter is to explore virtualization aspects of cybersecurity threats and solutions in the cloud computing environment. The authors also discuss the design of their novel 'Flush+Flush' cache attack detection approach in a virtualized environment.

INTRODUCTION

Cybersecurity in today's connected world is a basic component of any establishment. Weak security policies result in major service interruption and data breaches (Michelle, 2018). Cyberspace refers to the environment in which communication occurs over computer networks. The future of cybersecurity is firmly associated with the future of information technology and the advancements of the cyberspace. Cyberspace has become the most popular carrier of information exchange in every corner of our life. With the continuous development of science and technology, especially the virtualization technology, cyberspace security has become the most critical problem for the cloud computing environment (Zhou, Shen, Li, Wang, & Shen, 2018).

As an integral part of most of the business, virtualization is becoming more prevalent in various sectors of society. The virtue of virtualization rests on its ability to cut down operational costs and to provide an effective means of managing Information Technology (IT) resources (Francia, Garrett, & Brookshire, 2013). Virtualization has changed the landscape of technology and revolutionized computing capability. Virtualization has been widely adopted. An enterprise runs most of its workloads in a virtualization environment. A virtualized system has many advantages compared to traditional computing systems. The key benefit of virtualization is to reduce the overall operational cost.

Virtualization is a technique to separate multiple users on a single machine. Virtual Machines (VMs) share the underlying hardware and rely on the software level isolation provided by the hypervisor. The Hypervisor provides virtualization of hardware resources and thus enables multiple computing stacks called VMs to be run on a single physical host (Chandramouli, 2018). The sharing of hardware resources between multiple guest systems optimizes resource usage (Agarwal, 2018).

However, it has been discovered and proved that this isolation is not impenetrable (Paundu, 2018).

The objective of this book chapter is to explore virtualization aspects of cybersecurity threats and solutions in the cloud computing environment. The rest of this book chapter is organized as follows. First, we provide some background information on cryptography, cybercrime, and cyber-attacks in the context of cybersecurity. Second, we define cybersecurity and discuss why cybersecurity should be the biggest concern. Third, we narrate the importance of cybersecurity in the cloud computing environment. Fourth, we discuss guidelines and recommendations on the security aspects of virtualization provided by standard security agencies and present taxonomy of virtualization security issues. Fifth, we analyze virtualization specific cybersecurity threats, vulnerabilities, and mitigation techniques. Sixth, we compare various defense mechanisms pertaining to virtualization security. Next, we outline our proposed '*Flush+Flush*' cache attack detection approach. Finally, we conclude this book chapter and discuss future research directions.

BACKGROUND

Cryptography can be defined as a technique of securing private messages by using codes so that only those for whom the message is destined can read and process it. It converts ordinary plain text into impenetrable text and vice-versa. The concept of cryptography has been widely used for secure communication in computer networks. Current cryptographic techniques may be easily defeated by increasing computing power and thus not likely to be more secure.

Quantum cryptography is gaining importance among IT security practitioners. The theory of quantum cryptography is becoming quite a sound day by day and its practical implementations are also grown-up regularly. The concept of quantum cryptography is formed on the basic principles of quantum mechanics. Quantum cryptography has the capability to make a remarkable contribution to personal, business, and e-commerce security. It has the strength to provide security among government organizations.

Over the past few years, cybercrimes have been growing up to become one of the most compelling threats across the world. Cybercrime can potentially disrupt, damage the business operations as well as commercial losses and compromise well-established reputation. Cyber-attacks evolve every day as attackers are becoming more inventive. Not only the number of security violations are rising, but they're increasing in asperity, as well, leading to massive losses to businesses and organizations. In this section, we provide background information on quantum cryptography, cybercrime, and cyber-attacks in the context of cybersecurity.

Cybercrime

Cybercrime is an offense against the law involving computers and computer networks (Moore, 2005). This category of offense contains traditional crimes managed over the Internet (Beal, n.d.). The internet users are the main target of cybercrime. The computer can be treated as a tool rather than a target. (Kruse & Heiser, 2002). Halder & Jaishankar (2011) have defined cybercrime as *Offence against individuals or groups of individuals with a criminal motive to intentionally harm the reputation of the victim or cause physical or mental harm, or loss, to the victim directly or indirectly, using modern telecommunication networks such as the Internet and mobile phones*. Cybercrime may threaten a person, property, government, society or a nation's security and financial health (Morgan, 2016).

Figure 1 shows the figure for the number of losses induced by cybercrime announced to the IC3 for the year 2001 to 2018.

Cyber-Attacks

A cyber-attack is a spiteful strive to damage, destroy or alter: computer information systems, computer networks, network infrastructure, and computer gadgets. Recent surveys have shown that most of the businesses have unprotected data and poor cybersecurity systems in place, making them accessible to data and financial loss. Many internet users and <u>organizations</u> were affected by data breaches and cyber-

Figure 1. Cybercrime: reported damage to the IC3 2018 | Statista
(Clement, 2019)

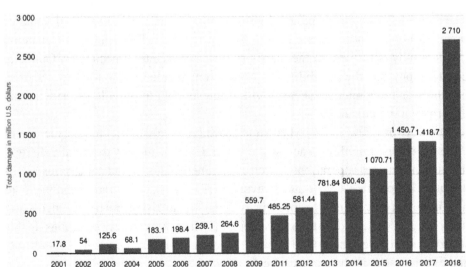

attacks during the past few years. A successful cyber-attack can cause major damage to businesses and organizations. The impact of a security violation can be broadly divided into three categories: financial, reputational and legal. Cyber-attacks often result in a substantial financial loss arising from the theft of corporate information, theft of financial information, theft of money, disruption to trading, and loss of business or contract. Cyber-attacks can damage a business's reputation and also erode the trust of customers. Businesses that suffered a cyber breach stand to lose sensitive data, and face fines and reputational damage.

Every business, regardless of its size, is a potential target of cyber-attack. Cyber-attacks against businesses are often deliberate and motivated by financial gain. Criminals launch cyber-attacks for many reasons: to steal money, to access financial and sensitive data, and personal information of staff and customers. Cyber-attack weaken integrity or disrupts the operations of a company or an individual. The motives behind cyber-attackers are to gain access to intellectual property, IT services, IT infrastructure, clients list, customer databases, customers' or staff email addresses and login credentials, sensitive personal data, customers' financial details, and business' financial details (Dcomisso, 2019).

WHAT IS CYBERSECURITY? WHY IS CYBERSECURITY AN IMPORTANT CONCERN?

Cybersecurity is an important concern for most businesses and organizations. Anything that relies on the internet for communication, or is connected to a computer or other smart device, can be affected by a breach in security. Agarwal (2018) has pointed out that cybersecurity is all about protecting computing devices and networks from unauthorized access or modification. Information security, network security, and application security are types of cybersecurity. Cybersecurity consists of technologies, processes, and controls designed to protect systems, networks, programs, devices and data from cyber-attacks ("What is Cyber Security?" n.d.). Effective cybersecurity reduces the risk of cyber-attacks and protects against the unauthorized exploitation of systems, networks, and technologies. Consultancy.uk (2018) has noticed five reasons, why cybersecurity is more important than ever: tighter regulations, a proliferation of IoT devices, widely available hacking tools, increasingly sophisticated hackers, and the rising cost of breaches. There are at least three main principles behind cybersecurity: confidentiality, integrity, and availability. Confidentiality involves any information that is sensitive and should only be shared with a limited number of people. Integrity involves keeping information from being altered. Availability involves ensuring those who rely on accurate information are able to access it.

Cyber Security in Cloud Computing

Cloud computing technology has made life much easier for internet users and organizations. Nowadays it is almost impossible to think about the digital transformation of businesses and organizations without cloud computing. Organizations have started to adopt cloud services to reduce their investment costs in infrastructures. Cybersecurity involves the security of interconnected systems which includes the physical hardware components and their software counterparts, as well as data and information against cyber-attacks (Lyke, 2018).

As defined by the Cisco Systems, Cyber Security is *the practice of protecting systems, networks, and programs from digital attacks.* Cyber-attacks can take form in many different shapes and sizes. Cloud Computing cybersecurity risks are continuously on the rise. Cybersecurity is an umbrella that captures all things necessary about security (Pramanick, n.d.). Cloud services provided by cloud service providers must comply with cybersecurity standards that guarantee the integrity of the data of the users and companies that contract the services (Marketing, 2018). Cloud computing must offer secure navigation, verification of the users trying to access the cloud service, multi-factorial authentication, firewalls, secure user groups, data encryption, and privacy policies (Marketing, 2018).

VIRTUALIZATION SECURITY

The primary objective of virtualization is to isolate the cloud-based users' environment. As an enabling technology, virtualization plays a very significant role in a cloud environment by supplying the competence of running numerous operating systems and applications on top of the same underlying hardware platform (Zhu et al., 2017). Virtualization in cloud computing can be categorized into three different types based on their characteristics i.e., server, storage, and network virtualization. The cloud service provider must ensure the security of its infrastructure by addressing the security issues confronted by the elements of a virtualization platform.

The standard security agencies in computing have developed several policies, guidelines, recommendations, and best practices to protect the computing environment against potential security threats. Recently National Institute of Standards and Technology (NIST) released security recommendations for hypervisor deployment on servers, a report that provides recommendations on ensuring the secure execution of baseline functions of hypervisors, enabling multiple computing stacks called virtual machines to be run on a single physical host (Chandramouli, 2018). Cloud Security Alliance (CSA) released a whitepaper on virtualization security best practices which provide direction on the recognition and administration of security threats particular to compute virtualization technologies that run on server hardware (CSA, 2015).

European Network and Information Security Agency (ENISA) released a report on the security aspects of virtualization. This report provides an analysis of the status of virtualization security. ENISA presents current efforts, emerging best practices and known security gaps, discussing the impact the latter have on environments based on virtualization technologies (ENISA, 2017). Information Systems Audit and Control Association (ISACA) provides the virtualization security checklist intended for use with enterprise full virtualization environments. This checklist is also intended to be product and vendor agnostic to provide the broadest coverage possible about full virtualization security issues (ISACA, 2010).

Taxonomy of Virtualization Security Issues

Several security threats, risks, and vulnerabilities exist in present virtualization infrastructure that an adversary can utilize to infiltrate the security and privacy of the systems in cloud computing environments. One can classify security issues into three categories. Figure 2 show these defined categories and their vulnerabilities and risks.

The authors have done a rigorous analysis of a number of peer-reviewed papers published in widely known international conferences and journals on security aspects of virtualization. The three dominant classes recognized were VM Image-based, Hypervisor-based, and VM-based attacks. The authors have also recognized possible sub-attacks at these categories and existing mitigation solutions to provide security to the virtualized environment. Table 1 shows three categories of cloud-based attacks on virtualization environments.

By doing the above analysis, one can conclude that attacks exploited on hypervisor have a much broader attack surface as compared to the VM-based and VM Image-based attacks.

VIRTUALIZATION SECURITY SOLUTIONS

Being a core component of cloud computing technology, cloud service providers must ensure the safety of their virtualized environment for the overall security of the cloud computing environment. Cloud service users may discuss and clear the security policies and standards with a cloud service provider before subscribing to their services. The virtualization element has a much larger attack surface than other elements of cloud computing. Cloud service models (i.e., Saas, PaaS, and IaaS) offer different levels of security services. Various techniques have been proposed by

Figure 2. Taxonomy of virtualization specific security threats and vulnerabilities

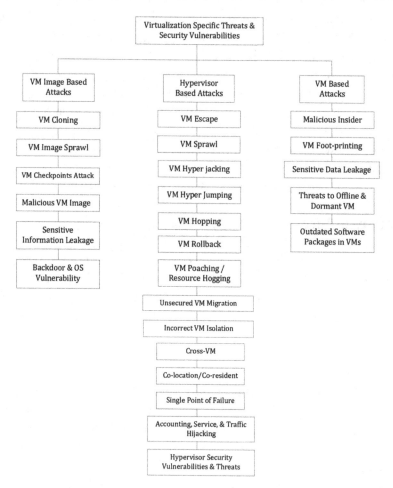

different researchers to solve virtualization specific threats and vulnerabilities in the cloud computing environment. In this section, we review mitigation techniques and solutions proposed in the research articles for enhancing the security of virtualization components. In Table 2, we compile our observations of defense mechanisms.

THE FLUSH+FLUSH CACHE ATTACK

The *Flush+Flush* attack was proposed by Gruss et al., and is a variant of *Flush+Reload* attack (Gruss et al., 2016). The *Flush+Flush* attack measures the execution time of the *CLFLUSH* instruction to decide whether the victim has accessed the

Table 1. Virtualization specific security threats, vulnerabilities, and mitigation techniques

Sr No	Attacks	Sub-Attacks	Existing Defense Mechanisms
1	VM Image-Based Attacks	VM Cloning	• Enforcing security policies and rules • Encrypting the checkpoints • Managing VM images • Cryptographic techniques • User awareness
		VM Image Sprawl	
		VM Checkpoint Attacks	
		Malicious VM Image	
		Sensitive Information Leakage	
		Backdoor & OS Vulnerability	
2	Hypervisor-Based Attacks	VM Escape	• Intrusion Detection/Prevention System (IDS/IPS) • Hypersafe • VMM patching • Encrypting VMsR • Proper configuration • Intrusion Detection System • Reducing the hypervisor attack surface • Protecting hypervisor integrity • Designing secure hypervisors • Security-aware development of VMMs • Hypervisor integrity checking and attestation • Identifying and enforcing security policies
		VM Sprawl	
		VM Hyperjacking and VMM Rootkits	
		VM Hyper Jumping	
		VM Hoping	
		VM Rollback	
		VM Poaching/Resource Hogging	
		Unsecured VM Migration	
		Incorrect VM Isolation	
		VM Information Leakage • Cross-VM • Co-location/Co-resident	
		Single Point of Failure	
		Account or Service Hijacking	
		Unauthorized Access to Hypervisor (Insecure Hypervisor)	
		Vulnerable cloud service provider's APIs (Insecure APIs)	
		The workload of Different Trust Levels	
		Hypervisor Security Vulnerabilities • SubVirt, Blue Pill, Vitriol	
		Hypervisor Security Threats • Hypervisor Introspection • Hypervisor Alteration • Hypervisor Denial-of-Service	
3	VM-Based Attacks	Inside VM attacks • Malware • Malicious insiders	• Using encryption and hashing of VMs state • A Security-Conscious Scheduler for VMs • Co-Residency Recognition via Side-Channel Analysis • Constructing a MAC-based security framework • Virtual Machine Monitor-Based Lightweight Intrusion • Introspecting VMs
		VM Foot-printing	
		Sensitive data leakage within a VM	
		Threats to offline and dormant VM	
		Outdated software packages in VMs	

Table 2. Comparison of various defense mechanisms

Sr No	Author	Defense Mechanisms	Security Criteria						
			Securing Hypervisor	Securing VM	Securing VM Image	Data Confidentiality	Data Integrity	Data Availability	Access Control
1	Azab et al. (2010)	HyperSentry	Y	-	-	-	-	-	Y
2	Wang and Jiang (2010)	HyperSafe	Y	-	-	-	Y	-	-
3	Zhang et al. (2011)	CloudVisor	Y	Y	-	-	Y	-	-
4	Jakub et al. (2011)	NoHype	Y	-	-	-	-	-	Y
5	Szefer and Lee (2012)	HyperWall	-	Y	-	Y	Y	-	-
6	Xiong et al. (2013)	CloudSafe	Y	-	-	Y	-	-	Y
7	Lee and Yu (2014)	Virtualization Introspection System (VIS)	-	Y	-	Y	-	-	-
8	MA and CD (2015)	Open Source SECurity Event Correlator	Y	-	-	-	-	Y	-
9	N.L and M. (2016)	Security Hypervisor	-	Y	-	-	-	-	Y
10	Dildar et al. (2017)	VMHIDS	Y	-	-	-	-	-	Y
11	Tang et al. (2018)	IHMI	Y	-	-	-	Y	-	-
12	Zhang et al. (2018)	VEDefender	Y	Y	-	-	-	-	-
13	Yadav and Challa (2018)	A two-level security framework	-	Y	-	-	Y	-	-

corresponding memory areas. If data is available in the cache, then the *CLFLUSH* instruction has to evict the data from all levels of the cache hierarchy. Therefore, the execution time of the *CLFLUSH* instruction will be a little longer. If data is not available in the cache, then the *CLFLUSH* instruction will take a shorter execution time. In this way, the length of the execution time can directly reflect the victim's memory usage patterns. There will be no memory access by the detective process in *Flush+Flush* attack. Thus *Flush+Flush* attack is more covert and harder to detect. Previous detection mechanisms using cache misses and cache references are unable to detect *Flush+Flush* attack. The *Flush+Flush* operation is depicted as a C language function in figure 3.

The cache-based attacks can threaten the security of cryptographic algorithms in any computing environment. Such types of attacks have been performed through programs written in C, C++ or JavaScript languages. The execution methods of attack may vary because of differences in how the various programming languages allow access to the cache memory.

Figure 4 shows the execution time (TSC cycles) of the CLFLUSH instruction on cached and uncached memory, run on the setup described in Table 3.

Figure 3. Definition of Flush + Flush function in C

```
1   void flush_and_flush (void* addr)
2 {
3       flush(addr);
4       sched_yield();
5       size_t time = rdtsc();
6       flush(addr);
7       size_t delta = rdtsc() - time;
8       if (delta >= MIN_CACHE_HIT_CYCLES) then
9           cache_hit()
10      else
11          cache_miss()
12      end if
13 }
```

Table 3. Our test system configuration

Host OS	Ubuntu 16.04 LTS Linux
Architecture	X86_64
Processor	Intel(R) Core™ i5-8265U CPU @ 1.60GHz x 4
OS Type	64-bit
Disk	1 TB
CPU (s)	4
CPU Core (s)	4
Core Private Level 1 and Level 2 caches	L1 I and L1 D: each 32 KB, 8-way set-associative L2 cache: 256KB, 4-way set-associative
Last Level Cache (LLC)	6 MB, 12-way set-associative
Cache-line size	64-Byte
Physical memory (RAM)	4 GB
Hypervisor (VMM)	KVM
VM – 1	OS - Ubuntu 16.04 LTS Linux Virtual CPU - 1 Memory – 1 GB Disk Size – 20 GB

Figure 4. The execution time of the CLFLUSH instruction on cached and uncached memory

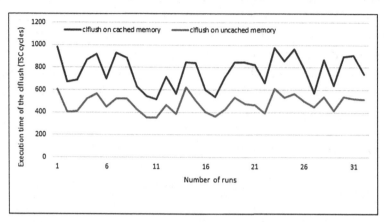

Detection Approach

We have successfully performed a *Flush+Reload* cache attack on our virtual machine. We have attacked OpenSSL's (version-1.1.0f) AES-128's t-table implementation. We are able to retrieve the secret key specified in the file. We want to put our efforts on the detection of *Flush+Flush* cache attacks in a virtualized environment. The *Flush+Flush* cache attacks are highly dependent on flush functions (*CLFLUSH*) and time functions (*RDTSC*).

Our recognition is to notice CPU operations for unique instruction execution patterns (i.e., *Flush + Flush* → *RDTSC–CLFLUSH–RDTSC*, *Flush + Reload* → *CLFLUSH – RDTSC – MOV – RDTSC*). The *Flush+Flush* cache attacks will significantly downgrade our system performance. By doing performance analysis, we can measure our system performance degradation while the *Flush+Flush* cache attacks are running. We can count the number of *VM-exits* caused by attempting to execute *RDTSC* instruction. *RDTSC* leads to *VM-exit* when guest application software tries to run it. To trace *RDTSC* instruction, we need to instrument our kernel to use the "*RDTSC exiting*" flag, then we can analyze *VM-exits* of the guest (using "*perf kvm stat report*") to see how frequently this flag shows up. The count of *VM-exits* reason would be a signal for us that someone runs suspicious code inside the VM. We then activate Intel Processor Trace and generate traces from the trace support on the CPU. If we can process the trace fast enough, it would be the most effective way to detect *Flush+Flush* cache attacks. We can bail out early if we haven't encountered any *RDTSC/CLFLUSH* instructions. This will probably yield linear complexity in the majority of cases.

CONCLUSION AND FUTURE WORK

In this book chapter, we have inspected the security aspects of virtualization in the cloud computing environment. Among other security threats, cache side-channel attacks try to break the isolation imposed by the hypervisor and pose a serious security threat to most cryptographic algorithms. There have been many countermeasures (i.e. software-based and hardware-based) proposed by the different researches in the past but, they fail due to the lack of effective implementation.

For all the other cache-based side-channel attack variants (*Prime+Probe, Flush+Reload, and Evict+Time*), the only research contribution left might be to design an effective or efficient detector application or implementation. Researchers also need to justify that any significant result improvements they got are worth the additional effort (computational cost) it takes. Researchers may apply their own perspectives and put their efforts forward to detect flush-based cache attacks in a virtualization environment, with the aim of low performance/computation overhead on the host and guest VM and with high true-positive and low false-positive rate.

ACKNOWLEDGMENT

The authors would like to thank the anonymous reviewers for their helpful and constructive comments. They would also like to thank the Editors for their generous comments and support during the review process.

REFERENCES

Aditya, J., & Rao, P. S. (2005). Quantum Cryptography. *Proceedings of the computer society of India*.

Bazm, M., Lacoste, M., Sudholt, M., & Menaud, J. (2017). Side-channels beyond the cloud edge: New isolation threats and solutions. *2017 1st Cyber Security in Networking Conference (CSNet)*. DOI:10.1109/csnet.2017.8241986

Bazm, M. M., Lacoste, M., Südholt, M., & Menaud, J. M. (2017). *Side Channels in the Cloud: Isolation Challenges*. Attacks, and Countermeasures.

Briongos, S., Irazoqui, G., Malagón, P., & Eisenbarth, T. (2018). CacheShield. *Proceedings of the Eighth ACM Conference on Data and Application Security and Privacy - CODASPY '18*. DOI:10.1145/3176258.3176320

Cache-based side-channel attacks. (n.d.). Retrieved from https://www.mikelangelo-project.eu/2016/09/cache-based-side-channel-attacks

Chaubey, N. K., & Tank, D. M. (2016). Security, Privacy and Challenges in Mobile Cloud Computing (MCC):- A Critical Study and Comparison. *International Journal of Innovative Research in Computer and Communication Engineering, 4*(2), 1259–1266. doi:10.15680/IJIRCCE.2016.0402028

Clement, J. (2019, July 9). *Amount of monetary damage caused by reported cybercrime to the IC3 from 2001 to 2018* [graph]. Retrieved from https://www.statista.com/statistics/267132/total-damage-caused-by-by-cyber-crime-in-the-us/

Consultancy.uk. (2018, August 30). *Five reasons cybersecurity is more important than ever.* Retrieved April 14, 2019, from https://www.consultancy.uk/news/18435/five-reasons-cyber-security-is-more-important-than-ever

Dcomisso. (2019, March 7). *Reasons behind cyber attacks.* Retrieved July 12, 2019, from https://www.nibusinessinfo.co.uk/content/reasons-behind-cyber-attacks

Gabel, D., Liard, B., & Orzechowski, D. (2015, July 1). *Cyber risk: Why cybersecurity is important.* Retrieved June 11, 2019, from https://www.whitecase.com/publications/insight/cyber-risk-why-cyber-security-important

6. Go-To Cybersecurity Apps 6 Go-To Cybersecurity Apps. (2019, May 24). Retrieved from https://www.cybintsolutions.com/go-to-cybersecurity-apps/

Gruss, D., Maurice, C., & Wagner, K. (2015). *Flush+Flush: A Stealthier Last-Level Cache Attack.* ArXiv, abs/1511.04594

Gruss, D., Maurice, C., Wagner, K., & Mangard, S. (2016). Flush+Flush: A Fast and Stealthy Cache Attack. *Detection of Intrusions and Malware, and Vulnerability Assessment,* 279-299. Doi:10.1007/978-3-319-40667-1_14

Irazoqui, G., Eisenbarth, T., & Sunar, B. (2015). S$A: A Shared Cache Attack That Works across Cores and Defies VM Sandboxing -- and Its Application to AES. *2015 IEEE Symposium on Security and Privacy.* 10.1109/SP.2015.42

Kulah, Y., Dincer, B., Yilmaz, C., & Savas, E. (2018). SpyDetector: An approach for detecting side-channel attacks at runtime. *International Journal of Information Security, 18*(4), 393–422. doi:10.100710207-018-0411-7

Litchfield, A., & Shahzad, A. (2016). *Virtualization technology: Cross-VM cache side-channel attacks make it vulnerable.* arXiv preprint arXiv:1606.01356

Michael, K. (2012). *How quantum cryptography works: And by the way, it's breakable.* Retrieved from https://www.techrepublic.com/blog/it-security/how-quantum-cryptography-works-and-by-the-way-its-breakable/

Murali, G., & Prasad, R. S. (2016). CloudQKDP: Quantum key distribution protocol for cloud computing. 2016 *International Conference on Information Communication and Embedded Systems (ICICES).* 10.1109/ICICES.2016.7518922

Mushtaq, M., Akram, A., Bhatti, M. K., Rais, R. N., Lapotre, V., & Gogniat, G. (2018). Run-time Detection of Prime + Probe Side-Channel Attack on AES Encryption Algorithm. *2018 Global Information Infrastructure and Networking Symposium (GIIS).* 10.1109/GIIS.2018.8635767

Nate, L. (2018). *Cryptography in the Cloud: Securing Cloud Data with Encryption.* Retrieved from https://digitalguardian.com/blog/cryptography-cloud-securing-cloud-data-encryption

Olanrewaju, R., Islam, T., Khalifa, O., Anwar, F., & Pampori, B. (2017). Cryptography as a Service (CaaS): Quantum Cryptography for Secure Cloud Computing. *Indian Journal of Science and Technology, 10*(7), 1–6. doi:10.17485/ijst/2017/v10i7/110897

Paundu, A. W., Fall, D., Miyamoto, D., & Kadobayashi, Y. (2018). Leveraging KVM Events to Detect Cache-Based Side Channel Attacks in a Virtualization Environment. *Security and Communication Networks, 2018,* 1–18. doi:10.1155/2018/4216240

Pearce, M., Zeadally, S., & Hunt, R. (2013). Virtualization: Issues, Security Threats, and Solutions. *ACM Computing Surveys, 45*(2), 1–39. doi:10.1145/2431211.2431216

Preventing CPU side-channel attacks with kernel tracking. (2018, September 18). Retrieved from https://www.slideshare.net/azilian/preventing-cpu-side-channel-attacks-with-kernel-tracking

Quantum Cryptography. (n.d.). In *American Heritage® Dictionary of the English Language, Fifth Edition. (2011).* Retrieved October 26, 2019, from https://www.thefreedictionary.com/quantum+cryptography

Quantum cryptography - Wikipedia. (n.d.). Retrieved from https://en.m.wikipedia.org/wiki/Quantum_cryptography

Ristenpart, T., Tromer, E., Shacham, H., & Savage, S. (2009). Hey, you, get off of my cloud. *Proceedings of the 16th ACM conference on Computer and communications security - CCS '09.* DOI:10.1145/1653662.1653687

Side-channel attack. (2004, May 20). Retrieved from https://en.wikipedia.org/wiki/Side-channel_attack

Tank, D., Aggarwal, A., & Chaubey, N. (2017). Security Analysis of OpenStack Keystone. *International Journal of Latest Technology in Engineering Management & Applied Science, 6*(6), 31–38.

Tank, D., Aggarwal, A., & Chaubey, N. (2019). Virtualization vulnerabilities, security issues, and solutions: a critical study and comparison. *International Journal of Information Technology.* Doi:10.100741870-019-00294-x

Tank, D. M. (2017). Security and Privacy Issues, Solutions, and Tools for MCC. *Security Management in Mobile Cloud Computing,* 121-147. Doi:10.4018/978-1-5225-0602-7.ch006

Valter, P. (2016). *Introduction to Quantum Cryptography.* Retrieved from https://howdoesinternetwork.com/2016/quantum-cryptography-introduction

Virtualization and Cloud Computing. (2014, April 15). Retrieved from https://resources.infosecinstitute.com/virtualization-cloud-computing/#gref

Wang, Z., Peng, S., Guo, X., & Jiang, W. (2019). Zero in and TimeFuzz: Detection and Mitigation of Cache Side-Channel Attacks. *Innovative Security Solutions for Information Technology and Communications,* 410-424. Doi:10.1007/978-3-030-12942-2_31

What is Virtualization Security? Definition from Techopedia. (n.d.). Retrieved from https://www.techopedia.com/definition/30243/virtualization-security

Xiaoqing, T. (2013). *Introduction to Quantum Cryptography.* Retrieved from https://www.intechopen.com/books/theory-and-practice-of-cryptography-and-network-security-protocols-and-technologies/introduction-to-quantum-cryptography

Yarom, Y., & Falkner, K. (2014). FLUSH+ RELOAD: a high resolution, low noise, L3 cache side-channel attack. *23rd USENIX Security Symposium (USENIX Security 14),* 719-732.

Zhang, T., & Lee, R. B. (2014). New models of cache architectures characterizing information leakage from cache side channels. *Proceedings of the 30th Annual Computer Security Applications Conference on - ACSAC '14.* 10.1145/2664243.2664273

Zhang, T., Zhang, Y., & Lee, R. B. (2018). Analyzing Cache Side Channels Using Deep Neural Networks. *Proceedings of the 34th Annual Computer Security Applications Conference on - ACSAC '18.* 10.1145/3274694.3274715

Zhang, Y., Juels, A., Reiter, M. K., & Ristenpart, T. (2012). Cross-VM side channels and their use to extract private keys. *Proceedings of the 2012 ACM conference on Computer and communications security - CCS '12*. DOI:10.1145/2382196.2382230

Zhou, T., Shen, J., Li, X., Wang, C., & Shen, J. (2018). Quantum Cryptography for the Future Internet and the Security Analysis. *Security and Communication Networks*, *2018*, 1–7. doi:10.1155/2018/8214619

Zhu, G., Yin, Y., Cai, R., & Li, K. (2017). Detecting Virtualization Specific Vulnerabilities in Cloud Computing Environment. *2017 IEEE 10th International Conference on Cloud Computing (CLOUD)*. DOI:10.1109/cloud.2017.105

Compilation of References

6 . Go-To Cybersecurity Apps 6 Go-To Cybersecurity Apps. (2019, May 24). Retrieved from https://www.cybintsolutions.com/go-to-cybersecurity-apps/

Abdul-Ghani, H. A., & Konstantas, D. (2019). A Comprehensive Study of Security and Privacy Guidelines, Threats, and Countermeasures: An IoT Perspective. *Journal of Sensor and Actuator Networks*, *8*(2), 22. doi:10.3390/jsan8020022

Abdul-Ghani, H. A., Konstantas, D., & Mahyoub, M. (2018). A Comprehensive IoT Attacks Survey based on a Building-blocked Reference Model. *International Journal of Advanced Computer Science and Applications*, *9*. doi:10.14569/IJACSA.2018.090349

Abinesh, K. K., & Shiju, S. (2017). Intrusion Detection System Using Big Data Framework. *Journal of Engineering and Applied Sciences*, *12*(12).

Ablayev, F., Ablayev, M., Vasiliev, A., & Ziatdinov, M. (2016). Quantum Fingerprinting and Quantum Hashing Computational and Cryptographical Aspects. *Baltic J. Modern Computing.*, *4*(4), 860–875.

Abood, O. G., & Guirguis, S. K. (2018). A Survey on Cryptography Algorithms. [IJSRP]. *International Journal of Scientific and Research Publications*, *8*(7).

Abouelmehdi, K., Beni-Hssane, A., Khaloufi, H., & Saadi, M. (2017). Big data security and privacy in healthcare: A Review. *Procedia Computer Science*, *113*, 73–80. doi:10.1016/j.procs.2017.08.292

Acar, A., Aksu, H., Uluagac, A. S., & Conti, M. (2018). A survey on homomorphic encryption schemes: Theory and implementation. *ACM Computing Surveys*, *51*(4), 79. doi:10.1145/3214303

Aditya, J., & Rao, P. S. (2005). Quantum Cryptography. *Proceedings of the computer society of India.*

Aggarwal, A., Chaubey, N., & Jani, K. A. (2013). A simulation study of malicious activities under various scenarios in Mobile Ad hoc Networks (MANETs). In Proceedings of the 2013 International Mutli-Conference on Automation, Computing, Communication, Control and Compressed Sensing (iMac4s) (pp. 827-834). IEEE.

Ahmad, F., Bhat, G. M., Khademolhosseini, H., Azimi, S., Angizi, S., & Navi, K. (2016). Towards single layer quantum-dot cellular automata adders based on explicit interaction of cells. *Journal of Computational Science*, *16*, 8–15. doi:10.1016/j.jocs.2016.02.005

Ahn, S.-H., Kim, N.-U., & Chung, T.-M. (2014). Big data analysis system concept for detecting unknown attacks. In *Proceedings of the 16th International Conference on Advanced Communication Technology* (pp. 269-272). IEEE. 10.1109/ICACT.2014.6778962

Al Omar, A., Rahman, M. S., Basu, A., & Kiyomoto, S. (2017, December). Medibchain: A blockchain based privacy preserving platform for healthcare data. In *Proceedings of the International conference on security, privacy and anonymity in computation, communication and storage* (pp. 534-543). Springer. 10.1007/978-3-319-72395-2_49

Alleaume, R. (2007). SECOQC white paper on quantum key distribution and cryptography.

Amiri, M. A., Mahdavi, M., & Mirzakuchaki, S. (2009). Logic-based QCA implementation of a 4. In Exhibition (pp. 1–5). IEEE. doi:10.1109/IEEEGCC.2009.5734314

Amorosi, D. (2011). *You Dirty RAT*. Elsevier. doi:10.1016/S1754-4548(11)70061-4

Ananthaswamy, A. (2019). *The Quantum Internet Is Emerging, One Experiment at a Time*. Scientific American. Retrieved from https://www.scientificamerican.com/article/the-quantum-internet-is-emerging-one-experiment-at-a-time/

Angizi, S., Alkaldy, E., Bagherzadeh, N., & Navi, K. (2014). Novel Robust Single Layer Wire Crossing Approach for Exclusive OR Sum of Products Logic Design with Quantum-Dot Cellular Automata. *Journal of Low Power Electronics*, *10*(2), 259–271. doi:10.1166/jolpe.2014.1320

Arias, O., Ly, K., & Jin, Y. (2017). Security and Privacy in IoT Era. In H. Yasuura, C.-M. Kyung, Y. Liu, & Y.-L. Lin (Eds.), *Smart Sensors at the IoT Frontier* (pp. 351–378). Cham: Springer International Publishing; doi:10.1007/978-3-319-55345-0_14

Arış, A., Oktuğ, S. F., & Voigt, T. (2018). Security of Internet of Things for a Reliable Internet of Services. In I. Ganchev, R. D. van der Mei, & H. van den Berg (Eds.), *Autonomous Control for a Reliable Internet of Services: Methods, Models, Approaches, Techniques, Algorithms, and Tools* (pp. 337–370). Cham: Springer International Publishing; doi:10.1007/978-3-319-90415-3_13

Atzori, L., Iera, A., & Morabito, G. (2010). The Internet of Things: A survey. *Computer Networks*, *54*(15), 2787–2805. doi:10.1016/j.comnet.2010.05.010

Au, M. H., Liang, K., Liu, J. K., Lu, R., & Ning, J. (2018). Privacy-preserving personal data operation on mobile cloud—Chances and challenges over advanced persistent threat. *Future Generation Computer Systems*, *79*, 337–349. doi:10.1016/j.future.2017.06.021

Azaria, A., Ekblaw, A., Vieira, T., & Lippman, A. (2016, August). Medrec: Using blockchain for medical data access and permission management. In *Proceedings of the 2016 2nd International Conference on Open and Big Data (OBD)* (pp. 25-30). IEEE.

Bacon, J., Evans, D., Eyers, D. M., Migliavacca, M., Pietzuch, P., & Shand, B. (2010, November). Enforcing end-to-end application security in the cloud (big ideas paper). In *Proceedings of the ACM/IFIP/USENIX 11th International Conference on Middleware* (pp. 293-312). Springer-Verlag.

Banafa, A. (2019). Internet of Things (IoT): Security, Privacy and Safety. Datafloq. Retrieved from https://datafloq.com/read/internet-of-things-iot-security-privacy-safety/948

Barnum, H., Caves, C. M., Fuchs, C. A., Jozsa, R., & Schumacher, B. (1996). Noncommuting mixed states cannot be broadcast. *Physical Review Letters, 76*(15), 2818–2821. doi:10.1103/PhysRevLett.76.2818 PMID:10060796

Barrett, J, Hardy, L, & Kent, A. (2005). No signaling and quantum key distribution. *Physical Review Letters, 95*(1).

Bass, T. (2000). Intrusion detection systems and multisensor data fusion: Creating cyberspace situational awareness. *Communications of the ACM, 43*(4), 99–105. doi:10.1145/332051.332079

Bazm, M., Lacoste, M., Sudholt, M., & Menaud, J. (2017). Side-channels beyond the cloud edge: New isolation threats and solutions. *2017 1st Cyber Security in Networking Conference (CSNet)*. DOI:10.1109/csnet.2017.8241986

Bazm, M. M., Lacoste, M., Südholt, M., & Menaud, J. M. (2017). *Side Channels in the Cloud: Isolation Challenges*. Attacks, and Countermeasures.

Beauregard, S. (2003). Circuit for Shor's algorithm using 2n+3 qubits. *Quantum Information & Computation, 3*(2), 175–185.

Bennett, C., & Brassard, G. (1984). Quantum cryptography Public key distribution and coin tossing. In *Proceedings of the International conference on computers, systems and signal processing*. Academic Press.

Bennett, C.H. & Brassard. (1987). Quantum Public key distribution. *Seget news, 18*(4), 51-53.

Bennett, C.H. & Shor, P.W. (1998). Quantum information theory. *IEEE Information theory, 44*(6), 2724-2742.

Bennett, C.H. (1985). Quantum public key distribution system. *IBM systems*.

Bennett, B., Brassard, G., Crépeau, C., Jozsa, R., Peres, A., & Wootters, W. K. (1993, March). Teleporting an unknown quantum state via dual classical and Einstein-Podolsky-Rosen channels. *Physical Review Letters, 70*(13), 1895–1899. doi:10.1103/PhysRevLett.70.1895 PMID:10053414

Bennett, C. H. (1992). Quantum cryptography using two non orthogonal states. *Physical Review Letters, 68*(21), 3121–3124. doi:10.1103/PhysRevLett.68.3121 PMID:10045619

Bennett, C. H., Bernstein, H. J., Popescu, S., & Schumacher, B. (1996). Concentrating partial entanglement by local operations. *Physical Review A, 53*(4), 2046–2052. doi:10.1103/PhysRevA.53.2046 PMID:9913106

Bennett, C. H., & Brassard, G. (1984). Quantum cryptography: Public key distribution and coin tossing. In *Proceedings of IEEE International Conference on Computers, Systems, and Signal Processing*. IEEE Press.

Bennett, C. H., & Brassard, G. (2014). Quantum cryptography: Public key distribution and coin tossing. *Theoretical Computer Science*, *560*(12), 7–11. doi:10.1016/j.tcs.2014.05.025

Bennett, C. H., Brassard, G., Breidbart, S., & Wiesner, S. (1982). Quantum Cryptography, or Unforgeable Subway Tokens, Advances in Cryptology. In *Proceedings of Crypto '82*. Plenum Press.

Bennett, C. H., Brassard, G., & Mermin, N. D. (1992). Quantum cryptography without Bell's theorem. *Physical Review Letters*, *68*(5), 557.

Bennett, C. H., Brassard, G., & Mermin, N. D. (1992). Quantum cryptography without Bell's theorem. *Physical Review Letters*, *68*(5), 557–559. doi:10.1103/PhysRevLett.68.557 PMID:10045931

Bernstein, D. J. (2009). *Introduction to post-quantum cryptography. Post-quantum cryptography* (pp. 1–14). Berlin: Springer. doi:10.1007/978-3-540-88702-7

Beth, T., & Gollman, D. (1989). Algorithm engineering for public key algorithms. *IEEE Journal on Selected Areas in Communications*, *7*(4), 458–466. doi:10.1109/49.17708

Bhagat, B. C. (2012). Patent No. 13/016,999. U.S.

Bhatia, A. S., & Kumar, A. (2018). McEliece Cryptosystem Based On Extended Golay Code.

Bhatia, A. S., & Kumar, A. (2019). Post-Quantum Cryptography. In *Emerging Security Algorithms & Techniques* (1st ed.). New York: Chapman and Hall/CRC Press. doi:10.1201/9781351021708-9

Biamonte, J., Wittek, P., Pancotti, N., Rebentrost, P., Wiebe, N., & Lloyd, S. (2017). Quantum machine learning. *Nature*, *549*(7671), 195–202. doi:10.1038/nature23474 PMID:28905917

Bilge, L., & Dumitraş, T. (2012). *Before we knew it: an empirical study of zero-day attacks in the real world. In Proceedings of the ACM conference on Computer and communications security* (pp. 833–844). ACM. doi:10.1145/2382196.2382284

Brandao, F. G., & Oppenheim, J. (2012). Quantum one-time pad in the presence of an eavesdropper. *Physical Review Letters*, *108*(4).

Brassard, G. (1996). Cryptography columns- 25 years of Quantum cryptography. *Sigact news*, *27*(3), 13-24.

Brassard, G. (2006). Brief history of quantum cryptography: a personal perspective.

Brassard, G. (1988). *Modern Cryptology*. New York: Springer.

Brassard, G. (2005). Brief history of quantum cryptography: A personal perspective. In *Proceedings of IEEE Information Theory, Workshop on Theory and Practice in Information Theoretic Security* (pp. 19-23). 10.1109/ITWTPI.2005.1543949

Brassard, G., & Crepeau, C. (1996). 25 years of quantum cryptography. *ACM Sigact News, 27*(3), 13–24. doi:10.1145/235666.235669

Braunstein, S. L., Cerf, N. J., Iblisdir, S., van Loock, P., & Massar, S. (2001). Optimal cloning of coherent states with a linear amplifier and beam splitters. *Physical Review Letters, 86*(21), 4938–4941. doi:10.1103/PhysRevLett.86.4938 PMID:11384386

Briongos, S., Irazoqui, G., Malagón, P., & Eisenbarth, T. (2018). CacheShield. *Proceedings of the Eighth ACM Conference on Data and Application Security and Privacy - CODASPY '18*. DOI:10.1145/3176258.3176320

Brogi, G., & Tong, V. V. (2016). TerminAPTor: Highlighting Advanced Persistent Threats through Information Flow Tracking. *In Proceedings of the 8th IFIP International Conference on New Technologies, Mobility and Security (NTMS)* (pp. 1-5). IEEE. 10.1109/NTMS.2016.7792480

Bruß, D., DiVincenzo, D. P., Ekert, A., Fuchs, C. A., Macchiavello, C., & Smolin, J. A. (1998). Optimal universal and state-dependent quantum cloning. *Physical Review A., 57*(4), 2368–2378. doi:10.1103/PhysRevA.57.2368

Buchmann, J. (2013). *Introduction to cryptography*. Springer Science & Business Media.

Buchmann, J., & Williams, H. C. (1988). A key-exchange system based on imaginary quadratic fields. *Journal of Cryptology, 1*(2), 107–118. doi:10.1007/BF02351719

Buhrman, H. Cleve, R. Watrous, J. & Wolf, R. (2001), Quantum Fingerprinting. doi:10.1103/PhysRevLett.87.167902

Bu, S., & Zhou, H. (2009). A secret sharing scheme based on NTRU algorithm. In *Proceedings of the 5th International Conference on Wireless Communications, Networking and Mobile Computing, WiCom'09*. IEEE. 10.1109/WICOM.2009.5302743

Buscemi, F., D'Ariano, G. M., & Macchiavello, C. (2005). Economical phase-covariant cloning of qudits. *Physical Review A., 71*(4), 042327. doi:10.1103/PhysRevA.71.042327

Buttler, W. T. (2003). Fast and Efficient error reconciliation for quantum cryptography. *Physical Review, 76*, 5.

Butun, I., Morgera, S. D., & Sankar, R. (2014). A survey of intrusion detection systems in wireless sensor networks. *IEEE Communications Surveys and Tutorials, 16*(1), 266–282. doi:10.1109/SURV.2013.050113.00191

Bužek, V., & Hillery, M. (1998). Universal optimal cloning of arbitrary quantum states: From qubits to quantum registers. *Physical Review Letters, 81*(22), 5003–5006. doi:10.1103/PhysRevLett.81.5003

Cache-based side-channel attacks. (n.d.). Retrieved from https://www.mikelangelo-project.eu/2016/09/cache-based-side-channel-attacks

Cai, J. Y., & Cusick, T. W. (1998). A lattice-based public-key cryptosystem. In *Proceedings of the International Workshop on Selected Areas in Cryptography* (pp. 219-233). Springer.

Caleffi, M., & Cacciapuoti, A. S. (2019). Quantum Switch for the Quantum Internet: Noiseless Communications through Noisy Channels.

Cárdenas, A. A., Manadhata, P. K., & Rajan, S. P. (2013). Big data analytics for security. *IEEE Security and Privacy, 11*(6), 74–76. doi:10.1109/MSP.2013.138

Castelvecchi, D. (2018). *Here's what the quantum internet has in store*. Nature. Retrieved from https://www.nature.com/articles/d41586-018-07129-y

Cavin, R. K., Lugli, P., & Zhirnov, V. V. (2012). Science and Engineering Beyond Moore's Law. *Proceedings of the IEEE, 100*, 1720–1749. doi:10.1109/JPROC.2012.2190155

Cerf, N., Durt, T., & Gisin, N. (2002). Cloning a qutrit. *Journal of modern optics, 49*(8), 1355-1373.

Cerf, N. J., Bourennane, M., Karlsson, A., & Gisin, N. (2002). Security of quantum key distribution using d-level systems. *Physical Review Letters, 88*(12), 127902. doi:10.1103/PhysRevLett.88.127902 PMID:11909502

Cerf, N. J., & Fiurasek, J. (2006). Optical quantum cloning. *Progress in Optics, 49*, 455–545. doi:10.1016/S0079-6638(06)49006-5

Cerf, N. J., & Iblisdir, S. (2000). Optimal N-to-M cloning of conjugate quantum variables. *Physical Review A., 62*(4). doi:10.1103/PhysRevA.62.040301

Cerf, N. J., Ipe, A., & Rottenberg, X. (2000). Cloning of continuous quantum variables. *Physical Review Letters, 85*(8), 1754–1757. doi:10.1103/PhysRevLett.85.1754 PMID:10970606

Cerf, N. J., Krüger, O., Navez, P., Werner, R. F., & Wolf, M. M. (2005). Non-Gaussian cloning of quantum coherent states is optimal. *Physical Review Letters, 95*(7), 070501. doi:10.1103/PhysRevLett.95.070501 PMID:16196769

Chakhchoukh, Y., & Ishii, H. (2014). Coordinated cyber-attacks on the measurement function in hybrid state estimation. IEEE transactions on power systems, 30(5), 2487-2497. doi:10.1109/TPWRS.2014.2357182

Chancellor, N. (2017). Modernizing quantum annealing using local searches. *New Journal of Physics, 19*(2), 23–24. doi:10.1088/1367-2630/aa59c4

Chandrashekhar, K. (2016, September 19). *Internet of Things (IoT) Characteristics*. Retrieved from [REMOVED HYPERLINK FIELD]https://www.linkedin.com/pulse/internet-things-iot-characteristics-kavyashree-g-c

Chang, V. (2015). Towards a Big Data system disaster recovery in a Private Cloud. *Ad Hoc Networks, 35*, 65–82. doi:10.1016/j.adhoc.2015.07.012

Chasin, C. (2005). Patent No. 10/888,370. U.S.

Chaubey, N., Akshai Aggarwal, S. G., & Jani, K. A. (2015). Effect of pause time on AODV and TSDRP routing protocols under black hole attack and DoS attacks in MANETs. In *Proceedings of the 2015 2nd International Conference on Computing for Sustainable Global Development (INDIACom)* (pp. 1807-1812). IEEE.

Chaubey, N. K. (2016). Security analysis of vehicular ad hoc networks (VANETs): A comprehensive study. *International Journal of Security and Its Applications*, *10*(5), 261–274. doi:10.14257/ijsia.2016.10.5.25

Chaubey, N. K., & Tank, D. M. (2016). Security, Privacy and Challenges in Mobile Cloud Computing (MCC):- A Critical Study and Comparison. *International Journal of Innovative Research in Computer and Communication Engineering*, *4*(2), 1259–1266. doi:10.15680/IJIRCCE.2016.0402028

Chaubey, N., Aggarwal, A., Gandhi, S., & Jani, K. A. (2015). Performance analysis of TSDRP and AODV routing protocol under black hole attacks in manets by varying network size. In *Proceedings of the 2015 Fifth International Conference on Advanced Computing & Communication Technologies* (pp. 320-324). IEEE. 10.1109/ACCT.2015.62

Chefles, A., & Barnett, S. M. (1998). Quantum state separation, unambiguous discrimination and exact cloning. *Journal of Physics. A, Mathematical and General*, *31*(50), 10097–10103. doi:10.1088/0305-4470/31/50/007

Chen, A. I. T., Chen, M. S., Chen, T. R., Cheng, C. M., Ding, J., Kuo, E. L. H., & Yang, B. Y. (2009). SSE implementation of multivariate PKCs on modern x86 CPUs. In *Cryptographic Hardware and Embedded Systems-CHES* (pp. 33–48). Berlin: Springer. doi:10.1007/978-3-642-04138-9_3

Chen, G., Dong, Z. Y., Hill, D. J., & Xue, Y. S. (2010). Exploring reliable strategies for defending power systems against targeted attacks. *IEEE Transactions on Power Systems*, *26*(3), 1000–1009. doi:10.1109/TPWRS.2010.2078524

Chen, J., Su, C., Yeh, K.-H., & Yung, M. (2018). Special Issue on Advanced Persistent Threat. *Future Generation Computer Systems*, *79*, 243–246. doi:10.1016/j.future.2017.11.005

Chen, K., Zhang, S., Li, Z., Zhang, Y., Deng, Q., Ray, S., & Jin, Y. (2018). Internet-of-Things Security and Vulnerabilities: Taxonomy, Challenges, and Practice. *Journal of Hardware and Systems Security*, *2*(2), 97–110. doi:10.100741635-017-0029-7

Chen, P. Y., Cheng, S. M., & Chen, K. C. (2012). Smart attacks in smart grid communication networks. *IEEE Communications Magazine*, *50*(8), 24–29. doi:10.1109/MCOM.2012.6257523

Chen, S. (2017). *Quantum Internet Is 13 Years Away. Wait, What's Quantum Internet?* Wired; Retrieved from wired.com/story/quantum-internet-is-13-years-away-wait-whats-quantum-internet/

Chinnaswamy, S. (2018). The Future is Calling: Using Voice Recognition for Authentication. TCS. Retrieved from https://www.tcs.com/blogs/using-voice-recognition-for-authentication

Choucair, M. (2016). *All you need for quantum computing at room temperature is some mothballs.* Phys.org. Retrieved from https://phys.org/news/2016-07-quantum-room-temperature-mothballs. html

Cisco. (2014). The Internet of Things Reference Model. In *Proceedings of the Internet of Things World Forum.* Academic Press.

Clement, J. (2019, July 9). *Amount of monetary damage caused by reported cybercrime to the IC3 from 2001 to 2018* [graph]. Retrieved from https://www.statista.com/statistics/267132/total-damage-caused-by-by-cyber-crime-in-the-us/

Comi, P. (2018). *Integration of classic cryptography with QKD.* Italtel. Retrieved from https://www.italtel.com/focus-integration-of-classic-cryptography-with-qkd/

Cong, I., Choi, S., & Lukin, M. D. (2019). Quantum convolutional neural networks.

Consultancy.uk. (2018, August 30). *Five reasons cybersecurity is more important than ever.* Retrieved April 14, 2019, from https://www.consultancy.uk/news/18435/five-reasons-cyber-security-is-more-important-than-ever

Crawford, K., & Schultz, J. (2014). Big data and due process: Toward a framework to redress predictive privacy harms. *BCL Rev., 55,* 93.

Critchley, L. (2018). *What are Quantum Networks?* AZO Quantum. Retrieved from https://www.azoquantum.com/Article.aspx?ArticleID=96

Curcic, T. (2004). Quantum networks: From Quantum cryptography to quantum architecture. *Computer Communication Review, 34*(5), 3–8.

D. Kundur, X. Feng, S. Mashayekh, S. Liu, T. Zourntos, K.L. Butler-Purry.(2011). Towards modeling the impact of cyber attack on a smart grid. *International Journal of Security and Networks (USN) special issue on security and privacy in smart grids, 6*(1), 2-13.

D'Ariano, G. M., Macchiavello, C., & Perinotti, P. (2005). Superbroadcasting of mixed states. *Physical Review Letters, 95*(6), 060503. doi:10.1103/PhysRevLett.95.060503 PMID:16090933

Das, J. C., & De, D. (2017). Nanocommunication network design using QCA reversible crossbar switch. *Nano Communication Networks, 13,* 20–33. doi:10.1016/j.nancom.2017.06.003

Das, J. C., De, D., Mondal, S. P., Ahmadian, A., Ghaemi, F., & Senu, N. (2019). QCA Based Error Detection Circuit for Nano Communication Network. *IEEE Access, 7,* 67355–67366. doi:10.1109/ACCESS.2019.2918025

Das, S. R., & Chandrashekhar, R. (2007). Capacity-Building for e-Governance in India. *Regional Development Dialogue, 27*(2), 75.

Davoli, L., Belli, L., Veltri, L. & Ferrari, G. (2017). THORIN: an Efficient Module for Federated Access and Threat Mitigation in Big Stream Cloud Architectures. *IEEE Cloud Computing.* doi:. doi:10.1109/MCC.2017.455155318

Dcomisso. (2019, March 7). *Reasons behind cyber attacks*. Retrieved July 12, 2019, from https://www.nibusinessinfo.co.uk/content/reasons-behind-cyber-attacks

De Busser, E. (2002). Big Data: The Conflict Between Protecting Privacy and Securing Nations. *Policy*, *9*, 330.

Debnath, B., Das, J. C., & De, D. (2017). Reversible logic-based image steganography using quantum dot cellular automata for secure nanocommunication. *IET Circuits, Devices & Systems*, *11*(1), 58–67. doi:10.1049/iet-cds.2015.0245

Deibert, R. J., Rohozinski, R., Manchanda, A., Villeneuve, N., & Walton, G. M. (2009). *Tracking ghostnet: Investigating a cyber espionage network*. Oxford: oxford university research archive.

Demertzis, K., Iliadis, L., & Spartalis, S. (2017). A Spiking One-Class Anomaly Detection Framework for Cyber-Security on Industrial Control Systems. *In* Proceedings of the I*nternational Conference on Engineering Applications of Neural Networks* (pp. 122-134). Springer.

Diffie, W., & Hellman, M. (1976). New directions in cryptography. *IEEE Transactions on Information Theory*, *22*(6), 644–654. doi:10.1109/TIT.1976.1055638

Dimitrov, D. V. (2019). Blockchain Applications for Healthcare Data Management. *Healthcare Informatics Research*, *25*(1), 51–56.

Ding, J., & Schmidt, D. (2005), Rainbow, a new multivariable polynomial signature scheme. In *Proceedings of the Conference on Applied Cryptography and Network Security ACNS 2005* (pp. 164-175). Springer. 10.1007/11496137_12

Dong, D., Chen, C., Li, H., & Tarn, T. J. (2008). Quantum reinforcement learning. *IEEE Transactions on Systems, Man, and Cybernetics. Part B, Cybernetics*, *38*(5), 1207–1220. doi:10.1109/TSMCB.2008.925743 PMID:18784007

Dorai, R. K. V. (2011). SQL injection—database attack revolution and prevention. *J. Int. Commercial Law Technol.*, *6*, 224.

Dowling, J. P., & Milburn, G. J. (2003). Quantum technology: The second quantum revolution. *Philosophical Transactions of the Royal Society of London. Series A, Mathematical and Physical Sciences*, *361*(1809), 1655–1674. doi:10.1098/rsta.2003.1227 PMID:12952679

Duan, L. M., & Guo, G. C. (1998). Probabilistic cloning and identification of linearly independent quantum states. *Physical Review Letters*, *80*(22), 4999–5002. doi:10.1103/PhysRevLett.80.4999

Dubbeldam, J. (2019). *The quantum Internet - A glimpse into the future*. Network Pages. Retrieved from https://www.networkpages.nl/the-quantum-internet-a-glimpse-into-the-future/

Duffield, N. G., & Presti, F. L. (2000, March). Multicast inference of packet delay variance at interior network links. In *Proceedings IEEE INFOCOM 2000* (Vol. 3, pp. 1351–1360). IEEE.

Dunjko, V., Taylor, J. M., & Briegel, H. J. (2017). Advances in quantum reinforcement learning. In *Proceedings of the IEEE International Conference on Systems, Man, and Cybernetics (SMC)* (pp. 282-287). IEEE Press. 10.1109/SMC.2017.8122616

Du, W., & Zhan, Z. (2003, August). Using randomized response techniques for privacy-preserving data mining. In *Proceedings of the ninth ACM SIGKDD international conference on Knowledge discovery and data mining* (pp. 505-510). ACM. 10.1145/956750.956810

Dwivedi, A. D., Srivastava, G., Dhar, S., & Singh, R. (2019). A decentralized privacy-preserving healthcare blockchain for iot. *Sensors (Basel)*, *19*(2), 326. doi:10.339019020326 PMID:30650612

Einstein, A., Podolsky, B., & Rosen, N. (1935). Can Quantum-Mechanical Description of Physical Reality Be Considered Complete? *Physical Review*, *47*(10), 777–780. doi:10.1103/PhysRev.47.777

Ekert, A. K. (1991). Quantum cryptography based on Bell's theorem. *Physical Review Letters*, *67*(6), 661–663. doi:10.1103/PhysRevLett.67.661 PMID:10044956

ElDahshan, K. A., Elsayed, E. K., Aboshoha, A., & Ebeid, A. E. (2017). Applying Quantum Algorithms for Enhancing Face Authentication. *Al Azhar Bulletin of Science*, *9*, 83–93.

Ellie, M. (2018). *4 Amazing Quantum Computing Applications*. DevOps. Retrieved from https://devops.com/4-amazing-quantum-computing-applications/

Elliott, C. (2002). Building the quantum network. *New Journal of Physics*, *4*(1), 46.

Elliott, C., Pearson, D., & Troxel, G. (2003). Quantum cryptography in practice. In *Proceedings of the conference on Applications, technologies, architectures, and protocols for computer communications*. ACM.

E-SPIN. (2017). *Definition and type of E-government*. Retrieved from https://www.e-spincorp.com/definition-and-type-of-e-government/

Esposito, C., De Santis, A., Tortora, G., Chang, H., & Choo, K. K. R. (2018). Blockchain: A panacea for healthcare cloud-based data security and privacy? *IEEE Cloud Computing*, *5*(1), 31–37. doi:10.1109/MCC.2018.011791712

Fan, H., Imai, H., Matsumoto, K., & Wang, X. B. (2003). Phase-covariant quantum cloning of qudits. *Physical Review A.*, *67*(2). doi:10.1103/PhysRevA.67.022317

Fan, H., Matsumoto, K., Wang, X. B., & Wadati, M. (2001). Quantum cloning machines for equatorial qubits. *Physical Review A*, *65*(1), 012304. doi:10.1103/PhysRevA.65.012304

Fan, H., Wang, Y. N., Jing, L., Yue, J. D., Shi, H. D., Zhang, Y. L., & Mu, L. Z. (2014). Quantum cloning machines and the applications. *Physics Reports*, *544*(3), 241–322. doi:10.1016/j.physrep.2014.06.004

Fan, Y., Zhang, Z., Trinkle, M., Dimitrovski, A. D., Song, J. B., & Li, H. (2014). A cross-layer defense mechanism against GPS spoofing attacks on PMUs in smart grids. *IEEE Transactions on Smart Grid*, *6*(6), 2659–2668. doi:10.1109/TSG.2014.2346088

Faraj, S. T., & Ali, M. S. (2011). Enhancement of E-Government Security Based on Quantum Cryptography. In *Proceeding of the International Arab Conference on Information Technology (ACIT'2011)* (pp. 11-14). Academic Press.

Feng, Q., He, D., Zeadally, S., Khan, M. K., & Kumar, N. (2019). A survey on privacy protection in blockchain system. *Journal of Network and Computer Applications, 126,* 45–58. doi:10.1016/j.jnca.2018.10.020

Fernandes, E., Jung, J., & Prakash, A. (2016, May). Security analysis of emerging smart home applications. In *Proceedings of the 2016 IEEE Symposium on Security and Privacy (SP)* (pp. 636-654). IEEE. doi:10.1109/SP.2016.44

Ferraiolo, D., Chandramouli, R., Kuhn, R., & Hu, V. (2016, March). Extensible access control markup language (XACML) and next generation access control (NGAC). In *Proceedings of the 2016 ACM International Workshop on Attribute Based Access Control* (pp. 13-24). ACM. 10.1145/2875491.2875496

Fette, I., Sadeh, N., & Tomasic, A. (2007). Learning to detect phishing emails. *In* Proceedings of the *16th international conference on World Wide Web* (pp. 649-656). ACM.

Feynman, R. P. (1982). Simulating physics with computers. *International Journal of Theoretical Physics, 21*(6), 467–488. doi:10.1007/BF02650179

Flick, T. & Morehouse, J. (2011). Attacking the utility companies in securing the Smart Grid. In Securing the smart grid: next generation power grid security (pp. 109-142). EPDF. doi:10.1016/B978-1-59749-570-7.00007-8

Fraenkel, A. S., & Yesha, Y. (1979). Complexity of problems in games, graphs and algebraic equations. *Discrete Applied Mathematics, 1*(1-2), 15–30. doi:10.1016/0166-218X(79)90012-X

Fuchs, C. A., Gisin, N., Griffiths, R. B., Niu, C. S., & Peres, A. (1997). Optimal eavesdropping in quantum cryptography. I. Information bound and optimal strategy. *Physical Review A., 56*(2), 1163–1172. doi:10.1103/PhysRevA.56.1163

Fu, Y., Ding, M., Zhou, C., & Hu, H. (2013). Route planning for unmanned aerial vehicle (UAV) on the sea using hybrid differential evolution and quantum-behaved particle swarm optimization. *IEEE Transactions on Systems, Man, and Cybernetics. Systems, 43*(6), 1451–1465. doi:10.1109/TSMC.2013.2248146

Gabel, D., Liard, B., & Orzechowski, D. (2015, July 1). *Cyber risk: Why cybersecurity is important.* Retrieved June 11, 2019, from https://www.whitecase.com/publications/insight/cyber-risk-why-cyber-security-important

Gahi, Y., Guennoun, M., & Mouftah, H. T. (2016, June). Big data analytics: Security and privacy challenges. In *Proceedings of the 2016 IEEE Symposium on Computers and Communication (ISCC)* (pp. 952-957). IEEE. 10.1109/ISCC.2016.7543859

Gentry, C. (2010). Computing arbitrary functions of encrypted data. *Communications of the ACM, 53*(3), 97–105. doi:10.1145/1666420.1666444

Gisin, N., Ribordy, G., Tittel, W., & Zbinden, H. (2002). Quantum cryptography. *Reviews of Modern Physics*, *74*(1), 145–195. doi:10.1103/RevModPhys.74.145

Goel, R., Garuba, M., & Girma, A. (2007, April). Research directions in quantum cryptography. In *Proceedings of the Fourth International Conference on Information Technology (ITNG'07)* (pp. 779-784). IEEE.

Goldreich, O., Goldwasser, S., & Halevi, S. (1997). Public-key cryptosystems from lattice reduction problems. In *Proceedings of the Annual International Cryptology Conference* (pp. 112-131). Springer.

Goldwasser, S., & Micali, S. (1984). Probabilistic encryption. *Journal of Computer and System Sciences*, *28*(2), 270–299. doi:10.1016/0022-0000(84)90070-9

Gonçalves, C. P. (2016). Quantum neural machine learning-backpropagation and dynamics.

Gottesman, D., Lo, H. K., Lutkenhaus, N., & Preskill, J. (2004). Security of quantum key distribution with imperfect devices. In *Proceedings of the International Symposium on Information Theory*. Academic Press. 10.1109/ISIT.2004.1365172

Goyal, A., Aggarwal, S., & Jain, A. (2011). Quantum Cryptography & its Comparison with Classical Cryptography: A Review Paper. In *Proceedings of the 5th IEEE International Conference on Advanced Computing & Communication Technologies ICACCT-2011*. IEEE Press.

Goyal, V., Pandey, O., Sahai, A., & Waters, B. (2006, October). Attribute-based encryption for fine-grained access control of encrypted data. In *Proceedings of the 13th ACM conference on Computer and communications security* (pp. 89-98). ACM. 10.1145/1180405.1180418

Grochocki, D., Ho Huh, J., Berthier, R., Bobba, R., Sanders, W., Cardenas, A., & Jetcheva, G. (2012). AMI threats, intrusion detection requirements and deployment recommendations. In *Proceedings of the 2012 IEEE 3rd International Conference on Smart Grid Communications, SmartGridComm 2012* (pp. 395-400). IEEE Press. doi:10.1109/SmartGridComm.2012.6486016

Gross, M. J. (2011). *Exclusive: Operation shady rat—unprecedented cyber-espionage campaign and intellectual-property bonanza. Vanity Fair.*

Gruss, D., Maurice, C., & Wagner, K. (2015). *Flush+Flush: A Stealthier Last-Level Cache Attack.* ArXiv, abs/1511.04594

Gruss, D., Maurice, C., Wagner, K., & Mangard, S. (2016). Flush+Flush: A Fast and Stealthy Cache Attack. *Detection of Intrusions and Malware, and Vulnerability Assessment*, 279-299. Doi:10.1007/978-3-319-40667-1_14

Gu, G., Porras, P. A., Yegneswaran, V., Fong, M. W., & Lee, W. (2007). Bothunter: Detecting malware infection through ids-driven dialog correlation. *In* Proceedings of the *USENIX Security Symposium* (pp. 1-16). Usenix.

Gubbi, J., Buyya, R., Marusic, S., & Palaniswami, M. (2013). Internet of Things (IoT): A vision, architectural elements, and future directions. *Future Generation Computer Systems, 29*(7), 1645–1660. doi:10.1016/j.future.2013.01.010

Habeeb, R. A. A., Nasaruddin, F., Gani, A., Hashem, I. A. T., Ahmed, E., & Imran, M. (2019). Real-time big data processing for anomaly detection: A Survey. *International Journal of Information Management, 45*, 289–307. doi:10.1016/j.ijinfomgt.2018.08.006

Hacherl, D. J., Garg, P., & Satagopan, M. D. & Reichel., R. P. (2007). Patent No. 7,200,869. U.S.

Hammoudeh, M., & Arioua, M. (2018). Sensors and Actuators in Smart Cities. *Journal of Sensor and Actuator Networks, 7*(1), 1. doi:10.3390/jsan7010008

Handa, A., Sharma, A., & Shukla, S. K. (2019). Machine learning in cybersecurity: A review. *Wiley Interdisciplinary Reviews. Data Mining and Knowledge Discovery, 9*(4).

Hardy, L., & Song, D. D. (1999). No signalling and probabilistic quantum cloning. *Physics Letters. [Part A], 259*(5), 331–333. doi:10.1016/S0375-9601(99)00448-X

He, H., & Yan, J. (2016). Cyber-physical attacks and defences in the smart grid: a survey. IET Cyber-Physical Systems: Theory & Applications, 1(1), 13-27.

Heath, T., & Rolington, A. (2018, July 30). News-News Analysis, Business-Services-IT & Telecoms. Cybersecurity Intelligence. Retrieved from https://www.cybersecurityintelligence.com/blog/what-is-digital-twin-technology-3564.html

He, H., & Yan, J. (2016). Cyber-physical attacks and defences in the smart grid: A survey. *IET Cyber-Physical Systems: Theory & Applications, 1*(1), 13–27.

Hoffstein, J., Pipher, J., & Silverman, J. H. (1998). NTRU: a ring based public key cryptosystem. In *Proceedings of ANTS-III* (pp. 267-288). Springer. 10.1007/BFb0054868

Horodecki, R., Horodecki, P., Horodecki, M., & Horodecki, K. (2009). Quantum entanglement. *Reviews of Modern Physics, 81*(2), 865–942. doi:10.1103/RevModPhys.81.865

Hu, V. C., Ferraiolo, D., Kuhn, R., Friedman, A. R., Lang, A. J., Cogdell, M. M., ... Scarfone, K. (2013). Guide to attribute based access control (ABAC) definition and considerations (draft). *NIST*.

Hughes, R. J., Alde, D. M., Dyer, P., Luther, G. G., Morgan, G. L., & Schauer, M. (1995). Quantum cryptography. *Contemporary Physics, 36*(3), 149–163.

Hülsing, A. (2013). W-OTS+–shorter signatures for hash-based signature schemes. *In Proceedings of the International Conference on Cryptology* (pp. 173-188). Springer. 10.1007/978-3-642-38553-7_10

Hur, J., & Noh, D. K. (2010). Attribute-based access control with efficient revocation in data outsourcing systems. *IEEE Transactions on Parallel and Distributed Systems, 22*(7), 1214–1221. doi:10.1109/TPDS.2010.203

Hu, V. C., Kuhn, D. R., & Ferraiolo, D. F. (2018). Access Control for Emerging Distributed Systems. *Computer*, *51*(10), 100–103. doi:10.1109/MC.2018.3971347 PMID:31092952

Irazoqui, G., Eisenbarth, T., & Sunar, B. (2015). S$A: A Shared Cache Attack That Works across Cores and Defies VM Sandboxing -- and Its Application to AES. *2015 IEEE Symposium on Security and Privacy.* 10.1109/SP.2015.42

Ishino, M., Koizumi, Y., & Hasegawa, T. (2014). A Study on a Routing-Based Mobility Management Architecture for IoT Devices. In *Proceedings of the 2014 IEEE 22nd International Conference on Network Protocols* (pp. 498-500). doi:10.1109/ICNP.2014.78

Jain, P., Pathak, N., Tapashetti, P., & Umesh, A. S. (2013, December). Privacy preserving processing of data decision tree based on sample selection and singular value decomposition. In *Proceedings of the 2013 9th international conference on information assurance and security (IAS)* (pp. 91-95). IEEE. 10.1109/ISIAS.2013.6947739

Jain, P., Gyanchandani, M., & Khare, N. (2016). Big data privacy: A technological perspective and review. *Journal of Big Data*, *3*(1), 25. doi:10.118640537-016-0059-y

Jerkins, J.A. (2017). Motivating a market or regulatory solution to IoT insecurity with the Mirai botnet code. doi:.2017.7868464 doi:10.1109/CCWC

Jiang, X., Zhang, J., Harding, B. J., Makela, J. J., & Domı, A. D. (2013). Spoofing GPS receiver clock offset of phasor measurement units. *IEEE Transactions on Power Systems*, *28*(3), 3253–3262. doi:10.1109/TPWRS.2013.2240706

Jing, L., Wang, Y. N., Shi, H. D., Mu, L. Z., & Fan, H. (2012). Minimal input sets determining phase-covariant and universal quantum cloning. *Physical Review A.*, *86*(6), 062315. doi:10.1103/PhysRevA.86.062315

Jing, Q., Vasilakos, A. V., Wan, J., Lu, J., & Qiu, D. (2014, November). Security of the Internet of things: Perspectives and Challenges. *Wireless Networks*, *20*(8), 2481–2501. doi:10.100711276-014-0761-7

Jin, X., Krishnan, R., & Sandhu, R. (2012, July). A unified attribute-based access control model covering DAC, MAC and RBAC. In *Proceedings of the IFIP Annual Conference on Data and Applications Security and Privacy* (pp. 41-55). Springer. 10.1007/978-3-642-31540-4_4

Jin, X., Wah, B. W., Cheng, X., & Wang, Y. (2015). Significance and challenges of big data research. *Big Data Research*, *2*(2), 59–64. doi:10.1016/j.bdr.2015.01.006

Jogunola, O., Ikpehai, A., Anoh, K., Adebisi, B., Hammoudeh, M., Gacanin, H., & Harris, G. (2018). Comparative Analysis of P2P Architectures for Energy Trading and Sharing. *Energies*, *11*, 1.

Jogunola, O., Ikpehai, A., Anoh, K., Adebisi, B., Hammoudeh, M., Son, S.-Y., & Harris, G. (2017). State-Of-e-Art and Prospects for Peer-To-Peer Transaction-Based Energy System. *Energies*, *10*(12), 12. doi:10.3390/en10122106

Johnson, J. R., & Hogan, E. A. (2013). A Graph Analytic Metric for Mitigating Advanced Persistent Threat. *In Proceedings of the IEEE International Conference on Intelligence and Security Informatics* (pp. 129-133). IEEE. 10.1109/ISI.2013.6578801

Johnson, R. C. (2002). *MagiQ employs quantum technology for secure encryption.* EE Times.

Joshi, A. P., Han, M., & Wang, Y. (2018). A survey on security and privacy issues of blockchain technology. *Mathematical Foundations of Computing, 1*(2), 121–147. doi:10.3934/mfc.2018007

Karpov, E., Navez, P., & Cerf, N. J. (2005). Cloning quantum entanglement in arbitrary dimensions. *Physical Review A., 72*(4), 042314. doi:10.1103/PhysRevA.72.042314

Katz, H. (2019, January 8). IoT Cybersecurity Challenges and Solutions. Allot. Retrieved from https://www.allot.com/blog/iot_cybersecurity_challenges_and_solutions/

Kelsey, J., Schneier, B., Wagner, D., & Hall, C. (n.d.). *Side Channel Cryptanalysis of Product Ciphers.* Retrieved from https://www.schneier.com/academic/paperfiles/paper-side-channel2.pdf

Kezunovic, M., Meliopoulos, S., Venkatasubramanian, V., & Vittal, V. (2014). *Application of time-synchronized measurements in power system transmission networks.* Springer; doi:10.1007/978-3-319-06218-1

Khezr, S., Moniruzzaman, M., Yassine, A., & Benlamri, R. (2019). Blockchain Technology in Healthcare: A Comprehensive Review and Directions for Future Research. Applied Sciences, 9(9), 1736. doi:10.3390/app9091736

Kianpour, M., & Sabbaghi-Nadooshan, R. (2014). A conventional design and simulation for CLB implementation of an FPGA quantum-dot cellular automata. *Microprocessors and Microsystems, 38*(8), 1046–1062. doi:10.1016/j.micpro.2014.08.001

Kim, K., Wu, K., & Karri, R. (2006). Quantum-Dot Cellular Automata Design Guideline. *IEICE Transactions on Fundamentals of Electronics, Communications and Computer Sciences, E89-A*(6), 1607–1614. doi:10.1093/ietfec/e89-a.6.1607

Kim, Y., Kim, I., & Park, N. (2014). Analysis of cyber attacks and security intelligence. In Mobile, Ubiquitous, and Intelligent Computing (pp. 489-494). Springer. doi:10.1007/978-3-642-40675-1_73

Kimble, H. J. (2008). The quantum internet. *Nature, 453*(7198), 1023–1030. doi:10.1038/nature07127 PMID:18563153

Kim, H. K., So, W. H., & Je, S. M. (2019). A big data framework for network security of small and medium enterprises for future computing. *The Journal of Supercomputing, 75*(6), 3334–3367. doi:10.100711227-019-02815-8

Kim, J., & Tong, L. (2013). On topology attack of a smart grid: Undetectable attacks and countermeasures. *IEEE Journal on Selected Areas in Communications, 31*(7), 1294–1305. doi:10.1109/JSAC.2013.130712

Kim, S. H., Kim, N. U., & Chung, T. M. (2013, December). Attribute relationship evaluation methodology for big data security. In *Proceedings of the 2013 International conference on IT convergence and security (ICITCS)* (pp. 1-4). IEEE. 10.1109/ICITCS.2013.6717808

Kim, S., Young Kwon, E., Kim, M., Hee Cheon, J., Ju, S. H., Lim, Y. H., & Choi, M.-S. (2011). A Secure Smart-Metering Protocol Over Power-Line Communication. *IEEE Transactions on Power Delivery, 26*(4), 2370–2379. doi:10.1109/TPWRD.2011.2158671

Kipnis, A., & Shamir, A. (1999). Cryptanalysis of the HFE public key cryptosystem by relinearization. In *Proceedings of the Annual International Cryptology Conference* (pp. 19-30). Springer. 10.1007/3-540-48405-1_2

Knezevic, D. (2018). Impact of Blockchain Technology Platform in Changing the Financial Sector and Other Industries. *Montenegrin Journal of Economics, 14*(1), 109–120. doi:10.14254/1800-5845/2018.14-1.8

Koashi, M., & Imoto, N. (1998). No-cloning theorem of entangled states. *Physical Review Letters, 81*(19), 4264–4267. doi:10.1103/PhysRevLett.81.4264

Koblitz, N. (1987). Elliptic curve cryptosystems. *Mathematics of Computation, 48*(177), 203–209. doi:10.1090/S0025-5718-1987-0866109-5

Kocher, P. C. (1996). *Timing Attacks on Implementations of Diffie-Hellman, RSA, DSS, and Other Systems* (pp. 104–113). Berlin: Springer. doi:10.1007/3-540-68697-5_9

Komninos, N., Philippou, E., & Pitsillides, A. (2014). Survey in Smart Grid and Smart Home Security: Issues, Challenges and Countermeasures. *IEEE Communications Surveys and Tutorials, 16*(4), 1933–1954. doi:10.1109/COMST.2014.2320093

Korolov, M. & Drinkwater, D. (2019). *What is quantum cryptography? It's no silver bullet, but could improve security.* CSO Online. Retrieved from https://www.csoonline.com/article/3235970/what-is-quantum-cryptography-it-s-no-silver-bullet-but-could-improve-security.html

Korolov, M., & Doug, D. (2019). What is quantum cryptography? It's no silver bullet, but could improve security. CSO Online. Retrieved from https://www.csoonline.com/article/3235970/what-is-quantum-cryptography-it-s-no-silver-bullet-but-could-improve-security.html

Ko, T., & Krishnan, R. (2003). Fingerprint and Face Identification for Large User Population. *Systemic. Cybernetics and Informatics, 1*(3), 87–92.

Kulah, Y., Dincer, B., Yilmaz, C., & Savas, E. (2018). SpyDetector: An approach for detecting side-channel attacks at runtime. *International Journal of Information Security, 18*(4), 393–422. doi:10.100710207-018-0411-7

Kumar, M., & Sinha, O. P. (2007). M-government–mobile technology for e-government. In *Proceedings of the International conference on e-government* (pp. 294-301). Academic Press.

Kumar, J. S., & Patel, D. R. (2014). A Survey on Internet of Things: Security and Privacy Issues. *International Journal of Computers and Applications, 90*, 20–26. doi:10.5120/15579-4304

Kumar, M. G. V., & Ragupathy, U. S. (2016, March). A Survey on current key issues and status in cryptography. In *Proceedings of the 2016 International Conference on Wireless Communications, Signal Processing and Networking (WiSPNET)* (pp. 205-210). IEEE.

Kute, S. S., & Desai, C. G. (2017). Quantum Cryptography: A Review. *Indian Journal of Science and Technology, 10*(3).

Kutvonen, A., Sagawa, T., & Fujii, K. (2018). Recurrent neural networks running on quantum spins: memory accuracy and capacity.

Labrinidis, A., & Jagadish, H. V. (2012). Challenges and opportunities with big data. *Proceedings of the VLDB Endowment International Conference on Very Large Data Bases, 5*(12), 2032–2033. doi:10.14778/2367502.2367572

Lakshmi, P. S., & Murali, G. (2017). Comparison of classical and quantum cryptography using QKD simulator. In *Proceedings of the International Conference on Energy, Communication, Data Analytics and Soft Computing (ICECDS)* (pp. 3543-3547). Academic Press. 10.1109/ICECDS.2017.8390120

Lamport, L. (1979), Constructing digital signatures from a one-way function. SRI International Computer Science Laboratory.

Langner, R. (2011). Stuxnet: Dissecting a cyberwarfare weapon. *IEEE Security and Privacy, 9*(3), 49–51. doi:10.1109/MSP.2011.67

Largman, K., More, A.B., & Blair, E. (2011). Patent No. 12/868,611. U.S.

Lee, H. (2016). *IoT: Architecture*. Juxtology. Retrieved from https://juxtology.com/iot-transformation/iot-world-forum/

Lee, J., Moon, D., Kim, I., & Lee, Y. (2019). A semantic approach to improving machine readability of a large-scale attack graph. *The Journal of Supercomputing, 75*(6), 3028–3045. doi:10.100711227-018-2394-6

Lemay, A., Calvet, J., Menet, F., & Fernandez, J. M. (2018). Survey of publicly available reports on advanced persistent threat actors. *Computers & Security, 72*, 26–59. doi:10.1016/j.cose.2017.08.005

Lenstra, A. K., & Hendrik Jr, W. (1993). The development of the number field sieve. Springer Science & Business Media. doi:10.1007/BFb0091534

Lent, C. S., & Tougaw, P. D. (1997). A device architecture for computing with quantum dots. *Proceedings of the IEEE, 85*(4), 541–557. doi:10.1109/5.573740

Lent, C. S., Tougaw, P. D., Porod, W., & Bernstein, G. H. (1993). Quantum cellular automata. *Nanotechnology, 4*(1), 49–57. doi:10.1088/0957-4484/4/1/004 PMID:21727566

Leverage LLC. (2018). An Introduction to Internet of Things. Retrieved from https://www.leverege.com/iot-intro-ebook

Li, M., Huang, W., Wang, Y., Fan, W., & Li, J. (2016). The study of APT attack stage model. *In* Proceedings of the *IEEE/ACIS 15th International Conference on Computer and Information Science (ICIS)* (pp. 1-5). Okayama, Japan: IEEE.

Liang, X., Zhao, J., Shetty, S., Liu, J., & Li, D. (2017, October). Integrating blockchain for data sharing and collaboration in mobile healthcare applications. In *Proceedings of the 2017 IEEE 28th Annual International Symposium on Personal, Indoor, and Mobile Radio Communications (PIMRC)* (pp. 1-5). IEEE. 10.1109/PIMRC.2017.8292361

Liang, G., Zhao, J., Luo, F., Weller, S. R., & Dong, Z. Y. (2016). A review of false data injection attacks against modern power systems. *IEEE Transactions on Smart Grid*, *8*(4), 1630–1638. doi:10.1109/TSG.2015.2495133

Li, H., & Zhang, W. (2010, December). QoS routing in smart grid. In *Proceedings of the 2010 IEEE Global Telecommunications Conference GLOBECOM 2010* (pp. 1-6). IEEE.

Li, J., Chen, X., Li, J., Jia, C., Ma, J., & Lou, W. (2013, September). Fine-grained access control system based on outsourced attribute-based encryption. In *Proceedings of the European Symposium on Research in Computer Security* (pp. 592-609). Springer. 10.1007/978-3-642-40203-6_33

Li, L., Qiu, D., Li, L., Wu, L., & Zou, X. (2009). Probabilistic broadcasting of mixed states. *Journal of Physics. A, Mathematical and Theoretical*, *42*(17), 175302. doi:10.1088/1751-8113/42/17/175302

Lin, F. X. (2014). Shor's Algorithm and the Quantum Fourier Transform. McGill University. Retrieved from www.math.mcgill.ca/darmon/courses/12-13/nt/projects/Fangxi-Lin.pdf

Lin, H., & W. Bergmann, N. (2016). IoT Privacy and Security Challenges for Smart Home Environments. *Information*, *7*, 44. doi:10.3390/info7030044

Li, P., Li, J., Huang, Z., Li, T., Gao, C. Z., Yiu, S. M., & Chen, K. (2017). Multi-key privacy-preserving deep learning in cloud computing. *Future Generation Computer Systems*, *74*, 76–85. doi:10.1016/j.future.2017.02.006

Litchfield, A., & Shahzad, A. (2016). *Virtualization technology: Cross-VM cache side-channel attacks make it vulnerable*. arXiv preprint arXiv:1606.01356

Liu, G., Chen, W., Chen, H., & Xie, J. (2019). A Quantum Particle Swarm Optimization Algorithm with Teamwork Evolutionary Strategy. *Mathematical Problems in Engineering*.

Liu, W., Srivastava, S., Lu, L., O'Neill, M., & Swartzlander, E. E. (2012). Are QCA cryptographic circuits resistant to power analysis attack? *IEEE Transactions on Nanotechnology*, *11*(6), 1239–1251. doi:10.1109/TNANO.2012.2222663

Liu, Y., Ning, P., & Reiter, M. (2011). False data injection attacks against state estimation in electric power grids. *ACM Transactions on Information and System Security*, *14*(1), 13. doi:10.1145/1952982.1952995

Lo, H.-K., & Zhao, Y. (2007). Quantum cryptography.

Lo, H.-K., & Chau, H. F. (1999). Unconditional Security of Quantum Key Distribution over Arbitrarily Long Distances. *Science*, *283*(5410), 2050–2056.

Lo, H.-K., & Chau, H. F. (1999). Unconditional security of quantum key distribution over arbitrary long distances. *Science*, *283*(5410), 2050–2056. doi:10.1126cience.283.5410.2050 PMID:10092221

Loidreau, P. (2000). Strengthening McEliece cryptosystem. In *Proceedings of the International Conference on the Theory and Application of Cryptology and Information Security* (pp. 585-598). Springer.

Loidreau, P., & Sendrier, N. (2001). Weak keys in the McEliece public-key cryptosystem. *IEEE Transactions on Information Theory*, *47*(3), 1207–1211. doi:10.1109/18.915687

Löndahl, C., Johansson, T., Shooshtari, M. K., Ahmadian-Attari, M., & Aref, M. R. (2016). Squaring attacks on McEliece public-key cryptosystems using quasi-cyclic codes of even dimension. *Designs, Codes and Cryptography*, *80*(2), 359–377. doi:10.100710623-015-0099-x

Longstaff, J., & Noble, J. (2016, March). Attribute based access control for big data applications by query modification. In *Proceedings of the 2016 IEEE Second International Conference on Big Data Computing Service and Applications (BigDataService)* (pp. 58-65). IEEE. 10.1109/BigDataService.2016.35

Lopez-Leyva, J., Talamantes-Alvarez, A., Ponce-Camacho, M., Garcia, E., & Alvarez-Guzman, E. (2018). *Free-Space-Optical Quantum Key Distribution Systems: Challenges and Trends. In Quantum Cryptography*. IntechOpen. Retrieved September 30, 2019 from https://www.intechopen.com/books/quantum-cryptography-in-advanced-networks/free-space-optical-quantum-key-distribution-systems-challenges-and-trends

Luitel, B., & Venayagamoorthy, G. K. (2010). Quantum inspired PSO for the optimization of simultaneous recurrent neural networks as MIMO learning systems. *Neural Networks*, *23*(5), 583–586. doi:10.1016/j.neunet.2009.12.009 PMID:20071140

Lunt, T. F. (1993). A survey of intrusion detection techniques. *Computers & Security*, *12*(4), 405–418. doi:10.1016/0167-4048(93)90029-5

Lu, R., Zhu, H., Liu, X., Liu, J. K., & Shao, J. (2014). Toward efficient and privacy-preserving computing in big data era. *IEEE Network*, *28*(4), 46–50. doi:10.1109/MNET.2014.6863131

Lu, X., Hinkelman, K., Fu, Y., Wang, J., Zuo, W., Zhang, Q., & Saad, W. (2019). An Open Source Modeling Framework for Interdependent Energy-Transportation-Communication Infrastructure in Smart and Connected Communities. *IEEE Access : Practical Innovations, Open Solutions*, *7*, 55458–55476. doi:10.1109/ACCESS.2019.2913630

Ma, C. Y., Yau, D. K., Lou, X., & Rao, N. S. (2012). Markov game analysis for attack-defense of power networks under possible misinformation. *IEEE Transactions on Power Systems*, *28*(2), 1676–1686. doi:10.1109/TPWRS.2012.2226480

Ma, C. Y., Yau, D. K., & Rao, N. S. (2013). Scalable solutions of Markov games for smart-grid infrastructure protection. *IEEE Transactions on Smart Grid*, *4*(1), 47–55. doi:10.1109/TSG.2012.2223243

MagiQ Technologies. (2003). [Press Release].

Mahalakshmi, S., Saiashwini, C., & Meghana, S. (2001). Research study of big data clustering techniques. *Int. J. Innov. Res. Sci. Eng*, 80-84.

Mahmood, T., & Afzal, U. (2013, December). Security analytics: Big data analytics for cybersecurity: A review of trends, techniques and tools. In *Proceedings of the 2013 2nd national conference on Information assurance (NCIA)* (pp. 129-134). IEEE.

Maier, M. J. (2001). Backdoor liability from Internet telecommuters. *Computer L. Rev. & Tech. J.*, *6*, 27.

Marchetti, M., Pierazzi, F., Guido, A., & Colajanni, M. (2016). Countering Advanced Persistent Threats through Security Intelligence and Big Data Analytics. *In* Proceedings of the *8th International Conference on Cyber Conflict* (pp. 243-261). NATO CCD COE Publications. 10.1109/CYCON.2016.7529438

Marchetti, M., Pierazzi, F., Colajanni, M., & Guido, A. (2016). Analysis of high volumes of network traffic for Advanced Persistent Threat detection. *Computer Networks*, 1–15.

Martinez-Mateo, J., Elkouss, D., & Martin, V. (2013). Key Reconciliation for High Performance Quantum Key Distribution. *Scientific Reports*, *3*(1), 1576. doi:10.1038rep01576 PMID:23546440

Masoodi, F., Alam, S., Siddiqui, S., & Liz, L. (2019). 3). Security & Privacy Threats, Attacks and Countermeasures in Internet of Things. *International Journal of Network Security & Its Applications*, *11*(02), 67–77. doi:10.5121/ijnsa.2019.11205

Mavroeidis, V., Vishi, K., Zych, M. D., & Jøsang, A. (2018). The impact of quantum computing on present cryptography. *International Journal of Advanced Computer science and Applications*, *9*(3).

Mayers, D. (1996). Advances in Cryptology. In N. Koblitz (Ed.), *Proceedings of Crypto'96* (pp. 343–357). New York: Springer.

Mayers, D. (1997). Unconditionally Secure Quantum Bit Commitment is Impossible. *Physical Review Letters*, *78*(17), 3414–3417. doi:10.1103/PhysRevLett.78.3414

Mayers, D. (2001). Unconditional security in quantum cryptography. *Journal of the Association for Computing Machinery*, *48*(3), 351–406. doi:10.1145/382780.382781

McEliece, R. J. (1978). A public-key cryptosystem based on algebraic coding theory. *Deep Space Network Progress Report*, *44*, 114–116.

Menezes, A. J., van Oorschot, P. C., & Vanstone, S. A. (2016). *A Handbook of Applied cryptography*. CRC press.

Meng, T., Cui, M., Dong, Z., Wang, X., Yin, G., & Zhao, L. (2019). Multilevel Programming-Based Coordinated Cyber Physical Attacks and Countermeasures in Smart Grid. *IEEE Access : Practical Innovations, Open Solutions*. doi:10.1109/ACCESS.2018.2890604

MErkle., R. C. (1989). A certified digital signature. In *Proceedings of the Conference on the Theory and Application of Cryptology* (pp. 218-238). Springer.

Mersin, A. (2007). The comparative performance analysis of lattice based NTRU cryptosystem with other asymmetrical cryptosystems [Master's thesis]. İzmir Institute of Technology.

Miao, F., Pajic, M., & Pappas, G. J. (2013, December). Stochastic game approach for replay attack detection. In *Proceedings of the 52nd IEEE conference on decision and control* (pp. 1854-1859). IEEE. doi:10.1109/CDC.2013.6760152

Micciancio, D. (2001). Improving lattice-based cryptosystems using the Hermite normal form. In *Cryptography and lattices* (pp. 126–145). Berlin: Springer. doi:10.1007/3-540-44670-2_11

Michael, K. (2012). *How quantum cryptography works: And by the way, it's breakable*. Retrieved from https://www.techrepublic.com/blog/it-security/how-quantum-cryptography-works-and-by-the-way-its-breakable/

Miller, L. (2016). IoT Security For Dummies, INSIDE Secure Edition. Learn ARM. Retrieved from https://learn.arm.com/iot-solutions-for-dummies.html

Miskinis, C. (2018, May). Incorporating digital twin into internet cyber security – creating a safer future. Challenge.org. Retrieved from https://www.challenge.org/insights/digital-twin-cyber-security/

Monojlovic, V. (2017). *Introduction to the Quantum Internet*. Retrieved from https://labs.ripe.net/Members/becha/introduction-to-the-quantum-internet

Moreno, J., Serrano, M., & Fernández-Medina, E. (2016). Main issues in big data security. *Future Internet*, *8*(3), 44. doi:10.3390/fi8030044

Morison, K., Wang, L., & Kundur, P. (2004). Power system security assessment. *IEEE Power & Energy Magazine*, *2*(5), 30–39. doi:10.1109/MPAE.2004.1338120

Mosavi, A., Salimi, M., Faizollahzadeh Ardabili, S., Rabczuk, T., Shamshirband, S., & Varkonyi-Koczy, A. R. (2019). State of the art of machine learning models in energy systems, a systematic review. *Energies*, *12*(7), 1301. doi:10.3390/en12071301

Mosenia, A., & Jha, N. K. (2017). A Comprehensive Study of Security of Internet-of-Things. *IEEE Transactions on Emerging Topics in Computing*, *5*(4), 586–602. doi:10.1109/TETC.2016.2606384

Mo, Y., Kim, T. H. J., Brancik, K., Dickinson, D., Lee, H., Perrig, A., & Sinopoli, B. (2011). Cyber–physical security of a smart grid infrastructure. *Proceedings of the IEEE*, *100*(1), 195–209. doi:10.1109/JPROC.2011.2161428

Mullins, J. (2003). *Quantum Cryptography's Reach Extended*. IEEE Spectrum Online.

Murali, G., & Prasad, R. S. (2016). CloudQKDP: Quantum key distribution protocol for cloud computing. 2016 *International Conference on Information Communication and Embedded Systems (ICICES)*. 10.1109/ICICES.2016.7518922

Mushtaq, M., Akram, A., Bhatti, M. K., Rais, R. N., Lapotre, V., & Gogniat, G. (2018). Run-time Detection of Prime + Probe Side-Channel Attack on AES Encryption Algorithm. *2018 Global Information Infrastructure and Networking Symposium (GIIS)*. 10.1109/GIIS.2018.8635767

Nabeel, M., Kerr, S., & Bertino, E. (2012). Authentication and key management for advanced metering infrastructures utilizing physically unclonable functions. In *Proc. IEEE Third Int. Conf. SmartGridComm* (pp. 324–329). IEEE Press. 10.1109/SmartGridComm.2012.6486004

Naik, N., Jenkins, P., Savage, N., & Katos, V. (2016, December). Big data security analysis approach using computational intelligence techniques in R for desktop users. In *Proceedings of the 2016 IEEE Symposium Series on Computational Intelligence (SSCI)* (pp. 1-8). IEEE. 10.1109/SSCI.2016.7849907

Nam, Y.S. (2012). Running Shor's Algorithm on a complete, gate-by-gate implementation of a virtual, universal quantum computer. Retrieved from http://citeseerx.ist.psu.edu

Nate, L. (2018). *Cryptography in the Cloud: Securing Cloud Data with Encryption*. Retrieved from https://digitalguardian.com/blog/cryptography-cloud-securing-cloud-data-encryption

National Institute of Standards and Technology. (2014). Framework for Improving Critical Infrastructure Cybersecurity, Version 1.0.

Nguyen, P. Q., & Regev, O. (2009). Learning a parallelepiped: Cryptanalysis of GGH and NTRU signatures. *Journal of Cryptology, 22*(2), 139–160. doi:10.100700145-008-9031-0

Niederreiter, H. (1986). Knapsack-type cryptosystems and algebraic coding theory. *Problems of Control and Information Theory, 15*, 19–34.

NIST. (2016). Recommendation for Key Management Special Publication (SP) 800-57 Part 1 Revision 4. doi:10.6028/NIST.SP.800-57pt1r4

Niu, C. S., & Griffiths, R. B. (1999). Two-qubit copying machine for economical quantum eavesdropping. *Physical Review A., 60*(4), 2764–2776. doi:10.1103/PhysRevA.60.2764

Olanrewaju, R., Islam, T., Khalifa, O., Anwar, F., & Pampori, B. (2017). Cryptography as a Service (CaaS): Quantum Cryptography for Secure Cloud Computing. *Indian Journal of Science and Technology, 10*(7), 1–6. doi:10.17485/ijst/2017/v10i7/110897

Ortiz, J., Sadovsky, A., & Russakovsky, O. (2004). *Modern Cryptography: Theory and Applications*. Retrieved from https://cs.stanford.edu/people/eroberts/courses/soco/projects/2004-05/cryptography/quantum.html

Padamvathi, V., Vardhan, B. V., & Krishna, A. V. N. (2016, February). Quantum Cryptography and Quantum Key Distribution Protocols: A Survey. In *Proceedings of the 2016 IEEE 6th International Conference on Advanced Computing (IACC)* (pp. 556-562). IEEE.

Paillier, P., & Naccache, D. (2003). Public Key Cryptography. *In* Proceedings of the *5th International Workshop on Practice and Theory in Public Key Cryptosystems.* Springer.

Pain, P., Das, K., Sadhu, A., Kanjilal, M. R., & De, D. (2019). Novel True Random Number Generator Based Hardware Cryptographic Architecture Using Quantum-Dot Cellular Automata. *International Journal of Theoretical Physics*, 1–20. doi:10.100710773-019-04189-2

Pal, A. (n.d.). *The Internet of Things (IoT) – Threats and Countermeasures.* CSO. Retrieved from [REMOVED HYPERLINK FIELD]https://www.cso.com.au/article/575407/internet-things-iot-threats-countermeasures/

Pal, S., Sikdar, B., & Chow, J. H. (2016). An online mechanism for detection of gray-hole attacks on PMU data. *IEEE Transactions on Smart Grid*, *9*(4), 2498–2507. doi:10.1109/TSG.2016.2614327

Panackal, J. J., & Pillai, A. S. (2015). Adaptive utility-based anonymization model: Performance evaluation on big data sets. *Procedia Computer Science*, *50*, 347–352. doi:10.1016/j.procs.2015.04.037

Pandey, R. K., & Misra, M. (2016, December). Cyber security threats—Smart grid infrastructure. In *Proceedings of the 2016 National Power Systems Conference (NPSC)* (pp. 1-6). IEEE. doi:10.1109/NPSC.2016.7858950

Parmar, P., & Udhayabanu, R. (2012), Voice Fingerprinting: A Very Important Tool against Crime. *J. Indian Acad. Forensic Med.*, *34*(1).

Parmar, P. V., Padhar, S. B., Patel, S. N., Bhatt, N. I., & Jhaveri, R. H. (2014). Survey of various homomorphic encryption algorithms and schemes. *International Journal of Computers and Applications*, *91*(8).

Parno, B., Perrig, A., & Gligor, V. (2005). Distributed Detection of Node Replication Attacks in Sensor Networks. In *Proceedings of the 2005 IEEE Symposium on Security and Privacy* (pp. 49-63). IEEE Computer Society. 10.1109/SP.2005.8

Patarin, J. (1997). The oil and vinegar signature scheme. *Presented at the Dagstuhl Workshop on Cryptography.* Academic Press.

Patarin, J., Courtois, N., & Goubin, L. (2001). Quartz, 128-bit long digital signatures. In *Cryptographers' Track at the RSA Conference* (pp. 282-297). Springer.

Patel, M., Aggarwal, A., & Chaubey, N. (2018). Variants of wormhole attacks and their impact in wireless sensor networks. In Progress in Computing, Analytics and Networking (pp. 637-642). Springer Singapore.

Patel, M., Aggarwal, A., & Chaubey, N. (2017). Wormhole attacks and countermeasures in wireless sensor networks: A survey. *IACSIT International Journal of Engineering and Technology*, *9*(2), 1049–1060. doi:10.21817/ijet/2017/v9i2/170902126

Patel, M., Aggarwal, A., & Chaubey, N. (2018). Analysis of Wormhole Attacks in Wireless Sensor Networks. In *Recent Findings in Intelligent Computing Techniques* (pp. 33–42). Springer Singapore.

Paundu, A. W., Fall, D., Miyamoto, D., & Kadobayashi, Y. (2018). Leveraging KVM Events to Detect Cache-Based Side Channel Attacks in a Virtualization Environment. *Security and Communication Networks*, *2018*, 1–18. doi:10.1155/2018/4216240

Pavlidis, N. G., Plagianakos, V. P., Nikiforidis, G., & Vrahatis, M. N. (2005). Spiking neural network training using evolutionary algorithms. *In Proceedings of the IEEE International Joint Conference on Neural Networks (Vol. 4*, pp. 2190-2194). IEEE. 10.1109/IJCNN.2005.1556240

Pawlick, J., Farhang, S., & Zhu, Q. (2015). Flip the Cloud: Cyber-physical Signaling Games in the Presence of Advanced Persistent Threats. *In Proceedings of the International Conference on Decision and Game Theory for Security* (pp. 289-308). Springer. 10.1007/978-3-319-25594-1_16

Pearce, M., Zeadally, S., & Hunt, R. (2013). Virtualization: Issues, Security Threats, and Solutions. *ACM Computing Surveys*, *45*(2), 1–39. doi:10.1145/2431211.2431216

Pearson, D. (2004, November). High-speed QKD Reconciliation using Forward Error Correction. *AIP Conference Proceedings*, *734*(1), 299–302.

Peev, M., Pacher, C., Alléaume, R., Barreiro, C., Bouda, J., Boxleitner, W., ... Zeilinger, A. (2009). The SECOQC quantum key distribution network in Vienna. *New Journal of Physics*, *11*(7), 075001. doi:10.1088/1367-2630/11/7/075001

Peikert, C. (2016). A decade of lattice cryptography. *Foundations and Trends in Theoretical Computer Science*, *10*(4), 283–424. doi:10.1561/0400000074

Perez, A. J., & Zeadally, S. PEAR: A privacy-enabled architecture for crowdsensing. In *Proceedings of the International Conference on Research in Adaptive and Convergent Systems* (pp. 166–171). Academic Press. 10.1145/3129676.3129685

Pham, D., Le Nguyen, T., Zhang, P. P., & Lo, M. (2005). U.S. Patent No. 6,931,530. Washington, DC: U.S. Patent and Trademark Office.

Pilkington, M. (2016). 11 Blockchain technology: principles and applications. In *Research handbook on digital transformations* (p. 225). Academic Press.

Poppe, A., Fedrizzi, A., Ursin, R., Böhm, H. R., Lorünser, T., Maurhardt, O., ... Jennewein, T. (2004). Practical quantum key distribution with polarization entangled photons. *Optics Express*, *12*(16), 3865–3871.

Postscapes. (n.d.). *Internet of Things Infographic*. Retrieved from [REMOVED HYPERLINK FIELD]https://www.postscapes.com/what-exactly-is-the-internet-of-things-infographic/

Preventing CPU side-channel attacks with kernel tracking. (2018, September 18). Retrieved from https://www.slideshare.net/azilian/preventing-cpu-side-channel-attacks-with-kernel-tracking

Prokofieva, M., & Miah, S. J. (2019). Blockchain in healthcare. *AJIS. Australasian Journal of Information Systems*, *vol*, 23.

Qi, H., Luo, X., Di, X., Li, J., Yang, H., & Jiang, Z. (2016, October). Access control model based on role and attribute and its implementation. In *Proceedings of the 2016 International Conference on Cyber-Enabled Distributed Computing and Knowledge Discovery (CyberC)* (pp. 66-71). IEEE. 10.1109/CyberC.2016.21

Quantum cryptography - Wikipedia. (n.d.). Retrieved from https://en.m.wikipedia.org/wiki/Quantum_cryptography

Quantum Cryptography by Brilliant.org (2019). *Quantum Cryptography.* Retrieved from https://brilliant.org/wiki/quantum-cryptography/

Quantum Cryptography. (n.d.). In *American Heritage® Dictionary of the English Language, Fifth Edition. (2011).* Retrieved October 26, 2019, from https://www.thefreedictionary.com/quantum+cryptography

Quantum XC. (2019). *Quantum Cryptography, Explained.* Retrieved from https://quantumxc.com/quantum-cryptography-explained/

Quantum XC. (2019). *What is Trusted Node Technology, and Why Does It Matter?* Retrieved from https://quantumxc.com/what-is-trusted-node-technology-and-why-does-it-matter/

Quantum-Safe Security Working Group. (2015). *What is Quantum Key Distribution?* Retrieved from https://www.quintessencelabs.com/wp-content/uploads/2015/08/CSA-What-is-Quantum-Key-Distribution-QKD-1.pdf

Rass, S., & Zhu, Q. (2016). GADAPT: A Sequential Game-Theoretic Framework for Designing Defense-in-Depth Strategies Against Advanced Persistent Threats. *In Proceedings of the International Conference on Decision and Game Theory for Security* (pp. 314-326). Springer. 10.1007/978-3-319-47413-7_18

Rastegin, A. E. (2003). Upper bound on the global fidelity for mixed-state cloning. *Physical Review A.*, *67*(1), 012305. doi:10.1103/PhysRevA.67.012305

RF Wireless World. (2012). IoT Architecture Basis- IoT Hardware Software Architecture. Retrieved from https://www.rfwireless-world.com/IoT/IoT-architecture.html

Riad, K., Yan, Z., Hu, H., & Ahn, G. J. (2015, October). AR-ABAC: a new attribute based access control model supporting attribute-rules for cloud computing. In *Proceedings of the 2015 IEEE Conference on Collaboration and Internet Computing (CIC)* (pp. 28-35). IEEE. 10.1109/CIC.2015.38

Richards, N. M., & King, J. H. (2013). Three paradoxes of big data. *Stan. L. Rev. Online*, *66*, 41.

Ristenpart, T., Tromer, E., Shacham, H., & Savage, S. (2009). Hey, you, get off of my cloud. *Proceedings of the 16th ACM conference on Computer and communications security - CCS '09.* DOI:10.1145/1653662.1653687

Rivest, R. L., Adleman, L. Dertouzos, M. L. (1978). On data banks and privacy homomorphisms. *Foundations of secure computation, 4*(11), 169-180.

Rivest, R. L., Shamir, A., & Adleman, L. (1978). A method for obtaining digital signatures and public-key cryptosystems. *Communications of the ACM, 21*(2), 120–126. doi:10.1145/359340.359342

Rosenberg, D., Harrington, J. W., Rice, P. R., Hiskett, P. A., Peterson, C. G., Hughes, R. J., ... Nordholt, J. E. (2007). Long-distance decoy-state quantum key distribution in optica fiber. *Physical Review Letters, 98*(1), 010503. doi:10.1103/PhysRevLett.98.010503 PMID:17358462

Rouhani, A., & Abur, A. (2016). Linear phasor estimator assisted dynamic state estimation. *IEEE Transactions on Smart Grid, 9*(1), 211–219. doi:10.1109/TSG.2016.2548244

Sabbaghi-Nadooshan, R., & Kianpour, M. (2014). A novel QCA implementation of MUX-based universal shift register. *Journal of Computational Electronics, 13*(1), 198–210. doi:10.100710825-013-0500-9

Sand, N.J. (2018). *Introduction to Quantum Cryptography*. Norwegian Creations. Retrieved from https://www.norwegiancreations.com/2018/11/introduction-to-quantum-cryptography/

Saponara, S., & Tony, B. (2012). Network architecture, security issues, and hardware implementation of a home area network for Smart Grid. *Journal of Computer Networks and Communications*, 1–19. doi:10.1155/2012/534512

Sarowar, M. G., Kamal, M. S., & Dey, N. (2019). Internet of Things and Its Impacts in Computing Intelligence: A Comprehensive Review–IoT Application for Big Data. In Big Data Analytics for Smart and Connected Cities (pp. 103–136). Hershey, PA: IGI Global. doi:10.4018/978-1-5225-6207-8.ch005

Saud, Z., & Islam, M. H. (2015). Towards Proactive Detection of Advanced Persistent Threat (APT) Attacks using Honeypots. *In Proceedings of the 8th International Conference on Security of Information and Networks* (pp. 154-157). ACM. 10.1145/2799979.2800042

Sayin, M. O., & Basar, T. (2017). Secure Sensor Design for Cyber-Physical Systems Against Advanced Persistent Threats. *In Proceedings of the International Conference on Decision and Game Theory for Security* (pp. 91-111). Springer. 10.1007/978-3-319-68711-7_6

Scarani, A., Acin, A., Ribordy, G., & Gisin, N. (2004). Quantum cryptography protocols robust against photon number splitting attacks. *Physical Review Letters, 92*(5), 057901. doi:10.1103/PhysRevLett.92.057901 PMID:14995344

Scarani, V., Bechmann-Pasquinucci, H., Cerf, N. J., Dušek, M., Lütkenhaus, N., & Peev, M. (2009). The security of practical quantum key distribution. *Reviews of Modern Physics, 81*(3), 1301–1350. doi:10.1103/RevModPhys.81.1301

Scarani, V., Iblisdir, S., Gisin, N., & Acin, A. (2005). Quantum cloning. *Reviews of Modern Physics, 77*(4), 1225–1256. doi:10.1103/RevModPhys.77.1225

Schrodinger, E. (1935a). Die gegenwärtige Situation in der Quantenmechanik. *Naturwissenschaften, 23*, 807–812, 823–828, 844–849.

Schrodinger, E. (1935b). Discussion of probability relations between separated systems. *Proceedings of the Cambridge Philosophical Society, 31*(4), 555–563. doi:10.1017/S0305004100013554

ScienceDaily. (2019). *Quantum Computer*. Retrieved from https://www.sciencedaily.com/terms/quantum_computer.htm

Shapsough, S., Qatan, F., Aburukba, R., Aloul, F., & Al Ali, A. R. (2015, October). Smart grid cyber security: Challenges and solutions. In *Proceedings of the 2015 international conference on smart grid and clean energy technologies (ICSGCE)* (pp. 170-175). IEEE. 10.1109/ICSGCE.2015.7454291

Sharma, A. (2018). *The Quantum Internet Is Still A Futuristic Dream, At Least A Decade Away*. Analytics India Mag. Retrieved from https://www.analyticsindiamag.com/the-quantum-internet-is-still-a-futuristic-dream-at-least-a-decade-away/

Shaw, K., & Fruhlinger, J. (2019, January). What is a digital twin? [And how it's changing IoT, AI and more]. Network World. Retrieved from https://www.networkworld.com/article/3280225/what-is-digital-twin-technology-and-why-it-matters.html

Shor, P. W., & Smolin, J. A. (1996). Quantum error correcting codes need not completely reveal the error syndrome.

Shor, P. W. (1994). Algorithms for quantum computation: discrete logarithms and factoring. In *Proceedings of 35th Annual Symposium on Foundations of Computer Science* (pp. 124–134). IEEE. 10.1109/SFCS.1994.365700

Shor, P. W. (1999). Polynomial-time algorithms for prime factorization and discrete logarithms on a quantum computer. *SIAM Review, 41*(2), 303–332. doi:10.1137/S0097539795293172

Shor, P. W., & Preskill, J. (2002). Simple proof of security of the BB84 Quantum key distribution protocol. *Physical Review Letters, 85*(2), 441–449.

Side-channel attack. (2004, May 20). Retrieved from https://en.wikipedia.org/wiki/Side-channel_attack

Sidelnikov, V. M., Vladimir, M., & Shestakov, S. O. (1992). On insecurity of cryptosystems based on generalized Reed-Solomon codes. *Discrete Mathematics and Applications, 2*(4), 439–444. doi:10.1515/dma.1992.2.4.439

Singh, A. K., & Misra, A. K. (2012). Analysis of Cryptographically Replay Attacks and Its Mitigation Mechanism. In *Proceedings of the International Conference on Information Systems Design and Intelligent Applications 2012 (INDIA 2012)* (pp. 787-794). Springer, Berlin, Heidelberg. doi:10.1007/978-3-642-27443-5_90

Singh, S. (1999). *The code book: the science of secrecy from ancient Egypt to quantum cryptography*. London: Fourth Estate.

Skowyra, R., Bahargam, S., & Bestavros, A. (2013). Software-defined ids for securing embedded mobile devices. *In Proceedings of the IEEE High Performance Extreme Computing Conference (HPEC)* (pp. 1-7). IEEE. 10.1109/HPEC.2013.6670325

Soltic, S., & Kasabov, N. (2010). Knowledge extraction from evolving spiking neural networks with rank order population coding. *International Journal of Neural Systems*, *20*(6), 437–445. doi:10.1142/S012906571000253X PMID:21117268

Sood, K. A., & Enbody, R. J. (2012). Targeted cyberattacks: A superset of advanced persistent threats. *IEEE Security and Privacy*, *11*(1), 54–61.

Spector, L., Barnum, H., Bernstein, H. J., & Swamy, N. (1999). Quantum computing applications of genetic programming. In *Advances in genetic programming* (pp. 135-160). Academic Press.

Sridhar, S., Hahn, A., & Govindarasu, M. (2012). Cyber–physical system security for the electric power grid. *Proceedings of the IEEE*, *100*(1), 210–224. doi:10.1109/JPROC.2011.2165269

Steane, A. M. (1996b). Error correcting codes in quantum theory. *Physical Review Letters*, *77*(5), 793–797. doi:10.1103/PhysRevLett.77.793 PMID:10062908

Steane, A. M. (1996c). Simple quantum error-correcting codes. *Physical Review A.*, *54*(6), 4741–4751. doi:10.1103/PhysRevA.54.4741 PMID:9914038

Sulkamo, V. (2018). IoT from cyber security perspective. Theseus. Retrieved from https://www.theseus.fi/bitstream/handle/10024/151498/IoT%20from%20cyber%20security%20perspective.pdf?sequence=1&isAllowed=y

Suthaharan, S. (2014). Big data classification: Problems and challenges in network intrusion prediction with machine learning. *Performance Evaluation Review*, *41*(4), 70–73. doi:10.1145/2627534.2627557

Swan, M. (2015). *Blockchain: Blueprint for a new economy*. O'Reilly Media, Inc.

Takabi, H., Joshi, J. B., & Ahn, G. J. (2010). Security and privacy challenges in cloud computing environments. *IEEE Security and Privacy*, *8*(6), 24–31. doi:10.1109/MSP.2010.186

Tang, Y.-L., Yin, H.-L., Chen, S.-J., Liu, Y., Zhang, W.-J., Jiang, X., ... Pan, J. W. (2014). Measurement device-independent quantum key distribution over 200 km. *Physical Review Letters*, *113*(19), 190501. doi:10.1103/PhysRevLett.113.190501 PMID:25415890

Tank, D. M. (2017). Security and Privacy Issues, Solutions, and Tools for MCC. *Security Management in Mobile Cloud Computing*, 121-147. Doi:10.4018/978-1-5225-0602-7.ch006

Tank, D., Aggarwal, A., & Chaubey, N. (2019). Virtualization vulnerabilities, security issues, and solutions: a critical study and comparison. *International Journal of Information Technology.* Doi:10.100741870-019-00294-x

Tank, D., Aggarwal, A., & Chaubey, N. (2017). Security Analysis of OpenStack Keystone. *International Journal of Latest Technology in Engineering Management & Applied Science*, *6*(6), 31–38.

Tan, X. (2013). *Introduction to Quantum Cryptography, Theory and Practice of Cryptography and Network Security Protocols and Technologies*. Intechopen.

Tariq, N., Asim, M., Al-Obeidat, F., Zubair Farooqi, M., Baker, T., Hammoudeh, M., & Ghafir, I. (2019). The security of big data in fog-enabled IoT applications including blockchain: A survey. *Sensors (Basel)*, *19*(8), 1788. doi:10.339019081788 PMID:31013993

Techechelons Infosolutioms Pvt Ltd. (2019). Cyber security in IoT: Why is it critical to understand and implement? Retrieved from https://www.techechelons.com/blog/cyber-security-in-iot-why-is-it-critical-to-understand-and-implement

Tene, O., & Polonetsky, J. (2012). Big data for all: Privacy and user control in the age of analytics. *Nw. J. Tech. & Intell. Prop.*, *11*, xxvii.

Terzi, D. S., Terzi, R., & Sagiroglu, S. (2015, December). A survey on security and privacy issues in big data. In *Proceedings of the 2015 10th International Conference for Internet Technology and Secured Transactions (ICITST)* (pp. 202-207). IEEE. 10.1109/ICITST.2015.7412089

Thapliyal, H., Ranganathan, N., & Kotiyal, S. (2013). Design of Testable Reversible Sequential Circuits. *IEEE Transactions on Very Large Scale Integration (VLSI) Systems*, *21*(7), 1201–1209. doi:10.1109/TVLSI.2012.2209688

Tomić, I., & McCann, J. A. (2017). A survey of potential security issues in existing wireless sensor network protocols. *IEEE Internet of Things Journal*, *4*(6), 1910–1923. doi:10.1109/JIOT.2017.2749883

Tourani, R., Misra, S., Mick, T., Brahma, S., Biswal, M., & Ameme, D. (2016, November). iCenS: An information-centric smart grid network architecture. In *Proceedings of the 2016 IEEE International Conference on Smart Grid Communications (SmartGridComm)* (pp. 417-422). IEEE Press. doi:10.1109/SmartGridComm.2016.7778797

U.S. Department of Homeland Security. (2014). Strategic principles For Securing The Internet of Things (IoT). Government of the USA. Retrieved from https://www.dhs.gov/sites/default/files/publications/Strategic_Principles_for_Securing_the_Internet_of_Things-2016-1115-FINAL_v2-dg11.pdf

Uchibeke, U. U., Schneider, K. A., Kassani, S. H., & Deters, R. (2018, July). Blockchain access control Ecosystem for Big Data security. In *Proceedings of the 2018 IEEE International Conference on Internet of Things (iThings) and IEEE Green Computing and Communications (GreenCom) and IEEE Cyber, Physical and Social Computing (CPSCom) and IEEE Smart Data (SmartData)* (pp. 1373-1378). IEEE. Retrieved from https://www.infosecurityeurope.com/__novadocuments/21994

Umesh, V., & Thomas, V. (2014). Fully Device-Independent Quantum Key Distribution *Physical Review Letters*, *113*(14), 140501. doi:10.1103/PhysRevLett.113.140501 PMID:25325625

Vacca, M., Wang, J., Graziano, M., Roch, M. R., & Zamboni, M. (2015). Feedbacks in QCA: A Quantitative Approach. *IEEE Transactions on Very Large Scale Integration (VLSI) Systems*, *23*(10), 2233–2243. doi:10.1109/TVLSI.2014.2358495

Valter, P. (2016). *Introduction to Quantum Cryptography*. Retrieved from https://howdoesinternetwork.com/2016/quantum-cryptography-introduction

van Kessel, P. (2015, March). EYGM Limited, Cyber Security and the Internet of Things. EY. Retrieved from https://www.ey.com/Publication/vwLUAssets/EY-cybersecurity-and-the-internet-of-things/%24FILE/EY-cybersecurity-and-the-internet-of-things.pdf

Van Waart, O., & Thijssen, J. (2015). Traditional Cryptography.

Vance, A. (2014). Flow based analysis of Advanced Persistent Threats detecting targeted attacks in cloud computing. *In Proceedings of the First International Scientific-Practical Conference Problems of Infocommunications Science and Technology* (pp. 173-176). IEEE. 10.1109/INFOCOMMST.2014.6992342

Varma, R. (2010). *McAfee Labs: combating aurora*. Retrieved from https://paper.seebug.org/papers/APT/APT_CyberCriminal_Campagin/2010/Combating%20Threats%20-%20Operation%20Aurora.pdf

Virtualization and Cloud Computing. (2014, April 15). Retrieved from https://resources.infosecinstitute.com/virtualization-cloud-computing/#gref

Vora, J., Nayyar, A., Tanwar, S., Tyagi, S., Kumar, N., Obaidat, M. S., & Rodrigues, J. J. (2018, December). BHEEM: A Blockchain-Based Framework for Securing Electronic Health Records. In *Proceedings of the 2018 IEEE Globecom Workshops (GC Wkshps)* (pp. 1-6). IEEE.

Vukalović, J., & Delija, D. (2015). Advanced Persistent Threats – Detection and Defense. *In Proceedings of the 38th International Convention on Information and Communication Technology, Electronics and Microelectronics (MIPRO)* (pp. 1324-1330). IEEE. 10.1109/MIPRO.2015.7160480

Vukovic, O., Sou, K. C., Dan, G., & Sandberg, H. (2012). Network-aware mitigation of data integrity attacks on power system state estimation. *IEEE Journal on Selected Areas in Communications*, *30*(6), 1108–1118. doi:10.1109/JSAC.2012.120709

Walus, K., Dysart, T. J., Jullien, G. A., & Budiman, R. A. (2004). QCADesigner: A Rapid Design and Simulation Tool for Quantum-Dot Cellular Automata. *IEEE Transactions on Nanotechnology*, *3*(1), 26–31. doi:10.1109/TNANO.2003.820815

Wan, K. H., Dahlsten, O., Kristjansson, H., Gardner, R., & Kim, M. S. (2017). Quantum generalisation of feedforward neural networks. *NPJ Quantum Information, 3*(1), 36.

Wang, Z., Peng, S., Guo, X., & Jiang, W. (2019). Zero in and TimeFuzz: Detection and Mitigation of Cache Side-Channel Attacks. *Innovative Security Solutions for Information Technology and Communications*, 410-424. Doi:10.1007/978-3-030-12942-2_31

Wang, L., Wijesekera, D., & Jajodia, S. (2004, October). A logic-based framework for attribute based access control. In *Proceedings of the 2004 ACM workshop on Formal methods in security engineering* (pp. 45-55). ACM. 10.1145/1029133.1029140

Wang, S., Zhang, Y., & Zhang, Y. (2018). A blockchain-based framework for data sharing with fine-grained access control in decentralized storage systems. *IEEE Access*, *6*, 38437–38450. doi:10.1109/ACCESS.2018.2851611

Wang, X.-B. (2005). Beating the Photon-Number-Splitting Attack in Practical Quantum Cryptography. *Physical Review Letters*, *94*(23), 230503. doi:10.1103/PhysRevLett.94.230503 PMID:16090451

Wang, Y., & Chakrabortty, A. (2016, July). Distributed monitoring of wide-area oscillations in the presence of GPS spoofing attacks. In *Proceedings of the 2016 IEEE Power and Energy Society General Meeting (PESGM)* (pp. 1-5). IEEE. doi:10.1109/PESGM.2016.7741175

Wang, Z., Cao, C., Yang, N., & Chang, V. (2017). ABE with improved auxiliary input for big data security. *Journal of Computer and System Sciences*, *89*, 41–50. doi:10.1016/j.jcss.2016.12.006

Wan, J., Zhang, D., Sun, Y., Lin, K., Zou, C., & Cai, H. (2014). VCMIA: A novel architecture for integrating vehicular cyber-physical systems and mobile cloud computing. *Mobile Networks and Applications*, *19*(2), 153–160. doi:10.100711036-014-0499-6

Ward, J. S., & Barker, A. (2013). Undefined by data: a survey of big data definitions.

Wehner, S. (2010). How to implement two-party protocols in the noisy-storage model.

Wehner, S., Elkouss, D., & Hanson, R. (2018). Quantum internet: A vision for the road ahead. *Science*, *362*(6412).

What is Virtualization Security? Definition from Techopedia. (n.d.). Retrieved from https://www.techopedia.com/definition/30243/virtualization-security

Wiesner, S. (1983). Conjugate coding. *SIGACT News*, *15*(1), 78–88. doi:10.1145/1008908.1008920

Wikipedia. (n.d.). Internet of things. Retrieved from https://en.wikipedia.org/wiki/Internet_of_Things

Wikipedia. (n.d.a). Cirq Documentation. Retrieved from https://en.wikipedia.org

Wikipedia. (n.d.b). Shor's algorithm. Retrieved from https://en.wikipedia.org

Wolfert, S., Ge, L., Verdouw, C., & Bogaardt, M. J. (2017). Big data in smart farming–a review. *Agricultural Systems*, *153*, 69–80. doi:10.1016/j.agsy.2017.01.023

Woodford, C. (2019). *Quantum computing*. Explain That Stuff. Retrieved from https://www.explainthatstuff.com/quantum-computing.html

Wootters, W. K., & Zurek, W. H. (1982). A single quantum cannot be cloned. *Nature*, *299*(5886), 802–803. doi:10.1038/299802a0

Xiaoqing, T. (2013). *Introduction to Quantum Cryptography*. Retrieved from https://www.intechopen.com/books/theory-and-practice-of-cryptography-and-network-security-protocols-and-technologies/introduction-to-quantum-cryptography

Xia, Q. I., Sifah, E. B., Asamoah, K. O., Gao, J., Du, X., & Guizani, M. (2017). MeDShare: Trust-less medical data sharing among cloud service providers via blockchain. *IEEE Access*, *5*, 14757–14767. doi:10.1109/ACCESS.2017.2730843

Xia, Q., Sifah, E., Smahi, A., Amofa, S., & Zhang, X. (2017). BBDS: Blockchain-based data sharing for electronic medical records in cloud environments. *Information*, *8*(2), 44. doi:10.3390/info8020044

Xu, J., Wang, W., Pei, J., Wang, X., Shi, B., & Fu, A. W. C. (2006, August). Utility-based anonymization using local recoding. In *Proceedings of the 12th ACM SIGKDD international conference on Knowledge discovery and data mining* (pp. 785-790). ACM.

Xu, L., Jiang, C., Wang, J., Yuan, J., & Ren, Y. (2014). Information security in big data: Privacy and data mining. *IEEE Access*, *2*, 1149–1176. doi:10.1109/ACCESS.2014.2362522

Xu, L., Wu, X., & Zhang, X. (2012, May). CL-PRE: a certificateless proxy re-encryption scheme for secure data sharing with public cloud. In *Proceedings of the 7th ACM symposium on information, computer and communications security* (pp. 87-88). ACM. 10.1145/2414456.2414507

Yamada, M., Morinaga, M., Unno, Y., Torii, S., & Takenaka, M. (2015). RAT-based malicious activities detection on enterprise internal networks. *In Proceedings of the 10th International Conference for Internet Technology and Secured Transactions (ICITST)* (pp. 321-325). IEEE. 10.1109/ICITST.2015.7412113

Yang, D., Usynin, A., & Hines, J. W. (2006, November). Anomaly-based intrusion detection for SCADA systems. In *Proceedings of the 5th intl. topical meeting on nuclear plant instrumentation, control and human machine interface technologies* (NPIC&HMIT 05) (pp. 12-16). Academic Press. doi:10.1109/GLOCOM.2010.5683884

Yang, L.-X., Li, P., Yang, X., & Tang, Y. Y. (2018). A risk management approach to defending against the advanced persistent threat. *IEEE Transactions on Dependable and Secure Computing*.

Yang, Q., Chang, L., & Yu, W. (2013). On false data injection attacks against Kalman filtering in power system dynamic state estimation. *Security and Communication Networks*, *9*(9), 833–849. doi:10.1002ec.835

Yang, Q., & Wu, X. (2006). 10 challenging problems in data mining research. *International Journal of Information Technology & Decision Making*, *5*(04), 597–604. doi:10.1142/S0219622006002258

Yarom, Y., & Falkner, K. (2014). FLUSH+ RELOAD: a high resolution, low noise, L3 cache side-channel attack. *23rd USENIX Security Symposium (USENIX Security 14)*, 719-732.

Yi, T., Wang, Q., Tai, W., Ni, M. (2018). A Review of the False Data Injection Attack Against the Cyber Physical Power System. *IET Cyber-Physical Systems: Theory & Applications*. doi:10.1049/iet-cps.2018.5022

Yimsiriwattana, A., & Lomonaco, S. J. Jr. (2004). Distributed quantum computing: A distributed Shor algorithm. *Quantum Information & Computation*, 2(5436), 60–372.

Yin, H.-L., Chen, T.-Y., Yu, Z.-W., Liu, H., You, L.-X., Zhou, Y.-H., ... Pan, J.-W. (2016). Measurement-device-independent quantum key distribution over a 404 km optical fiber. *Physical Review Letters*, *117*(19), 190501. doi:10.1103/PhysRevLett.117.190501 PMID:27858431

Zalka, C. (1999). Grover's quantum searching algorithm is optimal. *Physical Review A.*, *60*(4), 2746–2751. doi:10.1103/PhysRevA.60.2746

Zavalkovsky, A. (2017, July 25). Making IoT Secure: A Holistic Approach. Allot. Retrieved from https://www.allot.com/blog/making-iot-secure-a-holistic-approach/

Zhang, D. (2018, October). Big data security and privacy protection. In *Proceedings of the 8th International Conference on Management and Computer Science (ICMCS 2018)*. Atlantis Press.

Zhang, Q., Xu, F., Chen, Y. A., Peng, C. Z., & Pan, J. W. (2018). Large scale quantum key distribution: Challenges and solutions. *Optics Express*, *26*(18), 24260–24273.

Zhang, T., & Lee, R. B. (2014). New models of cache architectures characterizing information leakage from cache side channels. *Proceedings of the 30th Annual Computer Security Applications Conference on - ACSAC '14*. 10.1145/2664243.2664273

Zhang, T., Zhang, Y., & Lee, R. B. (2018). Analyzing Cache Side Channels Using Deep Neural Networks. *Proceedings of the 34th Annual Computer Security Applications Conference on - ACSAC '18*. 10.1145/3274694.3274715

Zhang, Y., Juels, A., Reiter, M. K., & Ristenpart, T. (2012). Cross-VM side channels and their use to extract private keys. *Proceedings of the 2012 ACM conference on Computer and communications security - CCS '12*. DOI:10.1145/2382196.2382230

Zhang, Z., Gong, S., Dimitrovski, A., & Li, H. (2012). Time Synchronization Attack in Smart Grid: Impact and Analysis. *IEEE Transactions on Smart Grid*, *4(1)*. doi:10.1109/TSG.2012.2227342

Zhao, Y., Cao, Y., Yu, X., & Zhang, J. (2018). *Quantum Key Distribution (QKD) over Software-Defined Optical Networks*. IntechOpen. Retrieved from https://www.intechopen.com/books/quantum-cryptography-in-advanced-networks/quantum-key-distribution-qkd-over-software-defined-optical-networks

Zhao, Y., Qi, B., Ma, X., Lo, H.-K., & Qian, L. (2006). Experimental quantum key distribution with decoy states. *Physical Review Letters*, *96*(7), 070502. doi:10.1103/PhysRevLett.96.070502 PMID:16606067

Zheng, Z., Xie, S., Dai, H., Chen, X., & Wang, H. An overview of blockchain technology: Architecture, consensus, and future trends. In *Proceedings of the 2017 IEEE International Congress on Big Data (BigData Congress)* (pp. 557-564). IEEE. 10.1109/BigDataCongress.2017.85

Zhou, T., Shen, J., Li, X., Wang, C., & Shen, J. (2018). Quantum Cryptography for the Future Internet and the Security Analysis. *Security and Communication Networks*, *2018*, 1–7. doi:10.1155/2018/8214619

Zhu, G., Yin, Y., Cai, R., & Li, K. (2017). Detecting Virtualization Specific Vulnerabilities in Cloud Computing Environment. *2017 IEEE 10th International Conference on Cloud Computing (CLOUD)*. DOI:10.1109/cloud.2017.105

Zych, M. (2018). Quantum Safe Cryptography Based on Hash Functions: A Survey [Master's Thesis]. University of Oslo.

Zyga, L. (2018). *New quantum repeater paves the way for long-distance big quantum data transmission*. Phys.org. Retrieved from https://phys.org/news/2018-02-quantum-paves-long-distance-big-transmission.html

Zyskind, G., & Nathan, O. (2015, May). Decentralizing privacy: Using blockchain to protect personal data. In Proceedings of the 2015 IEEE Security and Privacy Workshops (pp. 180-184). IEEE.

About the Contributors

Nirbhay Kumar Chaubey is currently working as a Dean of Computer Science, Ganpat University, Gujarat India. Prior to joining Ganpat University, he worked as an Associate Dean and Associate Professor of Computer Science at SSAICS College Code 554, Gujarat Technological University, Ahmedabad, Gujarat, India. Before joining as the Associate Professor, he was working as an Assistant Professor of Computer Science, at Institute of Science & Technology for Advanced Studies & Research (ISTAR), Vallabh Vidyanagar, affiliated to the Sardar Patel University, Vallabh Vidyanagar and then to the Gujarat Technological University, Ahmedabad, Gujarat, India. Before that, he has worked as a Lecturer, Computer Science Department, C.U. Shah College of Engineering and Technology, Surendranagar, Saurastra University, Gujarat, India. Professor Chaubey also worked as an Officer on Special Duty (OSD) to the Gujarat Technological University (GTU) for year 2011-2012. Professor Nirbhay Chaubey received his Ph.D in Computer Science, Faculty of Engineering, from Gujarat University, Ahmedabad, India. He has worked in the area of network communication and security for the past two decades. His research interests lie in the areas of Computer and Network Security, Cyber Security, Algorithms, Wireless Networks (Architecture, Protocol Design, QoS, Routing, Mobility and Security), Sensor Network and Cloud Computing. He has published several research papers in peered reviewed International Journals and Conferences, his published research works well cited by the research community worldwide which shows his exception research performance. Prof. Chaubey is a Senior Member of the IEEE, Senior Member of the ACM and a Life Member of Computer Society of India. He has been actively associated with the IEEE India Council and IEEE Gujarat Section and served IEEE in various volunteer positions. He has received numerous awards including IEEE Outstanding Volunteer Award- Year 2015(IEEE Region 10 Asia Pacific), Gujarat Technological University (GTU) Pedagogical Innovation Awards (PIA) -2015, IEEE Outstanding Branch Counselor Award - Year 2010 (IEEE Region 10 Asia Pacific).

Bhavesh B. Prajapati received his M.Tech from Rajiv Gandhi Proudyogiki Vishwavidyalaya, Madhya Pradesh in Information Technology. He is working in Information Technology department of Technical Education Department, Government of Gujarat, India since 2005. He is associated with L.D. College of Engineering, Ahmedabad and Government MCA College, Maninagar as Assistant Professor, IT department. His research areas are Quantum Computing, Quantum cryptography, Quantum teleportation and Quantum coding. He is pursuing his Ph.D. from Gujarat Technological University in Quantum computing domain.

* * *

Akshai Aggarwal has been working as Professor Emeritus in School of Computer Science in University of Windsor, Canada. Dr. Akshai Aggarwal had served Gujarat Technological University as Vice Chancellor for two successive terms (2010 - 2013, 2013-2016). Dr. Akshai Aggarwal holds Ph.D in Electrical Engineering from a prestigious Maharaja Sayajirao University of Baroda. In his dynamic career spanning over 45 years, he has served in premier institutions such as M.S. University of Baroda, Gujarat University, Gujarat Technological University and University of Windsor. He has also held membership of renowned institutions such as International Advisory Committee, Industries Affairs Committee etc. He has been honoured with Governor General's Award, Honorary Doctorate Degree, IEEE Millennium Medal and Fellowships of IETE, M.S. University and Punjab University.

Rengarajan Amirtharajan received his B.E. degree from P.S.G. College of Technology, Bharathiyar University, Coimbatore, India in 1997. He received M.Tech. and PhD degrees from SASTRA Deemed University, Thanjavur, India in 2007 and 2012, respectively. He is currently working as Professor in the School of EEE, SASTRA Deemed University. His research interests include image security, information hiding and information security. He has patented a novel embedding scheme which has been issued by USPTO during March 2015. He has also published more than 170 research articles in National & International journals.

B. Sathish Babu works as a professor in the department of computer science and engineering. He did his Ph.D. from Indian institute of science, Bangalore. He has published more than 50 research articles in reputed international journals and conferences, many of them are indexed in Scopus and web of science. He published two books and five book chapters. He has been awarded for best thesis for his Ph.D. research.

K. Bhargavi received her Mtech in the year 2012 and is working as an assistant professor in the department of CSE, siddaganga institute of technology, Tumkur. She is currently pursuing Ph.D. under Vevesvaraya Technological University, Belagaum, and has published around 25 papers in international conferences, 5 scopus indexed journals, and 3 book chapters. Her research interest includes machine learning, high performance computing, quantum computing.

Amandeep Bhatia is a visiting researcher in Prof Shenggen Zheng group at Center for quantum computing in Peng Cheng Laboratory, Shenzhen, China. He is also working as an Assistant Professor of Research at Chitkara University Research and Innovation Network, Chitkara University. Recently, he has received his PhD degree in the Department of Computer Science & Engineering Department from Thapar Institute of Engineering & Technology. His research focuses on quantum computation and information, quantum algorithms, post-quantum cryptography, quantum machine learning, formal languages, theory of computation, and computational complexity. He has five years of teaching and industrial experience. He has published more than 20 research articles in leading journals and conferences and 2 book chapters on different aspects of quantum computing.

Bhanu Chander completed his B.Tech from Acharaya Nagarjuna University, Andhrapradesh with specialization Computer Science and Engineering in 2013, M.Tech from Central university of Rajasthan with specialization Information security in 2016. Presently working as a research scholar in Pondicherry university, interesting research areas are information security, WSN, ML, DL, Cryptography.

Prisilla Jayanthi is a former Professor and Head Spatial Information Tech.; Head, Centre for Atmospheric Sciences and Weather Modification Technologies, JNTUH, India, Director (R&D) at Jawaharlal Nehru Technological University, Hyderabad. He worked on Hyperspectral Remote sensing during 2014-17 as Dr Raja Ramanna Distinguished Fellow at DRDO. Now, in 2018 onwards he is working as Independent Researcher and Open Innovation Consultant in the areas of Geospatial Technology, Environmental management, AI/ML applications. He is the coordinator & mentor of the national project related Public Health Data Analytics. 'Member of IBMOpenPOWER. He is Chief Advisor Berkeley Andhra Smart village project. He is the Active member of Triple Helix Institution. Professor of Excellence, Chiba University, Chiba, Japan. Adjunct Professor, Asian Institute of Technology Bangkok, Thailand. Member, GIS Academia Council of India.

Binod Kumar is Director & Professor at Jayawant Institute of Computer Applications (JSPM's Group), affiliated to Savitribai Phule Pune University, India. He is having more than 21 years of experience in various capacities in research, teaching and academic administration. He is recognized PhD guide in Computer Science & Computer Management under Savitribai Phule Pune University .He has been an evaluator for PhD dissertations of various Universities like Sardar Patel University (Gujarat), Bharathiar University (Coimbatore),Maharaja Sayajirao University of Baroda (MSU) (Gujarat), Karpagam University (Coimbatore), Banasthali University (Rajasthan) and Gujarat Technical University Ahmedabad. He is reviewer of Journals like Elsevier, SpringerPlus and Technical Program Committee member of various IEEE sponsored conferences. He is Editorial Board member of nearly 45 International Journals. He has been associated with Technical Program Committee member (TPC) of nearly 60 International Conferences in India and abroad. He is Senior Member of IEEE Computer Society USA, Senior Member of Association for Computing Machinery (ACM, USA).He has published nearly 45 papers in International & National Journals/Conferences. Under his guidance two students have completed PhD (Computer Science) and five students are currently pursuing PhD .His areas of interest are Internet of Things (IoT) and Machine Learning.

Kiritkumar J. Modi is a Professor at Parul University, India. He received his PhD in CSE from the Nirma University in 2016. His current research interests include service-oriented computing and cloud computing.

Ambika Nagaraj has completed her Ph.D. from Bharathiar University, Coimbatore. She has a good number of publications in International conference and Journals. She has 10+ years of experience in teaching and has guided BCA, MCA, and M.Tech students. Presently she is working as faculty for SSMRV college.

Zalak Prajapati works as an Assistant Professor at U. V. Patel College of Engineering since 2017.

Sheetal Prasad is 2nd Year student of B.Tech (Computer Science specialization in IoT) at SRM University, Chennai. She has qualified first level in National Engineering Olympiad 2.0 in 2019. She has completed ONLINE C PROGRAMMING TEST of NPTEL conducted by IIT Kharagpur. She has presented paper titled "IoT Required from an Embedded Design Prospective and Impact in Healthcare: A Survey" conducted by IEEE student chapter, SRM Institute of Science and Technology, Chennai. She is Vice President in CSI Student Chapter in SRM Institute of Science and Technology, Ramapuram. She got GOLD Certificate of MERIT in TIMES SPARK Scholarship Examination conducted by THE TIMES OF INDIA GROUP in class 11. She won GOLD MEDAL in 6th OF International English Olympiad in class 10. She has cleared first stage of NTSE in class 8.

Padmapriya Praveenkumar received her B.E (ECE) from Angala Amman college of Engineering and Technology and M.E (Communication system) from Jayaram college of Engineering and Technology. She has received her Ph.D in Wireless security from SASTRA Deemed University, Thanjavur in 2016. Currently, she is working as an Assistant Professor III in the Department of ECE in SASTRA University, Thanjavur. She has a teaching experience of 16 years and she has published 53+ Research articles in National & International journals. Her research area includes Image Encryption and Quantum Encryption.

Santhiya Devi R. received her B.Tech. (ECE) in 2014, from SASTRA University, Kumbakonam and M.Tech from SASTRA University, Thanjavur in 2017. She is currently working as Research scholar in SEEE, SASTRA University. Her research areas include information security, quantum cryptography, medical image security. She has published 7 research articles and authored two book chapters in the field of Quantum encryption.

John Bosco Balaguru Rayappan was born in Trichy, Tamil Nadu province, India in 1974. He received the B.Sc., M.Sc. and M.Phil. Degree in Physics from St. Joseph College, Bharathidasan University, Trichy and Ph.D. in Physics from Bharathidasan University, Trichy, Tamil Nadu India in 1994, 1996, 1998 and 2003, respectively. He joined the faculty of SASTRA University, Thanjavur, India in Dec 2003 and is now working as Professor & Dean Sponsored Research at SASTRA Deemed University, Thanjavur, Tamil Nadu, India. His research interests include Lattice Dynamics, Nanosensors, Embedded System and Steganography. So far he has published 251 Research articles in National and International journals and 14 conference papers. He has Supervised 8 Ph.D. Scholars, 25 Master Students and Supervising 8 Ph.D. Scholars. Currently he is working on four funded projects in the fields of Nanosensors and Steganography supported by DST and DRDO, Government of India, New Delhi. Indo-Swedish collaboration work.

Prachi Shah works as an Assistant Professor at U. V. Patel college of engineering since 2017. She perused he masters degree in Information Technology having major subject as Image Processing. Her technical interests are Database management system, Big data analytics, Machine Learning and Image processing.

Ayush Sinha is working as a full time research scholar at IIIT Allahabad in the Smart Grid Cyber Physical security domain. He has more than 8 years of R&D experience in the software industry.

K. N. Subramanya currently working as Principal, RV College of Engineering, Bengaluru. He did his B.E in Industrial and Production Engineering from Bangalore University, M.Tech in Industrial Management from IITM-Chennai, MBA from Karnataka State Open University-Mysuru, with HR specialization (5th Rank) and Ph.D. in Supply Chain Management. Has total 29 years of experience in Teaching, Training & Consultancy, Research and Administration. Academic and Research expertise includes Operations Management, Supply Chain and Logistics Management, e-Enterprise Modelling, Simulation Modelling and Analysis, Decision Sciences and Applied Ergonomics. Has guided more than 100 UG and PG projects. Actively involved in Research and guided/guiding four Research Scholars. Published 45 Technical Papers in Refereed National and International Journals and presented 81 Technical Papers in National and International Conferences. Executed several funded projects, consultancy assignments and co-ordinating the projects & consultancy worth more than 30 crores at the institution level since three years. Authored chapters in four books. He is a Member of various statutory committees both at the National and State level. Also, served as Member of various Autonomous Committees in the Country. Serving as member in Professional societies including ISTE, ORSI, IIMM, QCFI, IIIE, ISSE, CII and CS.

Darshan Tank currently working as a Lecturer at Government Polytechnic, Rajkot, Gujarat, India. He received his Masters in Computer Engineering from Dharmsinh Desai University, Nadiad in 2009. He is currently pursuing a Ph.D. degree in Computer/IT Engineering from Gujarat Technological University, Ahmedabad. He has 11 years of teaching experience and 3 years of industry experience. He has published several research papers in International Journals and Conferences. His areas of interest include cloud computing, security in virtualization environment, database management system and decision support system.

Manan Thakkar is an Assistant Professor in Computer Engineering branch with more than 3 years of experience. Manan Thakkar has secured gold medal during his master in Computer Science and Engineering branch from Ganpat University because of his overall scholastic performance. He is also a research scholar at Ganpat University. His major areas of interest are Wireless Networking, Machine Learning, Big Data Analytics and Security.

Rakesh D. Vanzara is an educationist and passionate teacher with 20 years of teaching and industrial experience. He has guided several undergraduates and postgraduates students for their project and research work. His research interest includes wireless networks, transport layer issues in heterogeneous networks, IoT and machine learning. He has published/presented several research papers in international/national journals and conferences. Currently, he is leading the Department of Information Technology at Ganpat University -U V Patel College of Engineering. He is also a Dean of Undergraduate programmes of Faculty of Engineering & Technology, Ganpat University. At the 20th Dewang Mehta Business School Awards in association with Business School Affairs and Hindustan Unilever Ltd. He was awarded with the prestigious 20th Dewang Mehta Business School Award for Best Professor in Information Technology on 24th November, 2012 at Hotel Taj Lands Ends, Mumbai.

S. Venkatesan is an Associate Professor in the Department of Information Technology, Indian Institute of Information Technology Allahabad, India. He received Ph.D from the Department of Computer Science and Engineering at Anna University, Chennai, India in the area of Mobile Agent Security. His current research is on Network Security and Blockchain technology.

O. P. Vyas has pursued M.Tech. in Computer Science from IIT Kharagpur and Ph.D. in Computer Networks from IIT Kharagpur in joint collaboration with Technical University of Kaiserslautern (Germany). Associated with IIIT-Allahabad since 2002 in different Faculty positions in the Department of Information Technology, before joining IIIT-Allahabad, he worked at Pt. R. S. University Raipur, where he successfully founded the School of Computer Science and was instrumental in introducing Computer Education in Chhattisgarh region since 1992. Prof Vyas worked at IIIT Naya Raipur as Professor (CS) and Dean (Academics) during 2015-2017 and was instrumental in structuring IIIT Naya Raipur acedemic wih novel academic paradigm of Fractal Academic. Prof. O. P. Vyas has been active researcher and had published more than 150 research papers, three books and completed one Indo-German Project under DST-BMBF and one Indo-French project with Inria-Lille, France (https://www.inria.fr/en/centre/lille). Currently he is Coordinator of DST-RCN funded Indo-Norway project combining Cyber Security and Machine Learning approaches. He has successfully guided Fifteen Scholars for award of Ph.D. degree whereas currently having three PhD scholars working under his Supervision. Prof. O. P. Vyas has worked in Academic Institutes / Universities of Italy, France, Japan and Germany in different academic assignments / collaborative projects as Guest Professor / Visiting Scientist. Prof. O. P. Vyas while being DAAD Fellow (Germany), AOTS Fellow (Japan) and EU Focalpoint coordinator under European Commission H2020, has also worked as member in many national statutory bodies like UGC Research Grants Committee, AICTE's expert committee and also worked as member of Review Committee for IIIT Bangalore and IIIT Hyderabad.

Shenggen Zheng received his Ph.D degree in computer science from Sun Yat-sen University in 2012. He did postdoc with Jozef Gruska and also a visiting researcher in Andris Ambainis' group from 2012 to 2015, he then joined Sun Yat-sen University as a Research Scientist from 2015 to 2018. From 2018 he joined Peng Cheng Lab and also Institute for Quantum Science and Engineering, Southern University of Science and Technology. Zheng is currently a Research Scientist in Center for Quantum Computing (CQC), Peng Cheng Lab (PCL) and assistant director of the Center.

Index

Recommended Reference Books

ISBN: 978-1-5225-8876-4
© 2019; 141 pp.
List Price: $135

ISBN: 978-1-5225-8100-0
© 2019; 321 pp.
List Price: $235

ISBN: 978-1-5225-7847-5
© 2019; 306 pp.
List Price: $195

ISBN: 978-1-5225-6313-6
© 2019; 349 pp.
List Price: $215

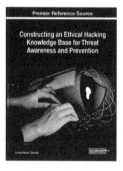

ISBN: 978-1-5225-7628-0
© 2019; 281 pp.
List Price: $220

ISBN: 978-1-5225-5855-2
© 2019; 337 pp.
List Price: $185

Looking for free content, product updates, news, and special offers?
Join IGI Global's mailing list today and start enjoying exclusive perks sent only to IGI Global members.
Add your name to the list at **www.igi-global.com/newsletters.**

Publisher of Peer-Reviewed, Timely, and Innovative Academic Research

www.igi-global.com   ✉ Sign up at www.igi-global.com/newsletters   **f** facebook.com/igiglobal   **t** twitter.com/igiglobal

Ensure Quality Research is Introduced to the Academic Community

Become an IGI Global Reviewer for Authored Book Projects

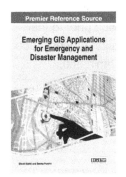
Premier Reference Source

Emerging GIS Applications for Emergency and Disaster Management

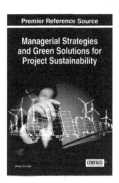
Premier Reference Source

Managerial Strategies and Green Solutions for Project Sustainability

Premier Reference Source

Comparative Approaches to Using R and Python for Statistical Data Analysis

Premier Reference Source

Solutions for High-Touch Communications in a High-Tech World

The overall success of an authored book project is dependent on quality and timely reviews.

In this competitive age of scholarly publishing, constructive and timely feedback significantly expedites the turnaround time of manuscripts from submission to acceptance, allowing the publication and discovery of forward-thinking research at a much more expeditious rate. Several IGI Global authored book projects are currently seeking highly-qualified experts in the field to fill vacancies on their respective editorial review boards:

Applications and Inquiries may be sent to:
development@igi-global.com

Applicants must have a doctorate (or an equivalent degree) as well as publishing and reviewing experience. Reviewers are asked to complete the open-ended evaluation questions with as much detail as possible in a timely, collegial, and constructive manner. All reviewers' tenures run for one-year terms on the editorial review boards and are expected to complete at least three reviews per term. Upon successful completion of this term, reviewers can be considered for an additional term.

If you have a colleague that may be interested in this opportunity, we encourage you to share this information with them.

IGI Global Proudly Partners With eContent Pro International

Receive a 25% Discount on all Editorial Services

Editorial Services

IGI Global expects all final manuscripts submitted for publication to be in their final form. This means they must be reviewed, revised, and professionally copy edited prior to their final submission. Not only does this support with accelerating the publication process, but it also ensures that the highest quality scholarly work can be disseminated.

English Language Copy Editing

Let eContent Pro International's expert copy editors perform edits on your manuscript to resolve spelling, punctuaion, grammar, syntax, flow, formatting issues and more.

Scientific and Scholarly Editing

Allow colleagues in your research area to examine the content of your manuscript and provide you with valuable feedback and suggestions before submission.

Figure, Table, Chart & Equation Conversions

Do you have poor quality figures? Do you need visual elements in your manuscript created or converted? A design expert can help!

Translation

Need your documjent translated into English? eContent Pro International's expert translators are fluent in English and more than 40 different languages.

Email: customerservice@econtentpro.com   www.igi-global.com/editorial-service-partners

Printed in the United States
By Bookmasters